German Essays
on Film

GERMAN ESSAYS
ON FILM

Edited by Richard W. McCormick and
Alison Guenther-Pal

CONTINUUM
NEW YORK · LONDON

2004

The Continuum International Publishing Group Inc
15 East 26 Street, New York, NY 10010

The Continuum International Publishing Group Ltd
The Tower Building, 11 York Road, London SE1 7NX

The German Library
is published in cooperation with Deutsches Haus,
New York University.
This volume has been supported by Inter Nationes.

Printed in the United States of America

Library of Congress Cataloging-in-Publication Data

German essays on film / edited by Richard W. McCormick and Alison
Guenther-Pal.
       p.   cm.
    Includes bibliographical references and index.
    ISBN 0-8264-1506-7 (hardcover : alk. paper)—ISBN 0-8264-1507-5 (pbk.
: alk. paper)
    1. Motion pictures.   2. Motion pictures—Germany.   I. McCormick,
Richard W., 1951–   II. Guenther-Pal, Alison.
PN1994.G425   2004
791.43'0943—dc22   2004001986

Acknowledgments will be found on page 319,
which constitutes an extension of the copyright page.

Contents

Critics, Scholars, and Theorists

Contents · ix

Introduction

... [T]hat which withers in the age of mechanical reproduction is the aura of the work of art. ... [creating] processes that lead to a tremendous shattering of tradition which is the obverse of the contemporary crisis and renewal of mankind. ... intimately connected with the contemporary mass movements. Their most powerful agent is the film. ... [T]he instant the criterion of authenticity ceases to be applicable to artistic production, the total function of art is reversed. Instead of being based on ritual, it begins to be based on another practice—politics.

—Walter Benjamin, *The Work of Art in the Age of Mechanical Reproduction (1936)*[1]

... [W]e do not want to restrict film or to place limits on filmmaking. We reject the authoritarian fixation on doctrine. ... One shouldn't think about political ideology from morning till night. We ourselves have sensitivities too light, too artistic for this. Art is free and art should remain free, yet it must accustom itself to certain norms.
—Joseph Goebbels, *Speech At the Kaiserhof (March 28, 1933)*[2]

Why juxtapose a visionary quote from Benjamin with a pedestrian one from Goebbels? We do so first to demonstrate the broad and dramatic range of political, aesthetic, and philosophical issues and positions that one finds when examining writing in German on the cinema, a quality that surely justifies a volume like this one and indicates its historical significance for the study of German culture. Another reason for this juxtaposition is to address a central dilemma of this volume, which includes the speech on film by Goebbels but not Benjamin's famous essay. This particular lack is very

---

1. In Benjamin, *Illuminations*. Trans. Harry Zohn. New York: Schocken, 1969, pp. 221, 224. Orig.: "Das Kunstwerk im Zeitalter seiner technischen Reproduzierbarkeit." Zeitschrift für Sozialforschung, V, 1, 1936.
2. See below, p. 153. Trans. Lance W. Garmer. Orig.: "Rede im Kaiserhof, 28 March 1933," in Gerd Albrecht, ed., *Der Film im 3. Reich* (Karlsruhe: Doku-Verlag, 1979), 26–31.

unfortunate but easily explained: we were unable to get permission to include the latter essay, which is in any case to be found in English translation in many anthologies currently available. But the larger dilemma—one that also has philosophical, political, ethical, and of course practical dimensions—is that of selection: how should one choose the pieces to fill a single volume (with a certain maximum word count) dedicated to "German Essays on Film"?

We did not try to choose only the "best" German writing on the cinema, and certainly not the "most accurate" (whatever that would be—were Benjamin's predictions about film "accurate"?). We opted instead for writing that had historical significance. This is what justifies including Goebbels, who is certainly not the best German thinker to articulate ideas about film—the juxtaposition of his conventional (yet insidious) remarks with Benjamin's ideas makes that abundantly clear. Nonetheless Goebbels's opinions had more historical significance for the course of German cinema than did Benjamin's—unfortunately. And as much as we still admire the latter's insights, his avant-garde, utopian optimism about film's revolutionary potential was perhaps a bit naïve.[3] On the other hand, to leave out Goebbels—and other functionaries and filmmakers who wrote about film in the Third Reich—would be a historical "whitewashing" of German thinking about the cinema to which we would not want to contribute.

Another guiding principle in selecting essays for this volume was our interest in some diversity with regard to the kind of writers selected; that is, not just intellectuals but also artists—and a bureaucrat or two. Not only film theorists, critics, and scholars (there are already a number of anthologies of film theory that include German writers) but also German authors—and of course filmmakers and screenwriters. Not just Kracauer, Balász, and Arnheim, but Hofmannsthal, Döblin, and Brecht; not just Lukács and Adorno, but Lang, Murnau, Staudte, Wolf, Fassbinder, Sander, and Kluge. And not just the liberal and leftist filmmakers, but also those who did well in the Third Reich: Riefenstahl, Harlan, and Hippler—and of course the politician Goebbels, who controlled the arts with an iron fist, meanwhile fancying himself the ultimate German film pro-

---

3. Lutz Koepnick has argued that Benjamin's famous essay was based mostly on ideas about silent cinema and thus was already anachronistic in 1936; see his "Benjamin's Silence," in Nora M. Alter and Lutz Koepnick, eds., *Sound Matters: Essays on the Acoustics of Modern German Culture* (New York: Berghahn Books, forthcoming).

ducer. Including such voices made it all the more imperative for us to include contributions from those whom the Nazis drove out of Germany; from the perspective of intellectual quality this of course was easy to do, because this meant including Kracauer, Adorno, Horkheimer, and Lotte Eisner. The latter was only one of the many voices of women we made a point of including: from Emilie Altenloh—who wrote one of the very first dissertations on film—and Malwine Rennert—a film critic who, like Altenloh, wrote in the 1910s—through Claire Goll, Riefenstahl, and Eisner, all the way to Helke Sander, Jutta Brückner, Gertrud Koch, and Heide Schlüpmann.

In attempting to assemble such a diverse group of historically significant voices, we also have construed the literary form of the essay as broadly and/or loosely as possible, including speeches, lectures, and manifestoes as well as excerpts from books (but, for obvious reasons, not interviews). We tried to select less well-known pieces by many writers, especially essays or excerpts from larger pieces that had not been translated. In the case of Arnheim's 1932 book *Film als Kunst* (Film as Art), for instance, we have included a section that was already translated in 1933 (titled *Film*) but was later eliminated by Arnheim himself when he created the famous (and abridged) English edition of the late 1950s, *Film As Art*. And while this volume is dedicated to English translations of writing about cinema in the German language, we have included the introductions by Kracauer and Eisner to their two famous postwar books on German film, neither of which was published first in German. How could we not include such influential works by two of the most important German writers on film who went into exile, Eisner to France and Kracauer to the U.S.? (Both would choose to stay in the nations that provided them refuge.)

We have treated the post-World War II era in general somewhat differently from the pre-1945 portion of the book. While we had no problem including pieces written by German film artists who are still alive, we have been more hesitant with regard to living scholars and critics. In the generation of German scholars who began writing about film in the 1970s and 1980s, we have chosen to focus on three in particular who have had an especially important influence on the development of academic film studies in Germany—Gertrud Koch, Heide Schlüpmann, and the late Karsten Witte, three members of what could be called the second generation of the Frankfurt School in Germany. These scholars are especially indebted to

Adorno and Kracauer and yet at the same time are pioneers in new directions: Schlüpmann's and Koch's works in feminist approaches to film history and theory are obvious examples.

There are undoubtedly gaps here. We have not included contributions by anyone born later than the middle of the twentieth century, and that limits the diversity represented in this volume. We probably should have included more artists or critics from the GDR[4] and at least some Austrian voices (beyond Fritz Lang, who left Austria just after World War I). But it was simply impossible to include all the pieces we wanted to include in this volume, and there were many more that we seriously considered. It is no easy task to fit into one volume all historically significant essays written in German on the topic of film. It is our hope that the volume that has resulted from the difficult work of selection is one that provides a vibrant, diverse, and eclectic introduction to what has been written in German about the ultimate art of the twentieth century, the cinema.

This volume has taken a long time (too long!) to produce, and we have many people to thank. First of all, we wish to thank Volkmar Sander for his support and patience, and then Anton Kaes and Eric Rentschler for all their help, advice, and contributions, both to this volume and to the study of German film and its history. Assenka Oksiloff, Barton Byg, and Beth Moore also provided helpful advice. Sabine Hake, Miriam Hansen, Patrice Petro, and Heide Schlüpmann have all done important work focused on writings about early German cinema that was very beneficial to this volume. There have been many research assistants here at the University of Minnesota who have worked hard on this volume over the years: Peter Mühle, Beth Kautz, Beth Muellner, Barbara Drescher, and Gundolf Graml, all of whom must be thanked. (Another research assistant became a co-editor of this volume: Alison Guenther-Pal.) Funding was provided at the University of Minnesota by the Graduate School, the Center for German and European Studies, and the Department of German, Scandinavian and Dutch. We thank Lance Garmer for his fine work on the translations; we thank Scott Witmer and Andrea Guenther-Pal for their editorial assistance. Finally, at Continuum we wish to thank Evander Lomke for his help and support, and Gabriella Page-Fort for her editorial work on the manuscript.

R.W.M.
A.G.-P.

---

4. The German Democratic Republic (*Deutsche Demokratische Republik*), i.e., East Germany.

1. Late Wilhelmine Germany

ARTISTS, CRITICS, AND SCHOLARS

Alfred Döblin

Though he studied medicine and was trained in neurology and psychiatry, Alfred Döblin (1878–1957) is known for his contributions to 20th-century literature, in particular, his participation in the Expressionist literary movement. His most famous work, the modernist classic Berlin Alexanderplatz *(1929), is influenced by cinematic montage, and it was adapted twice for film (first in 1931, and again by Rainer Werner Fassbinder in 1980). It tells the story of Franz Biberkopf, a proletarian recently released from jail. One day after the* Reichstag *was destroyed in 1933, Döblin, a Jew, left Berlin and ultimately settled in the U.S. until war's end. Though he was never able to achieve the renown he had attained during the Weimar period, his last published novel,* Tales of a Long Night (Hamlet oder Die Nacht nimmt ein Ende) *(1956; written 1945/46) was considered a success.*

The Theater of the Little People (1909)

The little man, the little woman knows no literature, no development, no direction. They weave through the streets in the evening, stand chattering under railroad bridges, look at a broken down horse; they want to be stirred, excited, shocked, to burst out in laughter. The strongest tobacco stands at the ready. It is a question of reaching torture chambers, sea animals, perhaps of participating in revolutions.

Consider the anatomical theaters, waxworks, and cinematographs. They are custodians of things most strange and completely dreadful. The quality of the offering is in direct proportion to the intensity of the intended goose bumps. Upon entry, the visitor of a waxworks is uncertain whether he should first pay his respects to a grimacing royal family or view the thumbscrew, and he sways between awe and horror. He sees a "mouth pear" there: "This was stuck into the delinquent's mouth and then screwed apart; it opened on four sides and spread a person's mouth so far apart that the wretched individuals were able to produce only whimpering tones, their mouth cavities often being ruptured." The stranger gazes at a doddering Prince Bismarck, a gigantic potato; he notices the dissected body of a sturgeon, which produces caviar, the beloved delicacy; under Number 486, he sees a mentally disturbed mother simmer her own child in a cauldron. Half dead, he drags himself in front of a penance cage from the region of Eisleben; finally at the end, the sight of Württemberg boots hits him like thunder—after all, the better educated person has very sensitive feet.

He is not up to the situation; with difficulty, he divines that these institutes provide a changing picture of advancing culture; and he drinks a glass of beer at moderate prices.

From now on, he flocks to the movie theaters. They are in the north, south, east and west of the city; in smoky rooms, sheds, unusable stores, in large halls, spacious theaters. The finest offer possibilities to enjoy this photographic technique, the fabulous fidelity to nature, optical illusions, including little light-hearted dramas, novels by Manzoni: very fine. Oh, this technique is very capable of being developed, and nearly verges on art.—In average theaters, the "burning of Rome" already glows, pursuers already hunt wild men across roofs, streets, trees.

Yet it is the dives in the north that have their special genre and are far above the level of the merely artistic. Garish lamps entice from across the street; in their light, one sees meter-high, colorful posters hanging in front of the door, a gigantic organ roars: "A murder has occurred." Stuffed beasts behind glass and game machines fill the corridor to the auditorium.—There, in the pitch-dark, low room, a square screen as tall as a man shimmers over a giant audience, over a mass that this white eye spellbinds with its vacant stare. In corners, couples embrace and, enraptured, keep their lascivious fingers to themselves. Consumptive children breathe shallowly and shake quietly in their evening fever; the eyes of foul-smelling workers nearly pop out of their sockets; the women with musty clothes, the made-up streetwalkers lean forward and forget to pull up their kerchiefs. One sees *panem et circenses* (bread and circuses) fulfilled: pleasure as necessary as bread; the bullfight, a need of the people. The instigating stimulus is simple, like reflective desire: criminal cases with a dozen bodies and grim hunts for criminals cascade over one another; then sentimental ties piled high: the blind, dying beggar and the dog that dies on his grave; a piece with the title "Pay notice to the poor" or the "crab catchers"; warships; no patriotism when seeing the Kaiser and the army; malicious amazement.

It becomes clear: the movie theater is an excellent remedy for alcoholism, keenest competition for six-pack gin mills; see whether cirrhosis of the liver and births of epileptic children decline in the coming ten years. Do not deprive the people and youth of trashy literature or the movie theater; they need this very bloody diet without the broad pap flour of folksy literature and the watery gushings of morality.

The better educated person, though, leaves the place, above all happy that the cinema—is silent.

Translated by Lance W. Garmer

Herbert Tannenbaum

Though not as well-known as other early theorists of the new medium of film, the contribution of Herbert Tannenbaum (1892–1958) to film criticism began in 1912 with the publication of his brochure "Film and Theater" (Kino und theater) in which he explicates the aesthetics particular to film as an art form and narrative medium. Before World War I, he wrote on film aesthetics for various journals and newspapers and finished his dissertation, one of the earliest on film. Plans to work in film production and found his own studio were interrupted by the war. When the Nazis came to power, Tannenbaum and his family fled to Amsterdam and later New York City, where he eventually opened an art gallery.

Art at the Cinema (1912)

One can recently dare to talk, and even to write, of movie *art* without running the danger of being declared uncultivated, coarse (and the like) by all those who must know. But only very recently: approximately in the last six months. Granted that the development of picture quality has made untold rapid advances in exactly these six months—so rapid that, in many regards, the criticism of yesterday has already become groundless today—it has nevertheless also again been noteworthy, that, in matters of art (and other things), there is indeed much lingering thoughtless chatter. After all this, it now doubly delights the person who has long been a friend of the movies when he sees how, slowly, yet very surely, dignified people who not long ago were still not showing their favor toward the movie theater are now doing so. This is sufficiently apparent from, among many other sources, resolutions of writers' associations and changes of opinion in leading journals. The scapegoat for all charges that are leveled against the motion picture stage is indeed constantly the movie *drama*. Surely, often not without justification. Primarily, though, it is necessary here repeatedly to fight against a mistake that is incessantly made by adult education committees and teachers' associations. The opinion that anything is served when people suggest that drama must be cut from the movie repertoire and that the movie theater public should be presented only with pictures of nature and scientific films in its place must be surrendered finally and forever. It is unquestionably something magnificent beyond all measure to allow oneself to be whisked off by the omnipotent cinematographer to foreign countries and marvelous regions, as if released from time and space. Yet, first of all, people never even realize (this is not the place to elaborate further) that not all beauties of nature give occasion for beautiful photographs; for, in general, the principle of nature is idyllic calm and the principle of the movie theater is liveliest motion—opposites rendered less noticeable when the photograph (as has hitherto frequently been done from an unconscious feeling) searches out nature where, as an exception, it is in motion. For that reason, mighty waterfalls and storm-swept landscapes with waving trees have the best effect on us. Secondly, though, those who want to generalize about nature and scientific films forget that the public in the theater seeks not instruction (or at least not *only*), but entertainment and excitement. No one stands for the one being foisted on him in place of the other, even if someone really wanted to impose (it) on him; but one should not attempt this.

The movie drama is capable of fulfilling so endlessly many artistic tasks incapable of being achieved by any other type of art that it is well-nigh inhuman to want to consider this as a *quantité néglige-able*. The photographic image is by no means an inferior imitation of the theater. As I attempted to show more precisely in a paper just published, one attempts with such a comparison to conflate two areas of human artistic endeavor that are built upon entirely different laws, that wish to achieve entirely different effects, and that do not at all mutually interfere with one another if only each type of art is conscious of its borders and strives, within its area of activity, toward the perfection that enables both, each for itself, to create for mankind beautiful hours of solemn artistic pleasure.

The movie drama lacks words, if we want to speak at all here of a lack. From the projection screen, therefore, mysteries of the world cannot be wrapped up and treated, as in the drama of the stage, nor can abnormally magnified sentiments of the human soul be interpreted. Nor will this be different if cinematography and the phonograph come together. We know that such a combination, which could be managed technically flawlessly and which has been undertaken often enough, is capable of offering us nothing in a purely artistic sense. We see the image and hear the sound, but the two do not come together; we do not experience a talking person. This is because, in the movie image, things and people do not have a plastic effect, but a two-dimensional one: as moving images. It is simply not possible for our consciousness to convince itself that this moving image is speaking. We must reign ourselves once and for all to the fact (and are glad to do so) that film art is a mute art.

The basis of the film drama is action. If nothing happens, then we see nothing. And in the movie theater, we know only what we see. This is why the action in the film drama must be so tremendously concentrated and succinct and why, in comparison to theater or even to reality, it takes place at an entirely unusual pace in its individual events. The protagonist of the movie drama lives, loves, takes a wife and dies, all in a film of a half-hour's duration. It is a life nearly like that of modern man that rushes by in the haste we so strongly condemn but basically love so dearly. A good part of the effect that the cinema exercises on us people of the twentieth century has its origin in this parallel. Thus, we enjoy it when we see how actions occur and how everything lives and is in flux. From there, though, it is only a small step to sensationalism, i.e., to pleasure in gruesome and nerve-wracking events. This cinema can and must avoid these unhealthy extremes as well as a fomentation of affective excitement to the point of sentimentality. Only writers can assist the cinema here—good writers who possess a fertile imagination and who are always able to show us occurrences that are grand and beautiful and who show us the occurrences and events in such a manner that, from these deeds, we recognize the people who perform them as unique flesh-and-blood humans, as people with a human soul.

In order for this to occur, though, the talented actor must lend his services to the talented writer. This actor has entirely different tasks from those on the stage. In this case, he has only his physical form, which he must use in such a way that the viewer knows what the person taking action wants. Through his mimicry and gestures, he must be able to show us the signs that every emotion in one's face and in the movements of one's hands produce. In a profound sense, he must be able to practice body art to such a degree that we sense in the image the aura of a real person emanating from it.

And another artist is necessary in the creation of the artwork called cinematic drama: the director, the man whom, as in the theater, no viewer sees and who, quite properly, is actually the creator of the entire artwork. Especially in the cinema. He produces the images and motivates the actors. He provides (and will have to provide much more in the future than already today) for the scenic apparatus, regardless of whether the action takes place between sets or in the open air. In American dramas, the art of film directing is to be most admired, and all the other nations will still have something to learn from them.

The cinematic image is a black and white image. Color is missing and will no doubt remain missing for a long time to come if we want to wait until colorization truly appears "natural" to us. Now, though, one must work with the given possibilities. Artistic photography shows us the guidelines that need to be observed here. If, for example, one sees a picture in which a somber figure is sitting in a dazed, dreamy spell, one might want this figure to rise and to walk through the room. One then senses what additional possibilities are at the disposal of the cinema if it constantly and consciously exploits the advances that artistic photography made not so long ago. The first requirement for a good cinematic scene is a distinguished, monumental simplicity. In the two-dimensionality of the objects in the picture, a complex tangle of lines in the background does not allow the gestures of the actor acting in the foreground to come forward; his acting is simply swallowed up. The basic law of the photographic image is contrast; for that reason, a quiet background must be present alongside an active actor. The lighting must also produce an effect rich in contrast. These days, we often see wonderful scenes in which the play of the image, the opposition and juxtaposition of light and dark, delights us. A comparison with work in black and white in the graphic arts automatically comes to mind when one entertains such notions. In this case, one has the opportunity to use colors, yet the drawer nevertheless foregoes them in order to create, with black pen on a white background, artworks that, in their own style, are not inferior in artistic value to color paintings. Accordingly, one should overcome the habit of addressing the absence of color in the cinematic image as an unqualified shortcoming. It is a matter of an art with rigidly determined boundaries, but it is certainly an art.

Undoubtedly, we stand at the very beginning of the development of artistic cinema. Yet all indications are that it will now advance rapidly with the help of the best efforts and that a time is coming when the cinema's achievements will exceed the expectations of even the most joyous optimists.

Translated by Lance W. Garmer

Malwine Rennert

An influential film critic before and during World War I, Malwine Rennert was the most important critic associated with the journal Bild und Film (Image and Film). *She was also one of the first women to review films.*

An Abyss Not to Be Bridged (1912–13)

It was after an evening of adult education. People had spoken about Italy. Cinematographic pictures of Venice, Florence and Rome had passed before people's eyes; young ladies had sung Italian folksongs. The few educated people among the public were delighted.

A worker, one of the better ones, indeed rather a leader, dryly said when he was asked how he had enjoyed it, "After a quarter of an hour I would have given four coins to have gotten out again."

His friend agreed, "If it hadn't been for the young gal who sang, I would have run away. People had already seen all the other stuff in other movie theaters."

"What? But the films were totally new; they were shown for the first time yesterday."

"Yeah, well, but houses and the sea, that's always the same."

The "drama" had been missing. These viewers were not receptive to images of culture and cities. People with untrained minds have only poor, empty schemes of form and time. They cannot differentiate and see less than the educated person. A hand—be it even the hand of Titian's "Christ With a Tin Coin"—is a hand to them, not this particular hand. Venice—whether in glimmering sunshine or in rose-colored twilight—Venice, the city of myriad moods, is a pile of stones on the water; the girl is young, otherwise nothing.

Did not Shakespeare already say, "Caviar for the people"?

If a movie theater becomes too refined, the people stop going; they will flock back to the ordinary movie theaters. Thus, one must not refine it too much, but only make it healthy. Later generations can think about caviar; for the people of today, what matters is healthy, yet robust strength.

Shakespeare shows the way. His public consisted of genteel youth and the rakish people of the docks. Women rarely attended and, even then, were veiled. Now observe how he simultaneously does justice to the highly educated, differentiated nobility of his time and the coarse seamen and warriors and, exactly because of this, seizes life at its zenith and nadir. In *The Tempest*, supernatural scenes alternate with sailor scenes. The crude antics and jokes still bring the people of our days to laughter and interest the educated person as well because they boldly depict the naivety of the persons speaking, their strange conception of the world of nature and man. The scenes of the masses and of craftsmen, the entire Falstaff comedy and everything connected with it, and the wet nurse and servant intermezzos all exhibit the same special dual character. Add to this the strong, powerful plot that also interested the uneducated public, if not as an artwork, then in terms of content, and raised it, in any case, into the domain of the true, living and organic.

What, in comparison, are the sensational, mendacious, brutal or sentimental "dramas" of the cinematographer?

The puppet theaters of the southern countries also indicate a viable path. Children and adults still press to the fore; they listen, rejoice, laugh and royally enjoy themselves if the player is a man of imagination. In political times, the puppet is often an effective agent; it achieves greater successes than the satirical magazines. But how does that work? Extremely lively, yet coarse and, in general contours, with a strong plot, such as is understandable to the people, who think only in general preconceived patterns. Just as little as one expects a callous fist to learn to wield a paintbrush, so can one not expect an untrained mind to become suddenly intoxicated by the subtleties of aesthetes. He is interested in landscapes only when the presentation about them is a happy mixture of gripping facts, stories and depictions. The empty mind desires facts, not reflections. He accepts these in the bargain only in so far as they bring him closer to the fact. One must *smuggle* them in, just like the salesman who first shows all sorts of stuff and, when he is sure of his clientele, carefully pulls out the showpiece last.

Indeed, the uneducated person is void of all mental associations that render a word, a phrase, a pause so dear to us and that suddenly resonate with us.

Only the simple love song and the sailor's, warrior's and wanderer's song awaken something of high spirits in him. As long as popular education ends at age 13, one cannot expect more.

Sempers Jugendland (Semper's Youth Land) is instructive in this regard. In the cigar shop where workers are so intoxicated by classical literary works that they believe that a reader, the protagonist, Ludwig Semper, has gone through secondary school and has become a worker only by necessity.

Compare the environment of a worker of our time with life at a Viking court and you will say to yourself that, despite popular education, despite all advances in technology and science, the worker occupies a mentally less advantageous position than a Viking who lived in and with nature and saw its becoming and passing: he lived his own life in struggle, on marches of conquest. At his court, skalds sang the praises of people of his race and of his kind; the saga men told him of deeds that had relation to his life. All this melded with his mind into a unity; it did not penetrate like an alien body of which his will and sentiment would not know what to make. We overestimate the knowledge that a popular school offers; furthermore, the little that is offered—it can be summarized in one volume—is offered in the form of excerpts and the most general preconceived patterns. Didactic material that is supplemented in educated circles by picture books, travels and discussions providing merely the building blocks upon which halls and columns are built, is for the children of the people nothing but a meager frame that never develops into a building.

Life brings no enrichment for most people. In the middle of our culture, they stand in a wasteland larger than the desert is for a Bedouin. In his book about the proletariat in London, *Across the Bridges*, Paterson says that a 40-year-old worker has fewer words and ideas at his disposal than he had as a 14-year-old schoolboy.

Nothingness, the void gapes before the worker and the small craftsman when he returns home. No gripping book, no music, no rich exchange of ideas awaits him—and this, not in a primeval forest with its endless enchantment, on a ceaselessly changing sea, in the desert with its radiant starry sky, but in a cramped, musty room full of screaming children! He prefers most of all to dash into the bar, into a café *chantant* or some such place in order to flee the nagging boredom. The extent to which the higher mental and emotional centers atrophy can be gathered from a fact also mentioned in *Across the Bridges:* during excursions into the countryside, a group of workers from London has nothing more urgent to do than to rush into the nearest pub and to stay there; one can observe the same phenomenon in Grunewald. Nature is alien, unimportant to them. The cinema could partially alleviate exactly this paucity of impressions and similar amazement if it were introduced already in school: history, literature and geography would have a different and longer-lasting effect, to say nothing of the natural sciences. And if the tender, still flexible organism had enriched itself in this manner and remained free from the yoke of lifeless, fruitless ideas, it would later approach attempts at adult education with an entirely different receptivity. School children who, for example, had seen their forefathers led along as bound slaves in the triumphal march of a Roman general on the cinema stage or had seen Queen Luise at Tilsit in conversation with Napoleon or Hermann and Dorothea and many other things would later presumably find little enjoyment in sultry, untrue or terrible representations from the sphere of the subhuman; they would have made the acquaintance of tragedy and poetry in lofty, pure forms.

The abyss cannot be bridged, yet can indeed be gradually filled.

Translated by Lance W. Garmer

Georg Lukács

Born in Budapest, Hungary, Georg (György von) Lukács (1885–1971) received his doctorate in law at the University of Heidelberg in 1906. He joined Hungary's Communist Party, but after the overthrow of the government in Hungary and his illegal work for the party in Budapest and Vienna, he was expelled from Austria and briefly moved to Moscow, where he worked at the Marx–Engels Institute. He then settled in Berlin, where he worked on leftist and literary projects. He returned to Hungary in 1944 to become a member of parliament and a university professor. Lukács's work after 1920 was greatly influenced by Marxism; his History and Class Consciousness (Geschichte und Klassenbewußtsein) *(1923), considered a standard work of Western Marxism, is an explication of the relationship between the arts and class.*

Thoughts on an Aesthetics of Cinema (1913)

We never get out of the state of conceptual confusions; something new and beautiful has arisen in our days, yet, instead of accepting it as it is, people want to classify it by all possible means in old, unfitting categories, to strip it of its true meaning and value. People today conceive of the "cinema" as an instrument of visual instruction one moment and as new and cheap competition for the theater the next—thus, pedagogically on the one hand and economically on the other. Today only the smallest number of people, though, thinks that a new *beauty* is indeed a beauty and that rules and valuations of *aesthetics* are befitting it.

A well-known dramatist occasionally fantasized that the "cinema" (through perfection of technique and through perfected reproducibility of speech) could replace the *theater*. If this succeeds—so he says—there will no longer be an imperfect ensemble: the theater is no longer bound to the spatial dispersion of good acting abilities; only the best actors will play in the pieces and they will play only well, for people just do not make recordings of performances in which someone is indisposed. The good performance, though, will be something eternal; the theater will lose everything merely momentary; it will become a large museum of all truly perfected accomplishments.

This beautiful *dream*, though, is a big *error*. It oversees the fundamental condition for all stage effects: the effect of the actually present person. For the root of the theater's effect lies not in the words and facial expressions of the actor or in the events of the drama, but in the power with which a person, the living will of a living person, emanates immediately and without hampering guidance to an equally living crowd. The stage is absolute *presence*. The transience of its accomplishment is not a lamentable weakness, but rather a productive limit: it is the necessary correlate and the evident expression of the fateful in drama. For fate is that which is present in itself. The past is merely framing, in a *metaphysical* sense, something entirely purposeless. (If a pure metaphysics of drama were possible, one that no longer required a merely aesthetic category, then it would no longer know concepts such as "exposition," "development," etc.) And a future is entirely unreal and meaningless for fate: the death that concludes tragedies is the most convincing symbol for this. Through the drama's being portrayed, this metaphysical feeling acquires a great enhancement toward the immediate and evident: from the deepest truth of man and his place in the cosmos arises a self-evident reality. The "presence," the *Dasein* of the actor, is the most evident and thus deepest expression of the fated doom of the characters of the drama. For to be present, that is, to live really, exclusively and most intensely, is already in and of itself fate—except that so-called "life" never attains such an intensity of living that could elevate everything into the sphere of fate. For that reason, the mere appearance of a truly significant actor on the stage (such as that of Eleanora Duse)[1] is itself, without great drama, already doomed by fate, already tragedy, mystery, and divine service. *Duse* is the fully present person in whom, according to Dante's words, the "essere" is identical with the "operazione." Duse is the melody of the music of fate that must resonate, regardless of the accompaniment.

The absence of this "presence" is the essential characteristic of the "cinema." Not because films are imperfect, not because the characters today must still move silently, but rather because they are only movements and deeds of people, but *not people*. This is not a shortcoming of the "cinema"; it is its limit, its *principium stilisationis*. In this manner, the eerily life-like images of the "cinema," identical in character to nature not only in their technique, but also

---

[1]Eleanora Duse, 1858–1924, famous Italian actress (translator's note)

in their effect, become by no means less organic and living than those of the stage, only they acquire a life of an entirely different sort; they become—in a word—*fantastic*. The fantastic, though, is not the opposite of living life, it is only a new aspect of it: a life without presence, a life without fate, without reasons, without motives, a life with which the innermost part of our soul will never become, nor can become, identical. And even if it—often—yearns for this life, the yearning is only for a strange abyss, for something far and internally distanced. The world of the "cinema" is a life without background and perspective, without difference of weights and of qualities. For only presence gives things fate and gravity, light and levity: it is a life without measure and order, without essence and value, a life without soul, of pure superficiality.

The temporality of the stage, the flow of events upon it is always something paradoxical: it is the temporality and the flow of great moments, something deeply quiet internally, nearly petrified, made eternal, precisely as a result of the torturously stark "present." Temporality and flow of the "cinema" is movement in itself, the eternal transience, the never-resting change of things. The *different basic principles* of composition on the stage and in the "cinema" correspond to these different concepts of time: the one is aloof toward everything metaphysically, everything empirically living, the other is so starkly, so exclusively empirically living and unmetaphysical that, indeed, another, entirely different metaphysics thereby arises through this, its most extreme intensification. In a word: the basic law of connection for stage and drama is inexorable necessity; for the "cinema," it is possibility restricted by nothing. The individual moments whose confluence brings about the temporal succession of "cinema" scenes are connected with one another only by their following one another immediately and without transition. There is no causality that would connect them with one another or, more precisely, their causality is inhibited or bound by no substantiveness. "Everything is possible": that is the worldview of the "cinema," and because its technique in every individual moment expresses the absolute (if only empirical) reality of this moment, the validity of the "possibility" as a category juxtaposed to "reality" is nullified; both categories are equated, they become an identity. "Everything is true and real, everything is equally true and equally real": the successions of images of the "cinema" teach this.

Thus, a new, homogenous and harmonic, uniform and varied world arises to which, in the worlds of literature and life, the fairy tale and the dream approximately correspond: great liveliness without an inner third dimension; suggestive connection by mere succession; austere reality attached to nature and the most extreme fantasia; the process of apathetic, of normal life becoming decorative. In the "cinema," everything that the romanticism of the theater had hoped—in vain—to achieve can be realized: the most extreme and least limited mobility of the characters, the complete vivification of the background, of nature and of the interior, of plants and of animals; a liveliness, though, that is by no means bound to the content and boundaries of normal life. For this reason, the Romantics attempted to force onto the stage the fantastic closeness to nature of their feeling for the world. The stage, though, is the realm of naked souls and fates; every stage is *Greek* in its innermost essence: abstractly clothed people walk onto it and perform their play of fate before abstractly grand, empty columned halls. Costume, milieu, wealth and variety of external events are a mere compromise for the stage; at the truly decisive moment, they always become superficial and thus distracting. The "cinema" merely depicts actions, but not souls, and what happens to them is merely event, but not fate. Therefore—and only seemingly because of today's imperfection of technique—the scenes of the "cinema" are silent: the spoken word, the articulated concept are vehicles of fate; only in them and through them does binding continuity arise in the psyche of the people of the drama. The *revocation* of the *word* and, with it, of memory, of duty and of faithfulness to oneself and to the idea of one's own selfhood makes everything, if the non-verbal develops into a totality, light, sprightly and quickened, frivolous and terpsichorean. That which is of importance to the portrayed events is and must be expressed exclusively through occurrences and gestures; any appeal to the word is a downfall out of this world, a demolishing of its essential value. Through this, though, everything that ever overwhelmed the abstractly monumental weight of fate flourishes into a rich and abundant life: what happens on the stage is not even important, so overpowering is the effect of its fatefulness; in the "cinema," the "how" of events has a power that dominates everything else. The animate in nature here acquires artistic form for the first time: the rushing of the water, the wind in the trees, the tranquility of the sunset and the raging of the thunderstorm as occurrences of nature become art here (not, as in painting, through pictorial values fetched from other worlds). Man has lost his *soul*, yet gains his *body* in return; his greatness and poetry lie here in the way in which his strength or his skill over-power physical impediments, and comedy consists in his failure in the face of them. The characteristics of modern technique, fully without significance for every great art, will here have a fantastic and poetically enthralling effect. Only in the "cinema" has the au-tomobile—to cite only one example—become poetic, such as in the romantically exciting event of a chase in racing autos. In this man-ner, even the normal activity of streets and markets here acquires a strong humor and an extremely powerful poetry: the child's naïve, animal glee over a successful prank or over the helpless fumbling of a ne'er-do-well is shaped in unforgettable form. In the theater, be-fore the great stage of the great drama, we gather and attain our highest moments; in the "cinema," we are supposed to forget these, our highpoints, and to become irresponsible: the *child* that is alive in every person is liberated here and becomes lord over the psyche of the viewer.

The *fidelity to nature* of the "cinema," though, is not attached to our reality. The furniture moves in the room of a drunken per-son, his bed flies with him—he was able to grab onto the edge of his bed at the last moment and his shirt waves around him like a flag—out over the city. The balls with which a group of people wanted to bowl become rebellious and chase them over mountains and fields, swimming through rivers, jumping onto bridges and chasing them up steep stairs, until finally the pins also become liv-ing and fetch the balls. Purely mechanically, too, the "cinema" can become fantastic: when films are rolled in reverse and people get up from under racing autos, when a cigar stub becomes larger and larger by smoking until, at the moment of lighting, the untouched cigar is finally laid back into the box. Or one turns the films upside down and strange creatures move, suddenly darting from the ceil-ing to the depths and crawling around there like caterpillars. These are pictures and scenes from a world like that of *E. T. A. Hoffmann* or *Poe*, like that of *Arnim* or of *Barbey d'Aurevilly*—only their great author who would have interpreted and ordered them, who would have retrieved their merely technically accidental fantasia into the meaningful metaphysical and into pure style, has not yet come. What has so far come arose naively, often against the will of people, only from the spirit of the *technique* of the "cinema": an Armin or a Poe of our days, though, would find an instrument ready for his scenic yearning, one as rich and as internally adequate as the Greek stage was for a *Sophocles*.

Granted: a stage for *recuperation* of the self, a place of amusement, at once of the most subtle and most refined, of the crudest and of the most primitive, and never one of edification and of elevation of any sort. Yet, precisely by these means, the truly developed "cinema," commensurate with its idea, can also open the way for *drama* (again: for truly great drama and not for what is today called "drama"). The invincible drive for amusement has virtually displaced drama from our stages: we can see everything on today's stage, from screenplay adaptations of trashy literature to heartfelt, anemic novellas or blustering, vacant brouhaha and ballyhoo—but not drama. The "cinema" can make a clear break here: more than the stage theater, it has in itself the ability to shape more effectively and, indeed, more gracefully everything that belongs in the category of amusement and that can be rendered obvious. No suspense of a theater piece can compete with the breathlessness of the tempo that is possible here; any closeness to nature in the nature brought to the stage is barely a shadow of what is attainable here and—instead of the crude truncations of souls that, because of the form of the stage drama, must inadvertently be measured against souls and must therefore be found repulsive—a world of intended and would-be soullessness arises, a world of the purely external: what was brutality on the stage can here become childlike, pure suspense, or grotesque. And when the popular literature of the stages has finally been slain—I am speaking here about a quite distant, yet all the more deeply desired goal of all who are seriously concerned with drama—then the stage will again be forced to cultivate that which is its actual calling: grand *tragedy* and grand *comedy*. And the amusement that was damned to crudity on the stage because its subject matter contradicted the forms of the drama stage can find an adequate form in the "cinema" that can be internally appropriate and thus truly artistic, even if it is quite rare in today's "cinema." And if the psychologists, refined and possessing talent for novellas, have been driven from both stages, then this can only be beneficial for the culture of the theater and a portent of clarity.

Translated by Lance W. Garmer

Walter Serner

*Born Walter Seligmann, the art critic and novelist Walter
Serner (1889–1942) took on the last name Serner when he
converted from Judaism to Catholicism in 1909. In 1914, the
pacifist Serner fled to Switzerland during World War I where
he met fellow Dadaists Hans Arp and Tristan Tzara with
whom he co-authored* Die Hyperbel vom Krokodilcoiffeur
und dem Spazierstock *(1919). During this same period, he
wrote reviews and essays on theater and the fine arts as well
as published a number of arts periodicals. Not content to
stay in one place for extended periods of time, Serner lived
throughout Europe and was active in the arts scene, especially
in the Dadaist movement wherever he lived. Several of his
works, including his crime novels and collections of short
stories, were banned by the Nazis. In 1942, he and his wife
were deported to the concentration camp in Theresienstadt;
he was transferred to a second concentration camp that same
year, where he was killed.*

Cinema and the Desire to Watch (1913)

It might have been just a few years ago that some variety program
concluded with the presentation of cinematographic pictures. That
was the beginning. And after a couple of years, the smallest provincial little town had its cinema and Berlin had three-hundred cinemas and small movie theaters. For sure: the bargain price, the
convenient location on the thoroughfare, the nearly unlimited leisure time, the ceaseless program being repeated only after hours
and, not least, the sweet darkness: all this must have already helped
in creating supranational success. Yet, at the same time, all this is
not able to explain the unprecedented triumphal march accorded
the cinema in all quarters. What is at work must lie deeper than
suspected. And if one looks yonder from where the last dime is fly-
ing toward the cinema, into these strangely flickering eyes that
point far back into the history of humankind, then it suddenly
stands there: the desire to watch . . .

Not the innocuous sort for which only movement or only color
or both are everything, but rather a desire that is terrible and no
less violent than the one most deep, which boils in the blood and

makes it bubble until that inexplicably powerful excitement common to all desire courses through one's flesh. That desire to watch which stood before flame-engulfed Troy and in the ancient world's wild splendorous festivals, which promenaded in the light of Nero's living torches and serenaded burning Rome with the red song of blood and fire, which howled around the execution site and the stake of the Middle Ages and entered the tournament in constantly new (and usually disappointed) expectation, which lay in a window at the Place de Louis Quinze and saw streams of blood gush from decapitated trunks and the most dissolute debaucheries behind windows across the way. And that today still possesses its old weighty bloodlust: it greedily drinks the red stream that shoots from the steer's neck and from the jugular vein of the victim of a salsa. Fire and blood: as in times past, they dominate the argot of the Faubourgs and the mob of Berlin, who provided themselves feeble recompense in the horrible *chahuts* of the *caveaux* and in the pugilistic jig of the gin mills and who not seldom afford themselves clattering knife fights and do mad things after great fires as if drunk. But this frightful lust in watching horror, fighting and death also lives faintly in every other person. This, nearly alone, is what hurries to the morgue and to the scene of the crime, to every chase and to every brawl and what, for a high price, slithers around the sodomy of the sexes. And it is what yanks the people into the movie theater as if possessed.

That which growing civilization day by day robs ever more from the people and which the tired sensations of neither circus, variety nor cabaret show are capable of replacing, here becomes, almost in aged gravity, the desire to watch. For this desire, the good stage, whose illusion is weakened by the powerful pressure of the milieu even for the person most inflamed with art, is disillusion. Whoever does not seek art, his ardent watching finds no glowing fire here. And the venal stages that serve the masses' dull madness for entertainment come to the eye in a cheap welter of movement and nonsensical action and garish gaudery all too richly reproachable. The will for illusion also fails here, and what remains is a bad joke that the public all too often bemoans for its lack of amusement value, only to get up finally with a wan feeling of dissatisfaction and half rage. Only nudities powdered and made-up as thickly as an arm, bawdily gyrating bellies and other dubitable stimulants are a final palliative to the complete éclat of these stages. And even this, long since bedraggled, totters only clatteringly through the nights. The imagination that comes into the room to be whipped up leaves him betrayed and in the bored mind to make the Sunday strength of this knee-weakening eroticism look ridiculous every day of the week. And the despaired raggedness of an American eccentric and his furious dives through open windows, the horseback vaulting exercises of leotard-clad abdomens on coughing pinzgauers and the breakneck leap from the highest pole of the circus tent in a quintuple pullover, buffalo baize, and larger-than-life mittens: they no less offer laborious surrogates to the famished eye of the lascivious onlooker. The movie theater probably was not required to make the cracked lapis lazuli of this putrescent apparatus of delectation gape completely. What effected this with one push was neither the rapid victory over something dying nor that of a perplexing profitability. It was the exciting adventurousness of a tiger hunt, of a mad, mad mountain ride, of a dead-tired automobile trip; it was the breathtaking pursuit of a shot, wounded and bleeding rowdy over the dizzyingly high roofs of New York; it was the eerie suburb with misery, disease and crime and all the ghastly detective romanticism with murder and fighting, Browning and Navajo; and it was all the bloody pictures of fire and death; horror and terror with which the eyes of all sated themselves after long deprivation. A watching, it was, that had tempo and life and that was lust.

With this, the cinema has won without a struggle: it surrenders only to the eye and the eye's desire. It serves this desire first of all with the ordinary experiences that nothing else less than the sense of sight for delusions is to be had. From this experience, it gains the courage to spit on the head of illusion. It throws the stage scenery out the window, bends over the street, and takes photographs. It thereby gives the eye what is the eye's and acts thanks to the eye; what the eye sees is no deception, and the greatest disillusion becomes for it the greatest illusion. Picture for picture in a true-to-life succession of movement: this is no stage and no picture, this is life. And into this life, which is a tasty appetizer *qua* exotic nature shot, *qua* interesting Pathé Journal, *qua* surprising film that teaches voyeurism, the cinema implants the life withdrawn, life horrible, bleeding, burning. That for this purpose it rushes uninhibited persons of no talent through its scenes cannot be an evil; the refreshing muteness puts at a distance even the most importunate lack of situationally appropriate gesture and mimicry and, affecting only the lips, lets contexts sink and arise that should neither sink nor arise. In addition to this, though, this muteness turns the actor into nothing, his action into the primary concern that is practically absolute, the means only to the deed, to the chase. And this is what is most important for the movie theater. Since the mighty veto of the censor usually washes away the blood of the deed from the cinema, it neutralizes the great danger of disappointing the eye by its very withdrawal of the frightful, through an overly long, obstacle-ridden path to the deed, and through the sheer endless chase that is all the more welcome to it as it knows the greatest constituent parts of the desire to watch and their innermost being in movement. And it masterfully understands how to peak the emotion of movement on a puddle, a bread roll, or a hairpin and to multiply it by means of the strangest incidents and racing events of nature in such a manner that the bloody deed, the terrible catastrophe could hardly have a more powerful effect and whose loss does not hurt all too badly. In this way, many a barren, improbably idiotic tragedy, whose ambition to be drawn from life would do better to take its own life, lives solely from the grace of the most higgledly-piggledy changes of scene and obstacle and from the mercy of the uninterruptedly interrupted gallop of the plot—indeed, many a dreary love drama is dedicated solely to a three-act flight at a constantly increasing speed. Love here appears as the most plausible pretense for riding down sheep, knocking down horses, and blowing up walls. And since the entire affair is contrived ethically, the censor lets the mutilated corpse of the evil rival lie here, since the censor sees moral values blossoming out of it for the public. The censor has no idea that this bloody corpse is always conceded in error. From it proceeds a rebellious effect by means of which Goethe's experience is proven: there is no crime that he would not have been able to commit. The crime is projected and the gratification that the real criminal savors is shared with the viewer and thus produces satisfaction for his rudimentary primeval urges in the image. All this naturally happens for the most part only subconsciously; the cinema is kept from reaching the quantum of baseness that alone can produce the total awareness and boundless power of this excitement. The level that it is allowed to achieve, though, is just low enough to favor the state of excitement that only then makes the desire to watch fertile in the first place and connects it with that desire to watch which was so frightful hundreds of years ago.

Fortunately, theatrical ambitions have been gaining a hold on the cinema for some considerable time. Insofar as they are associated with silly frivolities geared toward the most daredevil chase, they find their audience. But not over the long run, though, in the service of that desire to watch that is not content to feed on the nonsense of stage sets, music and color. What the set succeeds in doing on the stage, if need be, becomes only farce on the screen: the photographed stage picture is disillusion to the second power, and a cardboard Titanic sinking has some things on board whose loss will gradually have to be atoned for by the box office. Color is also a nasty affair. Nothing might be objected to color cinematography: perfected, it would offer the eye truly awesome effects; hand-colored film, though, to which an insane business spirit calls particular attention, is, incidentally, an affront that has already repeatedly failed. Color is capable of being not at all insignificant for the desire to watch; a painted shore scene, though, affects the eye that does not stand for being bamboozled like a decal in compensation for a high school diploma. And when the cinema gives monotonously pounding music the laudable task of engaging the ear to compensate for the distraction of the eye caused by silence, then this is achieved fairly flawlessly; yet not at all by an agonizing, puzzling droning of a gramophone, which provides so completely for the eye's diversion from a kitsch of movement occasioned by a rearranging of the set that one leaves the room. Yet the movie theater is not satisfied with this. On the rich field of love, it seeks to harvest what the censor does not allow it to sow even sporadically here. The eroticism that is provided thus stands on the same surface as that of the most forlorn night stage and is hopelessly on its last qui vive. Even the admittedly meager subsidy of illusion that here affords something to even the most played-up demoness cannot provide the missing increase in intensity. The fact that sensitive natures in Berlin cafés, eyes wet with tears, dream of an erotic cinema that perhaps even already exists somewhere, only confirms their special need for it and a visual lasciviousness that grabs with well-manicured fingers at the ultimate in excitement just as greedily as the red paws of the Jacobins. Nevertheless, this phenomenon can be generalized with broad probability; for the dalliance between cinema and the theater is not able to conjure up even the customary state of excitement that occasions the desire to watch in the first place. Rather, it recalls somewhat painfully the effect of the dead rival, which leads to the consideration that it is not worth paying three dimes to pursue feminine geography with the help of a translating *deshabillées*.

The competition that the cinema is creating for the theater is negative, by the way: seven-eighths of all moviegoers went just as seldom or just as frequently to the theater as before the appearance of the cinema. And the competition that the cinema program is attempting to create through its flirtation with the theater is unsuccessful: it causes no one to exchange the stage for the screen, but rather leads some to be untrue to the latter. A far cry from going to the theater, of course. The failures of the censor, which sometimes acts in excusable error yet all too often in oversensitive innocence, are thus balanced out to a certain degree. By this, though, the cinema should not be harmed. It only gives more than is required to the desire to watch, which previously had to go begging; additionally, it corresponds to a deep need that is undeniable and, if denied, will satisfy itself. The didactic and other valuable characteristics of the cinema do not by a long shot outweigh the possibility that the cinema might be able to satisfy the desire to watch even without sinking down to the lowly means that people permit it to use. In this culturally scandalous fact are rooted its greatest danger and its greatest attraction.

Translated by Lance W. Garmer

Hanns Heinz Ewers

After being imprisoned in Ehrenbreitstein following a duel, Hanns Ewers (1871–1943) gave up his career as a lawyer and began writing for the Berlin cabaret Überbrettl. He was an early proponent of the recognition of film as a legitimate art form. In 1913, he wrote the screenplay for The Student of Prague (Der Student von Prag, Rye), *about a young man who sells his image in the mirror only to be stalked by his double. His novel* Alraune *(1911) was also adopted for film a number of times. He wrote several novels, plays, short stories, and opera libretti, as well as the biography, supposedly commissioned by Hitler, of the Nazi martyr Horst Wessel, who penned the poem that eventually became the official song of the Party. Although he entered the Nazi party fairly early, in 1931, nearly all of his works were criticized and eventually banned by the National Socialists ostensibly because of their phantasmagoric thematizations of sexuality and moral transgression.*

Film and I (1913)

In spoken and written word, I have come out for the cinema so often that—from friend and foe—people repeatedly charged me, "So put it to the test!" What is the use, say the aficionados of the cinema, of you always rambling on in front of us something about the great possibilities of film if we can nowhere see these surprising possibilities? And the senior teachers in the press and in the public, those who know everything better and see a nasty annoyance in everything new, they screamed: Tomfool! Windbag! Charlatan! Cinema opener! Cin-e-ma o-pen-er!! This is, you see, the worst insult in the senior teacher's mouth today, even more contemptuous than scoundrel and rogue. It comes right behind matricide! Cinema opener, they screamed, babbler, phrasemonger, show us what you can do!

Truly, I had to do them the favor—the one as well as the other. And so I quickly decided, on the spur of the moment, and I wrote—screenplays and staged these scripts.—

Indeed, it was much, much, much more difficult than I thought. All the questions that I solved effortlessly at my desk became Gordian knots in front of the camera. Today, I know quite certainly that it is just as difficult, and requires just as much art, to write a good screenplay as it does to write a poem, a novel, a drama. And I also know that the director who truly wants to produce "art" in a film must be able to do not less, but rather much more than the person who has the *word* at his disposal on the stage!—But that was exactly what attracted me: finally the possibility, once and for all, to be able to dispense with the "*word*," this "word" that was hitherto everything for the writer and without which he did not even seem conceivable. With the "word"—which was nevertheless only a vague and never fully exhaustive surrogate for all *deepest* emotion! If it is true that the eye, that the quiet gesture of the hand can say the same—and sometimes more—than the most beautiful word of the poet, then the possibility exists for letting the soul speak without words as well. Rouff Sévérin and Wagner taught me this truth—and: does not a glance tell me more in the life of the day than the word?—

So I ventured it. I wrote a piece for film: *The Student of Prague*, it was called. I wrote it for *Paul Wegener*, and I worked long months on it with him in Prague and here in Berlin. It is intended to be a test case; it is supposed to prove to me that film can, as well as the stage, harbor great and good art. The "German Bioscope Company" believed me and placed at my disposal everything at all that I wanted and wished without asking about costs for even a moment. And I, for my part—well, whoever knows me knows what it costs me to stay in Berlin through the summer. And also knows that I would never bring this work to a conclusion if I were not strongly convinced that my work would have to turn out well. *I want to prove that, in the cinema, good art is also possible w i t h o u t the word—people can call me a scoundrel if I don't keep my word.*

Translated by Lance W. Garmer

Malwine Rennert

War Films (1914–15)

The movie theater, this guest unwelcome to so many, is still here and, indeed, it has become a household member whom one must suffer for good or ill. Impatiently, sometimes angrily, most educated people send it away, into the kitchen area, among the servants with their own backdoor entrance. Some people call for a surgeon who should remove this burdensome foreign body with a knife. Meanwhile, the movie theaters are fuller than ever before. If one wishes to draw conclusions about the audience from this, then one must admit that the healthy, working segment of the nation, the military one now standing in the field, has seldom gone to the movie theater. But just as little to the theater and to the concert halls, for these are also filled every evening. I asked myself as I heard this stated everywhere in large as well as in small cities whether the Greek theaters were also still as well-attended during the Persian or Peloponnesian Wars as during peace. One can assume with considerable certainty that no plays at all were performed. The theater was a national institution and suffered the repercussion of public events. And the women had neither the freedom nor the importance that they have in our country; no play would have been put on for them.

For the most part, though, it is women who now fill movie theaters, theaters and concert halls, in addition to some of the men who have stayed behind.

In the first months, the cinema-goers pardoned themselves by saying that the military films attracted them; they were "letters from the front." But then it turned out that the auditorium became empty before the war films: always just a lot of stuff about war! Hopes for real battles were not realized! There were people who had believed that the filmmaker could shoot battles!

The French army leadership has permitted no filmmakers at all; the German military leadership has permitted four, yet keeps all military significant films in a secret archive so that the enemy will learn nothing from them. There are a great deal of technical aids that every army would like to keep for itself.

It is not the war reports that draw the masses into the movie theater, but rather the *dramas*, as in the past. I am sorry for the movie haters that I must say this: even in war, the drama attracts the masses. In *Salambo*, I heard whispering voices to the left, to the right, in front of me and behind me that tremblingly asked whether Matho, the soldier leader in Carthage, would escape from the trap that his enemies had laid for him and that, breathing a sigh of relief, said, "Thank God, he's saved!" Now, during the war, when every day is rich in war dramas more important to us than Matho! The women were elegant and the ticket cost 3.60 marks.

For people with a strong, healthy national sense, such a state of mind is incomprehensible; they are entirely filled with the tragedy of the time. Only this is not the movie theater's fault; it is the standard, the indicator of this mawkish, insipid sentimentality, nothing more; the movie theater is directed at it, just as family magazines are. The adaptation of Flaubert's novel shows it: all hardships are left out and all that is horrible is settled to everyone's satisfaction in a wedding procession under blossoming almond branches and laughing faces.

As a study in history, the film is thus totally worthless. Carthage becomes an idyllic village. One can see in the adaptation, though, the difficulties with which the film drama had to struggle more than the stage drama.

The opening scenes of the film *Salambo* are of a wonderful beauty, fairy tales in light, dreams such as Wagner had perhaps imagined the scene of the flower girls in *Parsifal*. Beautiful people in beautiful gardens, transformed by unreal, rhythmic floods of light, a triumph of art. No educated person, were his imagination ever so great, could resist the magic of these scenes. They should be preserved in a museum. Since serious Germany does not go there, though, the film company only covers its expenses if it adds inferior material erected upon haste and sentimentality. Were the novel presented in its terrible seriousness exactly as Flaubert had it, only a few of the women who now fill the elegant movie theaters would hold out. They want idyllic contentment or even opium intoxication, and always in a new form.

Film distributors had thought, among other things, that the Italian drama *The Other's Memory* would find much approval and popularity in Germany because of its Venetian city and landscape images. That was the case in some cities; from others came protests that the landscape images were boring and should be cut out.

Are the gentlemen and ladies who make up the regular guests in the expensive movie theaters uneducated? Not by any means. One can sum up the movie situation in Germany in the following words: Serious Germany does not go.

Yet, serious Germany does not often go to the theater or to concerts. Sombart thinks that we cannot do without the Jews because no theater or concerts could survive financially without them. The movie theater thus shares the fate of all art institutions in the sense that serious Germany stays away from it. The production costs of a film, though, are significantly greater than those of a book, of a composition, or of a picture. Mrs. Maria Carmi cites as a factor for the undeniable, rapid improvement of film art in Italy something that is entirely missing here: the participation of art patrons and dilettantes in the production of films. They get together in film institutes, give advice, discuss, and are valuable assistants.

The procedure is similar in Italy at artistic events for philanthropic causes; dilettantes and people knowledgeable about art who possess much intelligence and financial means take charge. No one has time for that here. In the cosmopolis Rome, the magnificent, yet inartistic character of a festival immediately shows that some billionaire's daughter, not a Roman, drew up the plans.

The cooperation of professional artists, technicians and dilettantes eases and enriches the endeavor. It also cuts costs and is the reason that society is interested in the movie theater, as it extends into their own social strata.

It should now be the task of German film companies to create dramas of which the serious public approves and that the sentimental, idyllic, opium-addicted body of attendees does not reject. Film distributors smile at such a remark, saying that there is a total of 3,000 movie theaters in Germany, now a couple of hundred fewer during the war, and those do not cover costs and that film products must now count on the world market, which has rejected German taste in this area.

That might well be true of the past; after the war, the world market will long be closed to us for other reasons, anyway. Instead, Austria, Bulgaria, Turkey, China, Japan and a part of the United States are open to us. One can predict that the movie theater will offer war dramas for years to come *and the war will continue in the movie theater.* In the countries of the Triple Entente and their friends, the movie theater has already begun the task of glorifying their own armies.

It would be unforgivably careless if the German people did not notice the importance of the task at the right time. The masses will not see it; may the leading circles in good time become aware that arrogant rejection and isolation are not in the spirit of the age. They often produce unexpectedly heavy casualties that could have been avoided. Like song, the stage drama, music and the epic, the movie theater will also seize the topic of war—inexorably. If artists, writers and dilettantes stand to the side, if development is left to the *factory*, then it will result in scorn on our troops. Through cooperation with volunteer forces, epic film stories could be created worthy of being preserved in museums for posterity. Our warriors would later probably like to take on roles for mass movements, perhaps even for specific actions. The connection with life would be present.

We must be on guard because of other countries, as well. It is exhausting to hear people repeatedly saying, "It doesn't matter to us what our enemies say or how they smear our troops with words and images." Of course, it does not matter to us in the sense that we lose our peace of mind over it or get grey hair. But it must concern us as lies and bacteria and infections do: one holds them off and tries to destroy them. The air is so much purer, the earth so much more beautiful where one has become master of them. Wherever there are Germans, they should also have the opportunity to see the heroic age of their people in a worthy rendition, in contrast to the smears with which the enemy riff-raff at the movies will not be sparing.

The task is not easy in a people that has more sense for musical than for plastic beauty; but if there is no lack of good will and volunteers step forward, it can be done.

Detective dramas are still the favorite of the young people who go to the movie theater and, so they say, also of adults in America. How many thousands of real events and heroic deeds does this war now offer on land and on water, over and under the earth that are more suspenseful than the boldest detective novel. The abundance is so great that danger lies within; one can become confused and act hastily. If the movies do their job well, stick to what is essential and operate on a large scale, then the heroic deeds of Germans would *shine* over the entire world as far as China and Japan. Because the enemy's superior strength is so great and its malevolence so inexhaustible, the deeds of our men are imbued with so much spirit, exciting, suspenseful, uplifting, from beginning to end. It would be horrible if they were turned into the commonplace and the foolish in the movie theater. Indeed, we can attain the great and the beautiful only if many of the warriors cooperate. How are extras supposed to represent the looks, the facial expressions and the tension of the warriors? One can imagine that those who return home, among whom are so many artists and dilettantes, will later very much like to collaborate in producing memorial pictures; there will be a type of competition among Austria, southern Germany and northern Germany.—

The slideshow, which serious Germany has on its side and that knows none of the financial and technical difficulties with which the good sort of movie theater struggles, has not yet quite come as much into its own as one would wish. A rich historical subject would disappear into oblivion if scholars and art patrons do not set to work in good time. Battlefields and devastations in East Prussia, Upper Alsace, France and Belgium would later make clear more than all descriptions and assertions the difference in how the war was conducted. One would recognize the senseless destruction by the Russians and understand that the German army leadership limited itself to necessities of war. People just cannot get enough of the subject, even from foreign newspapers.

In *Modenwelt* (*Fashion World*), for example, there was a picture several months ago of Belgians stopping a German bicyclist and threatening him with revolvers. The picture had been taken from an English newspaper that certainly had not intended to portray the Belgians in a bad light, and yet—Belgium's worst enemy could not have done them any worse, so cruel and mean were the features and manner of the Belgians, so childlike the expression of the Germans. In a discussion, though, I heard that most of the viewers had found this out only after someone had drawn their attention to it. In film, it would have a much stronger effect and require no explanation. I have seen many instructive pictures of this sort and I always had to make the same observation: It is not enough to collect them; the collected images have an effect only as film images.

Translated by Lance W. Garmer

Emilie Altenloh

The dissertation on film by Emilie Altenloh (1888–1985), an excerpt of which is reprinted here, was the first book on film written by a woman. It remains of special interest today because it provides a glimpse into film production along with a profile of the film-going public in the early years of the cinema. In particular, Altenloh grants the reader important revelations about class. Altenloh's career ultimately turned toward politics and social policy where she worked in various administrative and elected positions, including a term in the German Federal Parliament (Bundestag) *from 1961 to 1965.*

From On the Sociology of the Cinema: The Cinema Business and the Social Strata of Its Audience (1914)

The Product

Two types of presentations are to be distinguished, as they arise in entirely different manners: the *plays* that contain *plots* and that are presented for the purpose of cinematographic recording, e.g., dramas, comedies, images set to sound, etc.; and *nature films* of landscapes, of daily events and from industry, as well as *scientific films* that show experiments.

The first group stands in the foreground, for it comprises 6/7 of the regular fare of the cinema, which offers an average of three dramas, three farces and one nature film. In order to make up for the lacking quality with great quantity, the so-called inserts (usually dramas, less often comedies) are added. Such long-running programs then extend to up to three hours. And the farther to the periphery of a city, the longer the program, the more numerous and more gruesome the pieces, and the less frequent the nature films. In the announcements of professional journals, too, nature films hardly appear, and the tremendous praises that fill the columns of newspapers already weeks before an opening are directed at the sensational dramas. Entire brochures with plot summaries and pictures about these are distributed in newspapers. The form in which the advertisements are penned often stands in strange contrast to the editorial component. If one reads at the front about attempts aimed at raising the standard of cinema presentations, about the high level that has already been reached, and about the unjust attacks by popular reformers, the advertisements, which are supposed, as it were, to present the illustrated film, are not quite able to confirm this notion. "The Cry For Happiness—presented under mortal danger to the actor personally" or "Morphine Addicts Are More Suspenseful Than the White Slave Woman, More Interesting Than the Temptations of the Big City and More Exciting Than Perilous Old Age" or "What the Titanic Taught Her: Mrs. Dorothy Gibson, a Survivor of the Titanic, in the Lead Role." These samples are by no means rare. The posters meet even modest aesthetic demands just as poorly; they bear striking resemblance to the illustrations of roving singers of thirty years ago, and one notices only in a few cases that a period of revolution within the industry has occurred in the meantime.

All this advertisement pertains primarily to drama and much less to comedies, and even the nature films lead an unknown Cinderella existence. The ratio of the actual numbers of the three types merchandised on the German market corresponds to this. Of all films that opened in the months of March, April, May, October, November, and December 1912, the ratio of drama to comedies to nature films was 12:11:5, and the comparison of the meter lengths—which offer such a splendidly mathematical measure of interest in a cinema presentation, as the time percentage of the individual types of program is derived from it—speaks every more clearly; it was 7:3:1.—The cinema is thus primarily a place of "dramas" and of "farces." These themselves and their origin shall now be the topic.

Drama and Comedy

One must set aside all ideas about poetic and literary creation and about the director's and actor's work that is subordinated to this creation and learn anew if one wants to understand the process by which a cinema piece is made. The writer is no longer an artist who produces on a freely creative basis when ideas are ripe and pressing for form; rather, the writer—specifically, the film writer—is for one thing a small part of a large industrial apparatus in which he is integrated with all his services. Primarily, therefore, he has to meet the demands that are necessary for the operation not to come to a halt. Just as in mechanical operations, the assets spent on salaries, on actors' and directors' pay, and finally also for the machines require an intensive use of labor, and this is the reason why several dramas, written by one and the same writer, often appear within one month. The division of labor among writers, directors and actors is also shifted in this novel manner. The "writer" or the director in his activity as writer—for these two functions are usually held by one person—supplies only the idea. Additional fashioning is not required. The director, and to a large degree the actors as well, have the greatest share in production. In part, they first appear during the performance of a drama or comedy. Director and actors work together in order to produce as effective an entirety as possible. A small act is repeatedly worked out, changed and again performed. The actors improvise words to it in order to render the gestures and facial expressions more plausible—until a short section is finally ready for filming. And this is how work is done in the large work studios at four or five places and on just as many pieces simultaneously. The directors who bring artworks from other genres into the form of cinema or, as is usually the case, use their own ideas, not infrequently also play the lead role in the pieces. This is how, for example, Urban Gad (Union Frankfurt) and Max Linder (Pathé Frères) combine all three activities. The majority of all dramas and comedies are produced in the manner described above mainly through the work of the director (who, as a rule, is bound to a company by long-term contracts) and of the actors, who, especially in the case of very large firms, are also continuously engaged.

Although the larger companies employ several directors and several troupes in delightful and diverse natural settings, there is something slightly pre-fabricated about such productions. The ideas, the faces and the scenes recur and finally no longer draw an audience if a particularly avid interest for individual popular actors does not replace the interest in content. In France, where the cinema became widespread much earlier, interest was so keen for so long that ideas were submitted by the audience. In Germany, on the other hand,

writers and dabblers initially stood entirely outside this development, partially shunning it. This was also probably due to the meager payment for sketches, as most of the work remained for the
director. According to the suitability of the piece, it was quite variable, of course, and ranged between 20 and 100 marks.

Important literary writers have only very recently placed their
power in the service of the cinemas; the psychology in their so doing
is complex. If people felt "responsible" for the intellectual nourish-
ment of the broad masses after they had realized that no expurgation of scenes of horror had been achieved by the strict rejection of
cinematographic dramas and by this purely negative position, they
might have thought to see the cinema as the path to a mass of people as yet entirely closed to art, even if this turn-around ultimately
lay in purely opportunistic motives. In short, after individual people
had already previously proclaimed the cinema to be a possibility
for a new type of artistic development, the Association of German
Writers finally abandoned its earlier position in October 1912 and
recommended that its members supply the cinema with material in
order to raise its existing level. Among the new allies are well-
known dramatists, such as Schnitzler, Gerhard Hauptmann, Suder-
mann, and others, and the first fruit of this new connection between
art and industry was the drama *The Other*, written by Paul Lindau,
in which the lead role was played by Alfred Bassermann. It was,
though, no more than a mediocre achievement, and better things
remain to be seen.

The Plot

Success would be of fundamental importance beyond any individual case, for the question of the day does indeed seem to be: Is it
possible to express the artistic qualities of a drama through film?
Can a literary artwork be conveyed without the means of language,
which differentiates all affects and feelings beyond crude outlines?
Are the cinema's means of expression, gesture, sufficiently nuanced
to dispense with the word?

Surely, this type of communication can still be developed beyond
its current capabilities. For individual situations, gesture is a more
perfect means of expression than language and is so omnipresent
where reactions are caused by sudden external influences, in which
case language usually fails in reality as well; this is the case, for example, with sudden fright, overwhelming pain, etc. For these states

of affect, typical movements—already set forth by actors and to some extent by painters, yet in very great measure by cinematographers—have been fixed that are generally understood, surely due not least to frequent repetition. In comparison to reality, though, these movements must also be greatly exaggerated in order to facilitate general understanding. Only painting still works in a similarly pronounced manner toward emphasizing the essential. Yet, because it always picks out only one moment and portrays nothing continuous, different difficulties arise than those that arise in the case of cinematographic recording. In the cinema, though, the psychology of the persons acting is necessarily coarsened by this constant emphasizing. All events before and after the effect, which are otherwise communicated in monologues or in conversation, can be expressed even less through mere gestures and facial expressions. This before and after, this *clair-obscure* of emotional and volitional effort in a person cannot be portrayed in this manner. The cement that joins the individual pieces is missing, as there is no standard and set language of gesture whose subtlest nuances would be developed. Words must enter so that these less emphatic events are also understandable to those who are not quite as attuned to the same tone of feeling as the actor is. Perhaps the people of today are more capable of comprehending in this manner than others were. Individual writers who create particularly strongly from their attitude toward the present, such as Hanns Heinz Ewers, Hermann Bahr, Johannes Schlaf and Stephan Zweig, see a new genre of art arising in the film drama, while others, such as Otto Ernst, Dr. Walter Bloem and Julius Stettenheim, are of an opposing view. A drama is not possible without the transitions and the internal revision of the external action, though. One need not go so far as to judge with the modern type of a Hofmannsthal or a Maeterlinck in mind, who probably stand at the opposite pole of drama possible for the cinema. It is therefore impossible because all progress of action today is only psychological development, in contrast to the so-called tragedies of fate, in which the progress of action is ushered in by external causes. But in order for there to be a resolution and thickening of the conflict, they, too, must have already affected a person who then acts accordingly. Yet we can witness this revaluation only through the mediation of language. Film can provide only the crudest outlines of this; it can reveal in a flash scenes typical for the course of action. According to his disposition, each viewer must provide the link between cause and effect that holds the structure together.

Furthermore: in part already purely externally, film's possibility of existence is rooted exactly in the primitive form of action, as it must be understood by people of all levels of culture and races. They all have no points of contact with one another beyond the most basic feelings.

So, is the film that contains a *plot* to be banned from the cinema as a matter of principle and the image of nature to be considered the only desirable form of representation? The majority of zealous reformers do indeed go so far; but that would entail making something else of the cinema than what it is today, and perhaps it would entail nipping the beginnings of artistic achievement in the bud.

Taste is the product of a long development. It modeled itself on the manifestations of art and has been determined by them. Our judgment is not geared to a type different from traditional and universally known concepts and only gradually adapts to something else. Such a modern cinema drama, though, does not wish to be considered as relying on the things that have hitherto been offered to us. If we draw a parallel to a stage drama or compare it with a series of paintings, we will hardly do it justice. But is it not because of the general, slow process of coming to understand the new that the essential element of the art of cinema is not yet at all recognized?—

All the previously made objections would not apply to *epic* film, which narrates without claim to dramatic development—it narrates in pictures and desires solely to entertain. Strictly speaking, every so-called cinematic drama is nothing else nor can be anything else, as the essential element of the conflicts cannot be reproduced at all. Caricatures such as those which one often sees arise only by the repeated use of such subject matters that do not bear the purely narrative character of the sort that the cinema is perhaps only able to portray. Precisely because it is possible for the image to represent all accompanying secondary circumstances in detail and to portray the context of the action and movement in a manner true to nature, the portrayal exceeds the liveliness of any spoken or read story. Within this context lie infinite possibilities for artistic development, something entirely new that lies between stage drama and the novel.

What has so far been not so clearly recognized in the case of drama—namely, that the essence of cinematic narration lies in the action and in an accumulation of events—has actually been long understood in the case of farce. Thus, we repeatedly encounter a more or less well-staged situational comedy. Even if not many new ideas beyond the usual chase scenes have yet surfaced, cinema comedy has at the outset developed on paths on which it is able to achieve the inimitable. For this reason, too, it has, despite many instances of bad taste, stirred less opposition among the critics.

The Image

Yet, the task that film can fulfill with respect to art is not yet completed with the working out of the subject matter in drama as well as in comedy. Particularly in the recent past, a part of the effect is increasingly being consciously sought in purely pictorial impact. The eye for the effect of space and lines has been trained by modern stage productions alone. One sees the same in the cinema, where the subject matter must also be conveyed in addition to any formal effect.

It was initially American companies that ushered in an entirely new era in film art through the combination of picturesque landscapes and movement. Considered solely in terms of their images, the well-known trapper and Indian stories, with their constantly repeating content, also have directly artistic effect. In order to achieve this, rather long training was first required, as there were no examples that one could have followed. Yet, artists today are consciously engaged in developing this facet of cinematographic representation. The film *Parsival*, for example, which was brought onto the market by the company Ambrosio of Turin, was quite exceptional in this regard.

There has been much controversy on all sides about the artistic value of the achievements of the cinema; in order to separate the wheat from the chaff, longer consideration is required. Yet, a large proportion of those who have approached the issue without prejudice fully and completely recognizes the type of artistic achievement just discussed. Friedrich Freksa once said, "The fantasy of the poet is still riding in the mail coach while the fantasy of the technician is already roaring along in the airplane. The wonderful invention of the cinema should not be damned for that reason; instead, time should endeavor to digest it." In the meantime, many people have already come to terms with it and, by recognizing the values that were contained in the new phenomenon, some of them set about assisting in the work in order to bring forth the authentic and the beautiful as purely as possible.

The Actors

It was initially the actors who saw in film drama a field for their artistic activity. They, like all who judged from the standpoint of acting, were not opposed to the film drama in principal; this is apparent from the various responses to an opinion poll in the international *Filmzeitung* (Film News): "Is the cinematographic drama an artwork?" Alfred Bassermann, Harry Walden, Richard Schultz (the director of the Berlin *Metropoltheater*), and Dr. Karl Hagemann (director of the German *Schauspielhaus* in Hamburg) did not, for example, rate the artistic value of the cinema drama as low as the majority of reviewers at the time did. The ability of the individual actor is also accorded infinitely more latitude precisely in this because that latitude becomes a contributing shaper of the work to the greatest degree, entirely different from the case on the stage, where the writer has at the outset determined the movements of the individual persons much more exactly. For this reason, people placed themselves in the service of the new art already quite early on, and the following list of several names shows that these people were not only unimportant figures: Asta Nielsen; Betti Nansen and Urban Gad from the Royal Theater in Copenhagen; Sarah Bernhard, who acted with her ensemble for the Charing Cross History Film Co.; Adele Sandrock, as Marianne in the drama *Marianne—A Woman of the People*; Grete Wiesental (Wiener Firma); Saharet (Messter Projektion); Ferdinand Bonn; Tilla Durieux; Alfred Bassermann; Giampietro; Clewing; Pallenberg; Madame Polaire (Royal Film Co., Düsseldorf).

This desertion was initially strongly disapproved of and energetically fought against by directors and professional organizations. In Vienna, the unfaithful were even threatened with dismissal. The Association of German Workers circulated a flyer that energetically took a position against the cinema. This speaks more loudly about concern for the endangered existence of the theaters than about concern for threatened art in general, though. The big names did not pay any attention to it and the small names went over to pantomime completely, where the revenues were better anyway. In any event, the cinema was the victor in this dispute, and, then as now, well-known men and women artists were won over for it.

The best-known cinema stars, though, were not former important figures of the stage, but rather became known only because of the cinema theaters. During the initial years, the actors appeared to retreat entirely behind their work; there were only unknown names that one could have cited. Over time, though, individual figures repeatedly returned. They broke off from the mass of indifferent cinema mimes, and the names Max Linder, Asta Nielsen or Wanda Treumann today conjure up very definite notions for any regular cinema viewer. Since the same writer usually works with a troupe over time, their names are the indication for a given particular type of pieces. Thus there are series with Asta Nielsen and Lissi Nebuschka.

The fees that these most famous people receive usually exceed the revenues at large theaters, and they can be paid only by large-scale companies with much capital. Max Linder draws a yearly salary of 330,000 francs; Fritzchen Abélard, a boy of about 10 years, draws 15,000 francs from the Gaumont company; and Asta Nielsen draws 85,000 marks for her work in ten dramas annually with a running time of approximately five months. Received for one performance: Giampietro, 10,000 marks; Pallenberg, 10,000; Fritzi Massary, 5,000; Kutzner, 3,000; Madame Polaire, 15,000. At the same time, nearly all these artists were also active on some stage.

Stage and cinema place entirely different demands on the abilities of the actor. "New dramatic laws come into effect here." Only a few people combine both qualities in themselves simultaneously, though. On the movie set, the actor will always miss being opposite the public, which he must win over and whose applause spurs him on. If he adheres too closely to theater technique by trying to make his gestures as natural as possible through improvised words, then the effect of the filming will frequently be greatly compromised. One then has the unpleasant feeling of sitting in front of a deaf mute who is making desperate attempts to communicate. In contrast, the cinematographic performance is afforded possibilities of expression that can be brought to highest perfection only through them alone; I would like to call it communicative sculpture—language of movement, and not only of facial expression (which is also seen much more clearly in an image), but also of the entire body. This special area of artistic activity has been recognized by only a few.

Yet, next to these main actors stands the large majority of cinema actors, whose lot is hardly distinguished advantageously from that of their colleagues on the stage. The largest companies, such as Pathé, Gaumont, Cines and others, maintain permanent troupes. The costumes are provided by the workshops. Smaller companies, and indeed the majority of all existing ones, which bring out a new film only weekly or usually less often, always employ people for one piece only. Attracted by occasional newspaper notices that tell of the fabulous salaries of individual cinema actors, the supply of workers grew enormously. It was increased more by the fact that many theaters, driven by the competition of the cinema, closed their doors and many actors became unemployed. Today in Berlin, approximately 2,000 people act for the cinema. A proletariat of actors arose whose economic situation was worse than that of any factory worker. Their existence is utterly insecure, as they are usually engaged only for the performance of one piece. Under these circumstances, a job placement service then developed, albeit an unlicensed one. Every evening in the Admiral's Café in Berlin, engagements are arranged by agents who take a 10% fee. If one considers that acting for the cinema was originally only a sideline and that this generally involved second- and third-tier people, then the individually paid salaries do not appear low in comparison to theater pay. One-third of theater actors earns less than 1,000 marks and only 10% over 3,000 marks. Except for the individual actors in lead roles, cinema actors draw 5–6 marks per day for a workday of approximately nine hours. This makes 20–50 marks for a film for which they are each time engaged for rehearsal.

Because of the dependency of such qualified labor, the industry has become concentrated in large centers, as only the large city brings together both types of workers that are of importance for it, i.e., the highly qualified work of artists on the one hand and the fluctuating element of the unemployed proletariat of actors on the other hand. So this, then, is why nearly all German film studios (I know of only four exceptions) have their headquarters in Berlin.

Furthermore, the industry is sales-oriented there, for approximately one-tenth of the 3,000 German cinemas are located in Berlin. Other factors have eventually become attached to this, such as the general recognition of the Berlin censor. On the other hand, the film distribution companies, which provide for distribution, lie largely strewn in the provinces.

Because of the actors' sometimes quite high salaries, a film negative represents a very high value that increases even more when distant trips are necessary to find a fitting background. In order to make these unnecessary, people seek to combine various motifs by constructing parks in which all sorts of sets stand next to one another. We walk, for example, out of an old castle that was originally the sole master of an area. A half-finished new building rises up right next to it and, just a bit farther, one enters the main yard of a small country farm. Chickens, ducks and geese, dogs and even two real bears live their artist's existence here. "The primeval forest," with an arm of a river running through it, borders the house, and ten steps farther we stand before a garage that contains the most important component of any cinema piece, the automobile. From a modern street, we immediately enter an old Rothenburg with pitched roofs and narrow lanes. Such museum parks exist only here and there, though, and they cannot meet the demands for realistic surroundings. The majority of filming is done in the middle of traffic on the street and wherever appropriate locations are found. The Parisian or Berliner is already entirely used to such pageants and the public, at most, makes up the extras necessary for any scene attracting attention. The huge costs involved for a drama run up to an average of 10,000–30,000 marks. Yet, up to 150 positives of a film are often ordered if the impact that makes it into a hit is correctly gauged and if the censor's scissors finally do not abruptly dash all hopes.

Nature Films

In conclusion, just a few words about nature films, this type of cinematographic recording that stirs up the least animosity and is least cultivated. The majority of reformers place their hopes particularly on its popularization and its perfection. If cudgels must be taken up on behalf of the cinema, then its merits and utility are praised. But one generally only first notices something of it when one is sitting in front of the screen and, between comedy and drama, sees distant lands and cities suddenly appear like a vision for ten minutes and disappear just as silently. For the manufacturers, they are the problem child, as has already been shown in one of the first chapters. One presents such subjects because one believes oneself to be indebted to the company's reputation, and only the largest ones can allow themselves such a luxury. Whereas a drama, if it is a big draw, sells up to 150 copies, even the best nature film seldom sells more than 50–60 copies. The huge costs for this are often out of all proportion, and only the development of the very modern reform movement, particularly the utilization of film for didactic purposes in school and in the army, seems to open new perspectives for the nature film.

The first cinematographic recordings actually were all nature films, according to our classification made above, in that the action was random or a reproduction of such random occurrences for the purpose of cinematographic recording. From this level, the development progressed to comedy on the one hand and to the modern portrayal of daily events on the other hand. Today, hardly anything happens in the world—be it the unveiling of a memorial in Lukau, a fire disaster in New York, a reception by an African chief or the launching of a ship—that is not swiftly captured on film and shown to a cinema audience in the whole world. In a *Festschrift* for the anniversary of the Kaiser's installation, a modern poet summarizes all these possibilities in the following highly poetic verse:

> *Hail to the film—it teaches us*
> Παντα ρει.
> *Sea storms and the bud's quiet stirring,*
> *Man and worm in movement*
> *And hooray—even Kaiser Willy*
> *The film shows.*

Rich people already today place value in conducting all important events of their lives in front of a cinematographic camera in order to be able to add illustrations to their memoirs, *My Life From the Cradle to the Grave,* and this fashion, which for the meantime is still reserved for multi-millionaires, surely has a great future.

Daily Events

For events of public interest, the film plays the role of the newspaper, and, with reports from all over the world, the cinema obliges a trend of the time "that wants to be informed about everything." The daily and weekly reviews are also very interesting where cinematographic reporting truly assumes the position of the newspaper. If pictures are old, the fleeting interest in the events is already long gone. It was for only the newest, the momentary present and not for the actual content. Only secondary moments, such as the surroundings in which an event takes place, or the purely pictorial attributes of the film still raise interest then. In order to ensure a total success, it is decisive who first shows the news item in film. In order to break the record, everything humanly possible is offered up on special occasions. So, for example, the Gaumont company entered into an agreement with the English railroad company on the occasion of the coronation ceremonies of George V of England according to which a railroad car was set up as a lab in order to develop and produce the film, which had been brought onto the train along with automobiles immediately after the ceremonies had concluded, during the trip to London in an express train in order to show it to the London public on the same evening. A few hours after the arrival of the first telegram that reported of the ceremony—six hours after the recording—the citizens of the capital could watch the coronation parade from their reclining chairs in the cinema.

Many entrepreneurs have built up quick reporting into a new type of news bureau. Instead of reading the newspaper, the stroller of Paris boulevards goes to the Pathé Journal for 10 centimes, looks at the posters with the telegraphically transmitted stock market reports at the entrance, ascertains in the cinema what has recently happened in the world, and leaves the room feeling entirely like an educated western European with cosmopolitan interests.

Over and above this momentary interest, individual films also have historical value for posterity as a veracious document of the events of our time. For this reason, the establishment of a film archive has on various occasions been suggested by the director of Berlin's Urania. Yet, it is said, celluloid film would not keep for more than a limited time and the value would thus be illusory.

Landscape Pictures

The interest in actual nature films and in pictures of places and foreign peoples is less fleeting and less temporally bound. It arises, though, from basically the same motives as what was previously described: from a need for an increase in knowledge. If one accorded nature films more space in an evening's program, then a new social stratum of devotees would certainly be won for the cinema, as a truly predominant interest in nature films and the demand for a reform of the program in this sense dominate almost without exception in educated circles. Yet, on the other hand, they would hardly provide a substitute for that social stratum of the public that goes to the cinemas solely for the dramas. One can more or less gauge the success that such a change would have by considering the importance of the panoramas, which, in comparison to the living images of the theaters, largely lead an extremely humble existence in some rear building. One may object that there is no climax, no movement here. In my view, though, this is not essential for mere nature films, as continuous film is not always determined by the portrayal. Movement enters a landscape only in a small proportion of the pictures, in flowing water, for example, and one of the most outstanding effects of cinematographic recording does indeed consist in this. It is not important whether a landscape is viewed in partial images of a somewhat smaller scale or in frequently discrete images. In so doing, one should not lose sight of the fact that the quality of what is offered in the cinema usually goes far beyond panoramic images. Yet this is a contingency determined by the large development and the capitalistic form of the company, and the great attractiveness of the cinema was long apparent even before film had surpassed technically the film slide.

Generally, the form of the presentation of nature films does not satisfy people's needs, and this is why it is basically a boring transition to the next shows for the majority of cinemagoers. As soon as action disappears from a film, talking in the room becomes livelier and attention drops off.

Scientific Films

Even scientific research work has become a tool in the apparatus of large-scale cinematographic companies. The French film companies have their own laboratories in which scientists do experiments or cultivate plants whose peculiarities enjoy popular interest and are easily understandable.

The significance of the cinema in the service of scientific research is much more important than these frivolities, though. Entirely new possibilities for knowledge have been opened through its utilization, in particularly great measure where it is necessary to gain a clear and absolutely accurate picture of the processes of motion that occur too quickly (flight of birds) or too slowly (growth of plants) to be captured in their individual phases. By means of cinematographic recording, the entire movement can now be adjusted to the eye's ability to perceive in slow or fast motion and each partial movement can be precisely studied.

The actual founder of scientific cinematography is Professor Marey, the same person to whom the perfection of cinematographic technique itself is greatly indebted.

In conjunction with Pathé Frères, Professor Commandon in Paris succeeded in constructing a device that made microscopic filming possible, and he first placed the new devices in the service of research in his examinations of the movement of blood in the vessels. Today, a central office for scientific cinematography has been created in the Marey Institute in which important scholars have the opportunity to conduct their research with the help of the most outstanding cinematographic devices. These devices themselves are being perfected more and more in the process. For years, experiments with the cinematographic recording of X-ray pictures have been made by Professor Carvallo and others. This procedure turned out to be very difficult, as the easily flammable film cannot withstand a luminosity of 2,000 candles, such as that of the X rays. Yet, he later succeeded with subsequent recordings that depicted stomach activity. Eykman-Scheveningen and Dessauer-Veifawerke Aschaffenburg brought the movement of the heart to film with the help of X rays.

When one speaks generally of scientific cinematography, though, then what is usually primarily meant is its capacity as a disseminator of popular scientific research that makes the insights of scholars into the processes of nature (which are gained only through great persistence and effort) accessible to a large public. As an instructional and educational factor in this sense, film is currently perhaps overrated. There is presently a real addiction to cramming huge amounts of material into people by, for example, suddenly instructing them for ten minutes during their entertainment in the cinema about the tsetse fly or incubation processes in a hen's egg or the fabrication of shoes. This might be quite entertaining; by the same token, though, a state of pseudo-education just as dangerous to culture as cinema dramas and comedies can result from an overestimation of what is achieved by this method. Deeper understanding is not possible in the face of the speed of the presentation and the rapid change of the most various impressions if an explanation is not provided. If, on the other hand, scientific pictures in the form of mere illustrations are added to a lecture or to a lesson, then this position changes, of course.

The Legal Framework

So far, the cinematographic industry has been considered as a private business enterprise of a small group of people. Yet, this manner of viewing the issue is decidedly insufficient to do justice to the cinema's impact. In a small book published by Gaumont, there is the sentence, "The cinema theater has outgrown the confines of a simple industry; it has become a factor, the common property of the entire world." It has thereby also become a public matter, though. If one conceives of the cinema theater industry as a mere business, as an opportunity to earn a living like many others that, while paying all attention to the best possible products, nevertheless, operate primarily according to economic principles, then the supreme law is big success at the cash register and high dividends. It goes without saying that first-class productions are not necessarily best suited for the attainment of this goal. Thus people made such large concessions to the taste of the broadest masses until a strong counter-current arose against the cinema itself. Under the pressure of public opinion and driven also by consideration of the ultimate interests of the industry itself, which must be concerned with maintaining the recognition won little by little from the side of the more judicious public, the idea of reform is also alive in the industry itself. Yet, despite all the speeches, despite all the conferences, it still sounds altogether like something unearned, like a certain concession that takes ethical and aesthetic demands into account at all against business interests. From this standpoint of the private enterprise, it is understandable if the measures taken by the legislature are felt to be extraordinarily severe and thus find incensed opponents, which is also why the first goal of all professional associations is then to reach an easing of the legal measures. Indeed, probably no industry is so greatly burdened. The cinema's impact extends far beyond that of similar business enterprises, and special laws and regulations have thus arisen that exert pressure on cinema theaters from three sides: (1) censorship; (2) child protection; (3) special taxation. For the time being, all these laws through which influence can be exerted are imperfect and hardly uniform. They have arisen for the most part in the form of ministerial decrees and police regulations in order to combat individual wrongs, as the cinema theater did not allow itself to be squeezed into existing laws. Eventually, all these special regulations will be unified by more rigid integration of the entire system and of locally variant individual regulations.

Censorship

I want first to say a few words about the censor, this much-deplored and much-desired institution. I am speaking primarily about Prussia, as it is important for the other federal states as well due to the centralization of the film business in Berlin. Prussian censorship regulations have developed in three stages. At the demand of schoolteachers and educators, preventative censorship was ordered for cinematographic products by a ministerial decree of December 11, 1911, for Prussia. This first ministerial decree stipulated that all films had to be submitted to the District Office for examination at the appropriate location twenty-four hours before screening, current films later. Many ill effects arose from this type of censoring, though. One and the same film had to be censored anew in every city in which it was to be shown, and that entailed much, partially wasted work. In addition, the decisions in various cities were different depending on the censor's disposition and financial losses thus followed upon the disruption of business activity, as well. For that reason, the call for a uniform Reich censor became loud. Under the pressure of the evils described above, the habit developed in business that nearly all films were submitted to the Berlin censor by manufacturers or importers and included a permit citing the production company, film length, film title, subtitle, and synopsis. Most police authorities then agreed with this decision. Everything was again censored only in individual places where the officials feared for the public's moral well-being. A further ministerial decree of April 30, 1912, followed the practice described above and provided that all films having the Berlin permit could be accepted without further examination. Yet, these rules were often circumvented. Films forbidden in Berlin were re-submitted in the province and frequently permitted there. In order to make better control possible and to render the censor more uniform, a refinement of the previous rules followed on July 6, 1912, that ordered, among other things, mutual notification among individual censorship authorities. A rather uniform administration of censorship was thereby achieved de facto, at least in Prussia. Although censorship will probably remain left to state legislature in the future as well, the states are seeking to achieve as much agreement as possible on the essential points.

The difficulty in administering all the laws determined by the censor is founded in the form of the object, i.e., of film. On the one hand, one cannot draw up a recipe according to which dramas may be made; on the other hand, though, the individual regulations just do not apply to the fundamental tendency of a piece. For only in consideration of this can one not do justice to the artistic qualities and, furthermore, pieces that do not offer any grounds for expurgation can indeed offend any moral and artistic sensitivity in the crudest manner. Thus, it is primarily up to the individual censor to achieve the intended goal to a greater or lesser degree with inadequate means. But in view of the mass of films presented (8 km per day) that are examined by four police councils, a schematic assessment is unavoidable even with the best of wills. So, the censor is then a constant bone of contention between both parties: the government on the one hand and the interested parties among the cinematographers on the other.

Child Protection

At the censor's office, films are divided into those allowed for children and those permitted only for adults. No effective protection against an unfavorable influence upon youth has yet been seen in this measure, though, and individual cities have thus entirely forbidden theater attendance by children at the demand of youth welfare organizations and teaching faculty. Child protection first had uniform regulation in Westphalia, then also in Schleswig-Holstein, where persons under 16 years are allowed to attend only shows for children. Wherever the prohibition was initially implemented, theater owners raised a protest, as they predicted a great decrease in their revenues. As the rules could not be effectively combated despite the attempts of several lawyers, though, insightful business people joined the efforts of the teaching faculty. First at the suggestion of Schools Chancellor Fricke in Hamburg and then of teachers and theater owners in Hannover and other cities as well, children's shows with selected film material were presented that, under the guidance of teachers, were viewed by school children for a low admission fee. This initially local arrangement has also become practical for other areas; for example, the magazine *Bild und Film*, published in Mönich-Gladbach, publicizes the selected films and thus provides all organizers of youth programs with suitable material. Such positive work—being seen as the lesser evil—has fostered further willingness to cooperate among theater owners, as could also be heard in the speeches given at the Cinema Convention in Berlin.

Taxes

City taxes appear to be the last and most effective means of keeping the ever-multiplying cinema theaters within bounds and have thus been most bitterly fought against by the interested parties—and, from the standpoint of business people, with justification; in some cities, they have indeed assumed a directly prohibitive character and have led to the destruction of a series of small businesses. Special cinema taxes have been levied against cinema theaters in addition to the high expenditures for entertainment taxes. They are a welcome supplement to the city purse especially in cities with high social service burdens, and these are mostly industrial cities in which cinemas are plentiful. The taxes are usually levied in the form of a ticket tax, i.e., five to ten percent or even twenty percent per ticket. This naturally results in very considerable sums, and so cinema theaters accounted for thirteen percent of all entertainment taxes in Cologne, for example, and ten percent in Elberfeld. The way in which these monies are used, though, is particularly bitter for those concerned. In Barmen, for example, the proceeds were spent to support the theater harmed by the cinema. Generally, this tax is successfully passed on to the public through an increase in admission prices.

The fact that educational films and nature films, in so far as they are shown at all, are tax-free also makes it apparent that the tax is intended to have the character of a repressive tax directed especially against presentations of sensational films. The impetus for this reform came from the Wiesbaden branch of the Organization Against Filth in Word and Image. They were guided by the notion that this type of presentation in particular could become a desirable means for enlightenment and the development of taste. The new tax was introduced in a similar form in Cologne on a trial basis, according to which presentations of exclusively scientific or didactic content were, upon application, to remain free of charge. Such applications were hardly filed, though. The radical change in programs intended by the elimination of dramas and comedies could not be so easily brought about, though. One should never lose sight of the fact that cinema theaters are generally popular as a means of entertainment and not as a means of education and, as such, have gotten such a strong foothold that their popularity surpasses that of anything that could come into question next to them.

Translated by Lance W. Garmer

2. Weimar Republic, 1918–33

WRITERS, CRITICS, AND ARTISTS

Herbert Ihering

Herbert Ihering (also spelled Jhering) (1888–1977) was one of the most influential film and theater critics of the Weimar Republic, and was published in such periodicals and newspapers as Sinn und Form, *the* Berliner Tageblatt, *and the* Berliner Börsencourier. *In addition to his work as a critic, he was active in theater and film production as dramaturg, casting director, and director. Belonging to the leftist circle of critics around Berlin, he was criticized for orienting his criticism after 1933 to the standards of the Ministry of Propaganda and continued to publish sanitized pieces during the Third Reich as was parodied in Klaus Mann's* Mephisto *(1936). It was also parodied in a poem by Alfred Kerr, a rival film critic with whom he had had a long-standing public disagreement about the function of the film critic. After the war, he wrote almost exclusively for the East German press although he lived in West Berlin. His collected works through 1932 were published in German in* Von Reinhardt bis Brecht. Vier Jahrzehnte Theater und Film (1958–1961).

An Expressionist Film (1920)

Expressionism and film mutually challenged one another. Film desired as a final consequence the exaggeration and rhythmization of gesture, expressionism the screen's possibilities of representation and variation. Particularly for the actor, film had to become a force for extensive performance and thus to accommodate the tendencies of a new stage art. If people had recognized the super-naturalistic demands of film in good time, the cinema—despite its artistic demoralization through business—could have assisted in the development of a precise, accentuated mimic art made fantastic by means of its objectivity. But people remained so far back and stuck to subject matter that expressionist film, which ought to be an organic development, is today considered to be a sensationalist experiment.

It is significant that the film *The Cabinet of Dr. Caligari* by Carl Mayer and Jans Janowitz was done in an expressionist manner only because it takes place in an insane asylum. One thus opposes the idea of healthy reality with the idea of sick unreality. Or: Impressionism exists where one remains accountable, expressionism where one remains unaccountable. Or: Insanity as an excuse for an artistic idea. But we want to assume that the expressionist risk does not appear so enormous to Robert Wiene the second time around and that he is laughing about the motivation for his venture. For expressionism is the requirement and law for all enhanced acting that overcomes content—and this is what film should provide. A good film is not one that, if need be, obscures the absence of the word, but the one whose actions would be disturbed by the word. The rhythm of the silence that voids language through the structure of gesture is the end and goal.

In particular, this goal is aspired to in *The Cabinet of Dr. Caligari*, but not always reached. When a sturdy naturalistic bed is in a set in which all lines intersect, then the rhythm is voided. When actors perform listlessly and indeterminately in landscapes and rooms that seek in their forms to extend beyond themselves, then the extension of the principle to bodily expression is absent. When actors made up to appear mask-like and rigid alternate with naturalistically made-up ones, then the style subverts itself. And what should engender mutual enhancement, inhibits. Aside from smaller roles—Fritz Fehér performs old, kitschy, plodding film mimicry and Lil Dagover is the sweet actress without talent who, with her expressionless fluidity, is generally insufferable but especially so here. Expressionism exposes. It requires an uncompromising selection of actors.

To their core, Conrad Veidt, who rose above his own body, had the style as the somnambulist, and Werner Krauss had the phenomenon as Dr. Caligari. But it is odd: Werner Krauss, who on the stage summons from the terrific intensity of his body any accent without diminishing nuance, is often unsettled in film, where his body's power of expression should attain its ultimate enhancement, and he grasps for support in overacting otherwise unknown to him.

Finally: This film is an advance in graphic terms—Hermann Warm, Walter Reimann, and Walter Röhrig are responsible for this—and promising in terms of directing. In order to achieve this, compromises must be eliminated and the typical racing around, embarrassing chases and banal groupings for the conclusion must be gotten rid of. Then film can break through the technical mastery represented by Lubitsch to a freer rhythmization and thus to an intellectuality that is appropriate.

Translated by Lance W. Garmer

Claire Goll

As a university student in Geneva where she studied philosophy, Claire Goll (born Clarisse Aischmann) (1891–1977), was active in the peace and women's movement. She later was involved with Dadaism and Surrealism. It was during this period that her first novellas and poetry were published. In 1939, Goll and her husband Yvan Goll, also a poet with whom she published love poems, fled the Nazis and emigrated to New York. Her mother did not survive the Holocaust and was murdered in Auschwitz. Later in life, Goll, who lived in Paris, primarily composed her poetry in French and won numerous literary prizes.

American Cinema (1920)

The Continent still has not realized that the cinema is not related to the theater. While Berlin is dripping wet with terrible series of anachronistic history films, the sentimentalities of Bernstein and Bataille are being photographed and pornographed for the cinema in Paris. While Balzac, Strindberg and Dostoyevsky are being filmed and turned into gelatin in Berlin, Zola's *Travail* is being produced in Paris! Here, *Morel: The Master of the Chain*; there, *Houdini: The Master of Mystery*. Bad, dopey sensations: detective, revolver, mask. Here, *Kohlhiesel's Daughter* for humor or real Bavarian alpine feelings; there, the vapid comedian's grimace of Rigadius. The actresses express the psychological moment by changing clothes and the actor through lighting cigarettes and words!

Whereas the old world endures this kitsch, America's healthy will has created true film. In the good American film, any literary element is left out, first of all. What is happening or rather racing by on the screen can no longer be called plot. It is a new dynamic, a breathless rhythm, action in an unliterary sense. Nor is it created and acted out in a glass house, but rather in the open air.

The American calls film "moving pictures," and not without reason do people in Paris compare the films from across the ocean with Manet, Cézanne, etc.

Advanced mechanics, technique, and primarily a foundation in grand style (in Los Angeles, for example, an entire film village with saloons, ranches, etc. was built) have produced truly miraculous works. America's great screen stars work exclusively for film, never for the theater. They themselves create their pieces and do almost entirely without the word, which they replace with concentrated movement and pantomime.

America's three most internationally famous and celebrated thespians are Douglas Fairbanks (Doug), Charlie Chaplin (Charlot) and Sessue Hayakawa (the Japanese). The genius among them is Charlot, the Molière of this century. In the clown's mask, completely doing without his own beauty (which of our actors would even do without his good ironing crease!), he has put his stamp on nearly every human weakness in the course of five years. His eccentric, mathematically construed movements, the psychological ones and the bodily ones, always contain a tragic comedy. For deep, knowing laughing that sticks not only to the surface, is born from melancholy and suffering. Charlot's irresistibility, though, lies not only in his explosive musical rhythm, but rather primarily in his face, which shows twenty nuances in a second. Every evening, the souls of Paris artists emigrate to America, off to Charlot, whose shadow is livelier than the bodies of all the thespians of the city on the Seine.

No physical feat is impossible for Charlot, nor for most Americans. He is an acrobat, athlete, and juggler, and this further increases the effect of his films.

In this, he is surpassed only by Douglas Fairbanks, who seems to put his life on the line in every film. He playfully executes the most superhuman things: he jumps with his horse from a racing express train or from one racecar into another. He climbs up a steep church or a skyscraper, hops from one roof over the street to the other. But these are only illustrations for the content of his films. (In our country, this would be the film itself and would be called "Leap of Death" by Fern Andra.) He mockingly imitates the ethical-social contents of five-act, tear-jerking films. He represents the American principle of taking nothing seriously, nothing narrowly. Like a jaguar, he lurks in a club chair, always ready to jump in and out of the so-called action into a joke or into the unusual. The American cinema has already accustomed its public to much. Tanks ride into houses, three cars race into one another or into the sea; 2,000 meters up, a man performs acrobatics from one airplane to another and comes down on a parachute over the ocean and New York without knowing whether and where he will land. Douglas Fairbanks breaks the record, though. He is the expression of a granite energy, of the heart-pounding life of a fresh world.

The great Japanese is all psychological effect: Sessue Hayakawa. No rinky-dink feelings, but primeval emotion. Not an art desecrated by civilization.

When he portrays grief, his pain is of ancient magnitude. When he plays the lover, his smile has the grace and fragrance of lotus and cherry blossoms. When he is the avenger, his body explodes in exotic savageness. Whoever sees him knows everything about Japan and the beauty of the mystical East.

These three people have raised film into the grandiose in all directions. The Continent will have something to learn from them for the future.

Translated by Lance W. Garmer

Hugo von Hofmannsthal

As a young high school student, Hugo (Hofmann Edler) von Hofmannsthal (1874–1929) had already published his first poetry. His early work earned him the reputation of being an aesthete, but in his 1905 fictional Letter of Lord Chandos (Ein Brief) *he tackles the modernist crisis of language. Hofmannsthal eventually focused his attention on the theater (operas, comedies, and dramas), much to the dismay of fellow poet Stefan George in whose literary magazine he frequently published. With such works as* Elektra *(1906) and* The Rosenkavalier *(1911), both of which were collaborations with Richard Strauss, and* Der Schwierige *(The Difficult One, 1917), he established his reputation as one of the most important figures in Austrian drama. His* Everyman (Jedermann, *1911) is staged every year at the Salzburg Festival Plays* (Salzburger Festspiele), *which he co-founded with Max Reinhardt. He is also represented in The German Library volumes 30 and 83.*

The Substitute for Dreams (1921)

What the people are looking for in the movie theater, said my friend with whom I came to this topic, what all the working people are looking for in the movie theater is a substitute for dreams. They want to fill their imagination with pictures, strong images in which the essence of life is summarized and that at the same time are constructed out of the viewer's inner being and go to his heart. For life owes them such images. (I am speaking of those people who live in the cities or large contiguous industrial areas, not of the others, the peasants, the shipmen, the woodsmen or highlanders.) Their heads are empty, not by nature, but rather because of the life that society forces them to lead. There are these conglomerations of coal-blackened places of industry with nothing except a small strip of withered meadow grass between them, and with the children who grew up there, of whom not one in six-thousand has in his life seen an owl or a squirrel or a spring—these are our cities, these lines of houses endlessly crisscrossing one another. The houses look similar to one another; they have a small door and lines of uniform windows and the stores are downstairs. Nothing speaks to the person who comes over or who is looking for a house: the only thing that speaks is the number. This is how the factory, the workroom, the machine, and the office where a person pays taxes or registers looks: nothing remains except the number. This is the workday: the routine of factory life or of the craftsman's trade; the couple of hand movements, always the same ones; the same hammering or swinging or filing or lathing. Then back at home: the gas cooker, the iron oven, the couple of appliances and small machines on which one is dependent and that require such practice to master that, finally, the person who constantly deals with them himself becomes a machine, a tool among tools. By the countless hundreds of thousands, they flee from this into the dark room with the moving pictures. It is one excitement more that these pictures are silent; they are silent like dreams. And at the most profound level, without knowing it, these people fear language; they fear in language the tool of society. The lecture hall is next to the cinema, the meeting-place is one small street farther, but they do not have this power. The entrance to the cinema attracts the steps of people with a power like—like the liquor cabinets; and yet, it is something different. Written in gilded letters over the lecture hall is "Knowledge is Power," but the cinema calls more strongly: it calls with images. The power that is imparted to them through knowledge—something about this power is unfamiliar to them, not entirely convincing, nearly suspicious. They feel that it leads only deeper into the machinery and farther and farther away from actual life, from that which their senses and a deeper mystery lingering under their senses tell them is actual life. Knowledge, education, the understanding of connections—all this perhaps loosens the shackles that they feel wrapped around their hands—perhaps loosens them—for the moment—in pretense—in order then perhaps to draw them together even more tightly. All this perhaps leads in the end to a new chain and even deeper bondage. (I am not saying that they say this, but a voice says it in them very quietly.) And their inner being would remain empty in the face of all this. (They say this as well to themselves without saying it to themselves.) The characteristic vapid emptiness of reality, the wasteland—out of which liquor leads—the few ideas that hang in the emptiness—all this is not really made whole by what the lecture hall offers. The slogans of the party congresses, the columns of the newspaper that appear daily—in these, too, there is nothing that would really cancel out the wasteland of existence. This language of the educated and semi-educated, whether spoken or written, it is something strange. It ruffles the surface, but it does not awaken what slumbers in the depths. There is too much algebra in this language; another numeral covers every letter, the numeral is an abbreviation for a reality; all this points from afar to something, also to power, even to power in which one has some share; but all this is too indirect, the connections are too non-material, this does not really lift up the spirit, does not carry it off to any place. All this rather leaves behind a despondency and again this feeling of being a powerless part of a machine, and they all know another power, a real one, the only real one: that of dreams. They were children, and they were powerful beings then. There were dreams, at night, but they were not limited to the night; they were also present by day: a dark corner, a breath of air, the face of an animal, the shuffling of a strange footstep sufficed to make their constant presence noticeable. There was the dark room behind the cellar stairs, an old barrel in the yard, half-full with rainwater, a chest with junk; there was the door to a closet, the attic door, the door to the neighbor's apartment out of which someone came before whom one anxiously ducked past, or a beautiful creature that cast the sweet, indefinable shudder of a dawning desire deep into the dark, quaking depths of the heart— and now it is again a chest with magical junk that opens: the cinema. There lies open everything that otherwise is hidden behind the cold, opaque facades of the endless houses, there all the doors open up, into the parlors of the rich, into the room of the young girl, into the halls of the hotels; into the hide-out of the thief, into the workshop of the alchemist. It is the trip through the air with the devil Asmodi, who takes all the roofs off and exposes all secrets. But it is not merely the pacification of a tormenting curiosity, so often disappointed: as with the dreaming person, a satisfaction is prepared here for a more secret desire: dreams are deeds, a sweet self-deception involuntarily mingles with this limitless watching, it is like having complete freedom to control these silent, graciously rushing pictures, complete freedom to control entire lives. The landscape, house and park, forest and port that race by behind the figures only add a new type of muffled music—stirring up God knows what kind of yearning and exaltation, down in the dark region into which no written and spoken word intrudes—in film, though, an entire literature meanwhile flies past in torn shreds, no, a whole tangle of literature, the remaining figures of thousands of dramas, novels, crime stories; the historical anecdotes, the hallucinations of spirit-seers, the reports of adventures, yet, at the same time, beautiful creatures and transparent gestures, miens and glances out of which the entire soul breaks forth. They live and suffer, struggle and pass away before the eyes of the dreamer; and the dreamer knows that he is awake; he need hide nothing of himself; with everything that is in him, into his innermost recesses, he stares at this flickering wheel of life that eternally turns. The entire person surrenders to this spectacle; there is not a single dream from the most tender childhood that would not resonate with this. For we have only seemingly forgotten our dreams. Of every one of them, including those that we had already forgotten upon awakening, there remains something in us, a quiet, yet decisive coloring of our affects; there remain the habits of the dream in which the whole person exists, more than in the habits of life, all the suppressed obsessions in which the strength and peculiarity of the individual develop inwardly. All this subterranean vegetation vibrates in harmony all the way to the darkest soil at the roots, while the eyes read the thousand-faceted image of life from the flickering film. Indeed, this dark soil at the root of life, it, the region where the individual ceases to be an individual, there where a word—even the word of the prayer or the stammering of love—so seldom reaches, this region vibrates in harmony. From it, though, proceeds the most secret and deepest of all of life's feelings: the sense of indestructibility, the belief in necessity, and contempt for the merely real that exists only contingently. Once it begins moving, there proceeds from it what we call the power of myth formation. In the presence of this dark glance, the symbol arises from the being's depths like lightening: the physical image for intellectual truth that is unattainable by reason.

I know, my friend concluded, that there are many ways of looking at these things. And I know there is a way of looking at them that is legitimate from another standpoint and that sees nothing in all of it except a wretched confusion of industrial greediness, the omnipotence of technology, the abasement of things intellectual, and dull curiosity side-tracked in any direction. To me, though, the atmosphere of the cinema seems to be the only atmosphere in which the people of our time—those who comprise the masses—enter into an entirely immediate, entirely unrestrained relationship with an enormous, albeit strangely formed spiritual heritage, life-to-life, and the jam-packed, half-dark room with the pictures flickering by is for me—I cannot say it otherwise—almost sacred, as the place where souls, in a vague urge for self-preservation, flee from the numeral to vision.

Translated by Lance W. Garmer

Carl Einstein

Carl Einstein (1885–1940) had a great influence on the avant-garde movement in Germany in the early part of the twentieth century. With his Negro Sculpture *(Negerplastik, 1915), in which he provided a theoretical basis for Cubism, he was one of the first to argue for the recognition of African art. He was also active in the Dada movement. Together with painter Georg Grosz, he published the periodical* Der blutige Ernst *(Bloody seriousness). During his time in Berlin (1919–28) he wrote his most successful book,* Twentieth Century Art *(Die Kunst des 20. Jahrhunderts, 1926) and published critical essays on art as well as monographs. From 1936 to 1938, he participated in the Spanish Civil War, was interned, and as the Nazi troops approached Spain he committed suicide.*

The Bankruptcy of German Film (1922)

The cinema is as old as the man who watches his life hurrying past, as old as our vanity that looks at itself in the mirror in low-burning candles before going to sleep. Whether mystery play, Egyptian relief series or Chinese makimono, it was cinema.

The easily overrated, yet manifold means of the cinema really narrowed, made one flat-headed, bustling, whereby one feeble idea is regularly sent running by an even more dim-witted one. The movie theater manager forces upon every person a level that he ridicules and has long since left behind as soon as the photographic suggestion releases him. When one enters the cinema, then one hands over at the checkroom, besides one's hat and walking stick, above all one's brain and learning in order to subject oneself to nearly painful idiocy, for the audience usually leaves the cinema precisely with a feeling of ridiculously tangible idiocy, and one often feels embarrassed shame, as if one were leaving an unseemly house, even though one has only watched atavistic childish pranks. Because one can never believe that two times two is four, though— for one could otherwise no longer live—so one runs to the next film; indeed, every film lives off of the empty disappointment that the previous one caused us.

First of all, the sentimental events of film. The greatest portion of all this rubbish is dripping with banally atavistic deception; we are expected to endure situations that perhaps happened to a retired assistant teacher of Stone Age hydrocephali, about which infants now already smile arrogantly. As if Mrs. X were wearing only a flaming red heart and carrying novels by Courths-Mahler or by Madeleine in aroused *combinaison*; perhaps also, tucked into her arched corset, a Strindberg—which was edited by a cadet, however.

If one films the soul, by which one usually means the close-up shot of a whimpering mouth or some teary waterworks, then one laughs the more despairingly the diva flinches. And even when the honest Thespian struggles inside instead of raising another drink.

Compared with the soul of film, the diagram of a children's reform school is confusing. The only thing that has an effect almost as idiotic as art is the amazingly insolent improbability of these things that are photographed as truly to reality as possible.

If—let them have it—art is created in film, though, people make use of the vulgarized means of some season long passed away. People say that the director must have a good nose; experience teaches that he is not allowed to have one.

People described the film director as a man who races in a hundred-horsepower car, roars through a megaphone and uses a general's mound. He races in gasoline because he has been crippled by bad strokes; megaphone because he has lost his voice due to old age and infirmity; general's mound due to advanced arterial sclerosis.

The only person who knows how to use the canonized idiocy of film: Chaplin. (Whereas the Germans let the great native of Munich Karl Valentin wail through Mr. P.)

Courths-Mahler, the sentimental picture postcard, bargain-basement expressionism—all this belongs together and lives from the exhausted boredom of contemporaries who do not know how they can spend their evenings.

And if nothing else attracts, people finance the historical costume film, i.e., circus reviews without technology and swanky Meiningen-like productions; in between, a few tempestuously pulsating rubber breasts, an "as-if" Sieglinde position and, in the orchestra, the Weser Song in whole-tone scale; or the chase, where one wishes that the cunningly righteous man would finally explode into a thousand pieces so that he would not besmirch the screen with even more grease and even more all-knowingly in the eighth part.

I do not doubt that world events—drawn-out funeral home—finally acquired meaning when Schulze had sucked off an autograph and free ticket from Yvonne Merdetti; in the end, though, our life is paid for too dearly with this. If one adores a boxer, then one respects the man who takes fantastically heavy blows, and takes them so long, until his brain, trained against beating, comes to itself and, in so doing, loses all consciousness. One respects this man all the more when he abides by the Bible quotation that should hang over every boxing ring, namely, that giving is more blessed than receiving. When I see what the stomachs and jaws of Criqui and Siki withstand, then a certain optimism carries over from them to me; I believe, thanks to them, that people will still endure life the next eight days. And that is a great deal. On the other hand, when I see what people call erotic passion in film, an incident almost uglier than unfilmed erotic insanity, then the only result is that I consume whiskey in order to forget this basic idiocy, which stands perfectly in inverse proportion to the means expended.

Film character types: the detective who knows everything and whom criminals get away from until the film company budget is used up. His intelligence is in a pipe bowl and the soot of the chimneys he has climbed through bleaches his shirts like chlorine.

A diva who loves the man whom she hates because she is married to the man whom she despises, while she pursues the man from whom she wants to flee in order to choose, exhausted, the man who in the first reel was already wearing the most modern cut or a woman's cape over a striped sport coat with pumps.

Or such a young man, right-thinking but without means, who wears soft collars and belts, fear not! The righteous man will only pretend for three reels that he is working; for only a rich heiress may fall in love with him, and the film is boring just like the morality of a type of aunt that, having disappeared around the time of the great Marlitt, is again electrically illuminated in film.

Proprietors of businesses betray a sensibility in film that would make it impossible for them to operate a match store and that is just as great as common boorishness.

If a person is engaged, then spring chirps on the Wannsee; people usually have a relationship in Friedenau or Tempelhof and renounce happiness in the presence of a frosted-glass screen and the moon, which rolls over Lake Müggel like an elongated blob of fat. Who would still dare make such oleographs? He would go broke.

That a crowd of two-thousand people forms is one of the more recent mysteries of film, given that the police have for thousands of years dispersed groups of two people with gracious skill.

Film has one thing in common with bad theater: One doubles over where one should bawl and one cries where, in terms of directing, one should die with laughter.

Dukes behave like a confused horde of evicted paupers, while lackeys exhibit the affable joviality of joking princes. Indeed, we would hang ourselves were life for one minute as boring as the typical film, and, in the end, most people tolerate this swindle out of respect for the enormous costs invested in it. There is said to be an artistic film, though, whose script is written by a tailor and in which an expressionist sculptor designs underpants and a writer has combed out the wigs. And always reliable living images.

Translated by Lance W. Garmer

Fritz Lang

Fritz (Friedrich) Lang (1890–1976) began his extraordinarily successful career in film as a screenwriter and director for Erich Pommer's Decla Film Company; he followed Pommer to Germany's largest film studio, Ufa. Before fleeing to the U.S. and divorcing his wife, collaborator and Nazi Party member Thea von Harbou, he directed some of the most well-known and visually stunning films of the Weimar era: Dr. Mabuse, the Gambler *(Dr. Mabuse, der Spieler, 1922),* The Nibelungen *(1924),* M *(his first sound film in 1931), and of course, the technically innovative film that bankrupted Ufa,* Metropolis *(1927). Lang's enormous success as a filmmaker continued in the U.S., where he directed films as diverse as the crime movie* Fury *(1936), the Western* Rancho Notorious *(1952) starring Marlene Dietrich, and such classics of film noir as* Secret Beyond the Door *(1948),* The Blue Gardenia *(1953), and* The Big Heat *(1953).*

The Artistic Composition of the Film Drama (1924)

To come quickly to the actual topic, the artistic composition of the film drama, I would like to define this topic somewhat more broadly than, going by the letter, it would appear at first sight. I would like, in particular, to put forward not only dramaturgic propositions, as it were, of how one structures a film drama—to put forward a cooking recipe, so to speak—as this is perhaps not even possible, since *every* film has *different* principles. I would like, rather, to speak primarily about the artistic composition of the film drama per se. And it is not difficult for me to speak about this. I may boast to have been one of those among the passionate pioneers for the development of film who fought most fiercely for the claim that film is called upon to develop itself from a vapid entertainment industry to an artwork, and I may well say with pride and pleasure that I have succeeded in this through the splendid association with Erich Pommer, the chairman of the board of my company, Dekla-Bioskop-Ufa.

Allow me first to utter the seemingly bold word—all the bolder as it comes in a city that is full of theatrical traditions—that film seems destined to depose the theater or, better said, the stage.

I would like to explain this to you with an example. If it is to be made clear on the stage that a mountain climber is falling down, then we are either told how terrible the danger was in which the person in question found himself and that he then fell down. If the person in question really "falls" down, then our brain cells must quickly translate that it is not a stage, but a mountain, and that I was told of this mountain that a very deep chasm lies behind it and the man has now fallen into this terrible chasm.—To perform so much mental work after a difficult day at work is out of the question for the brain of a person who works more than the obligatory eight-hour day—and nearly everyone does that today. He is simply too tired, too fatigued, too worn-out. With film, it is different. Film itself is what is evident and visual and is thus the immediate expression of an event that I can enjoy watching, and which possesses the powerful plasticity of what is experienced.—Consider the same image in film. You see a very high precipice and a small man on the edge of it. This automatically places the impression in your brain: the enormous precipice, the small man.—You identify with the man, and the reaction occurs immediately: For God's sake, don't let him fall!—A blaze that is *seen* has an effect a thousand times more vivid than one most brilliantly narrated!!!

After its marvelous successes—not least of all here in Vienna and Berlin under Reinhardt's brilliant direction—the stage has apparently fulfilled its mission and must learn that the people for whom the stage has until now meant detachment from the ego, shock or pleasure are now already turning—hesitantly at first, then irresistibly attracted—in hordes to the new art form: film.

With the peculiarly German ability to make the simplest things as complex as possible, people have now tried to turn film's intelligibility to the man on the street into a criticism and have presented it specifically as a product for the masses. This attitude seems to me to be a crude injustice with respect to the masses as well as to film. The strange mixture of essences that allows film to appear, its artistic mission notwithstanding, as an industrial product naturally entails its being able to be made easily and inexpensively available to the masses. And the working masses, i.e., what is fortunately by far the largest segment of a people, seem to me to have a totally unconditional right to be released, at least for a few hours, from the drudgery of everyday life with an art form that speaks to them most, and a right to partake of the best that their nervous systems can take in: relaxation, fortification, recuperation.

Unfortunately, I must protest here against an institution that boldly endeavors to do justice to the will of the people—I am referring to the censor. I myself have almost never had problems with the censorship authorities—except for *Dr. Mabuse*, in which case people were of the odd opinion that one could show people shooting firearms in street fights, but no corpses; yet the political era of the Spartacus battles was probably still too close in their memories. This was only an exceptional case, though. Otherwise, the Berlin censorship authorities were always friendly toward my mission, the development of artistic film.

I do not believe, though, that a people whose maturity has been politically documented by the state with universal suffrage, that this people would need a guardian because some claim that its members are not mature enough to know what hurts or helps them.—It is, for example, an impossible state of affairs that censorship authorities would object to a poster for the *Nibelungen* film because Siegfried is shown pierced by a spear and, at the same time, a poster for the *Bluebeard* circus pantomime hangs on outdoor advertising columns where skulls, naked women's bodies and blood come together to form a lovely still life.

It would be fine with me if the state would introduce a restriction for young people—I am in agreement—but it should not want to dictate to grown people what relaxation, what fortification, and what recuperation their brains need.

And here I have come to the point from which one must first start with the artistic composition of the film drama.

Among those people who wish to deny film any value, we repeatedly encounter the claim that film addresses itself to the so-called base instincts of people and owes its greatest successes to the offering of what is sensational, which is exploited by the film industry for economic reasons. Let us investigate this claim. It would, of course, be ridiculous to claim that the only forces at work in the film industry are those that produce films purely from an idealistic standpoint with no regard for business. This is nonsense, of course. But it has long since become apparent in the leading circles of the film industry—and everyone, including the film industry, learns from the tasks at hand—that an artistic film is just as good business as, if not better business than, a film that was made *purely* from a business standpoint. Please, do not condemn the sensational film of earlier years, for it alone made possible the rational composition of the artistic film drama, it alone made it possible for us to see the mistakes of this genre, and we learned the new forms of the new art from it. We learned that films have different principles from those of the theater, that the film drama has something to do with the theater drama only in a purely external sense; we learned that films have different laws from novels and novellas, that it was a new art form, and this was infinitely important for those who, out of the deepest heart-felt need, were involved with the artistic composition of film. It will perhaps seem ridiculous today, three, four or five years later. But I want to show you, you who are sitting here before me, how important it was with an example. When you go to the movies today, you say, "We're going to watch a film," and you don't even go so far as to classify as one does in the theater: drama, play, farce, comedy, slapstick, revue, or operetta. Instead you simply go and say to yourselves that you are going to watch a film. From this one example, imagine what this realization had to mean for us, for those of us people in the front row who fight for the artistic film with every nerve. And the artistic composition of the film began from this moment. And all these films, which I would evaluate as equivalent to any artwork, have demonstrably had the greatest successes in recent years. I choose randomly and would have to deem it nasty grandstanding were I to say nothing of several films that belong in this category because they are by me: take *Dr. Caligari*, the brilliant artistic idea of reproducing the visionary delusions of a madman through expressionism; *Golem* and *The Student of Prague*, the first attempt to express the magical and the spectral through this new art form;—*Madame Dubarry*, the only artistic work in which the so-called revolution manifested itself artistically; my *Destiny* [*Der müde Tod*, literally *The Tired Death*], in which I attempted to capture the German folksong in images; take *Sir Arne's Treasure*, *The Kid*, anything with Chaplin, the potential for making things ridiculous and for castigating our weaknesses; my *Dr. Mabuse*, which was to tear open the world around 1922 and to show us its hollowness; the *Lost Shoe*.—Does someone perhaps want to claim that Stiller's *Erotikon* is a sensational film? Grune's *Street* or Lubitsch's *The Flame*—or do you want to call my *Nibelungen* film a sensational film because Siegfried fights with the dragon? Certainly not. And yet these films were and are huge, commercially solid successes here and abroad, and the film industry did excellent business with these nonsensational films.

You have so far followed me in my remarks about the artistic composition of the film drama. It is anchored in the area of film most particular to it, in the limitlessness of its means of expression, which have left a completely new mark on the notion of magic, of the fabulous, in short, of the unusual. And secondly in the immediacy that I already mentioned and with which film orients itself toward the watching eye of man; it attests to our work in the artistic composition of the film drama that the public in our great first-run theaters rejects inferior films with the same energy, even boos them out, that it used to display in former times against affronts on the stage, and with the same energy, on the other hand, that it cheered *The Lost Shoe* in unconcealed rapture or applauded the *Nibelungen* film. To speak from my personal experience, it touched me with delight that, in Berlin as well as in London, the simple image of Siegfried from the second reel, in which the young dragon-slayer stops on the drawbridge with his heroes, that this image was accepted with ostentatious applause. And, in the case of this motionless image, one cannot speak of a sensation, try as one may.

Ladies and gentlemen, I am by no means one of those people who reject or even condemn sensational film in itself. Here as everywhere, it depends much more on the "how" rather than on the "what." Shakespearian dramas, separated from the brilliant mind of the great Englishman, display a continuous series of murder and manslaughter, poison and cruelty! It depends only on the "how"!! And the principle that good sensational films represent by placing black and white, good and evil next to one another; and by showing the bad guy leading the good and the honest ones into all conceivable dangers toward which the good one at first perhaps even succumbs, in order finally to overcome them victoriously; to harvest the reward of his honesty and of his good nerves and to see the evil rival punished and destroyed; all this seems to me to be an altogether healthy and acceptable world principle which one would heartily like to wish the widest circulation and fulfillment. It would also seem to me to be a serious endangerment of a good cause if one wanted to damn the artistic film to boredom by eliminating this great rule of the cinema and thereby render it incapable of survival.

In our efforts for the artistic composition of film drama, one man helped us to navigate past this cliff in the initial phases of film, a man to whom we owe thanks for the purest beauty and pure artistic sense in film even then. I am referring to Paul Wegener, who, at a time when hardly anyone took film seriously, created *Golem* and *The Student of Prague* and thereby uncovered one of the most essential peculiarities of film: the spectral, the process of making the unreal come alive.

Specifically on the occasion of the *Nibelungen* film, the question has been posed to me from various quarters of whether it was not tempting to me to try to get at the core of our century, the twentieth century, by means of the film and its unlimited technical possibilities and to make a film typically modern in every regard. I still am not able to comment on that today, although my internally formulated answer is already closer today to a "yes" than to a "no."

I have already said before that, just as everywhere, so also in the case of film, the "how" is of greater importance than the "what." My wife and most faithful co-worker, Thea von Harbou, whom I also thank for the script for the *Nibelungen,* is wont to express this a little drastically but correctly with the words, "One can make a fabulous film even of the Berlin address book if one goes about it in the right way." By this I would not like to have it said that the Berlin address book is the basis for my next film. It is true that no rules and no limits can be established for the composition of the artistic film drama: what is a sin against the spirit of art—and a sin that takes merciless revenge—is the economic activity created by any film hit without artistic conviction, without wanting to struggle out of inner necessity, to use a big word. One can bet 99-to-1 that the result will be a nasty defeat with respect to art and to business. In the case of every art, but quite particularly in the case of film, the highest law is that one must be riveted to the core and possessed by one's work and by one's labor itself. It can never be done by clever calculation. Whoever presumes to participate, and feels himself called to be involved, in the development of the artistic film must feel in his innermost being like the great pioneers who explored unknown parts of the world. There is no deprivation that must not be born, no labor from which one may withdraw, more sleepless nights than sleep, more work than rest, more bitter than sweet, as you may believe me. The world of the Bible applies to film as to hardly any other profession: "Whoever has laid a hand on the plough and looks back is not fit for this work."[1]

To every person who is involved with the task I love above everything else, the artistic development of the film drama and especially of the German film drama, I would like to cry out two words that always hovered before the eyes of my co-workers and me during the two-year production of the *Nibelungen* film, two words that, when I was in London for about ten days, I again found in German on the crest of arms of the Prince of Wales at the premiere of the *Nibelungen* film in the Royal Albert Hall: "I serve."

Translated by Lance W. Garmer

F. W. Murnau

One of the most influential filmmakers of the early German cinema, Friedrich Wilhelm Murnau (1888–1930) is most famous now for his adaptation of the Dracula story, Nosferatu *(1922), considered one of the classics of expressionist cinema;* The Last Laugh *(Der letzte Mann, 1924); and* Faust *(1925). He then went to the U.S., where he directed* Sunrise *(1927). In 1930, he directed the semidocumentary* Tabu *in the South Pacific. That same year he died in an automobile accident in California.*

The Ideal Picture Needs No Titles: By Its Very Nature the Art of the Screen Should Tell a Complete Story Pictorially (1928)

"It's another war picture." Of course it is! And there will be another, and another, and another.

---

[1] This is a reference to an actual passage from the Bible, Luke 9:62, which reads in the King James version as follows: "No man, having put his hand to the plough, and looking back is fit for the kingdom of God." (Translator's note)

It is as natural for this country to be flooded with war pictures, and continue to be for the next few years, as it is for a soldier to want to display his *Croix de Guerre*. War is new to America. It is an heroic event. America entered, not because it was forced to but because it volunteered—a demonstration of bravery, loyalty and martyrdom, each of these attributes a thread in the cloth called romance. Not so for Europe. Those countries are too full of it, too thoroughly immersed in the devastation of war any longer to see the romance of it. Don't you find that the man who has gone through the most horrible experiences is usually the one to say the least about them, and when asked whether he had suffered such and such a shock or witnessed such and such a catastrophe, will answer laconically: "Yes" or "No" and dismiss the subject.

Such is the position of the European countries, and that is the reason war is too real for them to idealize and romanticize over it in pictures and plays. It was an event to America, not a horror. Men enlisted bravely, hysterically; many returned in the same spirit, only more exalted for the thrills and frills that they could talk about after it was over.

I have become the most extreme pacifist because I have lived through the most lurid realities of its destructive force. It is my aim to do a war picture soon, but not the kind that would treat of the glorification of gore and wholesale slaughter, but rather disclosing its perniciousness and convincing people of the utter futility of physical combat.

What can the effect of the picture be that for two or two and one-half hours shows two nations at war, working up to its dramatic climaxes by bombing, blasting, shooting or wiping out armies of men, the helpless puppets of quarreling nations? And then waving the victorious country's flag and playing all the brasses of the orchestra *fortissimo*? At every showing of the picture, in every theatre where it is featured, at its two, three or four performances a day, there are from 2,000 to 3,000 susceptible people being stimulated into a bellicose attitude.

And the women, incredible as it may sound, play the most important part in battle. Just so long as they dub as a coward the man who refuses or hesitates to "fight," regardless of his ideals, just so long as they are proud to cling to the arm of a uniform, and they glory in the sacrifice of their sons, sweethearts, brothers and husbands for "the cause," just so long shall we continue to have war and continue to show pictures apotheosizing war.

As to the general future of motion pictures—I can say nothing definite; one can merely conjecture. The only point on which I would assert myself is that the ordinary picture, without movietone accompaniment, without color, without prismatic effects and without three dimensions, but with as few subtitles as possible, will continue as a permanent form of the art. Future developments may give birth to other forms, but the original form will continue with an identity of its own.

I hope to make the next picture after this without any titles whatever. *The Last Laugh* had only one. One way of eliminating titles is by showing two antagonistic thoughts as parallels; for example, by wishing to convey the wealth of a certain person as being extreme, I would show alongside of him a greatly impoverished character. Symbolism would obviate titles. I like the reality of things, but not without fantasy; they must dovetail. Is that not so with life, with human reactions and emotions? We have our thoughts and also our deeds. James Joyce, the English novelist, demonstrates this very well in his works. He first picturizes the mind and then balances it with the action. After all, the mind is the motive behind the deed.

I believe that in the future various theatres will be known for special grades of production. Just as the different publishing houses are each identified with certain types of books, running from trash to the classics, so there will be cinema houses identified with specific grades of pictures. A time will come when the moving-picture patron will become addicted to one grade of picture and will not patronize a theatre that shows cheap comedies one week and classic productions another week.

Real art is simple, but simplicity requires the greatest art. The camera is the director's sketching pencil. It should be as mobile as possible to catch every passing mood, and it is important that the mechanics of the cinema should not be interposed between the spectactor and the picture. The film director must divorce himself from every tradition, theatrical or literary, to make the best possible use of his new medium.

I find it preferable to work with actors and actresses who have had just enough experience to keep them from being great, but not enough to keep them from being pliable. Everything is subordinated to my picture, and just as I do not permit myself to be influenced away from what I think is the right thing to do and the right person to use, I will not do a picture that is based on a theme not to my liking or conviction.

THEORISTS

Béla Balázs

Béla Balázs, born Herbert Bauer (1884–1949), began his film career in his native Hungary as a director. But he is best-known for his works on film theory, an excerpt of which is reprinted. After the failure of the revolution in Hungary in which he participated, Belázs moved to Vienna and later to Berlin until 1933 to write screenplays, film reviews, and theoretical pieces as well as novels, novellas, and theatrical works. Committed to socialism and antifascism, Balázs wrote the screenplay for G. W. Pabst's adaptation of Bertolt Brecht and Kurt Weill's Three Penny Opera *(Dreigroschenoper, 1930/ 31), but also the screenplay for Leni Riefenstahl's* Bergfilm *("mountain film"),* The Blue Light *(Das blaue Licht, 1931/ 32), which was later heralded by the Nazis. After taking a position at the state film school in Moscow, where he taught film aesthetics, he returned to Hungary to build what he hoped would be a socialist film industry, but instead met with great resistance.*

From The Visible Human (1924)

Preface in Three Addresses

1. We Request Entry!

It seems quite appropriate to introduce my little book according to the old custom with the request to be heard. For your attentive listening is not only a precondition, but the actual, hoped-for, and ultimate goal of my immodest undertaking. You should not listen to me, but hear the matter; just as one creates, builds an object, so should one listen to the object.

For what I can provisionally tell you is not very much. Yet, once you have lent your ear to these things, once you have even noticed that there is something to be noticed here, then others will come and report more to you. But one becomes silent among the deaf.

I therefore begin this essay on a *philosophy of art* for film with a request of the learned custodians of aesthetics and the science of art, and I say: for many years, a new art has stood before the gates of your lofty academy and requests entry. The art of film requests advocacy, a seat and a word in your midst. It wishes to be deemed finally worthy of consideration by you at the level of theory, and you should devote to it a chapter in those grand aesthetic systems in which so much has been discussed, from carved table legs to the art of hair braiding, and in which film is not mentioned at all. Like the disenfranchised and despised mob before a grand manor house, film stands before your aesthetic parliament and demands entry into the sacred halls of theory.

And I wish to say a word on its behalf, for I know that theory is not at all grey, but rather represents the broad perspectives of *freedom* for every art. It is the map for the one who wanders through art that shows all paths and possibilities, and it reveals what appeared to be compelling necessity as a random path among a hundred others. It is theory that gives courage for the journeys of Columbus and makes every step an act of free choice.

Why the mistrust of theory? It does not even need to be true in order to inspire great works. Almost all great discoveries of mankind proceeded on a false hypothesis. A theory can also be easily dropped if it no longer functions. But the "practical experiences" of chance barricade the way like impenetrable walls. Never yet has an art become great without theory.

By this, I do not want to say that the artist must necessarily be "learned," and I also know the common (all too common!) view of the value of "unconscious creation." Yet, the level of consciousness of the mind at which one "unconsciously" creates is important. For the unconscious compositions of a naturalist have a different effect than the equally unconscious works of a musician who has studied counterpoint.

Yet, I need least of all to convince the learned gentlemen to whom I now address myself of the value of theory. But rather that *film* is worthy of an aesthetics.

But are there things, then, that are not worthy of a theory? For is it not the theory that first accords things dignity, the dignity of importance, the dignity of being the bearer of a meaning? And certainly you don't want to persuade yourselves that this interpretation is a magnanimous gift on your part? Interpretation is our self-defense against chaos. When an elementary being becomes so powerful that we can no longer either hinder or change it, then we rush to recognize a meaning in it so that it doesn't devour us. Theoretical knowledge is the cork that holds us above water.

Now, you gentlemen of philosophy, we must hurry, for it is high time. Film has become a fact, a fact so common and of such socially and psychologically profound effect that we, like it or not, must concern ourselves with it. For film is the *folk art* of our century. Not in the sense, unfortunately, that it arises from the spirit of the people, but that the spirit of the people arises from it. Of course, the one is determined by the other, for nothing can spread among the people that they do not already want to have in the first place. And the aesthetes might wrinkle their delicate noses, we cannot change anything about it. The people's imagination and emotional life are fertilized and shaped in the cinema. There is no point in talking about whether that is a fortune or a misfortune. For in Vienna alone, nearly 200—that is *two hundred*—cinemas with an average of 450 seats play every evening. They have three to four showings per day. With the houses three-quarters full, that makes nearly 300,000 (*three-hundred-thousand!*) people per day in a city that is not especially large.

Has any art ever been so widespread? Has any intellectual expression whatsoever (except perhaps the religious one) ever had such an audience? In the imagination and emotional life of the urban population, film has assumed the role that myths, legends and folk tales once previously played. Please, do not draw any wistfully nostalgic aesthetic and moral comparisons! We will get to that. For the time being, we have to consider it as a social fact and to tell ourselves that, just as the folk song and folk tale (which, by the way, were not always deemed worthy of attention) are a subject of folkloristic study and problems of cultural history, so henceforth it will not be permissible to write cultural history or ethnopsychology without devoting a large chapter to film. And whoever among you regards this fact as a great danger, it is precisely you who has the duty to jump in so as to exert serious theoretical control. For it is not an intimate affair of literary salons that is at issue here, but public health!

Now, even if cultural history—I hear you say—might concern itself with film, it is not a problem for aesthetics and the philosophy of art. Truly, aesthetics belongs among the proud, aristocratic sciences, for it is one of the oldest ones and still stems from the time when the ultimate question of meaning and being was intended with every question. For that reason, too, aesthetics has always entirely divided up the world and finds room for new phenomena with great difficulty. There is no such exclusive society as that of the muses. And not without reason. For every art signifies a unique relation of man to the world, a particular dimension of the soul. As long as the artist remains in these dimensions, his work can never have been present and new; his art is not. We can discover a thousand new things with the telescope and microscope, yet only the realm of the sense of sight will have been broadened. A new art, though, would be like a new sense organ. And these do not all too frequently become more plentiful. And nevertheless I say to you: film is a new art and as different from all others as music is different from painting and these are from literature. It is a fundamentally new revelation of man. I wish to attempt to prove this.

It may well be new, you say, but it is certainly not an art because, industrialized from the start, it cannot be an unconditioned and spontaneous expression of the mind. Not the soul, you say, but business interests and mechanical technology are the deciding factors here.

Now, it has not yet been settled that industry and technology must necessarily and forever be something foreign to man and thus to art. I do not wish to go into this here, though, but only to ask: *How do you know that a film is inartistic?* In order to be able to judge this, you must have a certain idea of the artistic, of the good film. I fear that you measure the quality of films according to a false norm and apply to it the measures of other arts essentially foreign to films. The airplane is not a bad automobile because it cannot be used well on a country road. And film too has different, unique ways.

But even if every film that has ever been made so far were bad and inartistic, is it not precisely the task of you theoreticians to search into its *possibilities in principle?* These would probably be worth knowing even if there were no hope for their realization. The good, the creative theory is not an empirical science and would be completely unnecessary if it had to wait until art were already perfectly present in everything. Theory is, if not the rudder, then at least the compass of the development of art. And only once you have gotten an idea of the right direction may you speak of aberrations. You must create this idea, the theory of film, for yourselves.

2. To the Directors and All Other Friends of the Field

You create the meaning; you do not need to understand it. You must have it in your fingertips, not in your heads. And yet, friends, it is part of the dignity of a given profession that it have its theory. For it is with praxis as it is with the art of the witch doctor. He knows no theory, experience dictates no prescriptions to him, and he often heals better than the learned physician. *But only cases that he has encountered before.* He stands helpless in the face of new problems. For, by its nature, experience can relate only to what has already been present, and he has no method for examining what is new. Film, though, is too expensive a thing for experimentation. Even in technology, there is never any random, free-wheeling experimenting. Theory first defines certain goals and calculates all possibilities and only the applications are tested out in experiment.

You know best that every day brings new problems in the young art of film which old experience does not know how to help. In these cases, the director must also first become conscious of the principles that he has unconsciously applied so that they become a practical method for him.

Nor will your brilliant, unconscious intuition be of much use to you if you want to create entirely new things. For standing opposite the "unconsciously" working director is usually a general director of the company who calculates in an extremely conscious manner, and the film director cannot prove the utility of his new idea to him only with the finished product. For he does not even get to start making the film if he does not have the possibility of convincing and reassuring that executive at the outset, i.e., theoretically.

And besides: you love the material with which you work. You think about it even if you do not have it right in hand, and you want to play with it in your thoughts. This playful thought, though, is already theory. (Only the word sounds so ugly.) You love the material, but it will only love you in return if you know it.

3. Of Creative Enjoyment

I shall indeed also have to direct a few words of apology and justification to the audience, for I feel almost guilty before it. I feel like the snake that wants to give child-like innocents to eat of the tree of knowledge of good and evil. For the cinema has until now been the happy paradise of naivety where one did not need to be clever, educated, and critical and in whose darkness, as in the intoxicated atmosphere of a den of iniquity, even the most cultivated and most serious minds could strip themselves of their obliging education and their austere taste without shame in order to surrender themselves to mere primitive viewing in naked, primeval childlikeness. One re-

cuperated there not only from work, but also from intellectual so-
phistication. One was allowed to laugh about a person falling on
his behind and was allowed (in the dark!) to cry great big tears
about things that, as literature, one was obliged to reject with contempt. One felt embarrassed to find pleasure in bad music. But the
cinema, thank God, was not a matter of education! It was a simple
agent of pleasure like alcohol. And now that, too, should become
an art about which one should know something? Should one now
be educated in that and recognize a difference between good and
bad like after the Fall?

No, truly, I have not come to disturb your enjoyment. On the
contrary. I wish to try to stimulate your senses and nerves to a
greater capacity for enjoyment. For an understanding of film is not
adverse to the state of being uninhibited, sweet, and childlike. Film
is a young, as yet unhackneyed art and works with new, primeval
forms of humanity. For that reason, a correct understanding of it
requires precisely that one be able to adapt oneself to the totally
primitive and naïve. You will continue to laugh and to cry and will
not have to decry it as a "weakness."

And as far as enjoyment is concerned, should one not "understand" that? Dancing must be learned, too. Is not the epicurean also
always a gourmet and connoisseur? And every lecher will tell you:
Conscious enjoyment is the highest pleasure. (Perhaps theory is also
just a refinement of the art of living?)

If you will separate bad from good, perhaps something will be
lost on you. In return, though, you gain the enjoyment of value.
You well know it when real or fake gemstones are at issue. Film
producers know it, too, and that is why they take care to advertise
their spectacular films that cost billions. For the value of something
makes it particularly appealing. But the billions indicate only the
price and not the actual value of the film; the film, though, costs not
only money, but also talent, intelligence, taste and passion, all of
which glow in it and shimmer as fire is reflected in a genuine gem
and are more visible to the connoisseur than the money invested.

For the gourmet, it is a particular pleasure to recognize the grape
and the vintage in a wine. He analyzes it with his tongue. Aesthetic
theory is also nothing else than such a careful savoring by means of
which one also wishes to feel and enjoy the hidden work of inner
life. The person who is incapable of this with art seems to me like
the person who sees only the end of the race while running. It is
however the path to the goal, the struggle for the goal that is actu-

ally exciting. For the connoisseur, though, every mere fact rises to an achievement, every phenomenon to a success, every deed to a victory in which there is still a trace of the living heat of struggle.

Yet you will say what the learned aesthetes say: film is simply not art because it is geared in advance toward an uncritical taste and places no demands whatsoever on a particular understanding. It is wrong to maintain this generally. But granted that there are nearly as many bad films as bad books, and granted that the production of a film is so tremendously expensive that the entrepreneurs cannot risk a failure and thus must necessarily count on already existing needs: what follows from that? Only that the type of films you will get depends on you, on your needs, on your capacity for enjoyment. Film, more than any other art, is a social art that is created to a certain degree by the audience. Every other art is essentially conditioned by taste, by the talent of the artists. With film, though, the taste and the talent of the audience will decide. In this cooperation lies your great mission. The fate of a new, great art offering immeasurable possibilities is placed into your hands. You must first understand something of good film art in order to receive it, you must first learn to see its beauty so that it can even arise. And when we learn to understand it, then we, we the audience, will become its creator with our capacity for enjoyment.

The Visible Human

The invention of the art of book printing has rendered the face of people illegible over time. They have been able to read so much from paper that they were able to neglect the other form of communication.

Victor Hugo writes somewhere that the printed book has assumed the role of the medieval cathedral and has become the bearer of the national spirit. However, a thousand books have torn the spirit of the cathedral into a thousand opinions. The word has smashed the stone (the one church into a thousand books).

Thus, a legible spirit has developed from the *visible spirit* and a conceptual culture has come from the *visible culture*. It is universally known that this transition has greatly changed the face of life. Yet, people think less often about how the face of the individual person, his brows, his eyes and his mouth had to change in the process.

Another machine is now at work giving culture a new turn toward the visual and humanity a new face. It is called cinematography. It is a technology for the duplication and dissemination of intellectual production, just like the book press, and its effect on human culture will be no less.

Not speaking hardly means not having anything to say. Someone who does not talk can nevertheless be brimming with things that can be expressed only in shapes, images, expressions, and gestures. For the man of visual culture does not replace words with his gestures as, for example, the deaf and dumb do with their sign language. He does not think words whose syllables he writes in the air like Morse code. His gestures do not at all signify concepts, but rather immediately his irrational self, and what is expressed on his face and in his movements comes from a depth in the soul that words can never reveal. Mind here immediately becomes body: wordless, visible.

It was the great age of the visual arts when the painter and the sculptor composed not only form and spatial relationships to abstract shapes, and the human being was not only a problem of form. Artists were allowed to paint spirit and mind without thereby becoming "literary" because soul and mind did not reside in concepts but rather could still completely become body. This was a fortunate age, for pictures were still allowed to have a "theme," an "idea," because the idea did not always first appear in concepts and words, and the painter with his picture was not merely adding an illustration afterwards. The soul, which directly became body, could be painted and sculpted in its primary manifestation. Since book printing, though, the word has become the main bridge between man and man. The soul has constituted itself and crystallized into the word. The body, though, has become bereft: without soul and vacant.

Our surface of expression has become reduced to our face. And not only because the other parts of our body are covered with clothes. Our face is now like a small, awkward, upward-stretched semaphore of the soul that gives us signs as well as it is able. The hands, whose expression always has the melancholia of maimed fragments, can only at times provide assistance. On the back of a Greek torso without a head, though, one can clearly see—we, too, can still see it—whether the lost face was crying or laughing. The hips of Venus smile no less full of expression than her face, and it would not have sufficed to have tossed a veil over her head in order not to know what she was thinking and feeling. For man was visible in his entire body. In the culture of words, though, the soul (since it has become so clearly audible) has become nearly invisible. The printing press has done this.

Now, film is engaged in providing culture once again with such a radical transition. Many millions of people sit there every evening and, through their eyes, experience human destinies, characters, feelings and moods of every sort without needing words. For the subtitles that films still bear are of minor importance, being in part transitory rudiments of as yet undeveloped forms and in part of a special significance that never wishes to be an aid for visual expression. All humanity is today already engaged in learning anew the often forgotten language of expressions and gestures. Not the verbal substitute of the language of the deaf and dumb, but the visual correspondence with the immediately embodied soul. *The human being is once again becoming visible.*

Modern philology and research into the history of language have determined that expressive movement is the origin of language. This means that the person who is beginning to speak (as well as the small child) moves his tongue and lips no differently than his hands and the muscles of his face, i.e., not originally with the intention of producing sounds. The movements of the tongue and lips are initially gestures just as spontaneous as any other expressive movement of the body. The fact that sounds arise through this is a secondary phenomenon that was, so to speak, put to practical use afterwards. The directly visible mind was then translated into an indirectly audible mind, whereby, as with every translation, some things had to be lost. The language of gesture, though, is the actual mother tongue of humanity.

We are now beginning to remember this language and are in the process of learning it anew. It is still awkward and primitive and far from approaching the diversity of modern linguistic artistry. But because it has older and deeper roots in human nature than spoken language and because it is nevertheless fundamentally new, it already frequently expresses things in its stammering that artists of the word vainly attempt to capture.

Is it a coincidence that, precisely in recent decades, artistic dance has also become a general cultural need at the same time as film? We apparently have many things to say that cannot be said with words. People revert to the original expressive movement whose secondary and derivative forms seem to have driven our culture into a great variety of dead-ends. The word seems to have violated humanity. Procrustean concepts threw much overboard that we still lack, and music alone does not suffice to give it back to us again. The culture of words is a de-materialized, abstract, intellectualized culture that has degraded the human body to a mere biological organism. But the new language of gesture that is coming arises from our painful yearning to be able to be a person with our entire body, to be ourselves from head to toe (not only in our words), and no longer to have to drag our own body around with us as a foreign entity, as some practical tool. It arises from the yearning for the silenced, forgotten, *physical* person that has become invisible.

There will yet be talk of why the decorative choreographies of men and women dancers will not bring this new language. It is film that will again raise up humanity, buried under concepts and words, to immediate visibility.

This visible human, however, is no longer present today and not yet entirely present. For it is a law of nature that every organ that is not used degenerates and becomes stunted. In the culture of words, our body was not fully used as a means of expression and, for that reason, it has also lost its capacity for expression and has become awkward, primitive, dumb and barbaric. How often is the abundance of gestures of entirely primitive peoples richer than that of a highly educated European who has the greatest vocabulary at his disposal. A few more years of good film art and scholars will perhaps see that people would need to compile an encyclopedia of gestures and expressions with the help of the filmmaker. The public, though, is not waiting for this new grammar of future academies, but is going to the cinema and learning by itself.

There has already been much talk about how the modern European is neglecting his body. And people have thrown themselves into sports with holy enthusiasm. Sports can indeed make the body healthy and beautiful, but they do not make it eloquent. For they enhance only the animal qualities. They do not make it a sensitive medium of the soul, an excitable mirror that shows every slightest emotion. Someone can also have a powerful and beautiful voice without being able to say precisely what he means.

Yet, not only the human body as an organ of expression has atrophied through this neglect, but so has the soul that would be expressed through it. For, mind you, it is not the same mind that expresses itself here one time in words and there the next time in gestures. Just as the same thing is not merely expressed differently in music from its expression in poetry. Buckets of words create from other depths and bring things to the surface different from those that gestures do. In this case, though, it is true that the fountain from which *nothing* is created runs dry. For the possibility of expressing ourselves already determines our thoughts and feelings in advance. This is the economy of our mental organization, which is capable of producing nothing unusable. Psychological and logical analyses have shown that our words are not just subsequent copies of our thoughts, but the forms that determine them in the first place. Bad writers and dilettantes do indeed speak much of their ineffable feelings and thoughts, but, in truth, it is the case that we can only very, very rarely think things that we cannot express, and then we do not even know what we have thought. Humanity's mental development here too, as in every other area, is dialectical. The growing, expanding human mind does indeed extend and increase its possibilities of expression, yet, on the other hand, it is exactly the increased possibilities of expression that make growth of the mind possible.

The image of the world in words yields a complete and meaningful system in which things that it does not contain are not quite *missing*, just as colors *are not missing* in music, although they are not present. The picture of man and of the world in immediate expressive movement yields precisely such a total, complete system. Human culture would be conceivable without language. It would indeed look entirely different, but it would not have to be inferior. In any case, it would be less abstract and less alienated from the tangible being of man and of things.

Ruth Saint Denis, this greatest genius of dance, writes in her autobiography that she did not learn to speak until the age of five, for she lived alone and secluded with her mother, who herself was long paralyzed in her arms and legs and thus had a quite special sensitivity to the meaning of movements. They communicated so well through expressions and gestures that Ruth very slowly learned speech, which she did not need. Her body became so eloquent, however, that she became a great, wonderful poet of gestures.

But the greatest dancer's expressive movements themselves always remain concert hall productions for the few; they remain a confined art separated from life. Only applied art signifies culture, however. Not the beautiful poses of the statues in galleries, but the walk and gesture of people on the street of everyday life while they work. Culture signifies the mind's permeation of the day-to-day material of life, and visual culture would need to give people different and new forms of expression in their normal contact with each other. Artistic dance cannot do this; film will do this.

In general, culture seems to be treading the path from abstract mind to visible body. Does one not see in a person's movements and delicate hands the spirit of his ancestors? The thoughts of the fathers become sensitivity of the nerves, taste and instinct in the children. Conscious knowledge becomes unconscious sensibility: *it materializes into culture in the body.* The physical capacity for expression is always the final result of a cultural development and, for that reason, while film today may still be a very primitive, barbaric stammering in comparison to the literature *of today*, it is nevertheless a cultural development because it signifies the immediate physical transubstantiation of mind.

This path leads in two seemingly opposite directions. For, at first sight, it appears as if physiognomic language would only increase and magnify even more the alienation and disintegration that began with the confusion of tongues in the building of the Tower of Babel. This path of culture seems on the one hand to lead farther in the direction of the isolation of individuality and loneliness. For, after the confusion of tongues at Babel, societies still remained that similarly maintained words and concepts from their common mother tongue, and the common lexicon, the common grammar saved man from the ultimate loneliness of not being understood. Mimic expression, though, is much more individual and personal than verbal language. Bodily expression also has its "interposed" forms generally used with a certain meaning such that one could, indeed ought to construct a theory of comparative bodily expression patterned after comparative linguistics. The language of gesture does indeed have its own traditions, but no laws, such as grammar has, that would be obligatory and from which, starting in school, one is forbidden to deviate under pain of punishment. This language is still so young that it lithely snuggles up to the idiosyncrasy of every unique individuality. It is still at the stage where, instead of creating mind, it is created by mind.

On the other hand, film in particular seems to promise us salvation from the curse of Babel. For *the first international language* is now developing on the screen of the cinemas of all countries: that of expressions and gestures. The reasons for this lie in the economic sphere, which always supplies the most solid reasons. The production of a film costs so much that it can be profitable only through international distribution. The few subtitles are quickly translated from one language into another. The artists' play of expressions must be equally understandable to all peoples, though. Strict limits are placed on national idiosyncrasy here, and it could still be seen in the first years of film how the Anglo-Saxon and French styles of expressive movement struggled against each other for hegemony. For the law of the film market tolerates only one general language of gesture that is commonly understandable in every nuance from San Francisco to Izmir, and which every princess and every grisette can equally follow. And today, film already speaks the only common world language. Ethnographic specialties and national intimacies are still used every now and then as local coloring, as ornamentation of a stylized milieu. But never more than as *psychological motifs*. The gesture that determines the course and the meaning of the action must be equally understandable to the most various peoples; otherwise, the film does not recoup its costs. The language of gesture was, so to speak, normalized in film. Accordingly, though, a certain normal psychology of the white race has developed that has become the foundation of every film story. This is the explanation for the present temporary primitiveness and stereotyped character of these stories. Nevertheless, this is of tremendous importance. Here lies hidden the first living seed of that normal white man who will eventually arise as the synthesis of all the various races and peoples. The filmmaker is a machine that, in its way, is creating living and concrete internationalism: *the single, common psyche of the white man*. And even more. By suggesting a uniform ideal of beauty as a general goal of selective breeding, film is bringing about a uniform type of the white race. The variety of facial expression and of movement, which have drawn sharper borders between peoples than the customs duty and the customs barrier, will be gradually retouched away by film. And once man becomes entirely visible, then he will always recognize himself in spite of the most different languages.

Sketches for a Dramaturgy of Film

The Substance of Film

If film is to be its own art with its own aesthetics, then it has to distinguish itself from all other arts. The special is the essence and the justification of every phenomenon, and the special is best represented by its difference. Thus, we now wish to delineate film art from its neighboring fields and thereby to demonstrate its autonomy.

People are primarily inclined to see in film a wayward and profligate child of the theater and are of the opinion that it is a question of a spoiled and mutilated subspecies, a cheap substitute for the theater that has the same relation to genuine stage art as, for example, photographic reproduction to an original painting. In both cases—so it seems—fabricated stories are portrayed by actors.

The Uni-Layered Nature of Film

Indeed. But not in the same material. Sculpture and painting also similarly portray people and yet have entirely different laws that are determined by their different material. The material of film art, though, its substance, is fundamentally different from that of the theater.

It is always a two-fold thing that we perceive at the theater: the drama *and* its portrayal. They appear to us independent, in a free relation to one another, always as a duality. The theater director is handed a finished piece, the stage actor a finished role. Their only remaining task is to fill out and vividly portray the *existing*, fixed meaning. In this process, the audience has the possibility of control. For we hear from the words what the writer intended and see whether the director and actors represent it correctly or incorrectly. They are only interpreters of a text that—shining through their portrayal—is accessible to us in the original. For the material of the theater is double-layered.

In the case of film, the matter is different. We cannot perceive an independent piece behind the portrayal nor consider and evaluate it independently of the presentation. With film, the audience has no possibility of any control over whether the director and actors have correctly or incorrectly portrayed the writer's work, for it is singularly and solely *their* work that the audience sees. They have made what pleases us and they are responsible for what displeases us.

Poeticizing Actors

This is why film directors are also much better known and more famous than their colleagues from the theater. Who, though, notices the name of a screenplay writer (if he is even named at all)? Much more fuss is also made about "film stars" than about stars of the stage. Is this an injustice that can be attributed only to advertisement? No. Even the greatest advertisement can only have a lasting effect if it is founded on existing interests. The fact is simply that the director and actors are the actual authors of film.

When an actor speaks a sentence and makes a face, then we gather meaning from his words, and his gestures are only a sort of accompaniment to it. If this accompaniment is wrong, it has an unpleasant effect exactly because we are in a position to determine that it is wrong. (For the bearer of the meaning is the word.)

In film, words give us no clue. We learn everything from facial expression, which is neither accompaniment nor form and expression, but rather the *sole content*.

Of course we can also notice when there is bad acting in a film. Bad acting, though, has another meaning here. It is not an incorrect interpretation of an existing character, but rather an incorrect treatment that utterly fails to create a character. It is a case of bad artistic creation. The mistakes are not contradictions with an underlying text, but rather contradictions of the acting with itself. It is also possible in the theater for an actor to falsify a fictional character consistently and well on the basis of a misunderstanding. If a film actor succeeds in doing this, we are not in a position to notice that it is a fake. For the original material, the poetic substance of the film is visible gesture. Film is shaped out of this.

Film and Literature

A director and actors (who stand in an entirely different relation to one another in film than in the theater) could most readily be compared to improvisers, who have perhaps gotten an idea, a short, general synopsis from someone else, but who *themselves compose the text*. For the text of a film consists of its texture, and of the language of pictures where every grouping, every gesture, every perspective, all lighting must radiate the poetic mood and beauty otherwise contained in the writer's words. Even in a poem or a novella, mere content is what matters least. Refinement and power of expression make the writer. Refinement and power of visual effect and gesture make up the art of film. *Therefore, it has nothing to do with literature.*

Film and Story

I must go into this analysis so thoroughly because herein lies the root of all misunderstandings and prejudices that render the majority of people of literary cultivation unable to perceive the art in film. They look only at the story content of film and find it certainly too simplistic and primitive. But they do not consider the visual treatment. It can thus happen that a litterateur who perhaps displays a highly differentiated sensitivity to books will write that the Griffith film *Way Down East* is tasteless, sentimental kitsch because it contains nothing more than a girl's being seduced and abandoned and then becoming miserable and unhappy. Yet, in the final analysis, Faust's Margarete is also just such a seduced and abandoned girl. What matters in both cases, though, is not the final outcome, but the text. What the words of a great writer make of this primitive, utterly simple story in the latter case, is made in this film by the deeply moving facial expressions of Lillian Gish and the masterful cinematography by Griffith, who links the rise and fall of every scene to this face.

A gentleman confesses his love to a lady. This fact appears in the greatest masterpieces of literature just as in the worst trashy novels. So wherein lies the difference? Exclusively in how the scene is described and what the gentleman in question says to that lady. Now, in the case of film, it also depends only on how the director portrays the scene visually and what the actor's face says. Created art consists in this and not in the abstract "facts" of an abstract content.

A good film has no "content" whatsoever, for it is "pit and peel in one." It has as little content as a painting or music or even—a facial expression. Film is a *surface art*, where "what's inside is outside." Nevertheless—and here lies its principal difference from painting—it is a temporal art of movement and of organic continuity and thus can have a convincing or false psychology, a clear or confused meaning. Except that this psychology and this meaning do not lie as "deeper meaning" in thoughts, but rather in obvious appearance completely on the surface.

This is the source of the primitiveness of the story content in film that so vexes the literati. There must indeed be a renunciation of purely intellectual values and of those psychological conflicts that are resolved only in thought. In exchange, though, we get to see things that cannot be thought and cannot be understood through concepts. And we get *to see* them, which is an entirely unique experience. Painting also imports neither thoughts nor refined psychological problems to us and yet it is not an inferior art because of that. Nor is it primitive because it can only ever represent one scene.

Parallel Story and Deeper Meaning

Nevertheless, film seems not to want to renounce entirely that "depth" of literature that allows one to sense another, hidden *action in the meaning* in a third intellectual dimension, namely, *behind* the superficially visible action. This is the reason for the advent in recent years of the fashion of films with stories running parallel in which two or even more stories from different historical time periods or different strata of society are shown and in which the same characters and types (played by the same actors) appear, and in which the similarity of experiences and the parallelism of the destinies are supposed, through repetition, to show a regularity, a common sense, and, in this, a deeper meaning to all that is happening.

Such attempts to create "*Weltanschauung* film" seem to be not at all hopeless. As there can be no "behind" and no "hidden" meaning on the two-dimensional surface of film, film attempts to dissolve into spatial juxtaposition that double layer of depth that appears in literature as temporal succession. Since the image does not signify in the same manner as the word, every other action must also be brought to the surface of visibility as a parallel. The law is in the common, and the deeper sense, which hides under the surface like the *one* root of many branches, is in the law. Film has no philosophical words to conjure this sense. It will show it in the common intersection of various lines of destiny.

Granted—and this danger is so imminent that every film of this type has so far fallen victim to it—the parallel story may not become a costumed repetition, not simply a parable. For the parable is only an illustration, which film requires least. As a parable, every story loses the weight of its reality. It becomes a symbol of another story and does not have its own reality. It repeats the meaning; the meaning does not repeat itself in it in new action. This parallel story would have to be not actually similar, but *related*, and to represent the other side of the same action. Unless in the belief in the transmigration of souls or in a mystical belief in the secret interweaving of all destinies. Why hasn't anyone yet made a "Déjà vu" film? Why hasn't anyone yet made into a filmic leitmotif this strange experience that, in its pure visuality, opens up the deepest levels of the soul, and through which a scene never before experienced suddenly appears eerily familiar to one, why hasn't anyone made into a filmic leitmotif the spectral penetration of one life by another as if by a dawning, this process by which surroundings become transparent?

Of Visual Continuity

There are films conceived from literature whose images are only a dense series of movable illustrations to a text that is shown in the subtitles. We are given every essential external and internal event to read in the title and only later do we get to see it, without the pictures further developing the plot in their own medium. Such films are bad, for they contain nothing that could be developed only in film. The justification of any art, though, consists in being an irreplaceable possibility of expression.

Even with the best directing and the best acting, the pictures of such literary films have something lifeless and choppy about them, for they lack *visual continuity*. A story conceived in words will jump over many moments that cannot be jumped over in an image. The word, the concept, the thought are timeless. The image, though, has its own concrete presence and lives only in it. Memory lies in words; one can refer and allude with them to that which is not present. The image, though, speaks only for itself. This is why film, particularly when portraying psychological developments, demands a seamless continuity of visible individual moments. Film must be fashioned out of the unadulterated material of pure visuality. For one immediately senses any merely literary bridging between moments like the coldness of an airtight space.

This continuity requires many meters of film. This is why a film that portrays a psychological development can have a very simple story. For, unfortunately, films in our country cannot be longer than 2,200 meters, and a presentation may last only one and one-half hours. The adaptations of the most beautiful film material undertaken with the best intentions (such as the sad series of failed Dostoyevsky film adaptations) had to fail because time was too short and the meters were too few in order to be able to portray the enormous abundance of motifs in this visual continuity. For this reason, these running times will certainly also not abide much longer, and instead of the six-reelers that last one and one-half hours, there will be three-reelers of two and one-half hours in which film art will finally be able to develop. Of course, this—like nearly everything with film—has to do with economic and social factors. The poor people who go to the movie theater could more easily come up with the double price of admission for a double feature than with twice as much time. This is certainly not possible with a ten-hour workday. Not only does man become stunted in this case, but so does art. But will it perhaps be different someday?

The Atmosphere

Atmosphere is indeed the soul of any art. It is the air and charm that, like a vapor of forms, surrounds all objects and creates a unique medium of a unique world. This atmosphere is like the nebulous primeval matter that condenses into individual forms. It is the common substance of various objects; it is the last reality of any art. Once this atmosphere is present, the inadequacy of the individual objects can no longer spoil what is essential. The question of the "origin" of this special atmosphere is always a question about the most profound source of any art.

Now, there are American films, for example, whose story content is empty and simplistic and in which the acting (which could replace much with its lyricism of gestures and expressions) is negligible, yet that nevertheless keep our interest awake from beginning to end. This comes from their living atmosphere. They have that dense, aromatic aura of sensuous life that only the greatest writers of all are sometimes capable of imparting with words. And then we say, "one really perceives the smell of the rooms when Flaubert describes an apartment" or "one's mouth waters when Gogol's peasants are eating." And behold, any of the better American directors creates this sensuous atmosphere that can be smelled and tasted.

The *entire* story is perhaps simplistic, perhaps also kitschy and contrived. The individual moments, though, are so full of warm life "that one really senses the aroma." *Why* the hero does something often has no reason, but *how* he does it has the warmth of nature. The hero's fate is empty, but his moments are richly shaped.

There was once a very insignificant film about the unhappy love of a cripple. This lame groom takes his bride out once to a fair, though, and then there follows an entire reel full of small, fleeting scenes that together create the animal vitality of the bustling activity of the fair. A flood and surge of images of strength that bury and oppress the physically impaired cripple. It is a thin hail of small moments of material life that ultimately must kill the weak man. An atmosphere is created in which he suffocates.

Or the girl afterwards goes to the groom to tell him that she does not want to marry him. The apartment, though, is decorated for the wedding. The wreaths and bouquets, the gifts and the hundred small *material* signs of tenderness are now shown individually. A thick mist of goodness arises around the girl in which she loses her way. Just as the many small particulars of the fair have condensed into an aura of life through which the weak and lame man could not wade, so does one feel in this wedding room the weight of things and facts against which the soul cannot prevail.

The Significance of Visible Things

It is a strong atmosphere that arises in film through the *vital role and significance of visible things*. In poetry, which is geared more toward an abstract meaning, things do not have this significance. It is for this reason, too, that no poetry can create this specific atmosphere, this "active essence of the material."

There is another reason for this, though. In the world of the speaking human, non-speaking things are much less lively and much less significant than the human. They acquire only a life of the second and third degree, and this only in the rare moments of particularly clairvoyant sensitivity of the people who consider them. In the theater, there is a difference of value between the speaking human and non-speaking things. They live in different dimensions. This difference of value disappears in film. Things there are not as slighted and degraded. *In shared silence, they become nearly homogenous with man and thereby gain in vitality and significance.* Because they do not speak less than people, they therefore say just as much. This is the riddle of that particular film atmosphere which lies beyond any literary possibility.

Filmed Literature

The essential difference between film and literature becomes most clearly evident when a good novel or a good drama is "filmed." In front of the movie camera, literary works become transparent as if before X-rays. The skeletal structure of the story remains, but the beautiful flesh of intellectual depth, the tender skin of lyrical sonority disappear on the screen. Of the most fragrant beauties, there remains only a naked, raw skeleton that is no longer literature nor yet film, but rather exactly this "content" that comprises the essence of neither. Such a skeleton would have to acquire new and entirely different flesh, another epidermis, in order to attain a visible living form in film.

True, there are also writers who have a particularly visual imagination and seem made for filming. There is Dickens, for example. Every page, even when read, is a visible picture. And yet no one, to my knowledge, has yet succeeded in making a good Dickens film, whereas I have already seen a whole series of bad Dickens films (competent directing and good actors notwithstanding).

This is because—as paradoxical as it sounds—Dickens's imagination is too vivid. For it is a technical impossibility to film an entire Dickens novel. No film today has room for the abundance of visions. It must thus be "abridged." In the case of other novels having a content "detachable" from their images and a story outline on which the individual scenes are merely attached, such an operation could easily be carried out. The images of a Dickens novel (as becomes apparent when trying to film one) are the living fibers of *one* organism, though. If one part is cut out, the next becomes lifeless, it dies off. One can abridge a story reflected in thought, for a definition can be formed more and more succinctly. *But one cannot abridge an image.* One would then have to paint the entire composition anew. Thus, exactly what makes Dickens so suitable for film, i.e., his visual imagination, renders his works unsuitable for treatment. He would have had to do it himself. For this is how the inner structure of the substance of film is.

Linguistic Gesture and Gesture Language

Is it permissible to regard expressive movement and the visual *in toto* as the material entirely unique to the art of film? After all, the actor in the theater also acts with his body, and the decorations of the stage are also present for the eye.

The speaking actor, though, has different expressions and different gestures. They express only the excess. What should be said but no longer fits into words is added with the facial muscles and the hands.

Mimicry in film is not a sacrifice and not an added remainder, and this difference means not only that film gesture is more extensive and clearer, but that it lies in an entirely different sphere. For the speaking person illuminates another level of the soul than, for example, the musician or the dancer does. Adjusted to language, his gestures, with which he accompanies his words, come from where his words come. As an optical phenomenon, they may be very similar to the gestures of the dancer, but they contain a different spirit. The gestures of the speaker have the same psychological content as his words, for the dimensions of the soul cannot be mixed. They merely indicate words that are still unborn.

The gestures of the dancer, though, come from elsewhere and have a different meaning. They are a unique expression of a unique soul and are thus a unique material of a unique art. They are just as unrelated to the gestures of the speaker as to his words.

I wish to make a comparison. Every language has a musical element and every word its melody. Yet, this melody of language—although acoustically similar to actual language—does not signify inner music. It carries the atmosphere of concepts and serves the purpose of rational nuance. Music is not only an acoustic matter, though, but a unique area of the soul. Now, expressions and gestures are also not only an optical matter.

Yet, I spoke of the dancer. But the actor in the film does not dance. Nevertheless, he, too, is not geared toward the word and does not appear to us in the rational dimension of concepts. Between the gesticulation of the speaker and the ornamental expressive movements of the dancer, there seems to be a third form of expression that corresponds to a unique inwardness. *The gestural language* of film is as principally different from the *linguistic gestures* of the theater as it is from dance.

Visual Language

But the actor in the film speaks exactly the same as in the theater. There is no difference whatsoever in the gestures. We simply do not hear him.

But we *see* him speak. This makes the big difference. In the theater, where we listen primarily to the words, we do not notice speech as expressive movement or as expressions of the mouth and of the entire face. Nor is there usually anything like this to notice in the theater. For the acoustic shape of the word is the goal, and the movement of the mouth only the means to an expression that does not itself intend to signify anything.

In film, though, speech is mimicry and immediate visual facial expression. Someone who *sees* speech experiences entirely different things from someone who hears the words. During speech, the mouth can also often show much more than its words can say.

This is why we understand American, French and Norwegian actors equally well in film. For we know what it means when someone gratingly mashes his words between lips pressed together or drunkenly babbles them with a heavy tongue or spits them out from his mouth with contempt like spittle or emits them between pertly pursed lips like thorns. We understand these linguistic gestures even if they are accompanied by Chinese words.

As soon as we notice the acoustic element because we see how the mouth forms vowels, though, then the mimic effect is over. Only then do we notice that we do not hear the actor, which we previously had not at all noticed, and he will have on us the effect of a mute who, with grotesque effort, wishes to make himself understood.

The good film actor speaks in an entirely different way from that of the good stage actor. He speaks clearly for the eye and not for the ear. But these two clarities do not seem capable of being combined. Just how independent the visible language of the mouth is from the audible is shown in the most grotesque manner when excellent film actors speak the most ridiculous nonsense as a replacement for dialogue during filming. The sight of their speaking in film, though, is deeply moving.

The Silent Art and the Art of Being Silent

Silence in pantomime is different. Pantomime is silent not only to the ear, but also to the eye. Not a silent art, but an art of silence. It is the dreamland of silence. Film, though, is merely soundless. It is not the soul of silence that it reveals to us. (Unlike music, for example, which, despite its sounds, nevertheless comes from this world of silence.)

When pantomime is performed in film, this difference is clearly seen. The audience sits around motionlessly. In the center, the pantomime might be performed with the wildest animation, but the dancers will always appear more distanced from life and relatively more rigid than their motionless audience. For the latter are nevertheless of our world.

It is a bad director who confuses film with pantomime and allows his characters to be silent too often. For silence is also not only a matter of acoustics, but a very pregnant and conspicuous expressive movement for the eye that always has its occasional and particular meaning in film. And speech is among the strongest means of mimic expression that film possesses.

In one film, *Die Galgenhochzeit* (*The Gallows Wedding*), Asta Nielsen wants to free her beloved from prison. She comes to him, the doors stand open, but only for a few minutes. There is no time to lose. The beloved lies apathetically on the ground, though, and does not stir. Asta Nielsen calls to him, once, twice. He does not stir. Then she begins to persuade him in frantic haste. What she is saying, we do not know. Apparently the same thing again and again: He should come, for time is wasting. There is a trembling fear, a mad desperation in this speech that could never have been expressed in audible words, though. This speech is *a sight*, as if she were tearing her hair out or scratching the skin of her face. She speaks for a long time. The words would have already bored us. The gestures become ever more exciting.

The Screenplay

From all this, it will be clear that the screenplay on the basis of which a film is made cannot be a product of literary imagination. An entirely special naïve and concrete imagination that need not first be transposed into the visual is required. It must be thought out with the vision of the director. A film cannot be really any good at all unless the director himself "composes" it and shapes it from his material. A musician, too, can never compose what a writer has conceived. The tonal possibilities of his instruments, material and technique are his muses. For the director, too, everything already lies contained in a black and white shadow theater, like in a block of stone for Michelangelo, which he only has to extract. This is why even the best screenplay is insufficient for the director. It will never contain precisely what is essential, because, in spite of everything, it has only words. The material, though, must show its will.

Type and Physiognomy

Motto: "For there has never been an animal that could have had the form of one animal and the nature of another, but always its own body and its own meaning. Every body necessarily determines its nature in this manner. Just as any expert judges animals according to their form. If this is true as it eternally remains true, then there is a physiognomy."—Aristotle in Goethe's *Physiognomic Fragments*

Already in the selection of actors, the film director is "composing" and giving his characters their crucial, most essential substance. In the theater, the director receives his figures and characters ready-made in the text of the drama and must find only one actor corresponding to the image that the words of the drama provide. In the theater, the figures characterize themselves and *one another* with their words.

In film, it is *their appearance* that determines their character for us from the first moment. The film director does not need to search out one "actor," but rather the character itself, and it is the director who creates the characters with his selection. As he imagines them, so will they appear to the audience, which has no possibility of comparing or controlling.

Since the film actor has to portray everything—racial as well as individual character—through his appearance, his acting must be made easier through the selection of an actor who need not even portray a racial character, but who possesses it from the outset and can concentrate entirely and in an uninhibited way on personal detail. He will not have to exaggerate and to pay heed to a series of stereotypical gestures, such as to a wig that sits too loosely on his head. The necessary gestures have just grown on him, and his acting has the weight of self-evident existence.

Only in the rarest cases can film make use of genuine theatrical actors, who are used to portraying the most diverse characters. For film tolerates disguises much less than theater (the close-up shots reveal everything fake!). And most actors simply have an "actor's face." It is always the same type that, like an officer in civilian clothing, can be recognized even through the most deceptive masking and in any costume.

Dangers of Pithiness

In the process, the figure selected also cannot be an overly pithy type, lest its mere appearance give it the overly rigid character of a carved figure. Anatomy must leave some latitude for physiognomy; otherwise, the figure in the rigid armor of a unique and fixed character becomes incapable of portraying external and internal transformations. (A common mistake of American directors who put very special emphasis on the selection of pithy types.)

Of course, the freezing of a basic character type on a face can have a very special charm if intended grotesquely or comically.

Clothes and Other Symbols

Striking the correct balance with this typification is not easy and is among the trickiest tasks for the director. For every character must also be typified in his clothing. In film, we judge exclusively according to what is external, and since no words give us information, every character must wear his symbols, lest we fail to understand the meaning of his action. For the same action can be meant for good or evil. We must simply see in the person how he intends it. Dressing up in costume in film always has the decisive meaning, albeit in a much more discreet form, as do the costumes of Bajazzo, Pantalone and Harlequin in old pantomimes or, if one wishes, of the even older Japanese or Greek theater masks. They indicate character to us at the outset.

Of course, this often has the effect in a naturalistic milieu of a grotesque prejudice, and people often enough ridicule the upturned shirt collar, which always indicates a ruffian, and the cigarette, which, in a woman's mouth, always indicates depravity.

But this ridicule is not always justified. Every art works with such symbols. They are often unconscious traditions and conventions of an entirely general sort, such as black for mourning and white as a sign of innocence. One would not think twice about them. They serve only as a shortened procedure for imparting general information and not for the actual characterization of people.

Typical outer appearance can indicate much more than the typical sign of a caste, though. Particularly in film, it must be shaped into an immediate expression of individual character. People of an "internalized," conceptual culture of words have an aversion to according such great significance to outer appearance. Yet the actor who does not speak becomes a homogenous canvas of expression in his entire body, and every crease of his clothing acquires the significance that a crease in his face has. Even if only unconsciously, we will judge him according to his outer appearance, regardless of whether the director so intended.

Goethe on Film

Permit me to reproduce here a few lines from Goethe, who has already written so many excellent things concerning our topic in his *Contributions to Lavater's Physiognomic Fragments.*

"What is a person's outer appearance? Truly, not his naked form and imprudent gestures that indicate his inner strengths and their play! Class, habit, possessions, clothing, everything modifies him, everything shrouds him. It seems most difficult, nearly impossible to penetrate through all these veils into his innermost being, even to find in these strange definitions fixed points that allow one to draw conclusions about his essence. Despair not! That which surrounds man affects not him alone; it also induces a reciprocal effect, and in being capable of modification, he in turn modifies all around him. A man's clothing and household goods thus surely allow one to draw an inference about his character. Nature shapes man, he reshapes it, and indeed this reshaping is in turn natural; he who sees himself placed in the great, wide world will fence and wall himself within a small world and appoint it in his likeness."

There is nothing more to add to this. Except this: The general physiognomy of a face is variable at any moment by facial expressions that transform the general type into a particular character. The physiognomy of clothing and of immediate surroundings is not so flexible. Thus, very particular foresight and very particular tact (qualities unfortunately all too rare) are necessary to give to this stable background only such characteristics that do not contradict lively animated gestures.

Of Beauty

A film star has to be beautiful. This requirement, which is never made so generally and unconditionally of theater actors, is also something that fills our literati and aesthetes with mistrust. One sees there, they say, that the soul and the mind, the meaningful, and real art are not what is important in film. The purely external and pure decorativeness decide.

"Despair not!" said Goethe. Film knows no "purely" external and no "empty" decorativeness. Precisely because everything internal in film must be recognizable in the external, *something internal* must also be recognizable in *everything external.* In beauty as well.

The beauty of facial features in film has the effect of physiognomic expression. Anatomical form has the effect of a physical expression. Kant's adage "Beauty is the symbol of the good" is realized in film. Where only the eye judges, beauty becomes the proof. The hero is externally beautiful because he is so internally. (In this light, the Luciferian beauty of evil and the resemblance to God in the Antichrist can achieve particularly eerie effects.)

Nevertheless, great beauty is also a decorative matter, an ornament unto itself that lives a life sometimes almost independent of the person who possesses it. And this life does not live in movement. "Je hais le mouvement, qui déplace les lignes," says Baudelaire's *Beauté*. And there are beauties (American films often suffer from this) whose forms swallow up facial expression. The anatomy of the face is so brilliant that the physiognomy of the face becomes nearly invisible. It wears its beauty like a hard mask. And it is also true that the greatest film actresses of all, such as Asta Nielsen or Pola Negri, are nothing less than beautiful. So the selection of type is an extremely delicate matter in this regard as well.

One's Own Face

No, not our *entire* face is our own. By merely looking, one cannot at all distinguish in our features the common property of family, race and class. And yet it is among the most interesting and psychologically relevant questions: How much in man is type and how much is individual, how much is race and how much is personality? Some writers have already attempted to portray this relationship in the soul. This relationship, though, is much more clearly visible in man's physiognomy and gestures and can be captured much more precisely and clearly by means of film than by the most refined words. And film has a mission here that extends far beyond the artistic and that can offer anthropology and psychology invaluable material.

Alien Races

For this reason, films in which people of alien races act, such as Negroes, Chinese, Indians and Eskimos, are tremendously interesting. In such films, it occasionally becomes clearly visible which expressions change not with the person, but with the race. In addition, certain prototypes of physiognomy that we do not at all notice in our own kind but that are present in alien races still make an impression with fresh significance. Most strange and most eerie, though, are the expressions that we initially do not understand at all because we have never seen a similar facial expression before.

The facial expression of an Indian actress who continued to smile in her desperate grief over her dead child once made an unforgettable impression on me. When one finally—it did not take long—recognized the expression of pain in it, this smiling affected one with the heart-rending intensity of a fresh gesture bearing nothing at all traditional and schematic and was no longer a sign and symbol of pain, but rather its sudden, naked manifestation.

Yet the greatest mystery here is this: How is it possible that one understands a *facial expression* that *one has never seen before*? We will never be able to fathom this mystery nor the others of physiognomy as long as we remain within a physiognomic and mimic system. Just as philology discovers the laws of language only with comparative linguistics, material for comparative physiognomic research would also need to be obtained with the help of film.

Soul and Destiny

The face of man wears both. In this visible relationship, in this interplay of facial features, type and personality, nature and nurture, fact and individual will, the "id" and the "ego" wrestle with one another. The deepest mysteries of life most intimate are revealed here, and this is as exciting to see as the beating of a heart in a vivisection.

And the picture also acquires a dimension of depth here. For the face can appear different at first glance than it is in reality. One first sees the type. Yet this can allow another hidden face to peer through gradually like a mask shimmering through. There are bad individuals of a noble race and vice versa. And on the face we see—like on an open battlefield—the wrestling of the soul with its destiny as no literature can portray it to us.

Similarity and the Doppelganger

Similarity is always the only possibility for recognizing very subtle and deep-seated differences. This is the particular attraction in the portrayal of different characters with very similar outer appearances, as can be the case with siblings, for example. One can then precisely see where the soul breaks from nature and individuality begins. What a task for an actor to play both characters! A wonderful technical possibility of film for doppelganger poetry that is among the most significant motifs of literature and that, by means of visible similarity, assumes an exciting reality in film that no literature can produce.

The attraction of doppelganger stories lies in the possibility of being able to live a "different" life from one's own. For it is a grave injustice that one can live only *one* life at a time. Imprisoned in my ego, I will never know how others look into the eyes of others while they are being kissed. I mix with unknown people in vain. I take myself with me everywhere, and every remark by others still applies only to me. I would have to be taken for someone else!

This is the indescribable attraction of being able to live the life of another, of a doppelganger without being recognized. This is the potential of the deepest psychology: how am I another and yet myself? And it will become apparent here how much in the outer appearance and even in the face of a person is only the reflection of surroundings and has only crystallized like the frost of the atmosphere. This is what makes this topic specifically filmic. The physiognomy of the most individual, most intimate character is released from its coincidental atmosphere as if by a sharp cut of scissors.

Facial Expression

There was once a French film in which Suzanne Després played the lead role although she did not at all participate in the "action." The film went like this: In a short prelude, we see a beggar woman imploring fate next to her dying child. Death appears and says to the mother, "I will show you the pre-ordained life of your child. Behold. And if you then still wish your child to remain alive, then so be it." And then the actual film begins, the fate of the child, a banal, empty story. Yet the mother, Suzanne Després, watches. In the left corner of the screen, we see the face of Suzanne Després, who watches the film as we do and accompanies the adventure of her child with facial expressions. For an hour and a half, we watch the play of a face in which hope, fear, joy, compassion, sorrow, courage, white-hot faith and black despair flicker. The actual drama and the essential content of the film play out on this face. The "story" provided only an opportunity.

And the audience, a very primitive audience, did not tire of watching these facial expressions for an hour and a half. The Gaumont Company knew why it had paid a large fee to Suzanne Després for this role. For the audience and the film businessmen have already figured out what our aesthetes and literati have not yet noticed: the important thing in film is *not the epic, but the lyric.*

Translated by Lance W. Garmer

Siegfried Kracauer

*Siegfried Kracauer (1889–1966) was a German–Jewish intel-
lectual associated with the Frankfurt School of critical theory
(see The German Library volume 78,* German 20th Century
Philosophy: The Frankfurt School) *who was a friend of, and
an intellectual influence upon Theodor W. Adorno. Having
studied architecture as a student, he also attended the lectures
of the sociologist Georg Simmel. Kracauer became an important film critic in Weimar Germany. In 1933, he left Germany
and went to the U.S., where he published books on German
cinema and on film theory.*

The Little Shopgirls Go to the Movies (1927)

Films are the mirror of the prevailing society. They are financed by
corporations, which must pinpoint the tastes of the audience at all
costs in order to make a profit. Since this audience is composed
largely of workers and ordinary people who gripe about the conditions in the upper circles, business considerations require the producer to satisfy the need for social critique among the consumers. A
producer, however, will never allow himself to be driven to present
material that in any way attacks the foundations of society, for to
do so would destroy his own existence as a capitalist entrepreneur.
Indeed, the films made for the lower classes are even more bourgeois than those aimed at the finer audiences, precisely because they
hint at subversive points of view without exploring them. Instead,
they smuggle in a respectable way of thinking. The fact that films
as a whole reaffirm the ruling system was demonstrated by the excitement over *Potemkin.* It was perceived to be different and was
aesthetically endorsed, but only for its meaning to be repressed. In
comparison with that film, the differences among the various types
of films produced in Germany or the United States evaporated, providing conclusive evidence that the cinematic productions of the latter countries are the homogeneous expression of one and the same
society. The attempts by some directors and authors to distance
themselves from this homogeneity are doomed from the start. Either such rebels are simply tools of society, unwittingly manipulated yet all the while believing they are voices of protest, or they
are forced to make compromises in their drive to survive (Even

Chaplin ends up as a millionaire in *The Gold Rush*, without having achieved any real goals.) Society is much too powerful for it to tolerate any movies except those with which it is comfortable. Film must reflect society whether it wants to or not.

But is it really society that manifests itself in sensationalist film hits? The breathtaking rescues, the impossible noblemindedness, the smooth young gents, the monstrous swindlers, the criminals and heroes, the moral nights of passion and the immoral marriages—do they really exist? They really do exist: one need only read the *Generalanzeiger* newspapers. There is no kitsch one could invent that life itself could not outdo. Servant girls do not imitate professional love-letter writers; rather, the opposite is true—the latter model their letters on those of servant girls. Virgins still drown themselves if they believe their bridegrooms have been unfaithful. Sensational film hits and life usually correspond to each other because the Little Miss Typists model themselves after the examples they see on the screen. It may be, however, that the most hypocritical instances are stolen from life.

Still, this is not to deny that, in the majority of contemporary films, things are pretty unrealistic. They give the blackest settings a pink tinge, and smear reds liberally everywhere. But the films do not therefore cease to reflect society. On the contrary: the more incorrectly they present the surface of things, the more correct they become and the more clearly they mirror the secret mechanism of society. In reality it may not often happen that a scullery maid marries the owner of a Rolls Royce. But doesn't every Rolls Royce owner dream that scullery maids dream of rising to his stature? Stupid and unreal film fantasies are the *daydreams of society*, in which its actual reality comes to the fore and its otherwise repressed wishes take on form. (The fact that major issues do get expressed—albeit in a distorted way—in both sensational film hits and in literary bestsellers does not detract from this claim.) Members of the higher and next-to-highest classes may not recognize their portraits in these films, but this does not mean there is no photographic resemblance. They have good reasons not to know what they themselves look like, and if they describe something as untrue, then it is all the more true.

Today's world can be recognized even in those films that are set in the *past*. It cannot examine itself all the time, because it may not examine itself from all sides; the possibilities for inoffensive self-portraits are limited, whereas the demand for material is insatiable.

The numerous historical films that merely illustrate the past (rather than showing the present in historical guise, as in *Potemkin*) are attempts at deception according to their own terms. Since one always runs the danger, when picturing current events, of turning easily excitable masses against powerful institutions that are in fact often not appealing, one prefers to direct the camera toward a Middle Ages that the audience will find harmlessly edifying. The further back the story is situated historically, the more audacious filmmakers become. They will risk depicting a successful revolution in historical costumes in order to induce people to forget modern revolutions, and they are happy to satisfy the theoretical sense of justice by filming struggles for freedom that are long past. Douglas Fairbanks, the gallant champion of the oppressed, goes to battle in a previous century against a despotic power whose survival is of no consequence to any American today. The courage of these films declines in direct proportion to their proximity to the present. The most popular scenes from World War I are not a flight to the far reaches of history but the immediate expression of society's will.

The reason this expression of societal will is reflected more directly in films than in theatrical works can already be explained simply by the greater number of elements that intervene between the dramatist and capital. It may seem to both the dramatist and the theater director as if they were independent of capital and thus able to produce timeless and classless works of art. Of course, this is impossible, but nevertheless shows are staged whose social determinants are harder to perceive than those in films, where the head of the corporation stands guard in person. This is particularly true of the social determinants of comedies, tragic dramas, high-class revues, and products of directorial artistry produced for the intellectual (Berlin) bourgeoisie—determinants that remain only partly unrefracted in society. In the end, the audiences for such works read a radical magazine and pursue their bourgeois profession with a bad conscience, in order to have a good conscience. The artistic qualities of a theater piece may also shift it outside the social sphere. Writers are often stupid, however, and if they renounce one aspect of traditional society, they are all the more taken in by another. (In the *Literarische Welt*, Bert Brecht called bourgeois lyricism suspicious and devoted himself instead to sports. Sports as a nonbourgeois phenomenon: Samson-Körner's biographer is not to be envied for making this discovery.) Apart from such exceptions, which consciously extricate themselves from some of the constraints, the majority of the remaining second-rate works for the stage are a precise response to the feelings of the theater crowds. They're just as indebted to the existing order of things as films, only they're more boring.

In order to investigate today's society, one must listen to the confessions of the products of its film industries. They are all blabbing a rude secret, without really wanting to. In the endless sequence of films, a limited number of typical themes recur again and again; they reveal how society wants to see itself. The quintessence of these film themes is at the same time the sum of the society's ideologies, whose spell is broken by means of the interpretation of the themes. The series "The Little Shopgirls Go to the Movies" is conceived as a small collection of samples whose textbook cases are subjected to moral casuistry.

Clear Road

A prison inmate who has seen better days is released and lands in a Zille-type milieu full of little shopowners, whores, proletarians, and shady characters. He had been wrongly convicted. In vain the fallen man looks for respectable work; only a whore takes pity on him. One day, he rescues a woman in a carriage whose horses have gone out of control in the Tiergarten park; she's the sister of a manufacturer, who expresses his thanks by giving the former inmate a job in his business. Now the road is clear for the diligent man: his achievements are recognized, his innocence considered proven. Following the timely death of the whore, who succumbs to consumption, the fellow—now dressed in a business suit—becomes engaged to the woman he rescued. A typical situation on screen, which attests to the social mentality of today's world. Using true-to-nature studio images of back-alley interiors, it depicts the impoverished conditions that give rise to transgressions which are not the real social crimes. It wanders without prejudice among the underprivileged classes, which provide gripping material for the film. The themes, however, have been carefully screened. All mention of class difference is avoided, since society is far too convinced of its first-class status to want to become conscious of the real conditions of its classes. Also avoided is any mention of the working class, which is attempting through political means to escape from the misery that the directors present so movingly. In films based on real-life situations, the workers are respectable lower-level railroad functionaries and patriarchal foremen; or, if they are supposed to be discontented, they have suffered a personal tragedy, so that the public misfortune can be all the more easily forgotten. One prefers the *Lumpenproletariat* as emotionally moving subject matter, because it is politically helpless and contains dubious elements who seem to deserve their fate. Society disguises the sites of misery in romantic garb so as to perpetuate them, and lavishes pity on them because here it doesn't cost a cent. It is full of pity, this society, and wants to express its emotional excess so as to soothe its conscience—assuming, of course, that everything can remain the way it is. Out of pity, it extends a hand to one or two of the foundering people and rescues them by pulling them back up to its level, which it really considers to be quite a height. This is how it assures itself moral support, while at the same time maintaining the underling as underling and society as society. On the contrary: saving individual people is a convenient way to prevent the rescue of the entire class; one proletarian who has been promoted to the drawing room ensures the perpetuation of many a beer joint. The manufacturer's sister will later go with her husband to visit his beer joint. Maybe these two will once again save another person. One need not fear that this is why the proletarians are dying out. The little shopgirls gain unexpected insights into the misery of mankind and the goodness from above.

Sex and Character

A young and pretty girl has made up her mind to win the heart of her cousin, who owns the adjacent property. She puts on pants, gets him to hire her as his domestic servant, and from then on appears as an ambiguous figure in the most unambiguous situations. The word "gay" is also ambiguous, its meaning depending on the context of its utterance. In order to establish the boy's true identity, the owner of the estate breaks into the servant's room. The half-undressed girl—from the waist up in livery, below the waist in lace panties—has crawled under the covers. The thorough master grabs her by the feet and; slowly and systematically, pulls her out. All out of love. The outcome: an engagement. The owner of the estate is rich. Before his domestic servant's hips began to arouse his suspicion, he had had an affair that began in a dance club. Dance clubs are no less numerous and no less important today than churches were in previous centuries. No film without a dance club; no tuxedo without money. Otherwise women would not put on and take off their pants. The business is called eroticism, and the preoccupation with it is called life. Life is an invention of the haves, which the have-nots try to imitate to the best of their inability. Since it is in the interest of the propertied classes to maintain society as it is, they must prevent others from thinking about that society. With the help of their money, they are able in their free time to forget the existence for which they slave during the day. They live. They buy themselves an amusement which allows the brain to take time off because it keeps the other organs so completely busy. If the dance clubs were not already fun in themselves, the state would have to subsidize them. Girls who disguise themselves as domestic servants and gentlemen whose ultimate goal can be grasped under bedcovers do not have evil thoughts—that are good thoughts. They might stumble upon such thoughts out of boredom. In order to alleviate the boredom that leads to the amusement that produces the boredom, the amusement is supplemented with love. Why did the girl do it? Because she loves the owner of the estate. Any objections to love are destroyed by the judgment of a society that has lost love. Out of the earthly realm of the club, society allows oaths of fidelity to blossom between lives that do not exist, and out of the revue environment it conjures up engagement apotheoses whose luster should not be dismissed as trivial. The light such apotheoses radiate is so festive that people no longer wish for society to conceive of things in a different light. Particularly if love is financially secure. In the dark movie theaters, the poor little shopgirls grope for their date's hand and think of the coming Sunday.

Nation in Arms

An impoverished hotel in eastern Austria during World War I has just been occupied by the Russians. Here, a servant lass hides an Austrian officer who has stayed behind. The Russian general who has taken up residence in the hotel harasses the patriotic lass with lascivious propositions. She resists, out of patriotism. Shortly thereafter the Austrians march back in and the officer and the woman who rescued him are honored by the entire company, to the tune of the Radetzky March. (A wartime wedding is in the offing.)—On another occasion, an intrepid East Prussian woman rescues her son (likewise an officer) during an enemy occupation. He wins his hardy cousin as his wife. The battle scenes are edited more decently than the uniformed acts of heroism.—These military and war films, which resemble each other down to the last detail, are a striking refutation of the claim that today's world is fundamentally materialistic. At the very least they prove that certain influential circles are very interested in having others adopt a heroic attitude instead of the materialism which these influential circles themselves support. In fact, those circles can achieve their aims—which may lead to new wars—only when the masses, which are still slightly contaminated by the revolution, have once again been morally purified; when the pleasure provided by war in the form of decorations and virgins replaces the memory of its horrors; when, once again, a new generation grows up which does not want to know what it is battling for, so that it can triumph and perish with all the more honor. The moral intent of these films is confirmed by the fact that they also acknowledge the humanity of the enemy. The Russian general who is after the patriotic lass is an honest man. Respect for the opponent makes war into an absurdity. This is precisely the aim of its producers, since, as such, war must be accepted as an inexplicable necessity. Only when the populace considers a heroic death a senseless fate can it endure it ethically. Military films serve to educate the populace. This is particularly true of the Friedericus Rex movies, in which—always according to the wishes of the same influential circles—the audience is once again treated to a king that inspires more enthusiasm than its real leaders, who, in turn, profit from this enthusiasm. When good old Sombart called the Germans "heroes" and the English "merchants" in a war pamphlet, he erred as profoundly as only a professor can. The film heroes of all countries unite as the propaganda bosses of their nation's businessmen. It is hard for the little shopgirls to resist the appeal of the marches and the uniforms.

The World Travelers

The daughter of an airplane engine manufacturer takes off on an air race around the world—a flight that is supposed to demonstrate the quality of daddy's motors. A competitor she has previously turned down tries to delay her all along the voyage. A young man whom she will assuredly not turn down helps her all along the voyage. Against the backdrop of India, China, the calm ocean, and America, a love affair develops with great speed, and great speed develops with this affair. The woman aviator always appears in the traditional garb of each respective country. In the end, triumph and an engagement. In other films, the characters get engaged on the shores of northern Italian lakes or in Spain (the choice of country depends on the whims of fashion.) Each engagement is linked with the continuous use of one's own car.—I have traveled around the entire world in order to find myself, Count Keyserling affirms in his philosopher's travelogue. Society likewise never finds itself through its voyages; but unlike the count, it travels precisely in order not to find itself. Whether at home or in some modern means of transportation, society's actions remain everywhere the same. Changes in the landscape, however, distract attention from the hypocrisy of societal events, whose monotony is forgotten in the adventure of the voyage. The woman aviator who overcomes danger in India pretends to be a modest damsel in distress; nobody recalls the capitalist transaction in Berlin that prompted her to take the trip in the first place. Travel is one of the best means for a society to maintain a permanent state of absentmindedness, which prevents that society from coming to terms with itself. It assists fantasy along mistaken paths; it occludes one's perspective with impressions; it adds to the wonder of the world, so that the world's ugliness goes unnoticed. (The concomitant increase in knowledge about the world serves to transfigure the existing system in which it is gained.) Some important social figures who can afford to spend their vacations in St. Moritz truly feel like human beings when they're there; they go to St. Moritz only to repress the fact that they really aren't human beings. Even the lower social classes, which have to stay at home, are sent away. The illustrated newspapers disseminate images among them from every country; and anyway, whom does the woman aviator fly for, if not for them? For the more they travel, the less they understand anything. When all geographic hideouts have been photographed, society will have been completely blinded. The little shopgirls want so badly to get engaged on the Riviera.

The Golden Heart

A young Berlin wholesaler, an industrious manager of a first-rate company, visits a business friend of his father's in Vienna; the paternal friend's firm is going to pieces because of the disorder in Austria. The guest would leave, if it were not for the business friend's daughter, a sweet Viennese gal who makes it clear to him that there are other things besides management: the waves of the Danube and the wine gardens specializing in new vintages. With delight, the young man from Berlin discovers his dormant feelings. He cleans up the company, which will soon be turning a profit again, and gets the gal for home use.—Even without close-ups, this course of events would be believable. Whether in the city of waltz dreams or on the beautiful beaches of the Neckar—someplace, but not here in the present, the rich are falling in love and discovering in the process that they have hearts. It is not true that they are heartless: films refute what life would make one believe. Outside business—which admittedly would not be the right place for heart—their hearts are always in the wrong place. They are brimming with feeling in situations where it is of little consequence and are often unable to do as they like, only because they waste their feelings so uneconomically in private affairs that their supply is continually running out. One needs to have experienced the tenderness and gentleness the young man from Berlin expresses to the Viennese girl under the Stephansturm in order to understand once and for all that his brutal behavior on the telephone does not indicate a lack of sentiment. The camera reveals this. What he really loves is operettas, and what he really longs for is an idyllic retreat in which, undisturbed, he can open his poor heart, which he has had to close off in all other situations. If there were no Viennese woman in the house to keep his heart from interfering in economic matters, it could, in a pinch, be well accommodated by the record player. Through films, one can prove on a case-by-case basis that with rising prosperity the number of emotional nature preserves is constantly growing. The little shopgirls learn to understand that their brilliant boss is made of gold on the inside as well; they await the day when they can revive a young Berliner with their silly little hearts.

The Modern Haroun al Raschid

A billionaire's daughter appears incognito as a poor girl, because she wants to be loved purely for who she is as a human being. Her wish is fulfilled by a rather plain young man who is actually an impoverished lord. Before he has even confessed his affection he learns, by chance, of the billions. He withdraws from his courtship in order to avoid any misunderstandings. Now, more than ever, the two come together, and since money loves to come into money, in the end the lord inherits an immense fortune.—In another film a young billionaire roams the world as a vagabond, because he wants to be loved purely for who he is as a person and so on. Incognito revealed, the girl hesitates, and a honeymoon on a comfortable yacht ensues.—As in the *Thousand and One Nights*, today's fairy tale prince also chooses discretion; but here the opulence of the ending stems from his billions, which outshine every social opulence. A huge fortune can be kept secret for instrumental reasons. The rich pauper and the tramp who isn't one do not appear incognito for any purpose other than perhaps wanting to be taken purely for who they are as human beings and so forth. Why don't they just throw the money away if they want to be loved as human beings? Why don't they demonstrate that they are something worth loving by doing something decent with their money? They don't throw it away, and they don't do anything decent with it. Instead, the feigned poverty serves to shine a bright spotlight on the luckiness of wealth, and the desire to be loved disinterestedly is a sentimentality that serves to obscure the lack of true love. For true love has interests; it is of great interest to it that its object be a worthy one. It might get uncomfortable for the billionaire's daughter if a suitor desired her out of real interest. So she hushes up the billions with which she has been provided and procures for herself, at the giveaway price of the open market, a husband whose unselfishness consists in the fact that he stumbles across a girl without billions who is nothing without her billions. But (so preach the moralists among the rich) what is important is the girl, not the wealth. According to the cinematic testimony, a human being is a girl who can dance the Charleston well and a boy who knows just as little. The love between one person and another—that is, between two private bagatelles—is therefore not superfluous but serves to justify property ownership. This ownership, in turn, is not nearly so aggravating to those without property if those who own property can show through so-called love that they can own it as human beings. The fairy tales have remained, while the theme of the incognito has been inverted. The authentic Haroun al Raschid traveled among the people anonymously in order to get to know them independently of property, and in the end revealed himself as their judge. The modern Haroun al Raschid presents himself independent of his wealth in order to be recognized as something special in this anonymity, and in the end reveals the only thing he really is: his wealth. If the little shopgirls were approached tonight by an unknown gentleman, they would take him to be one of the famous millionaires from the illustrated magazines.

Silent Tragedies

A banker goes bankrupt as a result of such immense incompetence that he commits suicide out of propriety. The insolvent estate includes a daughter. The first lieutenant who loves her must abandon his dreams of escorting her down the aisle; her lack of means and his career make this impossible. She goes on to earn her living as a dancer under an artistic pseudonym. The first lieutenant, who has long regretted his refusal of the relationship, meets her again after years of futile searching, and wants to be united with her at last. The only thing needed for a happy ending is his letter of resignation, which he has been planning to hand in. But the selfless dancer poisons herself in order, through her death, to force her lover to think only of his career. The officer, dressed in civilian clothes, stands wistfully beside the stretcher.—The young man need not be a first lieutenant; in other professions as well, an individual's career depends on marrying wealth. This leads to such tragedies, which really aren't tragedies. But for society's sake, it's imperative that they appear to be tragedies. If a woman kills herself so that a man can reach great heights, this guarantees the irrevocability of social structures. They are raised to the level of eternal laws, since, for their sake, people are willing to suffer a death reminiscent of a five-act tragic drama. The film companies know (or perhaps do not know) why they peddle such morbid fare. The death that confirms the power of the ruling institutions prevents a death in the course of a struggle against these institutions. In order to make the latter impossible, the former is glorified. The film producers glorify it, however, by passing off as tragic what is really lack of knowledge or, at best, a misfortune. The noblemindedness that the dancer wants to prove by voluntarily killing herself is a squandering of feeling, which is cultivated by the better classes because it weakens the feeling of injustice. There are many people who sacrifice themselves noblemindely because they are too lazy to rebel; many tears are shed which flow only because crying is sometimes easier than contemplation. Today's tragedies are private affairs with a bad outcome which society has metaphysically dressed up in order to preserve the status quo. The stronger the power positions of society, the more tragically weakness and stupidity will behave. And with every new international agreement that heavy industry reaches, the number of suicidal dancers will certainly rise. The audience is so touched by the signs of the poisoning by which these dancers take their leave that it no longer wants to get rid of the poison. Thus, only the attempts to detoxify society can be called tragic. Furtively, the little shopgirls wipe their eyes and quickly powder their noses before the lights go up.

Close to the Edge

At times, films go mad. They have terrifying visions and spew images that expose society's true countenance. Luckily, they are healthy at root. The schizophrenic outbursts are only momentary; the curtain is lowered once again, and everything returns to normal. A girl from the provinces, for example, comes to Berlin with her admirer, a clumsy young fellow. Since she is a beauty, a board chairman makes her into a revue star and gives the youth a job. He would be a bad businessman if he did not want to cash in on his investment. The girl, however, refuses his advances, packs up her young man, and turns her back on dirty favoritism. (The film's scriptwriter is a man of letters.) An unmasking of social practices? The film producer deserves to go broke, since nothing is more demoralizing for an audience than the revelation of immoral activities that are officially sanctioned so long as they take place in secret. The danger is avoided at the last minute, when the board chairman regrets his actions and catches up with the innocent couple, who, following his renunciation, happily allow him to drive them back to town. There have to be such board chairmen in order to whitewash favoritism. (The author is a man of letters.) The following case is even more drastic. The king of a tiny impoverished southern country has brought home a lover from Paris that an American billionaire wants to include among his possessions. In order to win her, the billionaire buys the cooperation of the discontented masses and bribes the king's general. A patriotic insurrection is quickly staged. Machine guns open fire, producing a picturesque distribution of corpses in the streets and squares. The general informs the billionaire that, thanks to the incarceration of the king, the girl is now free; his attitude toward his new patron is that of an obsequious servant. Is this how coups d'état and bloodbaths are staged by big capital? The film is insane. It portrays events as they actually happen, instead of maintaining the dignity usually accorded them such that they can continue to take place. Thank God the film recovers its rosy-cheeked smile immediately. The American is really a good person who deserves his billions. Upon learning that the Parisian woman is loyal to her lover, he frees the ex-king from prison and sends the happy pair on their honeymoon. Love is stronger than money when money is supposed to win sympathy. The little shop-girls were worried; now they can breathe easy again.

Translated by Thomas Y. Levin

Bertolt Brecht

As one of the most influential figures in twentieth-century the-ater, Bertolt Brecht (1898–1956) attempted to integrate his concept of the Verfremdungseffekt *into his dramas; this has often been translated as the "alienation effect," although "de-familiarization effect" would be more accurate. The purpose of this effect was to prevent viewers from losing themselves in emotional identification with the characters and events on-stage but rather to remain aware that they are watching a the-atrical production, thereby making the politics of the drama visible. He wrote the screenplay with Slatan Dudow to* Kuhle Wampe *(1932), and his famous 1928 play* The Three Penny Opera (Dreigroschenoper) *was the basis of G. W. Pabst's film of 1931—which Brecht rejected. His negative experience with the film industry led to the reflections below. On the day after the Reichstag was destroyed in 1933, Brecht emigrated to Denmark until 1939, then to Sweden and Finland, and by 1941 to the U.S., where he stayed until 1947. During his years in California, he worked as screenwriter, contributing to the screenplay for Fritz Lang's* Hangmen Also Die *(1943). Brecht's commitment to socialism—and the offer of a the-ater—ultimately led him to East Berlin, where, with his wife, Helene Weigel, he co-founded the Berlin Ensemble. Brecht is also represented in The German Library volumes 43, 53, 75, 83, 87.*

From The Three-Penny Trial: A Sociological Experiment (1931)

Contradictions are Hopes!

This winter, the filming of the theater piece *The Three-Penny Opera* afforded us the opportunity to encounter several ideas that are characteristic of the current state of bourgeois ideology. These ideas, drawn from the behavior of public institutions (the press, the film industry, the court), are a small part of the enormous ideological complex that comprises culture, and judgments can be made about culture only if this complex is observed in praxis, i.e., working, in full operation, constantly produced by reality and constantly producing it, and is made accessible to observation. Once one has dealt with these ideas in their entirety—those that reach into reality and those that do not reach into it—then one has also dealt with the image of culture, and one cannot arrive at such an image differently. Everything that is said about culture from a more remote, more general standpoint without consideration of praxis can only itself be an idea and thus must first be tested in praxis.

One must avoid seeking great conceptual things such as justice or personality where one finds them—in some mediocre heads or mouths—one must pursue them in common reality, in the dealings of film people and in the dealings of those who, by upholding the law, earn their bread. Sublime thoughts do not imply having culture. If the question of whether justice *or* the administration of justice exists (insofar as the two do not coincide) is raised, then the answer must be: the administration of justice. And confronted with the choice of the administration of justice or law (insofar as the two cannot be granted together), we would have to choose the administration of justice. In any event, we should say only as much about justice as there is of it in the administration of justice. Methods other than those of "objective, disinterested," passive observation are necessary in order to elicit the ideas held by constantly functioning reality, ever-adjudicating justice, the press expressing or producing public opinion, and industry incessantly and unstoppably producing art. In what follows, such a different, "non-objective," etc. method will be presented and called a "sociological experiment." A complete evaluation of the experiment will not be made; the experiment itself is very imperfect because it is carried out with too little planning and by too few people who are also not sufficiently specialized. Since they are subject to such great institutions as the press, the courts, and so on, one would need for such experiments a society that operates according to a plan and divides labor in order to make what is to be seen visible to everyone. All literary work, as performed by individuals, is becoming only increasingly dubious. . . .

Critique of Ideas

1. *"Art does not need film"*

"Honor unto the writer who on principle does not allow his works to be filmed ... He stands before the choice of not allowing his work to be filmed—which is his free will certainly to be highly esteemed artistically—or, if he wants to have the material reward, he must be content with it once and for all. . . ." —Frankfurter Zeitung, *"The Lawyer of the Film Company,"* Dr. Frankfurter

Many people tell us—and the court also represents this view— that, if we sell our work to the film industry, then we have to forego all rights; that the buyers gain the right through the purchase even to destroy what was bought; and that the money settles any further claim. If we become involved with the film industry, then we are acting, according to the view of these people, like a person who puts his laundry into a mud puddle to wash it and then complains that it is ruined. Those who advise against using these new machines grant these machines the right to work poorly and forget themselves out of sheer objectivity, for they are content with only filth being produced for them. They take the machines away from us at the outset, though, machines that we require for our production, for this method of production will replace the traditional method more and more; we will be forced to speak through increasingly closed media and we will be forced to express what is to be said with increasingly inadequate means. The old forms of communication do not remain unchanged by newly emerging ones and do not continue to exist next to them. The film viewer reads stories differently. But the person who writes stories is for his part also a film viewer. The technification of literary production can no longer be undone. The use of tools also leads the novelist who does not use them to want to be able to do what tools can do, too, and to add that which they show (or could show) to the reality that comprises his material, yet primarily to impart to his own stance in writing the character of the use of tools.

There is a great difference, for example, whether the writer approaches matters as if he had tools or whether he "produces" matters "from himself." What film itself does, that is, the extent to which it maintains its particular nature vis-à-vis "art," is not unimportant here. It is conceivable that writers of other genres, i.e., dramatists and novelists, can, at the outset, work in a more film-like manner than film people. They are in part more independent of the means of production. But they are indeed dependent on film and its progress or regress, and the means of production for screenwriters are thoroughly capitalized. The bourgeois novel today still shapes "one world" at a time. It does this purely idealistically from a world view, from the more or less private, but in any case individual view of its "creator." Within this world, all particulars are, of course, then correct and, ripped out of context, could not for a moment have a true-blue effect vis-à-vis the "details" of reality. One learns only as much about the real world as one learns about the author, the creator of the unreal world, in order not to have to say that one learns only something about the author and nothing about the world. Film—which cannot shape a world (the milieu of film is entirely different) and that allows no one to express himself (and nothing else) through a work and which allows no work to express a person—provides (or could provide): useful clues about human actions in detail. Its splendidly inductive method, which film at least makes possible, can be of immeasurable significance for the novel, in so far as the novel itself can still signify anything. For drama, film's position toward the acting individual, for example, is interesting. To imbue its characters (who are used only according to functions) with life, film simply uses ready-made types who come into particular situations and are able to assume particular positions in them. All motivation proceeding from the character is missing; the inner life of people never provides the primary impetus and is seldom the primary result of the action; the person is seen from the outside. Literature needs film not only indirectly. It also needs it directly. In the crucial widening of its social tasks, which result from a functional permutation of art into a pedagogical discipline, the means of representation must be multiplied or frequently changed. (To say nothing at all about actual didactic drama, which even demands that machines for filming be turned over to individual practitioners!) These machines can be used like hardly anything else for overcoming the old non-technical, anti-technical, "radiant" "art" connected with the religious. The socialization of these means of production is a question of life and death for art. To tell the person who works with his head that he is free to do without the new means of labor is to direct him to a freedom outside the production process. Just as the owners of the means of production tell the manual laborer that they are not forcing him to work for the wage they pay him and that he is "free" to go. The armed and the unarmed, the murderers and the victims thus face one another with equal entitlement; both are allowed to fight. The shift of the means of production away from the producer entails the proletarianization of the producer; the mental worker, like the manual laborer, has only to engage his naked labor more in the production process; his labor, though, is his self. He is nothing except this, and, just like the manual laborer, he increasingly requires (since production becomes increasingly "technical") precisely the means of production for the use of his labor: the terrible *circulus vitiosus* of exploitation has commenced here as well!

In order to understand the situation, one must free oneself of the common view according to which only a part of art has an interest in these struggles for modern institutions and machines. According to this view, there is a part of art—the authentic part—that, entirely untouched by the new possibilities of communication (radio, film, book clubs, etc.), uses the old ones (the printed book that comes freely onto the book market, the stage, etc.) and is therefore entirely free from any influence of modern industry. It is entirely different, according to this view, with the other part, the technological part, which has to do with the products created by these very machines. An entirely new issue that nevertheless owes its existence at the outset to certain monetary expectations and can therefore never be free of them. When works of the first type are turned over to machines, they thereby immediately become just *commodities*. This view, which then leads to complete fatalism, is wrong, for it excludes at least so-called "untouchable" art from all processes and influences of the age and considers it to be untouchable only because it withdraws from progress in communication. In reality, of course, all art without exception falls into the new situation. It has to come to terms with this as a whole and not in fragmenting parts; it becomes a commodity or does not become a commodity as a whole. Over time, the transformation leaves nothing untouched, but always comprises the whole.

The (commonly held) view discussed here is therefore injurious.

2. *"Film needs art"*

"A vitalization of sound film by means of the truly literary script would be an immeasurable gain."—Kölnische Zeitung (Cologne News)

"I find that this attitude of producers and their followers is entirely unproductive. As far as I am concerned, they need not understand

anything about art, but they would at least have to be able to take its economic value into account and to behave purely for utilitarian reasons like an advanced industrialist who entrusts real artists with tasks."—Frankfurter Zeitung (Frankfurt News)

The demand that film be art met with resistance nowhere. It came just as forcefully from the columns of newspapers as from the offices of film producers. Films were marketable only in the form of items for pleasurable consumption, so one had to rely from the beginning on the same market that art had, and the common notion that items for pleasurable consumption had to be ennobled and that this was a matter of art, that art was primarily the noblest of all items for pleasurable consumption, engendered further commitment by artists for film. An attempt should not be made here to make the well-known subtle distinction between true and false art in order to demonstrate that film instinctively reached for false art (in order to be marketable, art must first be for sale). Alone the definition as an item of pleasurable consumption accords both types of art quotation marks. "Art" has, in any case, prevailed against machines with force. Nearly everything that we see on the screen today is "art." Indeed, it must be "art": As "art," such a thing, even if in a somewhat different, slightly antiquated form as novel, drama, travelogue description and criticism, had already prevailed on the market and was therefore capable of being accommodated. The filmic form opened greater possibilities for distribution (in addition to gigantic capital turnover) and added the attractions of the new technical school to the old attractions. Only in this manner can a particular director prevail with his "art" against the new machines under the additional pressure of the sales department: What he successfully introduces is what he himself can make of what he, as a commonplace viewer, understands by "art." He will not know what art should do. He probably thinks: conjuring general feelings, compiling impressions or "all that sort of thing." In the area of art, he employs the understanding of an oyster; in the area of technology, he employs nothing better. He is incapable of understanding anything about the machines: he violates them with his "art." In order to capture reality with the new machines, he would have to be an artist or, in the worst of cases, a connoisseur of reality, but certainly not a connoisseur of art; therefore, he produces, which is simpler, "art" with them, the well-known, the tried-and-true, the commodity. He has the reputation of a tasteful arranger; people say that he "knows something about art!" As if one could understand something about art without understanding something about reality! And the machine here functions as reality simultaneously with the material. Such a situation did not create for the new machines the possibilities that would have existed for them in themselves. Entirely aside from the question of whether its primary task was to produce the social phenomenon art—they could have set about this more easily, too, if they had initially been able to ignore having to produce something like the old "art." Applied by science, for example, medicine, biology, statistics, and so on in order to determine visible behavior or to show simultaneous events, they could have learned to determine the behavior of people toward one another more easily than will be the case. The latter is difficult enough and cannot be solved without a very rigid, secure function within the tasks of total society. The situation thereby becomes so complicated that a simple "representation of reality" says something about reality less than ever before. A photograph of the Krupp Works or of A.E.G. yields nearly nothing about these institutions. Actual reality has slipped into the functional. The reification of human relationships, such as the factory, no longer produces the latter. So there is in fact "something to build up," something "artificial," "contrived." It is similarly a fact that art is necessary. But the old concept of art, drawn from experience, simply breaks down. For whoever presents of reality only what can be experienced from it does not represent reality itself. It has been a long time since it could be experienced in its totality. Whoever presents the dark associations and anonymous feelings that reality produces no longer represents reality itself. You will no longer recognize fruits by their tastes. But, in talking this way, we are talking of an art with an entirely different function in social life, e.g., the function of presenting reality, and we are doing this only in order to liberate what "art" in this country is doing from such claims that do not result from art's function.

It is not true that film needs art unless one creates a new idea of art.

3. *"One can improve public taste"*

"Whereas every better industrial firm today knows that quality goods increase profit and thus employs experts who produce this quality for it, the trade derides all expert assistance when possible

and sets its ambition in playing the arbiter of taste. To discuss the film distributor first of all, it amasses for itself functions for whose fulfillment it notoriously lacks the preconditions . . . It claims to know all about the needs of the public and influences the entire film production on the basis of this supposed knowledge. There would not be the least objection against such dilettantish ambitions if they produced great successes. But experience teaches that they—aside from those film producers who speculate in misguided instincts like Der wahre Jakob/The True Jacob *or* Drei Tage Mittelarrest/Three Days of Semi-arrest—*are at home in the lowest sphere and must make their way in desolate provincial cities because there are no other diversions there. Experience teaches that the distributor, which believes that it is supposed to determine of its own accord the type and quality of films in the interest of economics, thereby in truth acts against its economic interest and goes from one error to another. Many difficulties in the film industry have their root simply in the conceit of agents and salespeople that they are art experts and market researchers. The fact that they are not by no means sullies them; the fact that they nevertheless want to be proves their commercial ineptitude. In reality, they stand in many cases—numerous films bear out this thesis—at the lowest level of public taste, and the philosopher Georg Simmel made evident the fact that the average level always lies somewhat above the lower boundary. In practical matters, people should not hold philosophers in such contempt."*
—Frankfurter Zeitung (Frankfurt News)

If, in addition to the metaphysical discussions about film that our newspapers carry on the pages that are not filled with advertisements, one adds physics, i.e., insight into the actual mechanics, purpose and craft of film, since the issue cannot possibly have to do only with the charitable readiness of a few moneyed people to impart to the public the most recent ideas of technology and the loveliest thoughts of writers—if one, then, overlooking the "behind" so widely proffered up front, illuminates the "front" so fearfully hidden behind and conceives of film as a (badly running) business for incessantly pumping into a huge, amorphous, unimaginable public thoroughly predetermined, barely variable, yet, in effect, quickly worn-out entertainment, then one just as little avoids this last absolute obstacle to all progress called public taste as if one faithfully followed the usual metaphysical method. Public taste, this intricate, costly, and lucrative thing, hinders progress. There is no doubt about the increasing influence of buyers on the "how" of the product, and it has a reactionary effect. The necessity of fighting such an influence arises for our believers in progress. This influence is represented by the film buyers, provincial organizers of the market. Examined closely, there are even people who allow themselves to exercise the function to which the press itself and our metaphysicians in the feature article section are actually entitled, namely, to make a decision of what is right for the consumer. So one must fight them because they are reactionary. Now, it is not difficult for our metaphysicians to find them: they reside in the recesses of their newspapers, in the advertisement sections! The physicists sit together there and discuss public taste. They understand it just as little as the metaphysicians in the front room, but it is not so necessary to understand a thing in order to exploit it. For them, public taste, this costly and profitable thing, is the true expression of the real needs of the movie theater masses. One determines it empirically and, with their sharpened instincts, these people who rely *materially on the correctness of their analyses* act as if the roots of this taste lay in the social and economic situation of these masses; as if these buyers bought correctly; as if the item purchased were what was demanded by the buyer's situation; and therefore as if this taste could be changed not by courses in aesthetics or by the very able, lip-smacking spoon-feeding of our Kerrs and Diebolds,[1] but at most by a real, far-reaching change of the situation. Our metaphysicians, on the other hand, consider the arrangement of the world to be a matter of taste. They do not think of investigating the social use of, say, sentimentality; if they did want to do so, they would be lacking the methods of thinking and the necessary knowledge. A certain humor as well as its special coarseness are not only a product of material conditions, but also a means of production. Ihering has recently done some things for the theater in this regard when, on the occasion of *Hauptmann von Köpenick*, he determined that, and why, a parade march still has a rousing effect even as a caricature. As long as we fight against the consequences of causes unknown to us and only criticize symptoms in a purely conceptual world, our demands in the realm of things practical—where the thing we fight has a solid social function and is a real commodity that is profitable for buyer and seller—can at best be termed harmless. The struggle of progressive intellectuals against the influence of sellers is founded on the assertion that the masses do not know their interests as well as the intellectuals know them. But the masses have fewer aesthetic

---

[1] Theater and film critics. (Editor's note)

and more political interests, and at no time was Schiller's suggestion to make political education a matter of aesthetics so obviously
hopeless as today. Those who fight under this banner turn to people
who finance films with the request that they educate the buyers—
they appoint the capitalists as pedagogues of the masses! In practice, they imagine the great process of education (although they are
incidentally by no means obligated to imagine anything in practice)
such that like-minded intellectuals having the same taste who produce films upon the financers' order, directors, scriptwriters, and so
on should use the capital "placed at their disposal" for the education of the buyers. They are basically calling upon them to engage
in sabotage. It is no wonder that, with such a request, these people
almost always display a peculiar, far-reaching moral indignation.
The management of the *Three-Penny* film refused to endanger the
capital "entrusted" to it in this manner *out of decency,* and it is,
of course, just as impossible to undermine this decency as it is to
undermine the decency of demanding criticism. Concessions to
taste can be extorted, if need be. But is there more at stake? Should
one demand more than that items of pleasurable consumption be
ennobled? One will not improve public taste if one frees films of
tastelessness, but one will weaken the films. After all: Does one
know what one removes along with instances of tastelessness? The
tastelessness of the masses is rooted more deeply in reality than the
taste of the intellectuals. Under certain social conditions, the refinement of an item for pleasurable consumption causes it to become weaker. The concept "item for pleasurable consumption"
perhaps also contains too much luxuriousness to be applied to film
without hesitation. Film perhaps plays a much more important
role? Perhaps it is better to say that it provides relaxation? In any
event, it is absolutely necessary to examine the thing "public taste"
closely, especially where it involves the expression of social interests
that the public wishes to satisfy in movie theaters. One would have
to proceed absolutely experimentally to achieve this, though, and
thus in conjunction with certain movie theaters that especially
have a petit-bourgeois audience (and, within this group, specified
or proletarian audiences, etc., as well) and one would have to show
particular films and to gauge reactions through suitable means. Furthermore, the principles gained would necessarily have to meet the
demand for predictability, i.e., to be so formulated that industry
could adhere to them—that is, without absolute judgment.

The idea of the feature article writers is therefore inadequate: One can change the public taste of the audience not by means of better films, but only with a change of its circumstances.

4. *"Film is a commodity"*

". . . Accordingly, one cannot say that there is no reason to regard the screenplay writer differently or worse than the playwright . . . The former is the producer of a mass commodity that is to go out into the entire world. Because of this and the business risk engendered by it, greater economic emphasis falls on him; the financial expenditures for this are also to be judged differently . . . Yet the film producer's entire way of doing business, which is aimed at the production of a sales commodity, is a different one, as well. He must work up an inventory, and he depends on time, the public's taste, the timeliness of the material and competition on the world market much more than the theater director in his city." —Reich Court Judgment

"Anyone who enters into a work and business relationship with the cinema must understand that he is turning to an industry and to people who are betting their money and who afterwards either must find the approval of several thousand theaters or simply lose their money." —Kinematograph

Everyone agrees that film, even the most artistic, is a commodity. Some people, though, believe that this does it no harm; that it is a commodity only secondarily; that the form as a commodity is merely the form that brings film into circulation; and that this commodity form need not by any means utterly stigmatize film. They say that it is precisely the task of art to free it from this degeneration. Whoever believes this has no idea of the transformative power of the commodity character. The fact that, in capitalism, the world *in the form of exploitation and corruption* is transformed into a production is not as important as the fact of this *transformation*. Others say that film distinguishes itself from the artwork in that film may be more than an artwork, that it is a commodity, i.e., that its essence is determined by its commodity character. They lament this fact almost without exception. Apparently, no one can imagine that this manner of coming into circulation could be advantageous for an artwork. With the gesture of "heroic realism" (seeing things as they are), though, people overlook what no businessman overlooks, namely, that a thing is buyable. There are indeed artworks of other types that are not commodities, or only to a lesser degree, such that their commodity character hardly affects them, so to speak. But only the person who closes his eyes to the tremendous power of the revolutionary process that pulls all the things of this world into commodity circulation, without any exception and without any delay, can assume that artworks of any type could exclude themselves there. Indeed, the deeper meaning of the process consists in allowing nothing to be unrelated to anything else, but in connecting everything, just as it also delivers all people (in the form of commodities) up to all people; it is precisely and quintessentially the process of communication.

Thus, we have two incorrect ideas before us: (1) The ("bad") commodity character of the film work is nullified by art; (2) The artistic character of the other types of art is untouched by the ("bad") process in film.

5. *"Film provides relaxation"*

> *"The producers cannot act differently. A film entails such a great economic enterprise, represents such an amount of daring, capital and film labor that it may not be endangered by prima donna moods, ignorance of the requirements of film, or, as in the case of Brecht, even the wishes of political tendency."* —Frankfurter Zeitung; *the lawyer of the film company, Dr. Frankfurter*

As long as the social function of film is not criticized, film criticism is only a criticism of symptoms and itself has only a symptomatic character. It exhausts itself in matters pertaining to taste and, in so doing, remains entirely beholden to preconceptions provided by class. It does not recognize taste as a commodity or the weapon of a particular class, but rather posits it as an absolute (something everyone can buy is attainable by everyone, even if in reality not everyone can buy it). Now, taste could be thoroughly productive *within* a certain class (in this case, one with great purchasing power) by creating something akin to a "lifestyle." (Immediately after the bourgeois revolution of 1918, one could see the first signs of this in film. Broad segments of white-collar workers who saw in the inflation the opportunity to enter the ruling class learned a remarkably stylized behavior from Bruno Kastner and others that one could study in every café.) But primarily the sharp contrast between work and relaxation particular to the capitalist manner of production divides all mental activities into those that serve work and those that serve relaxation and turns the latter into a system for the reproduction of labor. Relaxation is not allowed to contain anything that work contains. In the interest of production, relaxation is dedicated to non-production. A uniform lifestyle cannot be created so naturally. The mistake consists not in the fact that art is pulled into the sphere of production, but rather in the fact that this happens so completely and that art is intended to create an island of "nonproduction." Whoever buys his ticket transforms himself into a loafer and exploiter in front of the screen. Since loot has been stashed in him here, he is, so to speak, a victim of "imploitation."[2]

6. *"The human dimension must play a role in film"*

"The human dimension must be deepened." —The Director

"As far as the story is concerned, it may even be thoroughly silly if, as is nearly always the case today, the silliness or sentimentality of its imaginative structure is embedded in scenic and mimic imaginative detail that is true to life and authentic, and through which the human dimension triumphs over the primitive inauthenticity of the entire organization in a hundred individual moments." —Thomas Mann

This idea cloaks itself with the idea that films need to be philistine. The general validity of this very reasonable tendency (reasonable, because who is supposed to make different films or, once they have been made, watch them?) is occasioned by the relentless demand for "deepening" made by the metaphysicians of the press who insist on "art." They are also the people who would like to see the "fateful" emphasized in the processes among people. Fate, once a grand concept, has long since become a philistine one in which resigning oneself to circumstances produces the particular "transfiguration" and "internalization" desired—and it has become a concept that involves pure class struggle, in which one class "prepares" the fate of the other. As usual, the demands of our metaphysicians are not very difficult to satisfy. One can easily represent everything that they reject in such a manner that they enthusiastically accept it. If one

---

[2] The German word Brecht uses is "Einbeutung," a sort of "reverse exploitation." (Editor's note)

shows them certain love stories like *Romeo and Juliet* or crime thrillers like *Macbeth,* i.e., famous pieces that need not contain anything else (that must show no other human behavior and that do not allow any other drives to determine the course of the world), then they will, of course, first scream that the "how" and not the "what" makes a philistine. "It depends on how," though, is itself nothing other than philistine. This "human dimension" so loved by them, the "how" (usually marked with the word "eternal," meaning something like color-fast dye) of the Othellos (my woman belongs to me!), of the Hamlets (better to sleep on it again!), of the Macbeths (I am called to something higher!) and so on appears today in large measure as philistinism and nothing else. If one insists on having it, then one can have it only in this form; insisting on it is simply philistine. The greatness of such passions, that which is not philistine, was once determined by the role that it had to play in society, i.e., by its revolutionizing role. Even the effect of *Potemkin* on these people is based on the outrage that they would feel if their wives wanted to put rotten meat in front of them (too much is too much!), and Chaplin knows well that he needs to be "human," i.e., philistine in order to be permitted to do other things, and occasionally alters his style rather unscrupulously to this end. (See the famous close-up of the doglike look with which *City Lights* concludes!)

In reality, film needs external action and nothing introspectively psychological. And capitalism operates with this intention by driving out, organizing and automating certain needs to a large degree—utterly revolutionizing things. It destroys wide swaths of ideology when—concentrating only on "external" action, dissolving everything into processes, and surrendering the hero as the medium and man as the measure of all things—it demolishes the introspective psychology of the bourgeois novel. Seeing from the outside is appropriate to film and makes it important. For film, the principles of non-Aristotelian drama (drama not based on sympathy and mimesis) are acceptable without hesitation. The Russian film *The Path to Life,* for example, demonstrates non-Aristotelian effects above all simply by the fact that the theme (the education of the neglected by particular socialist methods) leads the viewer to draw causal connections between the behavior of the teacher and that of his pupils. This control of causes thus becomes the viewer's primary interest by means of the crucial (educational) scenes to such an extent that the viewer "instinctively" rejects the reason for the neglect (domestic unhappiness plus mental anguish instead of world war or civil war) taken from the old sympathetic drama! Indeed, even the use of work as a means of education fills the viewer with skepticism simply because it is not shown that work in the Soviet Union, in absolute contrast to all other countries, does in fact determine morality. If man appears as an object, then the causal connections become crucial. The great American comedies also show man as an object and could have an audience of pure reflexologists. Behaviorism is a psychology that proceeds from the need of commodity production to be provided with methods with which one can influence the buyer, i.e., an active psychology, progressive and revolutionizing par excellence. In accordance with its capitalistic function, it has boundaries (reflexes are biological and are social only in a few Chaplin films). Here too, the path leads only over the corpse of capitalism, but here too, this is a good path.

7. *"A film must be the work of a collective"*

"I could imagine that it would be of great importance for those concerned, artists as well as producers, to come together in meetings concerning the question of the creation of a collective and its manner of operation." —Reichsfilmblatt

This idea is progressive. Indeed, film should do nothing that a collective cannot do. This limitation alone would already be quite a fruitful law and "art" would thereby be out of the question. In contrast to the individual, a collective cannot work without a fixed direction point and an evening's entertainment is no such fixed point. If the collective were to have certain didactic intentions, for example, it would immediately constitute an organic body. It is the essence of capitalism and by no means generally valid that everything "unique" or "special" can only be produced by isolated individuals and that collectives can produce only standardized mediocre goods. What sort of collective do we have today in film? The collective is composed of the financier, the sellers (market researchers), the director, the technicians and the writers. A director is necessary because the financier wants nothing to do with art; the seller, because the director has to be corrupted; the technician, not because the machinery is complicated (it is incredibly primitive), but because the director does not have even the most primitive idea about technical things; and, finally, the writer, because the public itself is too lazy to write. Who wouldn't want the individual's part in the production to be unrecognizable? At no point during work on the *Three-Penny* film, including the work done in the litigation, did the people involved have the same idea about material, the purpose of the film, the audience, the machinery, and so forth. Indeed, a collective can produce only works that can form collectives from the "public."

8. "A film can be regressive in content, progressive in form"

"Film is essentially the art form for which the material gravity of its artistic means puts the greatest limitations on the creative mind; the mind is not the master of film's means of expression; they are always a cumbersome, complicated and unmanageably expensive hand tool for it." —Reichsfilmblatt

"The Three-Penny Opera *provides us with an unheard-of wealth of perfected technology. As much as this perfected technology delights on the one hand, the conclusion that it was expended for something undeserved oppresses one on the other.* —Der Jungdeutsche

"What remains is an albeit disjointed, but grandiose film showpiece, crafted with such technical artistry that the substance nearly disappears." —8 Uhr-Abendblatt (Eight O'Clock Evening Paper)

"A gripping film experience, entirely regardless of what was intended." —Filmkurier

What is the purpose of this way of looking at things? Is it supposed to separate the wheat from the chaff? Then the form would be the wheat. Because the form of the presentation functions as "form." In practical terms, this formula also serves to create a market even for the most miserable trash. It could never be stated in a film "discussion" that the content of this or that film was good and the form bad. In reality, the appeal to quality (a senseless quality empty of content) serves retrogression simply and naively. For, in reality, there is no difference between form and content and what Marx says about form applies here, too: it is good only in so far as it is the form of its content. Film editing and an attitude that have the primary desire to be pleasant correspond to a dramaturgy that has the same primary desire. Our intellectuals consider the form of *Love Parade* or *The Brothers Karamazov* good because it is the form of its (reactionary) content. There is not the slightest difference between the content of any sort of ideas in, for example, *Old Heidelberg* and *The Brothers Karamazov*. The technology of the delivery has provided for this. Our critics all too much like to confuse this skill in delivering something tastefully with the improvement of machines. One can take the perfecting of photographic cameras as an example of technical progress that is actually a step back. They are much more sensitive to light than the old boxes used by people to make daguerreotypes. One can work with them almost without regard for lighting conditions. They also have a number of other advantages, especially for the photographing of faces, but the portraits that one can produce with them are doubtlessly much worse. With the old light-insensitive cameras, several expressions would go onto the rather long exposed plate; so, on the final picture, one had a more universal and livelier expression as well as something of function. Yet it would certainly be wrong to declare the new cameras worse than the old ones. Perhaps they are still missing something that will be found tomorrow, or one can do something else with them besides photographing faces. And perhaps faces after all? They no longer form a composite of faces—but do they need to be formed into a composite? Perhaps there is a new way of photographing, possible for the newer cameras, that breaks faces down? This way of using these cameras (which are in the grips of change), though, will certainly not be found without a new function for such photography. The intellectuals are uncertain about technology; its crude, but powerful interference in intellectual concerns fills them with a mixture of contempt and amazement; it is becoming a fetish to them. In art, this relationship to technology is expressed thus: one can forgive anything if it is "masterful." Such "technology" profits from the gleam of its isolatability ("It can be directed to better, more meaningful functions!"). What it makes possible could also be something else than nonsense. This is how nonsense acquires a gleam in actuality and on the market. Of course, one can toss the entire heap of masterfulness into the trash if the social function of film is changed. The operation of the cameras can be learned in three weeks: it is incredibly primitive. The typical director, endeavoring to work in a manner as true to nature as possible, nature in this case being what he has seen on the stage, endeavoring, therefore, to deliver an imitation of an artwork that is as easily mistakable for the real thing as possible, attempts to conceal all the shortcomings of his cameras, whereby everything that hinders the camera from producing that lifelike copy constitutes a shortcoming in this view. He considers the skill with which he extracts the lifelike imitation of real scenic magic from his very imperfect camera to be proof that he is an expert. The good one who, in addition to this, fights a bitter struggle for his art with several people from the sales department who know nothing about his work and who toss sticks between his short legs, he does not allow anyone near the camera who perhaps does not possess this skill. So engrossed in his work, he is miles away from any idea that exactly these shortcomings of his camera could be advantages, for this would presuppose a change in the function of film. The technology of film is a technology that makes something out of nothing. (The film *Karamazov* is something, i.e., a collage of various charms.) This something is made from nothing, i.e., from a heap of empty ideas, imprecise observations, inexact statements and unverifiable claims. This nothing has arisen from something, the novel *The Brothers Karamazov,* i.e., a series of precise observations, exact statements and verifiable claims. The film technology that was necessary to make something out of nothing was forced to make nothing from something beforehand. It cannot be transported away from this custom. It cannot be used for making something out of something. Thus, it is this technology that produces tricks, for making a tasty dessert from a helping of trash is not art, but a trick.

9. "Political censorship is to be rejected for artistic reasons"

The supporting evidence is known.

The struggle of intellectuals for better film is totally ill-fated where it is fought against the state and censorship. They must no longer fight against the public's patronization of film, but against the censor's patronization of the public. The true interests of the masses of viewers, who do not quite know about those interests, finally become apparent here, though, and it is the censor who does know. For here and nowhere else does the education take place that the "progressives" and those who march forward would so like to take over. The petit bourgeois masses of buyers are educated in a morality that, if strictly implemented, is suitable for guaranteeing them the satisfaction of their entertainment *and other* needs. The class that places value on the emotional and comic treasures of the studio lots and film student bars is not always entirely sure in selecting the political and cultural standpoints that guarantee such stimuli; it must appoint experts who provide enlightenment about this. Strangely enough, it is at first not even necessary to take the wishes of the upper middle class into account to understand the censor's process. It can be seen as a schizophrenic process within the petit bourgeoisie, loosely on the basis of "*I* tell *myself, I* have to hold *myself* back," and still be understandable. The petit bourgeois knows: Not everything that he would wolf down would be good for him. An "unimaginative," crude, pessimistic photograph of what can be photographed from the "life" of the student, i.e., of a type who, within the shortest time and at the sacrifice of a considerable part of his vital energy, must gather so much expert knowledge that is so expensive to buy and difficult to sell, or of the type of proletarian who is gotten ready and drilled for war against his relatives—this mere photograph would touch the basic condition of these ticket buyers, a situation that they can provisionally always imagine as being worse than it is as long as there are people who can no longer buy a movie theater ticket at all! In a world that had humor, people would need no humor! It is dimly dawning on these people that the unadorned photograph of the act of birth is a political act. The search for an answer to the "how" would lead to the ABCs of sociology, for it would have to be determined here what influence the political situation exerts on sensations, which are apparently determined entirely biologically. Everyone knows that the physical pains of the person giving birth are not the truth of births. Only something more complete is true here. But into which world do these uteruses cast creatures? From where should heroism vis-à-vis the partial truth come if it is not the heroism of total truth? What are our opponents of censorship fighting for then? Are they fighting to be allowed to see the act of birth? They would become sick to their stomachs. They are fighting to be allowed to become sick to their stomachs. They will have no success. Even if they utter threats, they will not be allowed to puke. The pricelessly ridiculous thing is this: They wish to reject the photographed act of birth for artistic reasons, whereas the censor rejects it for political ones. This is the reason for the struggle of the two "powers"! They are asking to interrupt the class struggle for artistic reasons! As regards taste, a true abyss separates them from the masses (since they wish to be the ideologues of the upper middle class in matters of taste, which, strangely enough, are the same as matters of culture), and as far as political understanding is concerned, an abyss separates them from the upper middle class (i.e., a dependence that gets itself paid). They do not understand that their own economic and social position depends on marriage (with the possible exception of their own) remaining untouched and motherhood remaining sacred. For once again—where do they belong? To those social strata that do not know their political interests. And so what do they need? They need to be educated. In what—once again—does their untenable situation consist? *They need to demand political art not for artistic reasons, but for political ones.* No arguments from aesthetics apply against political censorship. They would at least have to be in the position to understand critically and in political terms the cultural situation of these people (and thus their own) instead of criticizing only the symptomatic taste of those who buy art. They themselves have a difficult time raising themselves from this class of the petit bourgeois for whom film is primarily produced, the only class in which the concept "man" still resides *(man is the petit bourgeois),* and the only class that thinks retrogressively in principle because of its situation. But in this, the self-limitation of this type of thinking is not retrogressive. We are approaching the age of mass politics. What sounds strange in the case of the individual ("I don't allow myself freedom of thought") does not sound strange in the case of the masses. The masses do not think freely as individuals. Continuity is a precondition for thinking already in the case of the individual; it was long possible only for the individual. What our intellectuals, who comprise not a mass but a dispersion of individuals, understand by thought is merely inconsequentially reflexive because that thought has no backward, forward and lateral continuity. Anyone who really belongs to the masses knows that he cannot get any farther ahead than the masses can. Our intellectuals, who get farther only by separating themselves from the masses, each for himself, make no progress, but rather live only from a head start. The masses of our age—directed by common interests, constantly reorganizing themselves according to those interests, yet functioning as a unit—operate according to very definite laws of thinking that are not generalizations of individual thinking. These laws have so far been inadequately investigated. One can deduce them in part from the intellectual behavior of individuals in cases where these individuals think as representatives or deputies of mass units. In the next phase of development beyond capitalism, thought will not have the type of freedom that forces competitive lawfulness upon the capitalist. But another type.

10. "An artwork is the expression of a personality"

"An artwork is a living creature, and its creator, who will not toler-ate it becoming crippled, is right ten times over." —Frankfurter Zei-tung; *the lawyer of the film company, Dr. Frankfurter*

By maintaining the status quo in the use of film technology, the *Three-Penny Opera* could be transformed into a Three-Penny Film if its social intention was made the foundation of the adaptation. The attempt to assassinate bourgeois ideology had to be possible in film as well. Intrigues, milieus and characters could be treated en-tirely freely. This destruction of the work from the standpoint of maintaining its social function within a new machinery was rejected by the film company. Nevertheless, it did of course come to a de-struction of the work, and to be sure it was from a business stand-point. In order to reach the market, an artwork that is the adequate expression of a personality in bourgeois ideology must undergo a very definite operation that splits it into its parts; the parts come onto the market individually in a certain manner. The process that the artwork, "the adequate expression of a personality," must go through in order to reach the market should be clarified. . . .

The work can have one or several new authors (who are person-alities) without the original author being excluded for the commer-cialization on the market. His name can be used for the altered work and thus without the work. Even the rumor of his radical way of thinking can be used without the fruit of that way of thinking, the particular work. The work can find use as a literary work with-out his meaning, i.e., with another meaning or none at all. The in-tention collapses into a salvageable, socially approved intention reaching the market only by hearsay. The literary work can be pre-sented by its subject being given a different form or its form being given a different (or partially different) subject. As far as the form continues to be of concern, linguistic and scenic form can also ap-pear without one another. The story of the subject matter can be carried by other characters, the characters can be placed into an-other story, and so forth. This dismantling of artworks at first seems to occur in accordance with the same laws of the market as the dismantling of automobiles that, having become unusable, one can no longer drive and that one thus strips down into smaller parts (iron, leather upholstery, lights, and so forth) and sells as such. We are seeing the decay, relentless and thus to be countenanced, of the individualistic artwork. It can no longer reach the market as a unity; the state of tension of its contradiction-laden unity must be destroyed. Art is a form of human interaction and thus dependent on the factors determining human interaction in general. These factors are revolutionizing the old concepts. Several examples:

(1) An artwork is an invention that, once invented, immediately assumes commodity form, i.e., once separated from its inventor, it appears on the market in a form determined by sales potential. a) Court decision according to which the author must also permit such changes of his work that compromise its effect because another person—the screenplay writer—signs for it. b) Authors such as Heinrich Mann, Döblin, and Hauptmann demand no right to participate in the decision-making process.

(2) An artwork can be traced back to the invention of a story that is invented in accordance with the needs of the market. There is not any inseparable intention of an intellectual sort inherent in it. (Practice of the film companies that is not challenged by authors.)

(3) An artwork can be disassembled into parts from which individual parts can be removed. It can be disassembled mechanically, i.e., in accordance with the viewpoints of economics and the police. (Court decision according to which the author must allow the company to decide which parts of the manuscript do not seem usable to it.)

(4) Language is not at all important; it is to be separated from gesture and mimic art, which are important. (The court found our complaint with respect to the reworking of the text worthy of no answer.)

Nevertheless, the work operated upon in this manner comes as a unity onto the market. . . . For the issue is not the manner in which a certain artwork (such as the *Three-Penny Opera*) can be made marketable, but the manner in which, from a marketing standpoint, an artwork must be constructed. The breakdown process is accordingly a production. . . .

The idea that the artwork is an expression of a personality no longer applies for films.

Translated by Lance W. Garmer

Rudolf Arnheim

While still working on his doctoral dissertation in philosophy and psychology, Rudolph Arnheim (1904–) wrote critical pieces on film for the Berlin periodical Die Weltbühne *(The World Stage), some 70 of which became the basis of his most famous work,* Film as Art *(Film als Kunst), 1932 (the excerpt is from the 1933 English translation,* Film *not from the abridged and revised English edition of 1957). He was greatly influenced by Gestalt psychology and focused almost exclusively on the visual aspects of film in his work, ultimately arguing that sound negated the possibility of film being art. After the Nazis essentially prohibited him from working, Arnheim, who was both Jewish and leftist, emigrated to Italy in 1933 where he continued writing on film. Finally in 1940, he moved to the United States with only £10 in his pocket, eventually holding professorships at some of the most prestigious universities in the country.*

From Film (1932)

Part 1: Introduction

Something like twenty-five years have passed since both the author and the subject of this book came into existence. As I lay in my cradle, insignificant little films for which a great many more claims were made than could possibly be justified were clamoring for attention. On my attaining years of indiscretion the film also demonstrated its growing pains in the hysterical early postwar years by behaving in an unseemly manner, by exhibiting publicly and most blatantly all manner of callow suggestiveness akin to that hitherto kept under lock and key. These pictures must have been very flimsy: it takes practiced imaginative faculties to be successfully licentious—faculties that usually only develop at a rather later age. The scandal, however, was so great as to cause film to be considered a very doubtful subject of conversation for years to come.

When the Cinematograph Bill was being debated in the National Assembly at Weimar in 1920, the German nation was unanimous from Left to Right that a firm hand must be kept on the film industry. One Democrat member announced at the time that in the maternity ward of a Munich hospital the fact had been established that fifty per cent of the young women patients there had made the acquaintance of their seducers at a cinema (Hear! Hear!)—which still leaves open the question as to whether the fault lay with the bright screen or the dark auditorium. The German People's Party, living up to its name, based its demands for strict control upon the "general feeling among the people." A Socialist admitted that his party had hoped to avoid any censorship, but . . . And so the Bill was passed that has in effect kept the German film industry under martial law ever since. Although the theatre was relieved of all censorship, examining boards were set up to exercise a preliminary censorship on films; a general "juvenile prohibition" was issued; and the Board of Censors was alone given authority to license certain films for exhibition to young persons under eighteen years of age. Cinemas were burdened with a prohibitive amusement tax while theaters either went scot free or only paid a very small percentage.

These measures, which put a most restrictive moral ban on the film, are still in force, although they date from what are practically prehistoric days as far as the cinema is concerned. It is just as reasonable to retain them as it would be to forbid railway traveling on the ground that, according to experiments made between Nuremberg and Fürth a hundred years ago, the pressure of the atmosphere engendered by the rapid motion was injurious to the health of the passengers. This unfair discrimination as against the theatre is particularly absurd since the introduction of talkies. Every talkie comes under the censorship; so it is conceivable that a song incidental to some play—as for instance the "Beggar's Opera"—which had been sung hundreds of times all over Germany might be prohibited in the film version. Hence also this sort of thing may be found in the list passed by the Board of Censors:

"H. J. Ulm will play the Toccata in D Minor by John Sebastian Bach on the organ at the Ufa Theatre 'Universum' in Berlin. Soundfilm Co. Ltd., Berlin. Inland. 350 feet.—20.8.29.—23223—Purely educational. Sound film."

Is it possible that "public order and safety" could be disturbed, or "religious susceptibilities wounded," or that a "brutalising or demoralising effect" might be produced, or that "the prestige of Germany or her relations with foreign Powers" might be endangered by the playing of a Bach Toccata?

It must nevertheless be admitted that the severe control to which the film is subject accords with the reputation which it still bears among the majority of adult educated persons. They cannot forget its base origin and its youthful peccadilloes. Yet these are the very people who might give film its place among the arts: for it is they who are the repositors of the old authentic standards of culture. So many of us young people went to school rather desultorily in wartime; and the little we did learn was acquired from the point of view that the present *de*struction was infinitely more important than past *con*struction. Hence many young people's enthusiasm for film means very little; they have no standards of comparison and simply accept what is set before them. I hope to show in this book that film art did not spring into being ready-made, but that it follows the same age-old canons and principles as every other art. This book may even serve to convince some that there is more worthy of attention in art in general than many believe in these days of football clubs and OTCs.

Older people will, I hope, see from this book that film uses, or is capable of using, the same media of expression as those to which they are accustomed in the recognised arts; that Charlie Chaplin, Greta Garbo, constructive cutting, or the prevention of oscillation, may be discussed just as seriously as Titian, Cézanne, baroque, or sunbathing. I hope it may help them to feel that they can go to the pictures with a clearer conscience and fewer prejudices—and perhaps with a rather better understanding of the subject. There are, I am sure, plenty of "grown-ups" who have seen and enjoyed the great Russian and American films, and who know that Buster Keaton and Harry Piel, Asta Nielsen and Gerda Maurus cannot all be classed together, even if they happen to have been "featured" at the same picture house. Many others, however, go to a cinema once in a while, but quite unselectively, making no attempt to choose the programme. They do not know even the most important names, and just go to the nearest show if they happen to have an evening with nothing better to do. Then they come home bored and disgusted and more than ever convinced that "there's nothing like a good theatre." If you enquire what they have seen, it turns out to be " 'Twas in Springtime," an original drama in twelve reels, preceded by the two-act comic "Kandy Kids," starring one of the world's absolutely greatest humorists. . . . Those who abuse the cinema most blandly are the people who never go near one. They would no more go to a picture palace than they would to a gin palace. But it never seems to occur to them that the picture palace proves just as little against film art as a low public-house does against good wine.

I want to help all those who will accept a book but not a ticket for the "flicks," and those who still prefer the printed word to the moving picture, to understand film art. I want them to realise that it is not only words but also pictures and sounds that are capable of conveying profound intellectual impressions. They must, moreover, realise that the "plot," whatever its *genre,* does not particularly matter, but that it is essential to observe how an individual picture or an individual scene is mounted, photographed, acted, cut—as Stendhal says: *"Il n'y a d'originalité et de vérité que dans les détails"*—and that in the case of an art that is only twenty-five years old it is of very little importance how many masterpieces have been produced, but that it is indispensable to make certain that the first steps have definitely been taken in the right direction, and to have enough imagination to realise the marvellous potentialities of film as an artistic medium.

The younger generation has no excuse for despising the film. We see, of course, that as is the case in most other things much is produced that is bad and little that is good. But we realise that progress is rapid and the whole atmosphere vital—and that in itself is alluring. We had no part in the first epoch of German super-films. In the days when Lubitsch was working in Germany, when Emil Jannings played Henry VIII and Asta Nielsen Hamlet, we were not allowed to go to the pictures. That is not to say that we obeyed this injunction; there cannot have been many sixteen-year-olds in the big towns who did not go to the movies, carefully avoiding the performances "for the young"—classical patriotic tragedies interspersed with playfully educational films ("The Jolly Ploughboy") being voted hideously dull. So we looked as grown-up as we could, demanded the cheapest seats in deep manly voices, and feasted our eyes upon murderers and prostitutes, drunks and cops, millionaires' palaces and condemned cells, seductions and robberies. And all this wild nonsense may have damaged our eyesight but certainly not our morals. The cinema satisfies most thoroughly that desire for adventure and excitement that is part of the make-up of every normal child. And so one retains something of the same sentimental affection for the cinema that one has for old picture books, for the piratical doings of Long John Silver, for the wicked old Jew in "Oliver Twist." To this very day one sometimes goes and had "a bob's worth" down the road in order to sit spellbound through "Lord Jones' Night of Terror" or "Sweet Sins." . . .

We grew more receptive and the film acquired greater technique. Paul Wegener shot and played his "Golem" for the second time, Fritz Lang's "Destiny" stalked across the screen in grisly silence, and the mysterious Dr. Mabuse moved through his thrilling adventures in a marvellously handled crook film. Dr. Caligari displayed his cabinet of waxworks; and across the reopened frontiers came Charlie Chaplin, Fatty Arbuckle, and a hundred others, nameless clowns; motorcars exploded like so many crackers, and bearded men beat one another about the head with cudgels. The great American pictures of society life, with their tremendously refined direction and photography and the restrained art of their actors, demanded a very well-trained cinema sense on the part of the audience, for to the uninitiated they appeared like particularly silly comics. By way of light amusement for the jaded film fan followed the amazing capriccios of the French *avantgarde,* brilliantly fantastic finger-exercises for the well-tempered camera, expeditions into the realm of untried potentialities. The great Russian films eventually brought not only masterly mechanical control, but also wonderful raw material, both human and scenic, without making the slightest concession to the demand for entertainment or any conventional morality. They brought a breath of fresh air into the studios where film art was threatened with sterility through inbreeding. Gradually the film developed into something with a real aesthetic value. Then the invention of sound film revolutionised everything. All who are interested in the cinema are now putting every ounce of energy into proving that it can survive the new turn of events.

Authors have been quick to seize upon this fresh and fertile source of inspiration. Much that is both brilliant and ingenious has been written on the subject of films, though not as a rule by professional film-critics, whose opportunities for doing so one would suppose the greatest, though their capability apparently falls short. The smaller provincial papers, especially, contain articles on the cinema which cannot but injure the proprietors of picture houses who insert paid advertisements in their columns. Again, those who write movie reviews for the greater journals are more often than not men whose interests are primarily literary or dramatic and who have, therefore, no natural affinity with the new art form. Indeed, they frequently do not even understand its fundamentals, so that their criticisms are written from an outsider's point of view and are as a rule quite unprofitable. To say nothing of the artless babblers whose concern is rather with cunningly turned phrases than with honest criticism. Nevertheless, however good the literature on the subject, it is improbable that its effect on the philistines would be great unless some method could be evolved for giving these latter a thorough grounding in the principles. Neither brilliance nor ingeniously convolved ideas are necessary for the achievement of this object; and to this extent at least I believe that the present book fulfils its aim. As far as possible only the simplest language has been used in the description of everyday matters. If it should chance that in spite of this some passages prove obscure, it is probably due not only to the writer's imperfect powers of presentation but also to the difficulties surrounding a subject that as yet lacks an exact terminology. Even the most elementary conceptions are wanting, and it is as hard for the author to plough such virgin soil as it is for the reader— though perhaps this sense of adventure renders it the more exciting.

Of useful literature on film aesthetics there are really only the works of Béla Balázs, Léon Moussinac's *Panoramique du Cinéma,* and "Pudovkin on Film Technique"—a little volume that is a mine of practical information. For the rest, as on all aesthetic questions, the pronouncements of the artists themselves, in so far as they deal with the practical side, the so-called purely technical problems, are the most helpful.

This book will be much occupied with the faculties of sight and hearing and with the technical and psychological idiosyncrasies of the screen and the camera, and very little with metaphysics or the philosophy of art, with the mysteries of the craft or the irrationality of aesthetic qualities. It is one of the author's fundamental principles that art is just as much and just as little a part of material life as anything else in this world; and that the only way to understand art is to start from the simplest forms of sensory-psychological impressions and to regard visual and auditory art as sublimated forms of seeing and hearing. A man who considers the ordinary sensory processes as uncomplicated and unspiritual functions and art as a supernormal portent does justice to neither, and moreover denies himself the illuminating realisation of the close connection between the two. Obviously, the recognition of a definite tangible basis to an art does not imply an understanding of its full inwardness. But it is surely true in aesthetics as in natural science that it is the working out as much as the result that is important, and that the earlier steps of an argument are not to be considered as negligible because the later ones prove hard to follow. Philosophers are apt trium-phantly to indicate the difficulty of abstract conceptions—such as the idea of individuality—but these are not the only points that are important. Much has already been gained by realizing the presum-able trend of an argument. It is certainly not anyone's duty to deny himself what he can understand out of respect for what he cannot.

I gave myself a special "preliminary training" by going to the pictures frequently, often discussing practical details of their profes-sion with intelligent movie men, sometimes watching the work in the studios, and finally handling a camera myself and cutting a film. In making this book my acquaintance with some rudiments of mod-ern experimental psychology has seconded the familiarity I have ac-quired with the processes and the personnel of the film world. Far too many students of art neglect this aspect of their subject. Never-theless, though unconsciously, they do base their work on a definite psychological foundation, simply because they cannot avoid it; and this psychology is usually the atomic-mechanical doctrine of the classical school of the last century, which though it is still current among educated people has in fact been superseded. Many works on aesthetics are valueless purely on this account. If a simple con-cept such as seeing is misunderstood, how can a complicated one be explained and given its full aesthetic value?

In the field of aesthetics this book will endeavor to treat seriously the often carelessly expressed dictum that the laws governing an art must be determined by the character of its medium. It will be shown in part 2 that a film photograph is never the simple reproduction of nature; and divergencies of film from nature will be discussed. These differences, which at first may seem to evidence shortcomings in film-technique, will in part 3 be shown to be the means whereby reality is moulded and interpreted. For without such "shortcom-ings" art cannot exist at all. In part 4 will be shown how artistic form and significant content can be given, not only by exploiting the qualities of the camera, but also by selection of the shots. Part 5 applies these principles to sound film. Part 6 contains a prospect of the future.

The fact that so much space has been given to the discussion of silent film in this study needs particular justification.

We all labor so much under the tyranny of modern film industry that it seems strange to us to continue studying silent films now that one hardly ever sees them. But silent film still exists even though it is seldom shown. In no other branch of art is it customary to consign to oblivion past epochs and their achievements. On the contrary, greater value is usually laid on the work of the past than on that of the present—and rightly so. For great art never ages; and the long past must contain more good things than the short present. Good silent films therefore are not dead because they are rarely shown and no longer popular. They will be revived. They retain their value. It is undoubtedly worth while to study them analytically because the silent film represents a completely new artistic species, so that it is bound to give a fresh angle of approach to aesthetics even when it has ceased to be a living art form. As far as science is concerned, the important point is not whether or not a thing exists, but whether it is capable of existence. Moreover, as will be shown, an exact investigation of silent film will help considerably towards the evaluation of sound film. Silent film and sound film are, of course, in different classes. Since there have hitherto been but few sound films of any great merit a considerable amount of imagination is needed to derive laws from them. But, on the other hand, an immense material is ready to hand for the preparation of an aesthetic code of silent film. Hence the indirect method is still preferable, that is to say, the investigation of sound film as something not entirely separate from silent film, though possibly in antithesis to it. The very act of examining how the principles of silent film may be adapted to the needs of sound film is illuminating. Moreover, it is becoming increasingly clear that the essential principles of silent film which have hitherto been valid in the realm of optics, can now simply be carried over to the interplay of picture and sound. Besides, the methods and the basis from which we shall approach the aesthetic problems of silent film can be quite generally adapted to sound film. At the outset of an enquiry everything depends on getting the right angle of approach; and these aesthetic questions are the same for all arts—it is only the solutions that are different.

For this reason we may hope that not only what is said about sound film but also what is said about silent film is apposite and of practical utility. It is a fact that the postulates, reasonable or otherwise, of art-theorists have always had more influence on the work of the creative artist than is generally conceded. The views taken in various ages of the functions of art have always had their immediate effect on the works of art of that period. But perhaps there has never before been so definite a need for theoretical discussion as there is among the pioneers of sound film today. Shall it be silent film or tone film? Talkie or sound? Cutting or no cutting? Synchronism or asynchronism? All these are problems in the solution of which not only practical men but also theorists can assist. And the theorist, who in the domain of aesthetics generally confines his attention to the contemplation of what has already been achieved, rejoices that he is able to help in perfecting what is still to come.

Part 2: Film and Nature

The Psychology of the Mass-produced Film

A slight digression into extra-aesthetic matters is here necessary. If mass-produced films are under discussion it is essential to say something as to the tendencious nature of their subject-matter.

The public insists on having the films it likes. The maker produces his wares according to the dictates of the masses. He sees from the balance sheets which films have "gone over big" and arranges his output accordingly. The question is: what kind of films do the masses want?

We are discussing only the material level and not the artistic. What kind of material do the masses want?

Nearly all the stories of these films follow—consciously or otherwise—a definite trend. Not that they are preaching; on the contrary, the dangerous thing about this trend is that nothing is formulated theoretically, nothing is exacted; but the standpoint from which the things of this world are regarded, the choice of narrative and its implicit moral, are unilateral.

In real life it happens every day that worthy people are ruined by villains unavenged, that good deeds are rewarded by ingratitude, that the industrious man is unfortunate, the lazy or stupid man successful, that criminals drive in motorcars, and geniuses travel between decks. Not so in film. For as soon as we humans are given authority to make up stories, we mould them according to our desires. In film everything happens as it would in real life if all went just as seems right and pleasing to us. What God neglects, man makes up for in his own creations. And he is ingenuous enough to find comfort for real injustices in his make-believe justice; he cheerfully ignores the disparity between reality and appearance.

To please the public these films offer two things—they conjure up all the good and pleasant things that people wish for themselves and they show the punishment of wickedness and vice. To do this they work with very commonplace standards of value. The fact that in spite of this such films have a universal appeal shows how widespread is the taste for the hackneyed and retrograde. There are a great many people who in theory and principle are very modern, not to say revolutionary, but who fail when it comes to practice—who in theory would agree to a girl's giving herself to her lover, but who would thunder curses and have an apoplectic fit if their own daughter bore an illegitimate child; who in theory disapprove of armed soldiery treating free citizens roughly, but who cannot contain their enjoyment of a row when brawny soldiers and policemen come to blows in a film. The truth is that man really likes evil and is born stupid; anyone who wishes to improve the world has to effect his purpose in spite not only of external opposition but especially of himself. The mass-produced film titillates what is bad and stupid in man; it ensures that dissatisfaction shall not burst into revolutionary action but shall fade away in dreams of a better world. It serves up in a sugar coating what really needs combating.

And this not only because ninety per cent of film production is in the hands of people to whose interest it is to stabilise the social order in which they are comfortable, who have an interest in deflecting revolutionary energies and letting them run on to buffers. It would be impossible to get such productions accepted by millions if their own taste did not lie in the same direction. The average film encourages the lazy creature of habit that lies in man. Its effect is anticultural and antiprogressive since it nourishes the retrogressive tendencies that exist in every human being.

It is only necessary to pick out one or two of these film stories and to analyze them, and it will at once be seen how much secret poison there is in such apparently harmless entertainments. (The following are word-for-word quotations from trade papers.)

"Franz Rauch's scenario has no essential harmony, the richness of the themes is not always dramaturgically fully exploited. It is the story of the love of a suddenly impoverished nobleman for a girl of the middle classes. He gets to know her in his days of affluence; afterward coincidence makes him tutor in the house of the girl's brother. She has always been annoyed by his high-and-mighty ways. After various obstacles have been overcome, everything ends happily." Certainly that is a lively and exciting story with plenty of variety. But it is more than that—it is an excellent narcotic.

Just as an insignificant dream may discover the make-up of the patient's psyche to a psychoanalyst, so these idiotic film stories provide data for the psychology of the average man. There is anger at the arrogance of a rich nobleman. This arrogance is, in fact, unjustifiable, the patent of nobility is a scandal, the riches are bought with the destitution of many thousands—therefore the anger against it should become an incentive to overthrow riches and nobility in order that things might improve in this world. But beside the revolutionary fury slumbers laziness, which would prefer to assuage the wrath by pleasanter methods. The movies are not at all a bad means to this end. They divert anger at a general abuse by redressing the matter in a special case in a nonobligatory and nontypical way. By depriving the rich man of his money and breaking the pride of the nobleman, the public is satisfied with a trick of legerdemain. The rich Count got what he deserved when he fell on evil days—there is still justice in the world—and that pleases the poor discontented devils who have paid their money to see the film. The pleasure is worth the money—but outside the theatre the rich and the noble are just as arrogant as ever.

"Joe Dallman has written a light scenario which should be just to the taste of the general public. An old general, who is in financial straits, favors the suit of a rich diamond merchant for his daughter. On the day before the wedding the diamond merchant finds out that his fiancée loves another. He sends this man to take his place at the wedding ceremony; he personally resigns himself to the inevitable, renounces the girl, and goes away." It is, moreover, implied that before starting on his travels the diamond merchant writes out a large cheque for love of the girl. The rich man in this case is a pleasant character, and the concealed resentment in the story is directed not against him but against his wealth. The rich man does not get the girl, that is to say—he cannot get *everything* with this money of which other people are jealous. And that paralyses the envy of the unmoneyed. The injustice of there being rich and poor people in the world is compensated in a particular case which withholds something from the rich man that he particularly desires and gives it to the poor man. The trick once again lies in the fact that a typical abuse is remedied in a non-typical special case, that the part falsely represents the whole. And the poor man—this is the most curious part of the story—not only gets the girl but also gets money. For the possession of money is only disgusting when other people have it; it is quite pleasant to have it oneself. Thus film does not feed the revolutionary but the egotistic components of the hatred of riches. Finally, it is only necessary to indicate the interesting feature that the girl's father is a general, for poverty is disgraceful and the heroine of the film must not be disgraced in any way—so in this case military rank adjusts the matter. Now everything has been neatly tabulated; anger at the riches of the diamond merchant, justice being done by the fact that in spite of his money he is denied what he wants more than anything else, which incidentally proves the worthlessness of money; but at the same time satisfaction of personal desire for comfort and the shame and self-depreciation because of one's own poverty are shown. It cannot be said that film exposes and nourishes any very noble propensities!

Nine-tenths of all mass-production films deal with rich people, and are thus filmed visions of desire, which satisfy the longing for wealth. The patron of the movies is as pleased about the hero's car as if it were his own. He feels his own self-respect rise when a lady's maid attired in black silk helps the heroine into her cloak. It is quite obvious that these films are not intended to show rich people as they exist in real life, but simply to provide an imaginative, transcendent, visionary superfluity of all sorts of goods—an emancipation from economic troubles. Rich people in this kind of film are not rich because they earn a great deal of money, but because they live free. They are at home all day; they have time all day for friends and lovers; they never pay when they get out of a taxi; if supper in a fashionable restaurant whose manager has received them with low bows suddenly has to be interrupted because a rival or the mother-in-law turns up at the next table, no bill is presented; and the cloakroom attendant hands out the fur coat without requiring a ticket. If by any chance mention is made of the business or factory which finances this surprising display, it is only to show that bankruptcy is impending, which is brought in to give the unselfish daughter a chance to sacrifice her virgin person to a hard-hearted financier, or in order to bring the wicked and extravagant character of the wife into the limelight. Otherwise these people float like spirits through an opulent dream world without purses or note cases, and yet by having no worries fulfil their purpose with an audience that makes no demands for truth to nature so long as the subject of the story deadens anxiety and despair.

It is very instructive, too, to see how the ideology of bourgeois film production creeps in even in a film whose action takes place at the other end of the earth. The naked savage has to make his political morality palatable to occidentals. In Murnau's *Tabu* the islanders live as unconcernedly and happily as the princes of industry in society films. The natives—like the industrialists—concern themselves chiefly with affairs of love and honour. Just as the general manager in a film occasionally speaks down the telephone with a portentous frown in order that the spectator shall get an idea of him in his business capacity, so the islander throws a spear from time to time in a graceful attitude by way of earning his livelihood, and the rest of the time he spends courting his beloved with flowers in his hair. The economic motif only appears as an evil one—as when the sly Chinese publican waves his promissory note. Love rebels against the laws to enable dramatic excitement to be brought into the scenario, whether it be against the tabu of the South Seas or against the sacrament of Christian wedlock. But here as there the law triumphs in order that the populace may enjoy spiritual uplift; and the villain is eaten by sharks.

Thea von Harbou has given a characteristic example in *Metropolis* for the individual solution of general problems. Here the fierce struggle between the underworld of workers and the overworld of employers is brought to an end because the son of the king of industry makes friends with the workers, and to the ringing of bells joins the hands of the foreman and the manager. Thus the social question is abolished without a thought for tariff walls!

Very instructive, too, is the American story of the "Godless Girl." A dispute has arisen in a reformatory as to whether God exists. The dispute turns into a fight, and during the conflict the banisters on the stairs are broken and a little girl falls down. As she lies dying, she asks in terror whether she will go to heaven or whether there really is no God. The atheists are in a dilemma. Thus the distress of a child is cleverly enrolled as advocate for the solaces of the Christian faith.

The mass-produced film not only strengthens hereditary familiarity with Church and Capitalism; it also acts as propaganda for the sacrament of marriage and the sanctity of the home.

"A young nobleman runs away from home because he hates his stepfather, who finds him a nuisance. He is believed to be dead, but becomes a circus star of the first magnitude. After many years he returns to Europe. Here he finds again the girl who had grown up with him in the circus; he falls in love with her and marries her. His mother's marriage is very unhappy; her husband tries to prevent a meeting with the son. But mother-love cannot be denied, mother and son find one another. Then the stepfather tries to make away with the son but falls into the trap he set for the son and crashes from the roof of the circus." (Ms. by George Klaren and H. Jacobi)

It is to be observed that it is not a real father but only a stepfather who persecutes the son. Hence the axiom as to the love of parents for their children is not infringed. The reason for showing such an "immorality" is that, roughly speaking, a drama always consists in putting to rights again something that has got out of order. Family life is disturbed in order that the disturber may be punished. The cacophony is therefore necessary in order that the final chord may be harmonious. The unhappy marriage of the wicked man and his wife, which is an offence against the claims of the registrar's office, is avenged on the roof of the circus, together with his cruel behaviour to the son to whom he should have been a father. Mother and son, on the other hand, representing the principle of law and order, reap well-earned happiness.

"The film is excellently constructed, and it is no detriment that the plot is not new. It is the story of a man who deceives his best friend with the friend's wife, innocently, because he did not know that she was his wife. Neither is it new that in consequence of this the deceived man cannot make up his mind to save his comrades from a submarine that has gone down, because the one-time friend is on board." *(Submarine.)*

Of course in the end he does decide to effect a rescue. What before was caused by the lack of blood relationship is here paralleled by the ignorance of the adulterous friend—the wickedness of the deed is mitigated by the fact that it is done unintentionally. In any case the guilty friend has to expiate his crime by spending hours of torture in the submerged vessel—comparable with the tortures which, according to the priests, await adulterers in hell. In reality this submarine is nothing but a naive appropriation of the conventional idea of hell. The guilty wife, whom the film leaves, incidentally, without a rag of character, and whose life seems to be bounded by a lust for cigarettes, jazz and kisses, gets her punishment—she is left alone, while the two friends go off arm in arm.

In real life many fathers treat their sons badly without being punished for it; and numerous adulteries take place which are not atoned for in a submarine; but the mass-produced film knows no limits. The happy end brings not only an aesthetic but also a moral catharsis. It is never merely psychologically causal but always at the same time ethically valuable. It is not enough for it to show the development and upshot of a conflict; it must take sides and be careful that the decision should not fall unreasonably and casually as under the régime of Mother Nature, but wisely as under King Solomon.

The enemy of stable wedlock is represented by the "vamp," the vampire, the fiendish siren. She is the succubus of film mythology— she is the devil who prostitutes herself so that evil may ensue. But the devil is suitably punished. In *Flesh and the Devil* Greta Garbo deceives two friends alternately until they fight a duel in a scene which is reminiscent of the horrors of the submarine. But Good triumphs, God watches up aloft—the vamp drowns miserably among driving ice floes. If the vicious woman is not drowned, her soul is saved by a pure young man, and she gives up her wicked ways (*The Wonderful Lie of Nina Petrovna,* for instance, though this is complicated by various backslidings; however, it all comes right in the end). In "The Temptress" the vamp, Greta Garbo, falls a victim to drink. Her lover is rewarded for his sexual virtue with professional success—occult interdependence of cause and effect—but she is left glassy-eyed, sitting soullessly in a restaurant, calling for gin.

So also in *the Darling of the Gods* in which the story of the opera-singer Jannings proves that an adulterous mode of life has a detrimental effect upon the vocal chords. The throat specialist is the compurgator of good morals. Hardly has the singer renounced ballet girls and Russians—two types of women, incidentally, whom the movie psychologist knows at once to be tainted with evil—and settled down to an idyllic family life, than, altogether against the doctor's prognosis and for no earthly reason, his voice returns— doubtless from heaven, where lives a God who rewards virtue by suitable miracles.

"The plot is not new but is psychologically intensified. Owing to an unhappy marriage, the child suffers, because its father does not understand it. Mother and child are therefore made much happier when the father fails to return from a sea voyage on which he has taken his mistress, and is listed as dead. The wife is now free to marry the friend of her youth. But on the day of the wedding the first husband turns up again. He is ready to agree to a divorce if he has the custody of the child. The wife will not agree; and is willing to forgo her own happiness for the sake of the child. However, the mistress becomes *dea ex machina* and murders the first husband." ("A Mother's Heart's-blood.")

The guilty party is punished with banishment and death. The execution need not this time come from a Higher Power but can be carried out by the mistress, who is anyhow beyond the pale and need not be given a moral course of life. She is easily able to take the murder upon herself. If the wife were to play the part of avenger herself, one would suppose the situation to be morally the same. But not at all. A figure who has been properly legalized, and is therefore entered on the credit side of the transaction, must not be dismissed from the last Act with an unexpiated crime on her conscience. Anybody who is ready to love without marriage lines may also commit murder—a little thing like that would make no difference. (Similarly in Lupu Pick's *Street Song,* where a profligate is murdered, not by his wife, but by a woman who has kept house for him for many years.)

Adultery is frequently coupled with depravity. ". . . hardly has the wife departed than the husband shuts up his books and puts on his dinner jacket to go off on the spree. Suddenly he hears a noise in his strongroom that can only be caused by a burglar's blowlamp. He takes a flashlamp, puts out the light and creeps into the strongroom, where he catches the thieves just as they have opened the door of the safe. He is about to call in the police when a girl comes on the scene. It is the 'lady' whom he had arranged to take out to supper in a private room, but whose only intention had been to entice him away from the office in order to make things easy for her accomplices. She says to him cynically: 'Go on! Call the police! Your wife will be delighted!' But he only gestures feebly. . . ." *(Forgive Me.)*

The wickedness of the dissolute life is demonstrated by making the girl belong to the criminal classes. An offence of quite a different kind—which has no inherent connection with adultery but only appears combined with it in this particular story—serves as a dye to blacken what one wishes to see black, while the spectator gestures feebly. Truly a curious procedure!

It is seldom that anything particularly savoury emerges when the depths of human subconsciousness are stirred. So also in this case. We have shown what is the kind of moral to be drawn from the average popular film. We have picked our examples at random; but no one will say that we have wilfully taken exceptionally bad instances. On the contrary, anyone who has nothing better to do one evening than to go along to the nearest movie show will in nine out of ten cases see films which would yield similar results if analysed in this way.

To what conclusion has this led? That the films that please the greatest number of people all over the world reveal the following portrait of their audiences: rich people and noblemen are our foes and should be made to suffer; not so much because their advantages are undeserved as because we do not share them. We ourselves would also like high rank and riches, a lazy life and exemption from all occupation. We regard our own poverty and lack of gentility with the eyes of the mighty; we are ashamed of ourselves and try to cover our nakedness with motley. In our heart of hearts we are not proud, but humble and cringing. Our desires are so much stronger than our reason that we are perfectly satisfied if some state we consider desirable is held out to us as being true, and do not trouble whether this fulfilment has been achieved by means of a practicable and reasonable process. We are satisfied, for instance, if the balance between rich and poor is struck by means of a few love scenes, and in our pleasure at the satisfactory result we are not critical of the means.

Furthermore we believe that "God's in His heaven. . . ." For the weaknesses of our fellow men we have no understanding but only moral censure—the rules for which are drawn from a narrow-minded code of morality. Adultery or family quarrels are to us not misfortunes which arise when people whose characters are incompatible get together because Nature has made a mistake in her arrangements. They are punishable offences which should end in damnation or else with penance and repentance. People who are the causes of such misdeeds must, if we are not to be offended, live outside the pale of normal bourgeois conditions, must never belong to our own class, but must be criminals, swindlers, or prostitutes. A man running a wholesale business may indeed be tempted to stray once in a while, but will certainly return repentant, and from then on will live unto the Lord, as well as unto his wife and child.

Whose portrait is that? It is that of the ordinary everyday man. And from this emerges the dangerous fact that the many millions of people who enjoy the average film are secretly and without knowing it bourgeois of the most dangerous calibre. This is the more surprising since the proletariat forms the mainstay of the movie public; but in the subconsciousness of the proletarian soul, where reason has the least power, remains, as is hardly to be wondered if the historical background is considered, a plentiful allowance of bourgeois idealism. Reason—generally many decades ahead of feeling—is already class-conscious; feelings still wallow in the mental and moral outlook of the bourgeois past. This rot in the unconscious is the result of a centuries-old tradition which is carefully nurtured by schools, Church and State up to the present day. But luckily it is kept well down in the basement by a great number of people. Higher up, in the more ample spaces of reason, live discernment and well-directed revolutionary fury. People never realise that they are exposing a worse self when they go to the cinema and enjoy *The Prince and the Flower Girl*. The fact that they feel such a film to be full of justice, idealism and truth to life proves that somewhere in a hidden and therefore—since what is hidden is hard to attack—particularly dangerous corner of their souls is something which they must combat. Combat even though schools, Church and State make that task as difficult as possible.

The Case of Greta Garbo

The chapter on the present-day film industry must not be closed without giving a specially crass example of what happens when a real person, an up-to-date, natural being, gets into the toils of the film magnates. The case of Greta Garbo shows quite clearly how even a great and world-famous artist cannot guard against the shallowness, vitiation and standardisation which make the average film production so second-rate.

When Greta Garbo began to talk in *Anna Christie* in a deep, gruff, unpleasing voice, which was occasionally supple as the movements of an animal but never gracious and charming as a woman's voice should be—some people were shocked and disappointed; others were glad, because they now heard what they had long since seen.

Those who were disappointed showed thereby that they had for years allowed themselves to be talked into believing in a Greta Garbo who came from America and not from Sweden, a white silken, graceful creature, *soignée,* exquisite, superfluous, a rich man's plaything. They saw her appear among rough Wild West boys, walking down a flight of steps like an angel off a Christmas tree. They saw her standing by the piano in full evening dress with a flower on her shoulder, singing an aria from "Tosca" to diplomats in tailcoats. They saw her leaning over the edge of her box at the theatre, driving a car, wearing white trousers on a sailing boat—such a woman must have a clear flexible voice. But Greta Garbo in her first talkie sat, weary with watching, at a table in a public house and ordered "Whisky!" in a growl that tore like a needle into the sound strip.

The case of Greta Garbo is remarkably instructive. This really great—if not supreme—actress has never been offered what any ordinarily good theatrical artiste pretty easily gets in any ordinary city—a part which suits her, a reasonably high-class play, an intelligent director, an appreciative audience. Greta Garbo, who wandered about Berlin unnoticed and unemployed, and seemed to have no sort of film face, has been made a beauty queen in America—by barbers and electricians. They applied exquisite, delicate art to her, shaped her eyelashes and eyebrows, gave her a skin as of finely polished marble, laid her hair as a frame about her face, gleaming and soft, made her glow in a magical white light. They invented the Greta Garbo coiffure, copied by millions of girls. But Greta Garbo herself remained undiscovered—is undiscovered to this very day.

American film magnates have felt the special power of this woman without understanding or being able to apply it properly. Wherein lies her charm? Is Greta Garbo beautiful? Jeanette Macdonald is beautiful—of good figure, svelte and neat, charming and with delightful ways, and when she loves, she is another World's Sweetheart. Garbo is not in the least like that. If she looks at a man, or even kisses him, she does it with animal "deliberateness." Such grave abandon was not customary among flappers whose erotic education had been carried on at petting parties. The fact that someone was behaving like a human being—that is, that someone was not treating the most important things in life as an amusing game but as destiny—appeared both stimulating and indecorous.

The film industry, which does not like to let slip anything that is stimulating, though it cannot permit any indecorum, found a very characteristic method of employing Greta Garbo in spite of it. For the first time, a woman had appeared who was neither a part of the girl-cult, nor a humorous flapper à la Colleen Moore, nor a diabolical ice figure like Gloria Swanson, nor an exotic female such as Dolores del Rio, but simply a tender, sincere human being. It seems very strange that this woman has been used as the vamp, the destructive, immoral, dangerous principle. It was felt strongly that a real human being was the natural antithesis to everything that was considered right and seemly and pleasing in American film stories. And so Garbo was selected to upset the comfortable marriages of gentle dark-eyed girls, to drive hard-working men to fighting duels, and at the end of the film to go to hell—drowning either among ice floes or in alcohol.

At the same time the attributes of the ordinary vamp were seldom forced upon her—swaying hips, disdainful glances, and arms placed temperamentally akimbo. For in contrast to the German producer who likes to transform his performers into some type showing good business results—such as turning his beginners into Greta Garbo doubles—the Americans prefer to emphasise the idiosyncrasies of the actors and thus create fresh types within the limits set by morality and business. So Garbo nearly always represents women who, judged by bourgeois morality, are despicable and destructive, and therefore do not deserve a happy ending; but rightly regarded are nothing but the catspaws of Fate, which forces them to love against law and order, and to be loved by men who are already otherwise bound. The strong feelings of a real woman are misused for a dramatically quite fruitless attack on emptiness, on lifeless figures, who have a good name to lose but no heart.

If Greta Garbo may be described as a woman who takes life seriously enough to give it point, perhaps it is not too much to say that this actress, against a background of more or less superficial figures, is a type of the best modern youth. For young people nowadays are so constituted that they reject empty forms and ease, and try to take life seriously. Many arguments might be cited to prove it—the curious and exceptional position that Greta Garbo occupies in Hollywood, her almost morbid avoidance of people, her preference for simple clothes, and her uncouth manners—it all sounds familiar. And it seems all the greater pity that this woman should only be allowed to practise her art attired in inappropriate fashionable clothes, playing opposite palm-olive young men with moustaches.

In *Anna Christie* she has been dressed in a woolen sweater—no doubt with the director's recognition that a harsh material should go with a harsh voice. But it is very curious that the producer has gone to the other extreme, and has cast Garbo for the part of a prostitute and a proletarian, which suits her just as little as the gorgeous mannequin magnificence. It is to be hoped that one of these days—perhaps on account of her revealing voice—she may be seen as a human being among human beings, as a woman who not only knows how to love (which the directors have realized) but how to live, and whose glowing sympathy with all things living will shine from her eyes as a subtle enchantment.

Translated by L. M. Sieveking and Ian F. D. Morrow

3. Nazi Germany, 1933–45—And Those Who Fled. . . .

ARTISTS AND BUREAUCRATS
IN THE "THIRD REICH"

Joseph Goebbels

An early member of the National Socialist Party, Joseph Goebbels (1897–1945) rose from the bottom of its ranks to hold one of the most important political positions under Hitler, that of Reich's Minister for Public Enlightenment and Propaganda. With a doctorate in German, Goebbels had aspirations to become a writer, but published only one novel early in his life, Michael: A Novel (Michael. Ein deutsches Schicksal in Tagebuchblättern, *1929), before becoming the most infamous force behind the production of Nazi propaganda. As Minister of Propaganda, he was able to control nearly all aspects of the media and artistic production, which resulted in, among other things, the burning of purportedly subversive books and artwork deemed degenerate and the production of some of the most anti-Semitic films ever made, such as* The Eternal Jew (Der ewige Jude, *Hippler, 1940) and* Jew Suess (Jud Süß, *Harlan, 1940). In 1944, he became General Plenipotentiary for Total War Mobilization* (Generalbevollmächtigter für den totalen Kriegseinsatz) *and was to succeed Hitler as Reich's Chancellor, but instead followed the Führer's lead and committed suicide after having his six children fatally poisoned.*

Dr. Goebbels's Speech at the Kaiserhof
on March 28, 1933

I am grateful for the opportunity to express myself about the situation of German film and the presumable future tasks of German filmmaking. I am doing it as a man who has never stood distant from German film, but rather as a passionate lover of cinematic art. For many years, I have recognized the heights to which German film can be led by the strength and ingenuity of the German spirit.

One should dispense with the belief that the current crisis is a material one; the film crisis is much more a spiritual one; it will exist as long as we do not have the courage to reform German film from the roots up. For fourteen days, I have been speaking with representatives from all areas of German filmmaking; I have had to draw very amusing conclusions from this. These gentlemen from the cinema have formed a picture of National Socialism like the one reflected in the opposition press. The National Socialist movement and its supporters are unknown to the gentlemen of film, inwardly as well.

In all discussions, the fear of insecurity was repeatedly expressed. It is said that production has become insecure. It is said that the exact opposite must now be the case for film production. It is said that, in Brüning's or Müller's times, one had to be insecure because a person in production did not know after four weeks what exactly was modern.

Now *we* are here. And even the doubting Thomas will be convinced that we will be in power at least four years. That which is, will remain; we're not leaving!

Film production would thus have every reason to be secure on the basis of this fact. By the same token, though, there can be no doubt anywhere that the National Socialist movement will intervene in the economy and in general cultural questions and thus also in film. With the help of a couple of examples, I want to show what is artistic and what is dangerous in film. Several films have made an indelible impression on me.

First of all, *Panzerkreuzer Potemkin (The Battleship Potemkin)*. It is fabulously made; it is film art without parallel. The decisive "why" is the conviction. Whoever is not firm in terms of a world view could become a Bolshevist because of this film. This proves that a political bias can indeed be contained in an artwork, and even the worst bias can be propagated if it occurs through the means of an excellent artwork.

Then there is *Anna Karenina*. Greta Garbo has proven that decisive cinematic art exists. This film is not a surrogate for the theater and the stage. It is its own cinematic art.

The Nibelungen. Here is a film story not taken from our time, but crafted in a manner so modern, so close to the times, so topical that even the militants of the National Socialist movement were deeply moved within. Proof that it does not have to do with the theme in itself. Subject matter from Greek mythology can also have as modern an effect as subject matter from the present; it depends only on how it is captured.

As the new age approached, people in Germany began to produce so-called National Socialist films, yet these were so little imbued with the spirit of the time that one must experience an inner shudder. Such National Socialism is mere external veneer. The new movement is not exhausted in marching parades and the blare of trumpets.

Finally, there is a film that could knock over even someone who is not a National Socialist: *The Rebel.* One recognizes in this example that conviction alone does not make a film, but great skill.

It is not important that a film can be made—the inner greatness of the conviction must agree with the external means. Then German film can become a world power whose limit is still entirely unimaginable today. Wishy-washy and formless films also cannot make their way in the world. The more sharply a film reveals *völkisch* contours, the greater are the possibilities of conquering the world.

The state has the duty to step in as regulator in the event of dangerous effects of film.

I repeatedly hear the complaint: We lack subject matter.—That is not true! There is a lack of courage to grab hold of subject matter. The film producer has overlooked the task of being a pioneer of the time. Film should not fancy itself so above the fates that the German people are enduring. If film does not produce any subject matter to which the people (*Volk*) can relate, it will no longer fill the movie theaters. One can say: the people is better than its directors. One may not underestimate the taste of the public, and if it is in need of improvement, we are not too old for the young people of the new movement to set to work on the regeneration of public taste and gradually to improve that taste instead of continuing to lower it with bad films for economic reasons.

The German crisis has passed film by without a trace; while the German people, filled with worries and yearnings, endured the greatest drama of suffering in history, the gentlemen of cinema ignored it. They did not tackle life where it is interesting; they remained shallow and wishy-washy.

Whoever understands our time knows which dramas are at film's disposal. Every night on the streets outside. German film has no proximity to reality; it is without contact with actual events among the people. It is just terrible that the entire body of German films could have been a product of the pre-war period. One repeatedly hears the argument that the films we call for would not fill the movie theaters. People also told me that when I started talking in 1926. Imagination is required to make the inner sense and the inner shape of a new world come alive. Many filmmakers are still going around as if the seizure of power on January 30 were a phenomenon that one notices only by shaking one's head.

Because people tried to adjust themselves as quick as a flash, they cannot understand the spirit of the new age. Only whoever is imbued with it can shape it; whoever is living outside the times can never do it.

For that reason, the crisis is also one involving personnel.

Many people today must recognize that when the flag falls, the bearer must also fall. Whoever has not recognized the new age in good time has neither a political nor a cultural and moral right to hoist a different flag. A general lack of courage, civil courage, and eagerness to identify oneself with a cause characterize the film industry. Wash my fur, but don't make me wet, say the production circles and content themselves with hoisting a new flag. With a small jack from the old era, if at all possible. That is buried forever, that intellectual liberalism that, in truth, means anarchy of the spirit. The objections that claim that all art is apolitical are stupid, naïve and illogical.

Where is there absolute objectivity, then? It is exactly impartiality that is dangerous, and one must look more closely at those people who stand up for it. In truth, they want to prevent a thorough reform of the German people. This reform, though, is the common denominator of all public life.

Indeed, art is only then possible when it is rooted in the National Socialist soil. I warn against judging the German people as poorly as the other arts have unfortunately done before film.

We do not intend to tolerate at all in the least such ideas, which will be destroyed root and branch in the new Germany, again making their entry either in disguise or openly. Thereby a turning-point will indeed be achieved in film production.

The new age does not want to cut off cinematic art from the bottom, but rather to take measures for its promotion. In so doing, there need be no talk whatsoever of the material promotion of achievement. The German government can also promote ideally, and I believe it will soon be enveloped with such high stature that it will be considered the highest honor to be distinguished by it.

The artist and production have to draw the consequences from this situation. They must declare themselves followers of a new creative desire; courage vis-à-vis the new age is the precondition, and not only new ideas, but new people must also come.

The artistically creative person must proceed with his profession of allegiance to the new age. There is no more glorious feeling than to sit together at the loom of history, so to speak, and to be able to say for one's modest part, "We were there!"

Yet public taste is not as it plays itself out inside the mind of a Jewish director. One cannot gain a picture of the German people in a vacuum. One must look at the face of the people and have oneself planted one's roots in the German soil. One must be a child of this people.

People say that film is lacking money! When I look at some film and hear how much it cost, then I would like to say to the producer, "Get a refund of your tuition money!" When a government that is a heart-felt friend of film offers its hand, then one should be grateful to this government, for we do not want to restrict film or to place limits on filmmaking. We reject the authoritarian fixation on doctrine. But the precondition is repeatedly the closest connection with the wishes of new Germany. There will be nothing in the artistic realm without this direction of the will, without this intention and political tendency.

Nor do we wish to suppress the making of the tiniest amusement, of the daily requirement against boredom and tribulation. One should not think about political ideology from morning till night. We ourselves have sensitivities too light, too artistic for this. Art is free and art should remain free, yet it must accustom itself to certain norms. In a country other than Germany, it would be superfluous to emphasize this. But people have destroyed normal political thinking in recent years. From the point where the censor would begin all the way up to the film that will proceed as a model from the whole process of artistic creation, there is such a wide latitude that any artistic activity can develop itself freely.

There is no pardon beneath this cut-off line. Dangerous experiments begin there that can only too often be regarded as the excesses of a sick mind. Our film producers will have to get used to new standard bearers eventually arising.

If the government then brings forth from an entire year's production one film entirely in accord with its wishes, goals and tasks, then all filmmaking thereby gets a boost such as would never be attainable on a material path alone.

We do not have the intention of crippling production. We do not think of allowing a state of insecurity to arise. In this great upheaval of our time, film must move close to the life of the real existence of the people. Nor do we want to impede private initiative; on the contrary, it will acquire a great thrust from the national movement and from the secure foundation that these days have created for a new Germany.

It is not the intention of the government to interfere in the realms of professional organizations. Rather, the organizations will be provided with greater rights. The government wants to walk hand in hand with the creative film world and to tread a common path with it. Allegiance to the Party is not necessary for this, but the artist must clearly recognize the new foundations and raise himself entirely up to the generally spiritual level of the nation and acknowledge the demands of its world view. Do not believe that we feel ourselves called upon to make life miserable for you. The young men who now sit in the government are at heart fond of German film artists. I myself have sat with the Reich's Chancellor in the movie theater on many evenings spent after the nerve-racking struggles of the day and found relaxation. Do not think that we do not remember this in gratitude.

What we want is that you again have joy in your work. For the creative artist, it must be a great feeling to sit along at the loom of history and to be able to say that, for one's modest part, one has participated. I believe that a new moral ethos will also arise from such a new way of thinking.

I ask for trusting cooperation so that it can again be said of German film as it is said in other areas: May Germany lead the world!

Translated by Lance W. Garmer

Leni Riefenstahl

At once reviled and admired, Leni (Helene) Riefenstahl (1902–2003) is best-known for her bombastic, yet technically and aesthetically innovative propaganda film Triumph of the Will *(Triumph des Willens, 1933/34), which documents the Nazi Party's Sixth Congress in Nuremberg. Below she discusses her two-part film* Olympia, *documenting the 1936 Berlin Olympics. She began her career as a dancer, but quickly entered the movie industry as an actor making several mountain films* (Bergfilme), *a highly successful genre that prefigures the more well-known postwar* Heimatfilm. *In 1932, Riefenstahl produced, wrote the screenplay for, starred in, and directed* The Blue Light (Das blaue Licht). *Although her film career essentially ended after the war, she recaptured the public's curiosity in the 1960s with her photographs of the African Nuba tribe. She has been the subject of numerous documentaries, several biographies and an autobiography, and had in recent years before her death worked on a film about coral reefs.*

May the Strength and Beauty of Youth Have Found Cinematic Form (1937)

By New Year's 1938, almost two years will have passed since I began work on the film of the Olympic Games. For my studies and preparations commenced already with the 1936 Winter Olympics.

The new year should now see the conclusion of the production of both evening-long parts of the film already in the first six weeks. It should immediately afterward bring their premiere in Germany and the world. Presently, I am still intensely at work.

The preparations were great and the extent of the shots was unique, thus making the selection and editing doubly difficult, and just as multi-faceted, is that which is known as "synchronization" in a feature film or a documentary film, which must be accomplished in a couple of days. The "sound recording" here means the re-creation of the entire atmosphere, independent of the visual effect.

The sounds for the film of the Olympics are words and noises being created. The original sounds and reports that radio recorded during the Games constitute the foundation. Carefully selected music by Herbert Windt is added to this; I had to experiment a great deal with this new type of sports music. The new recordings of reports and commentaries to the matches, in part by foreign broadcasters, also require the ultimate accuracy and dramatic power in order to achieve the complete harmony of the synchronized image with all the elements having an impact.

My wish for the New Year and at the end of the final phase of work on my Olympic film: may the strength and beauty of the youth of the world have found cinematic form that is worthy of the high spirit of the Olympic Games. May the film delight millions of people in the whole world as it makes visible the ideals and strengths that the Olympic city of the New Germany provided with such an unforgettable setting.

Translated by Lance W. Garmer

Veit Harlan

Veit Harlan (1899–1964) is perhaps best-known for directing the infamously anti-Semitic film Jew Suess (Jud Süß, *1940). He began his career as an actor in both the theater and in film, but concentrated primarily on film direction after 1935 when his first work,* Trouble in the Back Building (Krach im Hinterhaus), *debuted. After his extremely successful career as the Third Reich's star director, Harlan was the subject of much controversy, and his first postwar films,* Immortal Beloved (Unsterbliche Geliebte, *1950) and* Hanna Amon *(1951), were nearly boycotted but were nonetheless commercial hits. During this same period, he stood trial no less than three times for his activities under National Socialism, but was acquitted each time; he was ultimately categorized as a "fellow traveler" (Mitläufer) by the denazification court. Harlan was never able to match the success of the films he directed during the Third Reich and made a series of unremarkable and largely unprofitable melodramas in the 1950s.*

History and Film (1942)

There are many who want artists in difficult times to place light fare in front of the public, a fare that brings enjoyment, one that makes the public laugh and lets it forget its difficult everyday life. Surely, there is a great deal of justification in such a demand. I nevertheless believe, though, that the German people in these fateful days want to sense a more noble elation in hours of artistic enjoyment because the people remain in a world of ideas that connects them with those toward whom their concern, their hope and their pride are directed. Artworks that endeavor to conquer the hearts of men may not aim for distraction. Distraction is flight, flight in the face of thoughts that hold our heart and mind captive. We do not want to flee in the face of our thoughts today, though. Our time and our thoughts are indeed not only difficult, but, what is much more, sublime, and it is a more sublime world into which I want to lead people with my film *The Great King (Der große König)*. It is an exalted song to a great man who unwaveringly led his people through his own painful doubts and struggles to a great victory and a great goal despite the most terrible setbacks and disappointments and despite the greatest misunderstanding on the part of his family and many of his generals. I was aware that I would have done the German people no service if I had presented them with a loose adaptation about Frederick II in a time of hard reality. For that reason, I have strictly kept to history in writing the screenplay. Yet the actual events of the Seven Year War often evince such an astonishing parallel to the events of our days that it seems necessary for me to emphasize: the most important statements by the king in my film come from his own mouth, and the historical events, up to contractions of time without which one cannot shape an artwork as a unity, are in accord with real events. Only the history of a miller's daughter and of a sergeant is freely invented. For the miller's daughter one hears the voice of the simple girl who is initially unable to cope in the turmoil of her fate and from the sergeant the voice of the brave, simple soldier who becomes involved in guilt because he does not understand the severe goodness of his king. But both sense the greatness of their king, and they find their way back to their belief in the justice of his cause, for which they are ready to die. These down-to-earth figures are not idealized heroically, but rather achieve their heroism through struggle; in order to possess it they earn it. They are simply Prussians—they are Germans. With their weaknesses and with their extraordinary strength of sacrifice and of love.

The historian has the task of telling people the truth; the artist has the task of elevating man and of giving him strength and belief. The creator of a historical artwork has both tasks. This principle does not apply as uncompromisingly to the stage drama as it does in film. With its set, the stage is so far removed from reality that one can indeed apply to it the law of inner truth, but not the strict standards of historical truth. It is an art form that strives more toward a stylization than toward a depiction of reality. Film, though, is much closer to reality and, for that reason, the screenplay writer and film director bear a different type of responsibility toward history from what the stage writer does. The art form of film does not yet have that centuries-old tradition and experience which theater has. Thus, we cannot yet establish any final laws for it, but one thing seems to me to be clear, namely, that film must bear the face of reality throughout all artistic revolutions that it has yet to pass through, regardless of whether it creates comedies, fairy tales or historical events. With this knowledge, I have endeavored to give the figure of the king the characteristics of reality. I have done without any heroic poses; I wanted to look into the careworn countenance of a man who, after the lost battle, utterly breaks down under the responsibility that he has placed upon himself. Fingers and a back bent with gout mark his character, but when he stands up straight or sits upon his horse, he overcomes his pain for the sake of his bearing and example. In his eyes shines love—as well as hate. His face is often contorted by anger, sometimes overcome by weakness, yet repeatedly strengthened and rejuvenated by belief in victory. One will find in my film none of the many famous anecdotes nor any amiable stories through which people previously have attempted to portray to the German people their greatest king; rather one will see the king the way that I believe he was—as he must have been.

Translated by Lance W. Garmer

Fritz Hippler

At 18, while still in secondary school, Fritz Hippler (1909–2002) entered the Nazi Party and remained an enthusiastic member until the end of the Third Reich. In 1932, he was expelled from the University in Berlin for hanging a flag with a swastika on it, and he later organized the burning of "un-German" literature (undeutsches Schrifttum), *though he would adamantly deny this in his autobiography. In 1942, he was appointed by Goebbels to the position of* Reichsfilmintendant, Reich's Supervisor of Film, *two years after making what is perhaps one of the most anti-Semitic films of all time, the pseudo-documentary* The Eternal Jew (Der ewige Jude). *Shortly after his appointment, it was discovered that his grandmother was "non-Aryan," and he had to vacate his position.*

The Formative Power of Film (1942)

Next to the personal connection of the viewer to the main actor during the course of a film, film also produces the attempt to be equal to him. How he clears his throat and how he spits, how he is clothed, how he behaves, whether and what he drinks, what and how he smokes, where he is a bourgeois philistine or a playboy—all this has its effect not only in the film, but also in the life of the viewer. A power-packed and triumphant film lets out a different audience than a tragic or a comic film. After a film by Albers, even a barber's assistant is an Albers; nobody had better dare to get into a fight with him.

It is similarly undeniable that the woman represented in film influences the broad masses' ideal of beauty. For this reason, enough heed cannot be paid to the casting of film roles. Not only that this or that woman should be in this or that film. No, the woman, correctly selected in her outer deportment as well as according to her inner qualities and attributes, can very advantageously influence the general level of taste and the ideal of beauty of a very large number of men quite unconsciously and yet strongly through repeated successive casting and thus have a valuable effect not only generally in terms of "population policy," but also in the special sense of a qualitative elevation.

It should be no different with the portrayal of children. It should by no means suffice here that the public perceive the child or children as a more or less *quantité négligeable* or find them at best "really nice." No, the selection as well as the way they are used and behave can and must promote love and the wish to have a child in the hearts of the viewers. Heaven forbid that an outright misanthropic confirmed bachelor and child-hater be created by this! But there are numerous transitional psychological states, an attitude that is only in a certain sense negative, an undecided perspective that can be altogether very forcefully managed and influenced in this regard.

And how is it ultimately with the portrayal of *family* in film? When is there ever a family in German film that ends its joyless existence without tension, envy, strife, tragedy, murder and inheritance hunting? If one speaks to authors or directors about this question, one usually receives the answer that this has to be done in this way and not differently, lest the *dramatic tension* be missing—an argument, as I already often attempted to point out, that is not absolutely valid and compelling for film. Furthermore, it would be entirely conceivable from a purely dramaturgical standpoint to use the organism of the *family,* united in itself, as a dramatic counter pole. This way of thinking, of course, is not meant to imply that there should no longer be any film with inner-family tensions and disputes. Such a line will not at all be avoidable in certain cases without endangering the essential kernel of the whole. On the other hand, though, the film's power to form types has its effect through the same considerations indicated above.

No one can deny that the continued portrayal of quarrelsome families in film at least does not have a positive effect on the will to start a family—and, correspondingly, vice versa. Or does anyone seriously wish to contend that a film acquires its artistic value only through a good family row? I know of very many Czech films of recent years, for example, that show a very harmonious family life and "nevertheless" are of high artistic value and, in contrast to this, many films with decidedly disharmonious marriages that "nevertheless" are simply very bad and inartistic.

One might perhaps counter that the consideration of choice of types, of women and children, of family, etc. arises from extra-artistic considerations. One can only plainly and simply reply here *that film now as ever is and will remain a folk art.* And the masses and the heart of the people are most readily addressed not so much by films with a basically negative attitude as by ones with a basically positive one.

It is said to be undisputed that there are extraordinarily many films that evince absolutely negative and morbid characteristics in their details and must be considered as great artworks from a purely aesthetic standpoint. Yet no one seriously wants to claim by this that these films are great for that reason. But such films are just not "pleasing." There are indeed certain circles that see the final revelation in them. The broad masses of the people, though, the so-called petit-bourgeoisie, the white-collar workers, the workers, and the peasants are not at all pleased by such films. And, furthermore, there are, as is known, very great film artworks with a basically positive attitude that are among the greatest commercial hits.

In recent years, France has produced several film works that have won national and international prizes, but that had to be banned even by the liberalistic French government at the outbreak of the war because of their basically pessimistic attitude, even though the basic attitude of these films by no means even tended toward the political. It should be noted in passing that France has lost the war; certainly not because of these films, but that they could have been made in this way and in this number is surely also a definite symptom of the general attitude from which they arose and on which they had an effect.

One might say in rebuttal to the criticism of such films with a decidedly morbid and pessimistic basic attitude and tendency that there are very many world-famous literary works that in themselves would deserve to become the basis of a film adaptation but that, without intending this and making a bias out of it, are purely amoral in terms of their facts; amoral, of course, not in the sense that they should be criticized for the absence of a good bourgeois or strict, Christian morality or the absence of justly granted praise or rebuke, or otherwise for the absence of a great guiding commandment. Yet the lives and fates as well as the outwardly manifested reactions and actions of the "actors" here are often not in harmony with that great general organizational structure that corresponds with the spirit of all men and that lies equally at the basis of *all* religions. It goes without saying that this is not an artistic criterion; on the contrary, the purely artistic value of such works is fully recognized and confirmed independently of these considerations.

Yet it is the task of the writer, for example, to depict the characters of the people he creates so scintillatingly, so interestingly, so intricately and yet, on the other hand, so simply and kind-heartedly, so child-like and piously or, for example, to measure out the impressions that enter the consciousness of his people and to allow these impressions to be so felt that an action arising from them and appearing outwardly and formally as a crime, can be accepted, indeed even affirmed, as necessarily and internally justified completely without the question of punishment and penance needing to be raised in the least. The impression of a particularly brutal realism then often arises from this for the external plot of such a literary work: the good person suffers, the bad person is happy, the crime finds no atonement, etc. All this in itself, though, has nothing to do with the artistic form, but rather is only its content, which first acquires luster and stature only in the literary work itself; otherwise, it would devolve into an element in a trashy story. In the effect of a literary work on the reader, there is also the fact that, with respect to the persons acting, the reader is moreover given the great opportunity to include his own impressions and his own imagination in the total artistic effect.

It is entirely different in the case of film, which can never provide such a *profound, almost analytical portrait of the soul* and such an inwardly compelling marriage of internal and external worlds without choking on dialogue, i.e., without having an excruciating and unsatisfying effect. This is not a limitation of its artistic character (just as, for example, visual art cannot be accused of representing only given fixed events while neglecting the passage of time before and after). But it is indeed a limitation of its goals, since its creative tools are at a loss here; in return, on the other hand, they extend into areas whose representation is barred to the writer.

The question of the "happy end" also belongs in the same context as what was said above. A great deal has already been said and written about this, and many overzealous critics see particularly in this a strong objection against the artistic character of film. This is altogether foolish, although it must be admitted that the actual formation of a given concrete "happy end" can be artistically unsuccessful. Moreover, the possibilities for subject matter in the "happy end" are more varied than people think; for example, it can consist in the kiss of a pair of lovers or in the death of "Annelie," who is reunited with her husband or, on the other hand, with the hanging of "Jew Suess" (*Jud Süß*), among many other things.

Film simply is and remains the art that has the most intense effect and that is made for the broadest masses. Its example and its impact all too easily become the inner property of millions. Apart from the arguments presented above, it thus also seems appropriate for purely external pedagogical and psychological reasons to craft the ending of a film in such a way that everyone affirms it from the heart completely—for example, by allowing selfless love to achieve fulfillment and letting a crime find its atonement. Should film not always correspond to the cruel realism of life in this regard, it would more than compensate for this shortcoming by imparting strength and the affirmation of life.

Translated by Lance W. Garmer

Helmut Käutner

Helmut Käutner (1908–80) began his career in entertainment as a member of several Munich cabaret groups, one of which was banned by the Nazis in 1935. Before the onset of World War II, he worked primarily in the theater as an actor and director, and in film as a screenwriter. By the war's end, he had made three films, Romance in a Minor Key *(Romanze in Moll, 1932),* Great Freedom Nr. 7 *(Grosse Freiheit Nr 7, 1943/44), and* Under the Bridges *(Unter den Brücken, 1944/45); the first brought him problems with Goebbels, who went on to ban the other two films. The piece below, from early 1945, clearly anticipates the defeat of Germany. In the postwar era, Käutner's successful films included* The Last Bridge *(Die letzte Brücke, 1953),* Ludwig II, *(1954),* The Devil's General *(Des Teufels General, 1954/55),* The Captain From Köpenick *(Der Hauptmann von Köpenick, 1956), and* The Affairs of Julie *(Die Zürcher Verlobung, 1956/57). By the time the New German Cinema emerged in the 1960s, Käutner's less political and less experimental style fell out of favor, though he remains one of the most significant German directors of the early postwar years.*

Gratitude toward the Theater (1945)

In these days, as the German theater is lowering its curtain between the stage and the auditorium for more than just a night and a day and leaving the word to time alone, everyone feels, next to sadness, a deep gratitude to the theater, a gratitude that has hope as its companion.

Of this gratitude we shall not speak here. We shall speak of the gratitude that the young art of film has to express to the old art of the theater independently of any current event.

This gratitude is almost never expressed, for between the two, film and theater, there gapes the rift between the generations, the age-old contrast between parents and children. If film and theater move apart in debate over the theory or practice of art, then they simply move apart. Unfortunately, they never get together. Were they to do so, they would realize that they have more in common than they have in opposition.

The art of the theater is as old as mankind itself. Thespis and his chariot is a sentimental legend. The first urge of the human race (to be observed atavistically in a child) is the urge to play. Play is the core of the theater. Originally an end in itself, it gradually becomes a purposeful, common activity under influences that are partially cultic, partially erotic, and partially political. The stylistic means of and basic elements of the art are initially mime and music. Later, the word is added, and gradually the total artwork of theater comes to be. It assumes such a rich development over the course of the centuries that it finally must divide into individual artistic genres. The word, ennobled by the poet, creates the spoken theater for itself through the drama; the mime finds his own art form in dance; and music creates opera for itself. Pantomime, melodrama, recitation and choral forms seek their stylistic ground between them.

Added to these inner divisions of the theater, as it were, are the hybrids that arise from the union of the theater with other areas. From the relation of the theater with sport arise the circus and the variety show, its younger sisters, and cabaret finally is the incestuous product, so to speak, of a *liaison dangereuse* of the variety show with a promiscuous member of the great theater family.

Film is the youngest of these descendants. It is the product of a late love affair of the theater with technology. Its youth makes much in its essence understandable. It is inexperienced and considers separation from the experienced maternal art necessary in order to find itself. This unfortunately often occurs in enmity because the son believes that the mother allows him neither the room to live nor the new discoveries of his subversive youth.

A look at the lineage and the development of the theater marks out the path for film. It provides film with the artistic goal of achieving a total artwork appropriate to its form. Through its centuries-long struggle for expression and appearance, the theater has smoothed the artistic paths for film to such an extent that film was able to succeed in reaching the vicinity of absolute art in the short time of its existence. It, too, needs the poet in order to raise itself, as the theater did in its time, from entertainment to an art form. It, too, needs uniquely creative personalities, as, for example, Neuberin and Lessing[1] were for the theater, in order to find the laws unique to it. It thanks the eloquent example of the theater for being able to walk these paths with a clear goal before its eyes.

Translated by Lance W. Garmer

---

[1] Caroline Neuberin, famous eighteenth-century German actress, and Gotthold Ephraim Lessing, famous German dramatist, aesthetic theorist, and thinker of the same period. (Editor's note)

INTELLECTUALS IN EXILE

Max Horkheimer and Theodor W. Adorno

Theodor W. Adorno, born Theodor Wiesengrund (1903–1969), was one of the main forces behind the Frankfurt School of critical theory, so-called because the Frankfurt Institute for Social Research, founded in 1923, was the center out of which this Marxist-oriented school of thought originated. After 1933 and as a result of his being banned from teaching at the university, he lived in Oxford and later in the U.S. where his work, combining sociological research and a philosophy of history, led to the publications of The Authoritarian Personality *(1950) and* Minima Moralia: Reflections on a Damaged Life *(1951). In 1949, he and Horkheimer returned to Frankfurt to reestablish the Frankfurt Institute, where Adorno eventually became director and published further influential works of social criticism, philosophy, and aesthetics, including* Negative Dialectics (Negative Dialektik, *1966) and* Aesthetic Theory (Ästhetische Theorie, *1970).*

Max Horkheimer (1895–1973) became the director of the Frankfurt Institute for Social Research in 1930 whose later members included Walter Benjamin, Theodor Adorno, and Herbert Marcuse. The intellectual focus of the Institute was to develop a social theory that combined the insights of Marxist materialism, empirical sociology, psychoanalysis, and aesthetics. After only three years as its director, the Institute was forced to close and Horkheimer fled to Switzerland, and eventually to the U.S., where he reestablished the Institute in New York City. After moving to Los Angeles, he collaborated with friend and Frankfurt School colleague Theodor Adorno on the influential Dialectic of Enlightenment (Dialektik der Aufklärung, *copyrighted 1944, published 1947, excerpted here). Horkheimer returned to Frankfurt after the war as a professor at the University of Frankfurt am Main. Horkheimer and Adorno are well represented in volume 78 of* The German Library.*

The Culture Industry: Enlightenment as Mass Deception (1944)

The sociological theory that the loss of the support of objectively established religion, the dissolution of the last remnants of precapitalism, together with technological and social differentiation or specialization, have led to cultural chaos is disproved every day; for culture now impresses the same stamp on everything. Films, radio and magazines make up a system which is uniform as a whole and in every part. Even the aesthetic activities of political opposites are one in their enthusiastic obedience to the rhythm of the iron system. The decorative industrial management buildings and exhibition centers in authoritarian countries are much the same as anywhere else. The huge gleaming towers that shoot up everywhere are outward signs of the ingenious planning of international concerns, toward which the unleashed entrepreneurial system (whose monuments are a mass of gloomy houses and business premises in grimy, spiritless cities) was already hastening. Even now the older houses just outside the concrete city centers look like slums, and the new bungalows on the outskirts are at one with the flimsy structures of world fairs in their praise of technical progress and their built-in demand to be discarded after a short while like empty food cans. Yet the city housing projects designed to perpetuate the individual as a supposedly independent unit in a small hygienic dwelling make him all the more subservient to his adversary—the absolute power of capitalism. Because the inhabitants, as producers and as consumers, are drawn into the center in search of work and pleasure, all the living units crystallize into well-organized complexes. The striking unity of microcosm and macrocosm presents men with a model of their culture: the false identity of the general and the particular. Under monopoly all mass culture is identical, and the lines of its artificial framework begin to show through. The people at the top are no longer so interested in concealing monopoly: as its violence becomes more open, so its power grows. Movies and radio need no longer pretend to be art. The truth that they are just business is made into an ideology in order to justify the rubbish they deliberately produce. They call themselves industries; and when their directors' incomes are published, any doubt about the social utility of the finished products is removed.

Interested parties explain the culture industry in technological terms. It is alleged that because millions participate in it, certain reproduction processes are necessary that inevitably require identical needs in innumerable places to be satisfied with identical goods. The technical contrast between the few production centers and the large number of widely dispersed consumption points is said to demand organization and planning by management. Furthermore, it is claimed that standards were based in the first place on consumers' needs, and for that reason were accepted with so little resistance. The result is the circle of manipulation and retroactive need in which the unity of the system grows ever stronger. No mention is made of the fact that the basis on which technology acquires power over society is the power of those whose economic hold over society is greatest. A technological rationale is the rationale of domination itself. It is the coercive nature of society alienated from itself. Automobiles, bombs, and movies keep the whole thing together until their leveling element shows its strength in the very wrong which it furthered. It has made the technology of the culture industry no more than the achievement of standardization and mass production, sacrificing whatever involved a distinction between the logic of the work and that of the social system. This is the result not of a law of movement in technology as such but of its function in today's economy. The need which might resist central control has already been suppressed by the control of the individual consciousness. The step from the telephone to the radio has clearly distinguished the roles. The former still allowed the subscriber to play the role of subject, and was liberal. The latter is democratic: it turns all participants into listeners and authoritatively subjects them to broadcast programs which are all exactly the same. No machinery of rejoinder has been devised, and private broadcasters are denied any freedom. They are confined to the apocryphal field of the "amateur," and also have to accept organization from above. But any trace of spontaneity from the public in official broadcasting is controlled and absorbed by talent scouts, studio competitions and official programs of every kind selected by professionals. Talented performers belong to the industry long before it displays them; otherwise they would not be so eager to fit in. The attitude of the public, which ostensibly and actually favors the system of the culture industry, is a part of the system and not an excuse for it. If one branch of art follows the same formula as one with a very different medium and content; if the dramatic intrigue of broadcast soap operas becomes no more than useful material for showing how to master technical problems at both ends of the scale of musical experience—real jazz or a cheap imitation; or if a movement from a Beethoven symphony is crudely "adapted" for a film soundtrack in the same way as a Tolstoy novel is garbled in a film script: then the claim that this is done to satisfy the spontaneous wishes of the public is no more than hot air. We are closer to the facts if we explain these phenomena as inherent in the technical and personnel apparatus which, down to its last cog, itself forms part of the economic mechanism of selection. In addition there is the agreement—or at least the determination—of all executive authorities not to produce or sanction anything that in any way differs from their own rules, their own ideas about consumers, or above all themselves.

In our age the objective social tendency is incarnate in the hidden subjective purposes of company directors, the foremost among whom are in the most powerful sectors of industry—steel, petroleum, electricity, and chemicals. Culture monopolies are weak and dependent in comparison. They cannot afford to neglect their appeasement of the real holders of power if their sphere of activity in mass society (a sphere producing a specific type of commodity which anyhow is still too closely bound up with easygoing liberalism and Jewish intellectuals) is not to undergo a series of purges. The dependence of the most powerful broadcasting company on the electrical industry, or of the motion picture industry on the banks, is characteristic of the whole sphere, whose individual branches are themselves economically interwoven. All are in such close contact that the extreme concentration of mental forces allows demarcation lines between different firms and technical branches to be ignored. The ruthless unity in the culture industry is evidence of what will happen in politics. Marked differentiations such as those of A and B films, or of stories in magazines in different price ranges, depend not so much on subject matter as on classifying, organizing, and labeling consumers. Something is provided for all so that none may escape; the distinctions are emphasized and extended. The public is catered for with a hierarchical range of mass-produced products of varying quality, thus advancing the rule of complete quantification. Everybody must behave (as if spontaneously) in accordance with his previously determined and indexed level, and choose the category of mass product turned out for his type. Consumers appear as statistics on research organization charts, and are divided by income groups into red, green, and blue areas; the technique is that used for any type of propaganda.

How formalized the procedure is can be seen when the mechanically differentiated products prove to be all alike in the end. That the difference between the Chrysler range and General Motors products is basically illusory strikes every child with a keen interest in varieties. What connoisseurs discuss as good or bad points serve only to perpetuate the semblance of competition and range of choice. The same applies to the Warner Brothers and Metro Goldwyn Mayer productions. But even the differences between the more expensive and cheaper models put out by the same firm steadily diminish: for automobiles, there are such differences as the number of cylinders, cubic capacity, details of patented gadgets; and for films there are the number of stars, the extravagant use of technology, labor, and equipment, and the introduction of the latest psychological formulas. The universal criterion of merit is the amount of "conspicuous production," of blatant cash investment. The varying budgets in the culture industry do not bear the slightest relation to factual values, to the meaning of the products themselves. Even the technical media are relentlessly forced into uniformity. Television aims at a synthesis of radio and film, and is held up only because the interested parties have not yet reached agreement, but its consequences will be quite enormous and promise to intensify the impoverishment of aesthetic matter so drastically, that by tomorrow the thinly veiled identity of all industrial culture products can come triumphantly out into the open, derisively fulfilling the Wagnerian dream of the *Gesamtkunstwerk*—the fusion of all the arts in one work. The alliance of word, image, and music is all the more perfect than in *Tristan* because the sensuous elements which all approvingly reflect the surface of social reality are in principle embodied in the same technical process, the unity of which becomes its distinctive content. This process integrates all the elements of the production, from the novel (shaped with an eye to the film) to the last sound effect. It is the triumph of invested capital, whose title as absolute master is etched deep into the hearts of the dispossessed in the employment line; it is the meaningful content of every film, whatever plot the production team may have selected.

The man with leisure has to accept what the culture manufacturers offer him. Kant's formalism still expected a contribution from the individual, who was thought to relate the varied experiences of the senses to fundamental concepts; but industry robs the individual of his function. Its prime service to the customer is to do his schematizing for him. Kant said that there was a secret mechanism in the soul which prepared direct intuitions in such a way that they could be fitted into the system of pure reason. But today that secret has been deciphered. While the mechanism is to all appearances planned by those who serve up the data of experience, that is, by the culture industry, it is in fact forced upon the latter by the power of society, which remains irrational, however we may try to rationalize it; and this inescapable force is processed by commercial agencies so that they give an artificial impression of being in command. There is nothing left for the consumer to classify. Producers have done it for him. Art for the masses has destroyed the dream but still conforms to the tenets of that dreaming idealism which critical idealism balked at. Everything derives from consciousness: for Malebranche and Berkeley, from the consciousness of God; in mass art, from the consciousness of the production team. Not only are the hit songs, stars, and soap operas cyclically recurrent and rigidly invariable types, but the specific content of the entertainment itself is derived from them and only appears to change. The details are interchangeable. The short interval sequence which was effective in a hit song, the hero's momentary fall from grace (which he accepts as good sport), the rough treatment which the beloved gets from the male star, the latter's rugged defiance of the spoilt heiress, are, like all the other details, ready-made clichés to be slotted in anywhere; they never do anything more than fulfill the purpose allotted them in the overall plan. Their whole *raison d'être* is to confirm it by being its constituent parts. As soon as the film begins, it is quite clear how it will end, and who will be rewarded, punished, or forgotten. In light music, once the trained ear has heard the first notes of the hit song, it can guess what is coming and feel flattered when it does come. The average length of the short story has to be rigidly adhered to. Even gags, effects, and jokes are calculated like the setting in which they are placed. They are the responsibility of special experts and their narrow range makes it easy for them to be apportioned in the office. The development of the culture industry has led to the predominance of the effect, the obvious touch, and the technical detail over the work itself—which once expressed an idea, but was liquidated together with the idea. When the detail won its freedom, it became rebellious and, in the period from Romanticism to Expressionism, asserted itself as free expression, as a vehicle of protest against the organization. In music the single harmonic effect obliterated the awareness of form as a whole; in painting the individual color was stressed at the expense of pictorial composition; and in the novel psychology became more important than structure. The totality of the culture industry has put an end to this. Though concerned exclusively with effects, it crushes their insubordination and makes them subserve the formula, which replaces the work. The same fate is inflicted on whole and parts alike. The whole inevitably bears no relation to the details—just like the career of a successful man into which everything is made to fit as an illustration or a proof, whereas it is nothing more than the sum of all those idiotic events. The so-called dominant idea is like a file which ensures order but not coherence. The whole and the parts are alike; there is no antithesis and no connection. Their prearranged harmony is a mockery of what had to be striven after in the great bourgeois works of art. In Germany the graveyard stillness of the dictatorship already hung over the gayest films of the democratic era.

The whole world is made to pass through the filter of the culture industry. The old experience of the movie-goer, who sees the world outside as an extension of the film he has just left (because the latter is intent upon reproducing the world of everyday perceptions), is now the producer's guideline. The more intensely and flawlessly his techniques duplicate empirical objects, the easier it is today for the illusion to prevail that the outside world is the straightforward continuation of that presented on the screen. This purpose has been furthered by mechanical reproduction since the lightning takeover by the sound film.

Real life is becoming indistinguishable from the movies. The sound film, far surpassing the theater of illusion, leaves no room for imagination or reflection on the part of the audience, who is unable to respond within the structure of the film, yet deviate from its precise detail without losing the thread of the story; hence the film forces its victims to equate it directly with reality. The stunting of the mass-media consumer's powers of imagination and spontaneity does not have to be traced back to any psychological mechanisms; he must ascribe the loss of those attributes to the objective nature of the products themselves, especially to the most characteristic of them, the sound film. They are so designed that quickness, powers of observation, and experience are undeniably needed to apprehend them at all; yet sustained thought is out of the question if the spectator is not to miss the relentless rush of facts. Even though the effort required for his response is semi-automatic, no scope is left for the imagination. Those who are so absorbed by the world of the movie—by its images, gestures, and words—that they are unable to supply what really makes it a world, do not have to dwell on particular points of its mechanics during a screening. All the other films and products of the entertainment industry which they have seen have taught them what to expect; they react automatically. The might of industrial society is lodged in men's minds. The entertainments manufacturers know that their products will be consumed with alertness even when the customer is distraught, for each of them is a model of the huge economic machinery which has always sustained the masses, whether at work or at leisure—which is akin to work. From every sound film and every broadcast program the social effect can be inferred which is exclusive to none but is shared by all alike. The culture industry as a whole has molded men as a type unfailingly reproduced in every product. All the agents of this process, from the producer to the women's clubs, take good care that the simple reproduction of this mental state is not nuanced or extended in any way.

The art historians and guardians of culture who complain of the extinction in the West of a basic style-determining power are wrong. The stereotyped appropriation of everything, even the inchoate, for the purposes of mechanical reproduction surpasses the rigor and general currency of any "real style," in the sense in which cultural *cognoscenti* celebrate the organic pre-capitalist past. No Palestrina could be more of a purist in eliminating every unprepared and unresolved discord than the jazz arranger in suppressing any development which does not conform to the jargon. When jazzing up Mozart he changes him not only when he is too serious or too difficult but when he harmonizes the melody in a different way, perhaps more simply, than is customary now. No medieval builder can have scrutinized the subjects for church windows and sculptures more suspiciously than the studio hierarchy scrutinizes a work by Balzac or Hugo before finally approving it. No medieval theologian could have determined the degree of the torment to be suffered by the damned in accordance with the *ordo* of divine love more meticulously than the producers of shoddy epics calculate the torture to be undergone by the hero or the exact point to which the leading lady's hemline shall be raised. The explicit and implicit, exoteric and esoteric catalog of the forbidden and tolerated is so extensive that it not only defines the area of freedom but is all-powerful inside it. Everything down to the last detail is shaped accordingly. Like its counterpart, avant-garde art, the entertainment industry determines its own language, down to its very syntax and vocabulary, by the use of anathema. The constant pressure to produce new effects (which must conform to the old pattern) serves merely as another rule to increase the power of the conventions when any single effect threatens to slip through the net. Every detail is so firmly stamped with sameness that nothing can appear which is not marked at birth, or does not meet with approval at first sight. And the star performers, whether they produce or reproduce, use this jargon as freely and fluently and with as much gusto as if it were the very language which it silenced long ago. Such is the ideal of what is natural in this field of activity, and its influence becomes all the more powerful, the more technique is perfected and diminishes the tension between the finished product and everyday life. The paradox of this routine, which is essentially travesty, can be detected and is often predominant in everything that the culture industry turns out. A jazz musician who is playing a piece of serious music, one of Beethoven's simplest minuets, syncopates it involuntarily and will smile superciliously when asked to follow the normal divisions of the beat. This is the "nature" which, complicated by the ever-present and extravagant demands of the specific medium, constitutes the new style and is a "system of non-culture, to which one might even concede a certain 'unity of style' if it really made any sense to speak of stylized barbarity."[1]

The universal imposition of this stylized mode can even go beyond what is quasi-officially sanctioned or forbidden; today a hit song is more readily forgiven for not observing the 32 beats or the compass of the ninth than for containing even the most clandestine melodic or harmonic detail which does not conform to the idiom. Whenever Orson Welles offends against the tricks of the trade, he is forgiven because his departures from the norm are regarded as calculated mutations which serve all the more strongly to confirm the validity of the system. The constraint of the technically-conditioned idiom which stars and directors have to produce as "nature" so that the people can appropriate it, extends to such fine nuances that they almost attain the subtlety of the devices of an avant-garde work as against those of truth. The rare capacity minutely to fulfill the obligations of the natural idiom in all branches of the culture industry becomes the criterion of efficiency. What and how they say it must be measurable by everyday language, as in logical positivism. The

---

[1] Nietzsche, *Unzeitgemässe Betrachtungen, Werke,* Vol. I (Leipzig, 1917), p. 187.

producers are experts. The idiom demands an astounding productive power, which it absorbs and squanders. In a diabolical way it has overreached the culturally conservative distinction between genuine and artificial style. A style might be called artificial which is imposed from without on the refractory impulses of a form. But in the culture industry every element of the subject matter has its origin in the same apparatus as that jargon whose stamp it bears. The quarrels in which the artistic experts become involved with sponsor and censor about a lie going beyond the bounds of credibility are evidence not so much of an inner aesthetic tension as of a divergence of interests. The reputation of the specialist, in which a last remnant of objective independence sometimes finds refuge, conflicts with the business politics of the Church, or the concern which is manufacturing the cultural commodity. But the thing itself has been essentially objectified and made viable before the established authorities began to argue about it. Even before Zanuck acquired her, Saint Bernadette was regarded by her latter-day hagiographer as brilliant propaganda for all interested parties. That is what became of the emotions of the character. Hence the style of the culture industry, which no longer has to test itself against any refractory material, is also the negation of style. The reconciliation of the general and particular, of the rule and the specific demands of the subject matter, the achievement of which alone gives essential, meaningful content to style, is futile because there has ceased to be the slightest tension between opposite poles: these concordant extremes are dismally identical; the general can replace the particular, and vice versa.

Nevertheless, this caricature of style does not amount to something beyond the genuine style of the past. In the culture industry the notion of genuine style is seen to be the aesthetic equivalent of domination. Style considered as mere aesthetic regularity is a romantic dream of the past. The unity of style not only of the Christian Middle Ages but of the Renaissance expresses in each case the different structure of social power, and not the obscure experience of the oppressed in which the general was enclosed. The great artists were never those who embodied a wholly flawless and perfect style, but those who used style as a way of hardening themselves against the chaotic expression of suffering, as a negative truth. The style of their works gave what was expressed that force without which life flows away unheard. Those very art forms which are known as classical, such as Mozart's music, contain objective trends which represent something different to the style which they incarnate. As late as Schönberg and Picasso, the great artists have retained a mistrust of style, and at crucial points have subordinated it to the logic of the matter. What Dadaists and Expressionists called the untruth of style as such triumphs today in the sung jargon of a crooner, in the carefully contrived elegance of a film star, and even in the admirable expertise of a photograph of a peasant's squalid hut. Style represents a promise in every work of art. That which is expressed is subsumed through style into the dominant forms of generality, into the language of music, painting, or words, in the hope that it will be reconciled thus with the idea of true generality. This promise held out by the work of art that it will create truth by lending new shape to the conventional social forms is as necessary as it is hypocritical. It unconditionally posits the real forms of life as it is by suggesting that fulfillment lies in their aesthetic derivatives. To this extent the claim of art is always ideology too. However, only in this confrontation with tradition of which style is the record can art express suffering. That factor in a work of art which enables it to transcend reality certainly cannot be detached from style; but it does not consist of the harmony actually realized, of any doubtful unity of form and content, within and without, of individual and society; it is to be found in those features in which discrepancy appears: in the necessary failure of the passionate striving for identity. Instead of exposing itself to this failure in which the style of the great work of art has always achieved self-negation, the inferior work has always relied on its similarity with others—on a surrogate identity.

In the culture industry this imitation finally becomes absolute. Having ceased to be anything but style, it reveals the latter's secret: obedience to the social hierarchy. Today aesthetic barbarity completes what has threatened the creations of the spirit since they were gathered together as culture and neutralized. To speak of culture was always contrary to culture. Culture as a common denominator already contains in embryo that schematization and process of cataloging and classification which bring culture within the sphere of administration. And it is precisely the industrialized, the consequent, subsumption which entirely accords with this notion of culture. By subordinating in the same way and to the same end all areas of intellectual creation, by occupying men's senses from the time they leave the factory in the evening to the time they clock in again the next morning with matter that bears the impress of the labor process they themselves have to sustain throughout the day, this subsumption mockingly satisfies the concept of a unified culture which the philosophers of personality contrasted with mass culture.

Translated by John Cumming

Siegfried Kracauer

Introduction to From Caligari to Hitler: A Psychological History of the German Film (1947)

Introduction

1.

When, from 1920 on, German films began to break the boycott established by the Allies against the former enemy, they struck New York, London and Paris audiences as achievements that were as puzzling as they were fascinating.[1] Archetype of all forthcoming postwar films, *The Cabinet of Dr. Caligari* aroused passionate discussions. While one critic called it "the first significant attempt at the expression of a creative mind in the medium of cinematography,"[2] another stated: "It has the odor of tainted food. It leaves a taste of cinders in the mouth."[3] In exposing the German soul, the postwar films seemed to make even more of a riddle of it. Macabre, sinister, morbid: these were the favorite adjectives used in describing them.

With the passage of time the German movies changed themes and modes of representation. But despite all changes they preserved certain traits typical of their sensational start—even after 1924, a year considered the beginning of a long period of decline. In the appraisal of these traits complete unanimity has been reached

---

[1] Lubitsch's historical costume film PASSION—the first German production to be brought to this country—was shown at New York late in 1920. In April 1921, there followed the New York release of *The Cabinet of Dr. Caligari*.

[2] Rotha, *Film Till Now,* p. 178.

[3] Amiguet, *Cinéma! Cinéma!,* p. 37.

among American and European observers. What they most admire is the talent with which, from the time of *Caligari,* German film directors marshaled the whole visual sphere: their outspoken feeling for impressive settings, their virtuosity in developing action through appropriate lighting. Connoisseurs also appreciate the conspicuous part played in German films by a camera which the Germans were the first to render completely mobile. In addition, there is no expert who would not acknowledge the organizational power operative in these films—a collective discipline which accounts for the unity of narrative as well as for the perfect integration of lights, settings and actors.[4] Owing to such unique values, the German screen exerted world-wide influence, especially after the total evolution of its studio and camera devices in *The Last Laugh* (1924) and *Variety* (1925). "It was the German camera-work (in the fullest sense of that term) which most deeply impressed Hollywood."[5] In a characteristic expression of respect, Hollywood hired all the German film directors, actors and technicians it could get its hand on. France, too, proved susceptible to screen manners on the other side of the Rhine. And the classic Russian films benefited by the German science of lighting.[6]

Admiration and imitation, however, need not be based on intrinsic understanding. Much has been written about the German cinema, in a continual attempt to analyze its exceptional qualities and, if possible, to solve the disquieting problems bound up with its existence. But this literature, essentially aesthetic, deals with films as if they were autonomous structures. For example, the question as to why it was in Germany that the camera first reached complete mobility has not even been raised. Nor has the evolution of the German cinema been grasped. Paul Rotha, who along with the collaborators of the English film magazine *Close Up* early recognized the artistic merits of German films, confines himself to a merely chronological scheme. "In surveying the German cinema from the end of the war until the coming of the American dialogue film," he says, "the output may roughly be divided into three groups. Firstly, the theatrical costume picture; secondly, the big middle period of the studio art films; and thirdly, the decline of the

---

[4] Rotha, *Film Till Now,* pp. 177–78; Barry, *Program Notes,* Series I, program 4, and Series III, program 2; Potamkin, "Kino and Lichtspiel," *Close Up,* Nov. 1929, p. 388; Vincent, *Histoire de l'Art Cinématographique,* pp. 139–40.

[5] Barry, *Program Notes,* series I, program 4.

[6] Jahier "42 Ans de Cinéma," *Le Rôle intellectuel du Cinéma,* p. 86.

German film in order to fall into line with the American 'picture-sense' output."[7] Why these three groups of films were bound to follow each other, Rotha does not try to explain. Such external accounts are the rule. They lead straight into dangerous misconceptions. Attributing the decline after 1924 to the exodus of important German film people and American interference in German film business, most authors dispose of the German pictures of the time by qualifying them as "Americanized" or "internationalized" products.[8] It will be seen that these allegedly "Americanized" films were in fact true expressions of contemporaneous German life. And, in general, it will be seen that the technique, the story content, and the evolution of the films of a nation are fully understandable only in relation to the actual psychological pattern of this nation.

2.

The films of a nation reflect its mentality in a more direct way than other artistic media for two reasons:

First, films are never the product of an individual. The Russian film director Pudovkin emphasizes the collective character of film production by identifying it with industrial production: "The technical manager can achieve nothing without foremen and workmen and their collective effort will lead to no good result if every collaborator limits himself only to a mechanical performance of his narrow function. Team work is that which makes every, even the most insignificant, task a part of the living work and organically connects it to the general task."[9] Prominent German film directors shared these views and acted accordingly. Watching the shooting of a film directed by G. W. Pabst in the French Joinville studios, I noticed that he readily followed the suggestions of his technicians as to details of the settings and the distribution of lights. Pabst told me that he considered contributions of that kind invaluable. Since any film production unit embodies a mixture of heterogeneous interests and inclinations, teamwork in this field tends to exclude arbitrary han-

---

[7] Rotha, *Film Till Now*, p. 177.—It should be noted that Rotha expresses the views then held of the German movies by French and English film aesthetes, although his book is more vigorous and perceptive than those which had preceded it.

[8] Bardèche and Brasillach, *History of Motion Pictures*, p. 258 ff.; Vincent, *Histoire de l'Art Cinématographique*, pp. 161–62; Rotha, *Film Till Now*, pp. 176–77; Jeanne, "Le Cinéma Allemand," *L'Art Cinématographique*, VIII, 42 ff.; etc.

[9] Pudovkin, *Film Technique*, p. 136.

dling of screen material, suppressing individual peculiarities in favor of traits common to many people.[10]

Second, films address themselves, and appeal, to the anonymous multitude. Popular films—or, to be more precise, popular screen motifs—can therefore be supposed to satisfy existing mass desires. It has occasionally been remarked that Hollywood manages to sell films which do not give the masses what they really want. In this opinion Hollywood films more often than not stultify and misdirect a public persuaded by its own passivity and by overwhelming publicity into accepting them. However, the distorting influence of Hollywood mass entertainment should not be overrated. The manipulator depends upon the inherent qualities of his material; even the official Nazi war films, pure propaganda products as they were, mirrored certain national characteristics which could not be fabricated.[11] What holds true of them applies all the more to the films of a competitive society. Hollywood cannot afford to ignore spontaneity on the part of the public. General discontent becomes apparent in waning box-office receipts, and the film industry, vitally interested in profit, is bound to adjust itself, so far as possible, to the changes of mental climate.[12] To be sure, American audiences receive what Hollywood wants them to want; but in the long run public desires determine the nature of Hollywood films.[13]

3.

What films reflect are not so much explicit credos as psychological dispositions—those deep layers of collective mentality which extend more or less below the dimension of consciousness. Of course, popular magazines and broadcasts, bestsellers, ads, fashions in language and other sedimentary products of a people's cultural life also yield valuable information about predominant attitudes, widespread inner tendencies. But the medium of the screen exceeds these sources in inclusiveness.

---

[10] Balázs, *Der Geist des Films*, pp. 187–88.

[11] See the analyses of these films in the Supplement.

[12] Cf. Farrell, "Will the Commercialization of Publishing Destroy Good Writing?" *New Directions*, 9, 1946, p. 26.

[13] In pre-Hitler Germany, the film industry was less concentrated than in this country. Ufa was preponderant without being omnipotent, and smaller companies carried on beside the bigger ones. This led to a diversity of products, which intensified the reflective function of the German screen.

Owing to diverse camera activities, cutting and many special devices, films are able, and therefore obliged, to scan the whole visible world. This effort results in what Erwin Panofsky in a memorable lecture defined as the "dynamization of space": "In a movie theater . . . the spectator has a fixed seat, but only physically. . . . Aesthetically, he is in permanent motion, as his eye identifies itself with the lens of the camera which permanently shifts in distance and direction. And the space presented to the spectator is as movable as the spectator is himself. Not only do solid bodies move in space, but space itself moves, changing, turning, dissolving and recrystallizing. . . ."[14]

In the course of their spatial conquests, films of fiction and films of fact alike capture innumerable components of the world they mirror: huge mass displays, casual configurations of human bodies and inanimate objects, and an endless succession of unobtrusive phenomena. As a matter of fact, the screen shows itself particularly concerned with the unobtrusive, the normally neglected. Preceding all other cinematic devices, close-ups appeared at the very beginning of the cinema and continued to assert themselves throughout its history. "When I got to directing films," Erich von Stroheim told an interviewer, "I would work day and night, without food, without sleeping sometimes, to have every detail perfect, even to descriptions of how facial expressions should change."[15] Films seem to fulfill an innate mission in ferreting out minutiae.

Inner life manifests itself in various elements and conglomerations of external life, especially in those almost imperceptible surface data which form an essential part of screen treatment. In recording the visible world—whether current reality or an imaginary universe—films therefore provide clues to hidden mental processes. Surveying the era of silent films, Horace M. Kallen points to the revealing function of close-ups: "Slight actions, such as the incidental play of the fingers, the opening or clenching of a hand, dropping a handkerchief, playing with some apparently irrelevant object, stumbling, falling, seeking and not finding and the like, became the visible hieroglyphs of the unseen dynamics of human relations. . . ."[16] Films are particularly inclusive because their "visible hieroglyphs" supplement the testimony of their stories proper.

---

[14] Panofsky, "Style and Medium in the Moving Pictures," *transition*, 1937, pp. 124–25.

[15] Lewis, "Erich von Stroheim . . ," *New York Times*, June 22, 1941.

[16] Kallen, *Art and Freedom*, II, 809.

And permeating both the stories and the visuals, the "unseen dynamics of human relations" are more or less characteristic of the inner life of the nation from which the films emerge.

That films particularly suggestive of mass desires coincide with outstanding box-office successes would seem a matter of course. But a hit may cater only to one of many coexisting demands, and not even to a very specific one. In her paper on the methods of selection of films to be preserved by the Library of Congress, Barbara Deming elaborates upon this point: "Even if one could figure out . . . which were the most popular films, it might turn out that in saving those at the top, one would be saving the same dream over and over again . . . and losing other dreams which did not happen to appear in the most popular individual pictures but did appear over and over again in a great number of cheaper, less popular pictures."[17] What counts is not so much the statistically measurable popularity of films as the popularity of their pictorial and narrative motifs. Persistent reiteration of these motifs marks them as outward projections of inner urges. And they obviously carry most symptomatic weight when they occur in both popular and unpopular films, in grade B pictures as well as in superproductions. This history of the German screen is a history of motifs pervading films of all levels.

4.

To speak of the peculiar mentality of a nation by no means implies the concept of a fixed national character. The interest here lies exclusively in such collective dispositions or tendencies as prevail within a nation at a certain stage of its development. What fears and hopes swept Germany immediately after World War I? Questions of this kind are legitimate because of their limited range; incidentally, they are the only ones which can be answered by an appropriate analysis of the films of the time. In other words, this book is not concerned with establishing some national character pattern allegedly elevated above history, but it is concerned with the psychological pattern of a people at a particular time. There is no lack of studies covering the political, social, economic and cultural history of the great nations. I propose to add to these well-known types that of a psychological history.

---

[17] Deming, "The Library of Congress Film Project: Exposition of a Method," *Library of Congress Quarterly*, 1944, p. 20.

It is always possible that certain screen motifs are relevant only to part of the nation, but caution in this respect should not prejudice one against the existence of tendencies affecting the nation as a whole. They are the less questionable as common traditions and permanent interrelationship between the different strata of the population exert a unifying influence in the depths of collective life. In pre-Nazi Germany, middle-class penchants penetrated all strata; they competed with the political aspirations of the Left and also filled the voids of the upper-class mind. This accounts for the nation-wide appeal of the German cinema—a cinema firmly rooted in middle-class mentality. From 1930 to 1933, the actor Hans Albers played the heroes of films in which typically bourgeois daydreams found outright fulfillment; his exploits gladdened the hearts of worker audiences, and in *Mädchen in Uniform* we see his photograph worshiped by the daughters of aristocratic families.

Scientific convention has it that in the chain of motivations national characteristics are effects rather than causes—effects of natural surroundings, historic experiences, economic and social conditions. And since we are all human beings, similar external factors can be expected to provoke analogous psychological reactions everywhere. The paralysis of minds spreading throughout Germany between 1924 and 1929 was not at all specifically German. It would be easy to show that under the influence of analogous circumstances a similar collective paralysis occurs—and has occurred—in other countries as well.[18] However, the dependence of a people's mental attitudes upon external factors does not justify the frequent disregard of these attitudes. Effects may at any time turn into spontaneous causes. Notwithstanding their derivative character, psychological tendencies often assume independent life, and, instead of automatically changing with ever-changing circumstances, become themselves essential springs of historical evolution. In the course of its history every nation develops dispositions which survive their primary causes and undergo a metamorphosis of their own. They cannot simply be inferred from current external factors, but, conversely, help determine reactions to such factors. We are all human beings, if sometimes in different ways. These collective dispositions gain momentum in cases of extreme political change.

---

[18] Of course, such similarities never amount to more than surface resemblances. External circumstances are nowhere strictly identical, and whatever psychological tendency they entail comes true within a texture of other tendencies which color its meaning.

The dissolution of political systems results in the decomposition of psychological systems, and in the ensuing turmoil traditional inner attitudes, now released, are bound to become conspicuous, whether they are challenged or endorsed.

5.

That most historians neglect the psychological factor is demonstrated by striking gaps in our knowledge of German history from World War I to Hitler's ultimate triumph—the period covered in this book. And yet the dimensions of event, milieu and ideology have been thoroughly investigated. It is well known that the German "Revolution" of November 1918 failed to revolutionize Germany; that the then omnipotent Social Democratic Party proved omnipotent only in breaking the backbone of the revolutionary forces, but was incapable of liquidating the army, the bureaucracy, the big-estate owners and the moneyed classes; that these traditional powers actually continued to govern the Weimar Republic which came into shadowy being after 1919. It is also known how hard the young Republic was pressed by the political consequences of the defeat and the stratagems of the leading German industrialists and financiers who unrestrainedly upheld inflation, impoverishing the old middle class. Finally, one knows that after the five years of the Dawes Plan—that blessed era of foreign loans so advantageous to big business—the economic world crisis dissolved the mirage of stabilization, destroyed what was still left of middle-class background and democracy, and completed the general despair by adding mass unemployment. It was in the ruins of "the system" which had never been a true structure that the Nazi spirit flourished.[19]

But these economic, social and political factors do not suffice to explain the tremendous impact of Hitlerism and the chronic inertia in the opposite camp. Significantly, many observant Germans refused until the last moment to take Hitler seriously, and even after his rise to power considered the new regime a transitory adventure. Such opinions at least indicate that there was something unaccountable in the domestic situation, something not to be inferred from circumstances within the normal field of vision.

---

[19] Cf. Rosenberg, *Geschichte der Deutschen Republik;* Schwarzschild, *World in Trance;* etc.

Only a few analyses of the Weimar Republic hint at the psychological mechanisms behind the inherent weakness of the Social Democrats, the inadequate conduct of the communists and the strange reactions of the German masses.[20] Franz Neumann is forced to explain the failure of the communists partly in terms of "their inability to evaluate correctly the psychological factors and sociological trends operating among German workers. . . ." Then he adds to a statement on the Reichstag's limited political power the revealing remark: "Democracy might have survived none the less— but only if the democratic value system had been firmly rooted in the society. . . ."[21] Erich Fromm amplifies this by contending that the German workers' psychological tendencies neutralized their political tenets, thus precipitating the collapse of the socialist parties and the trade-unions.[22]

The behavior of broad middle-class strata also seemed to be determined by overwhelming compulsions. In a study published in 1930 I pointed out the pronounced "white-collar" pretensions of the bulk of German employees, whose economic and social status in reality bordered on that of the workers, or was even inferior to it.[23] Although these lower middle-class people could no longer hope for bourgeois security, they scorned all doctrines and ideals more in harmony with their plight, maintaining attitudes that had lost any basis in reality. The consequence was mental forlornness: they persisted in a kind of vacuum which added further to their psychological obduracy. The conduct of the petty bourgeoisie proper was particularly striking. Small shopkeepers, tradesmen and artisans were so full of resentments that they shrank from adjusting themselves. Instead of realizing that it might be in their practical interest to side with democracy, they preferred, like the employees, to listen to Nazi promises. Their surrender to the Nazis was based on emotional fixations rather than on any facing of facts.

Thus, behind the overt history of economic shifts, social exigencies and political machinations runs a secret history involving the inner dispositions of the German people. The disclosure of these dispositions through the medium of the German screen may help in the understanding of Hitler's ascent and ascendancy.

---

[20] Outstanding among these analyses is Horkheimer, ed., *Studien über Autorität und Familie;* see especially Horkheimer, "Theoretische Entwürfe über Autorität und Familie," pp. 3–76.

[21] Neumann, *Behemoth,* pp. 18–19, 25.

[22] Fromm, *Escape from Freedom,* p. 281.

[23] Cf. Kracauer, *Die Angestellten.*

Lotte H. Eisner

In 1927, Lotte H. Eisner (1896–1983) became the first woman film critic in Germany (at Film Kurier*), and her work on the early German cinema remains relevant to film scholarship today. Along with Kracauer's* From Caligari to Hitler *(1947), her* Haunted Screen *(L'Écran démoniaque, 1952), first published in France where she emigrated in 1933, is a seminal work on the art cinema of the Weimar Republic and traces its roots to the theater of Max Reinhardt and expressionist art. In 1940, Eisner was interned in the Jewish section of the concentration camp in Gurs at Pau from which she fled, to live under the pseudonym Louise Escoffier in the south of France. After the war she worked at the* Cinemathèque française, *ultimately becoming its director.*

Introduction to The Haunted Screen: Expressionism in the German Cinema and the Influence of Max Reinhardt (1952)

1. The Predisposition toward Expressionism

The years immediately following World War I were strange ones in Germany. The German mind had difficulty adjusting itself to the collapse of the imperial dream; and in the early years of its short life the Weimar Republic had the troublesome task of meeting outside demands (the onerous terms imposed on Germany at Versailles), while at the same time maintaining equilibrium internally (the Spartacist revolt of 1919, the unsuccessful Kapp Putsch of 1920). In 1923, after Germany had failed to pay the war reparations laid down at Versailles, French and Belgian troops occupied the Ruhr, and inflation, which had always been a serious danger, could not be stopped. The material conditions that resulted led to a general decline of values, and the inner disquiet of the nation took on truly gigantic proportions.

Mysticism and magic, the dark forces to which Germans have always been more than willing to commit themselves, had flourished in the face of death on the battlefields. The hecatombs of young men fallen in the flower of their youth seemed to nourish the grim nostalgia of the survivors. And the ghosts which had haunted the German Romantics revived, like the shades of Hades after draughts of blood. A new stimulus was thus given to the eternal attraction toward all that is obscure and undetermined, toward the kind of brooding speculative reflection called *Grübelei,* which culminated in the apocalyptic doctrine of Expressionism. Poverty and constant insecurity help to explain the enthusiasm with which German artists embraced this movement which, as early as 1910, had tended to sweep aside all the principles which had formed the basis of art until then.

Rather than give an account of Expressionism in terms of sculpture or painting, we need, in order to analyse the phenomenon in all its complexity and ambiguity, to follow its track through the literature of the period. This may appear paradoxical; the reason is that, for the Germans, that "race of thinkers and poets," every manifestation in art is immediately transformed into dogma: the systematic ideology of their *Weltanschauung* is wedded to a didactic interpretation of art.

But finding one's way through the tangled phraseology of the German Expressionists is not an easy task. At first sight, their telegraphic style, exploding in short phrases and exclamations, seems to have simplified the labyrinthine syntax of classical German; but this apparent clarity is misleading. Expressionist phraseology is ruled by a desire to amplify the "metaphysical" meaning of words. Its exponents juggle with vague expressions, strings of words which have little orthodox relationship to each other, and invent mystical allegories which amount to little once we attempt to translate them. This language of symbols and metaphors is intentionally obscure, designed to be intelligible only to the initiated.

As an example let us listen to the dithyramb intoned in 1919 by a fervent theorist of this style, Kasimir Edschmid, in his *Über den Expressionismus in der Literatur.* Here we may detect, more clearly than anywhere else, the keystone of the Expressionist conception.

Expressionism, Edschmid declared, is a reaction against the atom-splitting of Impressionism, which reflects the iridescent ambiguities, disquieting diversity, and ephemeral hues of nature. At the same time Expressionism sets itself against Naturalism with its mania for recording mere facts, and its paltry aim of photographing nature or daily life. The world is there for all to see; it would be absurd to reproduce it purely and simply as it is. The Expressionists also oppose the effeminacy of neo-Romanticism.

The Expressionist does not see, he has "visions." According to Edschmid, "the chain of facts: factories, houses, illness, prostitutes, screams, hunger" does not exist; only the interior vision they provoke exists. Facts and objects are nothing in themselves: we need to study their essence rather than their momentary and accidental forms. It is the hand of the artist which "through them grasps what is behind them" and allows us to know their real form, freed from the stifling constraint of a "false reality." The Expressionist artist, not merely receptive but a true creator, seeks, instead of a momentary, accidental, form, the *eternal, permanent meaning* of facts and objects.

We must detach ourselves from nature, say the Expressionists, and strive to isolate an object's "most expressive expression." These rather confused stipulations were explained by Béla Balázs in his book *Der Sichtbare Mensch* (1923); an object can be stylized by the accentuation of (in Balázs's words) its "latent physiognomy." This will permit the penetration of its visible aura.

Edschmid proclaimed that human life, transcending the individual, participates in the life of the universe; our hearts beat with the rhythm of the world itself and are linked with everything that happens: the cosmos is our lung. Man has ceased to be an individual tied to concepts of duty, morality, family and society; the Expressionist's life breaks the bounds of petty logic and causality. Free from all bourgeois remorse, admitting nothing but the prodigious barometer of his sensibility, he commits himself to his impulses. The "world-image" is reflected in him in its primitive purity; reality is created by him and the "world-image" exists solely in him. This intense longing to lose all individuality in a total extravasation of self, to feel pervaded by the destiny of the universe, is a characteristic common to many German intellectuals toward the end of World War I. Most were beginning to cry out against the absurd slaughter taking place; soon German poets, wishing like Schiller before them to embrace the whole of humanity, were to write, as Werfel had already written in 1910: "My only happiness, O Man, is to feel myself your brother."

The contrasts and contradictions in all this will be readily apparent. On the one hand Expressionism represents an extreme form of subjectivism; on the other hand this assertion of an absolute totalitarian self creating the universe is linked with a dogma entailing the complete abstraction of the individual.

The Germans, themselves steeped in contradictions, felt the need for a compromise. Thus the art critic Paul Fechter, in a work called

Der Expressionismus (1919), distinguished between (1) an "intensive Expressionism" characterized by extreme individualism, such as that of the painter Kandinsky who, at the apogee of feeling, deliberately ignores the exterior world and, remote from logic and causality, strives for transcendentality and the chaos of form and color; and (2) the "extensive Expressionism" of a Pechstein, whose creative impulse flows from a cosmic feeling which his will fashions and transforms. On the other hand the Expressionists distinguished between two opposing tendencies. As early as 1910 one of the two groups which had gathered around two literary reviews had taken the name Aktion. This group, led by Franz Pfemfert in opposition to the purist ecstatic Expressionists, pursued anti-bourgeois social and political aims while claiming absolute intellectualism with the catchword Gehirnlichkeit (cerebrality). The other group had taken the name Sturm (storm). Its programme was more artistically inclined than that of Aktion, and promulgated the Expressionist doctrine of ecstatic creation based on visions. The leader of Sturm, Herwart Walden, wrote in a pamphlet Die neue Malerei (1919): "Expressionism is neither a fad nor a movement; it is a Weltanschauung."

Nature is not alone in being proscribed. Psychology, the handmaiden of Naturalism, is also condemned, along with the laws and concepts of conformist society and the tragedies provoked by petty social ambitions. Edschmid proclaimed the dictatorship of Mind. Mind has the mission of giving form to matter. He also exalted the attitude of constructive Will, and called for a total revision of the whole of human behavior. The same stereotyped vocabulary crops up time and again in German Expressionist literature: words and phrases such as "interior tension," "force of expansion," "immense accumulation of creative concentration" or "metaphysical interplay of intensities and energies"; much is also made of expressions such as "dynamism," "density," and above all of the word Ballung, a well-nigh untranslatable concept which might be rendered as "intensive crystallization of form."

A few words are needed here about the "abstraction" so frequently referred to by the theorists of Expressionism. In his doctorate thesis Abstraktion und Einfühlung, published in 1921, Wilhelm Worringer anticipated many of the Expressionists' precepts, proving how close to the German Weltanschauung these aesthetic axioms were.

Abstraction, Worringer declared, stems from the great anxiety that man experiences when terrorized by the phenomena he perceived around him, the relationships and mysterious polarities of which he is unable to decipher. This primordial anguish, which man feels when confronted with unlimited space, makes him want to detach the objects of the exterior world from their natural context, or better still, to free the individual object from its ties with other objects, to make it "absolute."

Nordic man, Worringer continued, is constantly aware of the presence of a "veil between himself and nature"; this is why he aspires after abstraction in art. Inwardly discordant, always striving for the unattainable, he needs that spiritual unrest which is an incentive to the "animation of the inorganic." Mediterranean man, so perfectly harmonious, can never know this ecstasy of "expressive abstraction." Such was the paradoxical formula that the troubled mysticism of Expressionism preached.

According to Worringer, Nordic man's desire for abstraction reaches its climax in the living abstraction of Gothic art, in the "extensive dynamism of energies," and in that intensity of expression which leads him, "beatified and quivering with spasmodic ecstasy, enthralled by a vertiginious intoxication, toward the heavens opened up for him by a thundering orchestration of mechanical forces."

To come back to Edschmid, we find him stipulating that everything must remain "sketchy" and quiver with immanent tension; a perpetual effervescence and excitation must be carefully maintained.

From the *élan* of Gothic art to the Expressionist ecstasy is not such a far cry as might be thought. According to Wolfhart Gotthold Klee (in *Die charakteristischen Motive der expressionistischen Erzählungsliteratur,* 1934), Gothic, Baroque, *Sturm und Drang,* Romanticism and Expressionism are interrelated: they are periods of the *Werden* (becoming) and not, like the Renaissance for example, periods of the *Sein* (being). Nietzsche maintained that the German *is* not, he *becomes,* he is forever in the process of evolving.

The Expressionists, who liked to call themselves "apocalyptic adolescents," display an almost childlike love of youth; they abhor old people, those representatives of a chilly conformism which reproves their unbounded high spirits. Two generations separated by an unbridgable gulf bear a mortal hatred for each other: poignant examples are Werfel's poem *Vater und Sohn,* Kafka's novellas *The Metamorphosis* and *The Judgment,* and the plays *Der Sohn* by Hasenclever and *Vatermord* by Bronnen.

The paroxysm that the Germans take for dynamism is found in all the drama of this period, which has since been called the *O Mensch Periode*(the "O Man period"). Of *Der Bettler* by Reinhard Sorge, a play written in 1912 and a prototype of the genre, it has been said—and the remark holds good for all the artistic activity of this period—that the world has become so "permeable" that, at any one moment, Mind, Spirit, Vision and Ghosts seem to gush forth, exterior facts are continually being transformed into interior elements and psychic events are exteriorized. Is this not precisely the atmosphere we find in the classic films of the German cinema?

Translated by Roger Greaves

4. Postwar Germany: 1945 to the Present

FILM ARTISTS

Wolfgang Staudte

After the National Socialists banned him from the theater for leftist activities in 1933, Wolfgang Staudte (1906–84), worked as an actor in Nazi cinema. However, he achieved renown as a director and screenwriter of such socially critical, critically acclaimed, and commercially successful postwar films as Germany's first postwar production The Murderers Are among Us *(Die Mörder sind unter uns, 1946); the antifascist* Rotation *(1948/49);* The Subject *(Der Untertan, 1951), an adaptation of Heinrich Mann's novel; and* The Story of Little Mook *(Die Geschichte vom kleinen Muck, 1953), a popular children's film. All of these were made for DEFA in the GDR, although Staudte always lived in West Berlin. In 1955, Staudte was no longer able to make films in the GDR, and he began making films in West Germany. One of the most successful was* Roses for the State Prosecutor *(Rosen für den Staatsanwalt, 1959). In the mid-1960s he began working as a director in television.*

A Letter to the Central Military Commander of the Soviet Occupation Zone (October 9, 1945)

To: The Central Military Commander of the Soviet Occupation Zone
Berlin-Mitte
Luisenstrasse
Dept. of Film, Theater, and Educational Affairs

In contrast to the areas of theater, opera, and musical life, where the helpful support of the representatives of the Soviet Union was able to achieve visible successes, filmmaking in the sector of Berlin has so far demonstrated no signs of a positive development.

In view of the undeniable political and cultural significance that will be attached to new filmmaking in Germany, the dangerous threat of a splintering of the productive forces of film must be energetically countered. I therefore suggest the establishment of an organization that would have its seat and a site of operation on the studio grounds of the former Tobis Film in Johannisthal and that, working from there—analogous to the directorship of a theater— would assume the systematic leadership and central organization of filmmaking in the sector of Berlin and that would answer for this work to the representatives of the Red Army as well as the representatives of the Berlin municipal authorities.

The organization sees its task and duty in the following points:

(1) The immediate establishment and development of a production plan for some 4–5 films, whereby the best suggestions and projects of the various workgroups and small associations that have come together in Berlin might be realized.

(2) The greatest possible centralization and concentration of filmmaking in the workplaces in Johannisthal and a reorganization of the working conditions there.

These studio locations are presently the only useable production sites and have been administered for months under the direction of Mr. Koslowsky without artistic initiative and without a vision beyond a purely commercial standpoint. The increasingly frequent dismissals of qualified film personnel to which management has thus been forced represent a considerable endangerment to filmmaking. At the moment of starting the first feature film, these highly trained personnel must again be found and brought back to film production. Thus, this first production group would stand before the difficult task of acquiring the building materials, raw film, props, etc. necessary for its film plans. Naturally, it would see to it that this were carried out only to the extent as would be absolutely necessary for the completion of its first film. Without systematic central management and planning, the second film company then has to do the same difficult preliminary work, which, in turn, will happen only insofar as it accords with its interests. It is beyond question that the artistic realization of new films will be compromised by such unnecessary economic and labor-related obstacles.

Furthermore, from a social as well as an artistic standpoint, it must be deemed an unacceptable fact that a large segment of the most capable filmmakers has been working for months on projects of all sorts out of idealism without being able to count on even the least economic security because all technical and economic preconditions for the practical implementation of these film plans will be absent. If, however, the possibility of forward-looking planning is provided, the speediest remedial measures can be taken through contractual agreements here as well.

(3) The establishment of a separate script department that will concern itself with the development of new film material, bear responsibility for additional screenplays ready for filming, and examine submitted film suggestions in terms of their artistic quality and political orientation. Close cooperation with the representatives of the Soviet Union and of the Berlin municipal authorities will be aimed for here, too. The urgent challenge of bringing young, talented writers to the new German film is another essential task of this dramaturgical department.

(4) Studio management, in cooperation with architects as a result of uniform planning, will be much better able to create the technical conditions for the execution of a planned film program than if architects alien to the studio are each time placed before this task from the beginning. Considerable savings can be made in the acquisition of building materials in this manner as well as through appropriate repeated use of studio sets.

(5) In a school for the advancement of the new generation, the best instructors, directors and cameramen will be employed in order to actively address an urgent problem here as well: the renewal of German film.

Not all arguments that speak for a centralization of filmmaking in the sector of Berlin can be cited here, yet, from the experiences of recent months, it is clearly recognizable that, without the help of the representatives of the Soviet Union and without uniform leadership and planning, the advent of successful film production will remain questionable for a long time to come. On the basis of these considerations, the suggestion for a central organization has arisen that would consist of the following members: Wolfgang Staudte as artistic director; Alf Teichs as director of production and chief script editor; Fritz Mauruschat as architect and technical director of studio operations; Peter Pewas as director and head of the school for the new generation; Eberhard Keindorff and Johanna Sibelius as script editors and authors; and Friedl Behn-Grund as lead cameraman.

Executive and business management would lie in the hands of the first two persons named.

The engagement of directors Helmut Käutner and Josef von Baky is envisioned. The following films are planned for the first echelon of the production program: *The Man I'm Going to Kill*, director W. Staudte; *The Second Shot* (Pushkin), director Josef von Baky; a film by Helmut Käutner; *Dawn Is Breaking*, director Peter Pewas; *Victory of Youth*, a film for pupils, director Werner Hochbaum; *Second-hand Fate*, director Helmut Käutner.

Demo Film is working independently, but will be looked after by the planned umbrella organization when it uses Jofa's studio sets in its work. Obviously, though, the wish there is to work in the studios in Tempelhof. A clarification with respect to this will be supplied after approval of this suggestion.

I believe that I am speaking in the name of all filmmakers when I emphasize that a quick decision is necessary here in order to remedy a social malady and to take an important step—on the path to the political renewal of Germany.

Translated by Lance W. Garmer

Gunter Groll, Helmut Käutner, and Walter Talmon-Gros

The published dissertation by Gunter Groll (1914–82) has been called the most significant work on film theory published during the Third Reich, which is not to say that he was in agreement with the National Socialist government. As a university student in Vienna, he protested against the Nazis and was critically injured when a member of the SA ("brownshirts") stabbed him. In 1945, Munich's Süddeutsche Zeitung

(South German Times) was founded, and Groll was one of its first writers. There he initially contributed pieces on the theater and cabaret, but eventually concentrated his efforts on film. He is known as one of the most important film critics of the 1950s if not the most important, whose journalistic work was praised as elevating film criticism to a literary art form. In 1961, Groll suffered a heart attack and was unable to continue in his career for health reasons.

Walter Talmon-Gros (1911–73) was an author, translator, and film historian. For many years, he was the director of the Mannheim Film Festival. With Günter Groll and Helmut Käutner (see above) he wrote the following essay in the new film journal they edited, Monatshefte für Film und Fernsehen (Monthly Journal for Film & Television).

Every Audience, as Everybody Knows, Has the Films It Deserves (1956)

Every audience, in the long run, also has the magazines it deserves . . . Jane Doe, for example, the allegorical Jane,[1] has her films by the lot, and she also has her magazines. Things are going well for them, the Jane magazines, and we, for our part, wish them no harm whatsoever.

They should not be the only ones, though.

The friend of good film unfortunately did not have what Jane had, at least not in Germany. He came away once again empty-handed—quite empty-handed in the movie theater and absolutely empty-handed at the magazine stand.

There have been, of course, numerous attempts in recent years. Theoretically, a serious film magazine was supposed to have been started again and again, but, practically, something always got in the way. Each of the three signatories below has seen such attempts made and fail. All three of us—three people who attempt to work for good film in three different areas and through various means—have in the meantime become extremely distrustful of new attempts. It looks as though no one wanted to have such a magazine.

---

[1] In the original German, the name "Lieschen Müller" is used. (Editor's note)

One day, though, the people from the Institute for Film and Television in Munich, led by Eberhard Hauff, came along with people from film clubs and art film movie theaters and said that they wanted to give it a new try. We were very skeptical. One year later, they were still saying the same thing. They were very persistent. And something astonishing happened: after yet another year, they did in fact produce this magazine, supported by the Süddeutscher Verlag (South German Publishing). Film journalists from the entire world promised to contribute. Film directors and screenplay writers were keenly interested, joyful noise was made in film clubs, and a great deal of friendly encouragement surrounded the laudable Institute—it looked as though there really were people who wanted to have such a magazine.

When we say this, we were delighted and participated.

Nevertheless, we, the editors, wish to admit quietly that we are still a bit skeptical. Will you, esteemed reader, not become bored if the ominous words "film art" appears on many occasions in these pages? It will hardly be avoidable. Will you be interested if films are not only discussed and criticized here but also analyzed through and through and if there will be talk here not only of the very newest films, but also of old ones, even the very oldest ones? Will you not be missing something if you find fewer film bosoms and similar pictorial attractions in this magazine than there doubtlessly are elsewhere? And as good as no film gossip? And will you even show understanding for the fact that the first issues cannot turn out quite as we imagine? Will you give the magazine a little time to develop?

Please, do not think that we are confusing you with Jane Doe. (She does not even pick up this magazine because there is such an unattractive picture on the front—from *La Strada*, namely, a film that a proper Jane can hardly approve of.) No, we already more or less know who you are.

You are the man, or the woman, or the by no means rowdy *(halbstark)* young person to whom we owe it that the number of good films has grown in recent years—because the audience that wished them grew. You are the regular attendee of art film theaters; you are most probably a film club member, in the newspaper, you prefer to read film reviews (with which you presumably by no means always agree, as you yourself are critical) more than film gossip (about which the veiled advertisement presumably annoys you most); you find De Sica or Chaplin or René Clair much more exciting than beauty queens; you are not at all a so-called fan; and you are interested in many other things in addition to film—is that right? We owe much to you. Your mere existence results in the fact that movie theaters do not show exclusively tear-jerkers; that anti-tear-jerker directors are not boycotted, at least not always; that critics have not been silenced by advertising bans, at least not all; that the art film theaters are far from bankrupt, but, quite to the contrary, are finding more and more followers (namely, you and your friends)—no, we are not confusing you with anyone else. But none-theless—of course, we do not exactly know whether you have been missing a film magazine up till now, or whether you don't perhaps think that things would be fine even without one. . . . We shall see.

So, we set to work, and this seems entirely reasonable to us, not without skepticism, but also, of course, with trust: in you, dear reader, in the young editors who produce this magazine, and in film, which has so often disappointed us and which we so doggedly love.

We hope that this independent magazine will become a rallying point for genuine friends of film and that, in the worst of cases, it will not go bankrupt until it has already demonstrated the justification for its being—it would at least comfort us if people were then to say, "Too bad. That was a decent magazine."

But perhaps a long-term acquaintanceship is also starting between you and us with these lines (in case you read introductory words), who knows, and perhaps all of us together—film critics, film people, moviegoers—can work together a bit in the common pursuit of good film. It certainly needs it. Let's try!

Translated by Lance W. Garmer

The Oberhausen Manifestor (1962)

At the Oberhausen Film Festival in 1962, the manifesto below was signed by a number of young West German filmmakers, many of whom had recently won international awards for their short, experimental films. The young filmmakers were attacking the commercialism and aesthetic mediocrity of the West German film industry, controlled by an older generation of artists the younger directors rejected as being politically

and aesthetically compromised by its work in the film indus-
try during the "Third Reich." The manifesto is often consid-
ered the beginning of what became known as the "Young
German Cinema," the first phase of a cinematic "new wave"
that by the 1970s gained international acclaim and which we
now call the "New German Cinema."

The collapse of the conventional German film finally removes the
economic basis for a mode of filmmaking whose attitude and practice we reject. With it the new film has a chance to come to life.

German short films by young authors, directors, and producers
have in recent years received a large number of prizes at international festivals and gained the recognition of international critics.
These works and these successes show that the future of the German film lies in the hands of those who have proven that they speak
a new film language.

Just as in other countries, the short film has become in Germany
a school and experimental basis for the feature film.

We declare our intention to create the new German feature film.

This new film needs new freedoms. Freedom from the conventions of the established industry. Freedom from the outside influence of commercial partners. Freedom from the control of special
interest groups.

We have concrete intellectual, formal, and economic conceptions
about the production of the new German film. We are as a collective
prepared to take economic risks.

The old film is dead. We believe in the new one.

Oberhausen, February 28, 1962

Bodo Blüthner	Walter Krüttner	Detten Schleiermacher
Boris v. Borresholm	Dieter Lemmel	Fritz Schwennicke
Christian Doermer	Hans Loeper	Haro Senft
Bernhard Dörries	Ronald Martini	Franz-Josef Spieker
Heinz Furchner	Hansjürgen Pohland	Hans Rolf Strobel
Rob Houwer	Raimond Ruehl	Heinz Tichawsky
Ferdinand Khittl	Edgar Reitz	Wolfgang Urchs
Alexander Kluge	Peter Schamoni	Herbert Vesely
Pitt Koch		Wolf Wirth

Translated by Eric Rentschler

Alexander Kluge

Though trained as a lawyer, the film career of Alexander Kluge (1932–) began with an internship at CCC-Film where he had the opportunity to work with Fritz Lang on The Indian Tomb *(Das indische Grabmal, 1959), and it was shortly afterward that he directed his prize-winning first short film* Brutality in Stone *(Brutalität in Stein, 1960, with Peter Schamoni). As one of the forces behind the Oberhausen Manifesto, which was written at the 1962 Oberhausen Film Festival, Kluge and twenty-five other filmmakers sought to distance themselves from what they perceived to be a preoccupation with escapist themes and lack of originality in the films of the 1950s. His first feature film,* Yesterday Girl *(Abschied von Gestern, 1966), based on one of his short stories, established him as one of the major figures of the New German Cinema and remains one of his most accessible films. He is also the author of numerous theoretical works on film as well as important works of fiction.*

What Do the "Oberhauseners" Want? (1962)

West German Film is in a crisis: its intellectual content was never more lacking, but today its economic status is equally threatened. This is happening at a time when in France and Italy, in Poland and Czechoslovakia, but also in many other countries, film has assumed a new artistic and political importance. Films like Italy's *Salvatore Giullano*, which was just shown in Berlin, or *Ashes and Diamonds* from Poland, indicate that film has been able to interact with literary and other art forms as well as with political consciousness. We have had numerous conversations with members of Group 47 and have seen that there exists a quite extraordinary interest in film among people working in other sectors. It therefore is crucial that we (1) free film from its intellectual isolation in the Federal Republic; (2) militate against the dictates of a strictly commercial orientation operative in the film industry today; (3) allow for conditions which make film aware of its public responsibility and, consequently, in keeping with this responsibility, to seek appropriate themes: film should embrace social documentation, political questions, educational concerns, and filmic innovations, matters all but impossible under the conditions that have governed film production.

For an Intellectual Transformation

In the film industry today there are two main groups: the producers associated with the Head Organization of the German Film Industry (SPIO) and their affiliated distributors; the young directors organized around the Oberhausen group, who also have their own distributors (e.g., Atlas-Film, but also to a degree Gloria-Film). The Oberhausen group in the meanwhile is not only limited to the signatories of the Oberhausen Manifesto this last February, but also includes all those forces who want not only a reorganization of previous practice in German film, but also a structural change in film production and an intellectual transformation in film activity. This group has among its members directors, producers, and authors. The group seeks close working relations with Group 47, with the so-called "Cologne School" (Stockhausen), and with other intellectual forces outside of the film industry. We are also seeking close contacts with [Wolfgang] Staudte, [Bernard] Wicki, [Helmut] Käutner, and [Hans] Abich, because we think that the failures these outstanding filmmakers have had recently are not due to personal shortcomings, but rather are a result of the faulty system governing the film industry.

The program called for by the Oberhausen group can in the long run finance itself. In the early phase, where new types of film will have to be developed in a comparatively short time (in France and Italy one took the last six years to do so, in the Eastern Bloc countries the state pays for this development work anyway), the program will at least in part have to rely on public subsidies. That means we will have to maintain a definite *noncommercial* position within the framework of a free-market economy. For these reasons the Cultural Minister Conference has recommended the support of culturally significant films in the discussions about the 1963 budget.

Three Goals

The Oberhausen group has pursued three tasks since this spring:

(1) The founding of a public foundation for "Young German Film." This foundation should enable each new generation of Ger-

man filmmakers to complete their first feature film, granted that the filmmaker in question has proved himself in the short film realm and finished a short film. A jury will monitor the quality of the projects submitted. This foundation has in the meanwhile been established. It needs, though, further public monies. On the other hand, it is clear that no one will make money from this foundation, particularly because the profits of each film subsidized must be passed on back to the foundation in keeping with the amount of support granted. We have calculated that three successful films out of every ten subsidized will suffice to maintain a constant fund for upcoming young German filmmakers.

(2) Subsidization of independent short films. The independent short film is the natural experimental field of film, just as the private school is the carrier of independent impulses and reformist endeavor in the field of education, an institution which cannot be governed by the large state school apparatus. This independent short film is seriously threatened today, particularly since the abolishment of the entertainment tax. Due to the loss of the entertainment tax in several states, the predicates no longer mean so much to distributors. The box-office returns for "particularly noteworthy" short films in this way have sunk well below the production costs. It is important that we not lose this short-film basis, even when we go on someday to make feature films. In this way the Conference of Cultural Ministers and the responsible social powers cannot make it any clearer how potentially dangerous the diminishing importance of the Film Rating Board (FBW) is. The Film Rating Board is in any case the single institution in the film branch which is not strictly commercial in its orientation.

(3) To create an intellectual center for film, in which new generations can be trained and in which theoretical work and developmental work have their place, things that are necessary for every industry, even the film industry. This institution has been established as of October 1 and it consists of twelve instructors, i.e., two film scholars and ten directors, and to all appearances, it is off to a good start. This Department for Film Design in connection with the Scholl-Siblings Foundation (in keeping with the *Bauhaus* conception) links new filmic models with instruction in film design. This department likewise, as of December 1, will have an experimental studio based in Munich, in which the practical experimental work and further training of Ulm students with two years of previous

course work will be carried out. The film department and the experimental studio fit into the overall framework of the film and television academy which will be established with branches in Munich, Berlin, and Ulm.

The idea of founding a film and television academy initially caused us a lot of misgivings. The problem lies in a potential academization of the already wretched film situation we have in Germany, and it's exactly that which we cannot want. Along with this came the competition between the cities Berlin and Munich, which each with a certain ambition sought an advantage in the academy question, so that discussion on this level is not free from certain prestige considerations. This was one of the reasons why we particularly concentrated on the educational model linked to the Institute for Film Design (although right now we are very much involved in film productions of our own), because it seemed necessary to us, from the very beginning, to maintain our own and independent model of creative education in a more modest form above and beyond any likely large academy apparatus. From the cooperation between the academy and the film department in Ulm a positive influence can be generated toward film. This cooperation will be made easier insofar as the *Bundestag* representative Dr. Martin has intervened continually, working on a national basis to support and encourage independent endeavors.

Translated by Eric Rentschler

Wolfgang Staudte

A Reflection: Befouling Our Own Nest? (1964)

When the war was happily lost, our nest was hopelessly filthy from top to bottom. And since no large-scale revolutionary cleaning took place, the filth was hidden as well as was possible, but it stayed in our own nest. . . .

Those, though, who nevertheless seized the moment and tried to sweep the filth out of their own corners—there were, thank God, not a few—often had to make do without the gratitude of the fatherland and to learn that their need for political hygiene was being accompanied by exactly the commentary that is the occasion for these lines: He's befouling his own nest!

Soon after the film *Die Mörder sind unter uns* (*The Murderers Are among Us*) premiered, this charge surfaced against me, albeit in a relatively timid way. Today, I know that the concerned objections came primarily from those who themselves had to fear being caught between a broom and a dustpan.

The fact that, twenty years later, the murderers are still among us, strolling out of prison cells, receiving Federal Crosses of Merit, and being placed on ministerial seats means only that there is still dirt in our nest that should be removed.

Whoever undertakes this work, which is certainly not always thankful, however, incurs displeasure in a strange, often disquieting manner from some quarters.

He is seen as an alien bird from an alien nest that crows with malicious pleasure, "Look how dirty your nest is!" But it is his own nest and thus also his own dirt.

As far as those people are concerned whose hastily renewed national consciousness is beginning to totter and who look beyond the "provisional" national borders with their brows furrowed in worry, they can easily be shown that films such as *Rosen für den Staatsanwalt* (*Roses for the State Prosecutor*) or *Kirmes* (*Fairground*), for which I am responsible, have brought more respect to the German image abroad than those hopeless attempts to reinterpret German guilt as tragic entanglement.

Yet even poor Heinrich Mann had to put up with a caption before *Der Untertan* (*The Subject*) that more or less said that the whole thing had no real, malicious intent, and that the story to a certain extent was only the depiction of an isolated case. Philistine cautiousness about not befouling one's own nest led to a conscious falsification here. Hitler was an isolated case, too. But his monstrous spirit set Europe aflame. And it is only a short way from the idiotic ideology of the "master race" back to that arrogant phrase of Wilhelmine coinage, "the German essence," which was supposed to make the world get better.

Political films are a part of the historical representation of the present. Insofar as they are art, they will be partisan, challenging and subjective, but always engaged and concerned with the state of their "own nest."

The film *Herrenpartie (Gentleman's Outing)*, which is going to the starting line as a German contribution, is such a film. A satirical attack against German tourists' lack of political sensitivity in formerly occupied territory. On the other hand, though, it directs itself against the hatred of Germans that is set in concrete, and against irreconcilability and delayed revenge. Not only the perpetrators, but also the victims have a past with which they must come to terms, and we, I think, all have good cause to help them in this. There can be no doubt that there is such a great lack of sensitivity here in our country among a handful of philistines when ministers can give speeches that smash political porcelain so loudly that the crashing can be heard even in the Pentagon!

—Surely it is not the films that are befouling our nest.

Translated by Lance W. Garmer

Wim Wenders

One of the most important directors of Germany's New German Cinema, Wim (Ernst Wilhelm) Wenders (1945–) began making films in the 1970s, including his critically acclaimed road movie trilogy—Alice in the Cities (Alice in den Städten, *1974),* Wrong Move (Falsche Bewegung, *1975), and* Kings of the Road (Im Lauf der Zeit, *1976). In the early 1980s he had international success with* Paris, Texas *(1984) based on Sam Shepard's screenplay and filled with desolate images of the U.S. Southwest. After completing his education at the newly founded* Hochschule für Fernsehen und Film *in Munich, he directed* The Goalie's Anxiety at the Penalty Kick *(*Die Angst des Tormanns beim Elfmeter, *1971) based on a novel by Peter Handke, with whom he again collaborated on the international hit,* Wings of Desire (Himmel über Berlin, *1987). Wenders continues to make films, including the sequel to* Wings of Desire, Far Away, So Close! (In weiter Ferne, so nah!, *1993), and* Buena Vista Social Club *(1999), a documentary about the music scene in Cuba that was nominated for an Academy Award.*

That's Entertainment: Hitler (1977)

Obscenity, who really cares?
Propaganda, all is phony.—
"It's Alright, Ma (I'm Only Bleeding)—Bob Dylan

The Hitler film by Joachim C. Fest and Christian Herrendoerfer was premiered at the Berlin Film Festival.[1] With a set of program notes in hand chock-full of explanations I awaited the film with great expectations. In the notes I read: "This film depicts the Hitler era dispassionately, objectively and rationally. It conveys the fascination of Hitler's career without in any way being tempted to fall prey to this fascination.

"This film does not manipulate our history. It does not transfigure either. It explains." Why all these words of defense for something one hadn't even had a chance to attack yet?

My consternation became all too justified, however, when the film started, and it soon grew into an incredible dismay. At the end of the film a short applause, then the otherwise so outspoken festival audience headed for the exists, perplexed and disconcerted. Someone cracked, *"That's Entertainment, Part 3,"* but that didn't make things any better. Something had happened here almost beyond belief, no, it was not so much a matter of what we had seen as much as the way, HOW we had seen all this. It was hard to sort out, to be sure, for that reason the difficulty and the reluctance to give it a name.

With growing exasperation I followed the discussion about the film over the next few weeks: frivolous or impudent acclamations for the most, inoffensive cultural page rhetoric (in *Stern*: "If the Führer were to find out") or the positivism of *Der Spiegel*: "He has moved the filmic coming to grips with recent German history in a new direction."

You can say that again.

Then the first decided rejection, with no ifs, ands, or buts, in *Die Zeit*, where Karl-Heinz Janssen expressly terms the film dangerous and also carefully explains his judgment.

Finally, in the *Frankfurter Rundschau*, the most painstaking analysis by Wolfram Schütte, who shows "how greatly this film's

---

[1] The complete title of the film under discussion is *Hitler—eine Karriere (Hitler—A Career)*. Fest, one of the editors of the conservative daily newspaper, the *Frankfurter Allgemeine Zeitung*, was the author of *Hitler*, translated into English by Richard and Clara Winston (New York: Random House, 1975).

aestheticization of reality resembles a similar penchant inherent in fascism."

Of course the film is doing well. To expect anything else would be childish. This is how fortunes are made.

I finally became furious last week after watching the wretched performance on television, the program *Aspekte*, where the Hitler film was supposed to be discussed. The good will behind this boomeranged. The program devolved into an extended advertisement for the film. As soon as the evening news was over, we were already graced with clips from the film as a trailer, and Janssen repeated his theses from *Die Zeit* sitting in front of a studio wall draped from top to bottom with the Hitler poster. At least one should have learned one thing from this film: you cannot show something at considerable length if you want to distance yourself from it. In film (in television no doubt as well) what we see is above all the crucial representation, only secondarily what we think about it. And instead of discussing the formal means of the Fest film, HOW this film had been made, one limited the debate to matters of content and historical fact: WHAT the film was about or was supposed to be about. The same old television setting, then, diverse OPINIONS and the historian Fest could be seen in the circle, smiling forbearingly. Whether Lubitsch emigrated in 1923 or 1932 ("change the two and the three around!"). Passed off as a bit of trivia, "a give-away." One didn't even get around to talking about Fritz Lang. Taking up their side, however, I would like to say a few words about this non-film (*Unfilm*), as someone who makes films in Germany. I speak for everyone who in recent years, after a long drought, has started once again to produce images and sounds in a country which has an unceasing distrust of images and sounds that tell its story, which for this reason has for thirty years greedily soaked up all foreign images, just as long as they have taken its mind off itself. I do not believe there is anywhere else where people have suffered such a loss of confidence in images of their own, their own stories and myths, as we have. We, the directors of the New Cinema, have felt this loss most keenly, in our own persons in the lack, the absence of a tradition of our own, as a fatherless generation, and in the spectators with their perplexed reaction and their initial hesitation. Only gradually has this defensive attitude, on the one hand, and this lack of self-confidence, on the other, broken down, and in a process that will perhaps take several years more, the feeling is arising here again that images and sounds do not have to be only something imported, but rather can be something concerned with this country that also comes out of this country.

There is good reason for this distrust. Because never before and in no other country have images and language been abused so unscrupulously as here, never before and nowhere else have they been debased so deeply as vehicles to transmit lies. And now a film comes along which, with an incomprehensible thoughtlessness, wants to sell exactly these images as the heart of the matter and as "documentary footage," SOLD, and in the process once again, ONCE AGAIN, several lies are transmitted. "Having come from Germany—after running out on Goebbels, who had offered me the leadership of the German film industry—I was very, very happy to get a chance to live here and become an American. In those days, I refused to speak a word of German. (I was terribly hurt—not personally—about what had happened to Germany, which I had liked very much . . . and about what had been done to the German language.)" (Fritz Lang in an interview, 1965.)

The "career" that Fest and Herrendoerfer wanted to investigate was above all possible because there was a total control of all film material, because all of the images of this man and his ideas were made in a clever manner, were chosen skillfully and used tactically. As a result of this thoroughgoing demagogic treatment of images, all of those people in Germany involved with the conscientious and equally competent production of film images left this country. Fest and Herrendoerfer, almost without exception, can therefore only cite the images of Nazi sympathizers in their "comprehensive documentation," the gaze of the complicitous, in a phrase, propaganda footage, the most despicable meters of celluloid ever shot here. They use all of this in an uncritical fashion, not bothering in the least to draw the necessary consequences for their presentation, not even stopping at making the claim at the start: "This film contains no dramatized footage," dressing things up even more (which moves the producer to proclaim proudly, "No expenses spared"), heightening and replicating the propaganda value in so doing and making themselves in the process once again accomplices after the fact.

To repeat myself: because of these images we see before us for two hours there was a hole in the film culture of this country which lasted thirty or forty years. Fest and Herrendoerfer, smiling the whole while, tear it open again, proud of their gruesome discoveries. As a dam for all the things that come gushing out they only have a commentary. Does this suffice to stop the flow of these images, which are anything but innocent and harmless?

Where is the author of this film if not in this commentary? Or, more precisely: in the VOICE that speaks this commentary. Because it is its USE which causes a reaction in the spectator. I watched the film a second time, armed with a cassette recorder. Free of the tensed-up agitation of the first viewing, I am this time more able to comprehend what is going on here. And that is the voice. It leads the spectator by the hand and seduces him in a way that is not much different from the other voice one constantly hears. In the same way it is less and less important what it says and more important how it says what it does. It too gradually pulls the spectator in and puts one to sleep. Which I only gradually am able to perceive: it in fact does not stand "soberly and objectively" above its object, but rather tries to illustrate it, to enter into it, to change its modalities: sometimes reverent, sometimes casual, sometimes mournful, then suddenly hopeful, occasionally amused, occasionally angered, also bold or mocking. . . .

Sometimes a subterranean tone of sympathy or comradeship resounds: "Everything Hitler hated: bickering between parties, communists, Jewry . . ." or even: "He couldn't stand the countenance of party comrades who had grown corpulent while in office." Or a sympathetic recognition: "He could neither be bought nor was he in league with big business." (I am only talking here about HOW things are being said.) The voice is at its worst when it says: "In the early part of '33 the first concentration camps are established. No one at the time wanted to see such images. There were reasons: embarrassment, fear, shyness."

The voice goes silent, one sees the front of a KZ (concentration camp) accompanied suddenly by a glockenspiel playing the melody, "Freut euch des Lebens" . . . (Can I believe my eyes and ears? I look around in the cinema: no one really seems to be getting what's happening here. What sorts of MEANS are there anyway in a film made "without emotion, with almost scientific reserve"? Irony, perhaps? Or pure mockery?), and then this infamous voice actually goes on to say in a RELIEVED tone, I swear it, in a relieved tone, I repeatedly listened to it on the cassette player, continues in a relieved tone: "What happened behind the barbed wire was obscured by popular amusements and all sorts of simple pleasures. The Germans were among themselves." The embarrassment, fear, and shyness mentioned several moments ago are here no longer a matter of content, but rather a form of speech, here the repression of a theme has become a method and has only joined together with arrogance. . . .

Given the way this film is organized, quite simply due to customary ways of seeing and the most simple patterns of identification, one has to be frankly relieved, for instance, that Hitler survives the assassination attempt of July 20. I too notice how I respond to this with a certain, so to speak, completely formal satisfaction as Hitler reports to a just arrived Mussolini about the great bit of luck he has just experienced. Given the way this film is organized the assassins remain exactly that: assassins. The narrative stance, emanating from Hitler, makes us see them as such. This film about the "career" comes at the cost of all those who suffered because of this career, who were murdered or forced out of the country. For this reason they only are marginal presences here.

This film is so fascinated by its object, by its importance, in which it takes part ("He gave truth to the phrase that history on occasion loves to take shape in a SINGLE person"), that this object again and again takes control of the film, becoming its secret narrator.

Here someone thought, arrogantly and with outrageous stupidity, having already tested the waters successfully with a best seller, that his language was superior to the language of demagogic images, thought that with a superior commentary he could put everything in its correct place, like a god from on high.

Blindly he stepped into all the traps that a much more clever god from on high set for him forty years ago. Without noticing it, he performs the same acts of homage as did all of the sorrowful masses from whose reproduced faces he cannot tear himself loose. At one point we hear the phrase: "He who had let out the cry knew the magic of simple images. He loved to come down to his people like a kind of god." I have a hard time understanding this except as a description of Fest's own method.

During the second viewing I am occasionally so overcome by nausea that I leave my cassette player running and go out. On the toilet wall in the cinema a couple of dumb phrases are scribbled on the wall, a swastika as well. Of recent vintage. I sit there numbed by it all. A bit of graffiti occurs to me, a stupid wordplay using "business write-off company" (*Abschreibungsgesellschaft*): that one could write off this film as a film about fascism. And right away then the next step: that this film was copied (*abgeschrieben*) from the fascists, every single image. Somewhat relieved I go back into the cinema, just in time to change the cassette.

At one point toward the start the authors seemed to have realized something. "Scores of cameramen constantly surrounded him. Their photographs stylized him into a sort of monument." But this film stylizes every bit as firmly (*fest*). "As a monument, that's how he wanted to go down in history." What is this film if not a monument?

I think I am in my own way too only advertising the film. NOT to see the film is perhaps the only recommendation one can make. Or, if one wants to see it *partout* with one's eyes and above all: to hear it with one's own ears, then only as a testament of the kind of fascination which this film succumbs to and reflects.

Wait for Theo[dor] Kotulla's film, *Aus einem deutschen Leben* (*Death Is My Trade*), which has more to say about this fascination by refusing to share it. I hope this film will soon come to the cinemas as a sort of correction. But even if there were many other sensible films like this: one does not so easily make up for the set-back which the film by Fest and Herrendoerfer has brought to cinema in Germany.

I am ashamed of the decision of the FBW, which deemed this film PARTICULARLY NOTEWORTHY and allowed it to be played on holidays and for youths twelve years and older. On the other hand, films that are so peaceful, careful, and humane as Wolfgang Berndt [and Doris Dörrie]'s *Ob's stürmt oder schneit* (*Whether It Storms or Snows*) are denied such a predicate for purely formal reasons and there are others which are forbidden to youths under eighteen (*Im Lauf der Zeit/Kings of the Road*).

These, too, are reasons to emigrate, Rainer Werner.

(*I'm only bleeding.*)

Translated and abridged by Eric Rentschler

Helke Sander

Born in Germany in 1937, Helke Sander lived in Finland in the early 1960s. She completed her film studies in 1969 at Berlin's Film and Television Academy (Deutsche Film und Fernsehakademie Berlin), *where she had been briefly banned from attending, after she and other students occupied the building as part of a protest. In 1974, Sander founded* Frauen und Film (Women and Film), *Europe's first feminist film journal, which is still in publication. In 1977 she directed her first feature film,* The All-around Reduced Personality—REDUPERS (Die allseitig reduzierte Persönlichkeit—Redupers), *which was a critical success. She has continued making films and is currently a professor at the* Hochschule für bildende Künste *(Academy for the Creative Arts) in Hamburg.*

Feminism and Film (1977)

> *"i accept chaos. i am not sure it accepts me."*
> —*From a paper given in Graz, Austria in November 1977, on the occasion of the annual fall literature and theater festival there—the so-called "Steirischer Herbst"—on the topic, "Is There and What Is Feminine Imagery?"*

After thinking about it for a long time, I have come to doubt whether this question makes any sense. But it is so frequently posed, along with its variations about the forms of feminine aesthetics and feminine creativity, that it has come to belong to the repertory of many festivals, seminars, and symposia; and the very peculiar conclusions arrived at at these conferences have also begun to work their way into professional terminology, where they tend to confuse rather than clarify concepts as well as to distract attention away from other more pressing questions.

In posing the question, people often make no distinction between *feminine* and *feminist* imagery; they use the words interchangeably, even though one word is a biological and psychological term and the other a political one.

As for feminism, the most contradictory and utterly irreconcilable definitions of the term are represented among women's groups that call themselves feminist, whose only common denominator is that they see all women oppressed by patriarchal power structures. But in defining causes, political consequences, and relations to other theories about society, opinions diverge so widely that thus far we have not been able to use an exact terminology or refer to a single predominating position which might have set definitions of these terms.

And there has not yet been a feminist art manifesto of the sort that either directly or indirectly political movements bring about, as for example the manifesto of Russian artists shortly after the revolution or of the many European artist groups in the twenties.

But perhaps the initial question also implies that through the feminist movement, certain as yet unrealized feminine qualities—that is, characteristics which have been socially smothered in men, such as sensitivity, fantasy—can be expressed with confidence first in art works by women.

The question about feminine imagery cannot even begin to be answered due to the lack of film-producing women, and it would break all rules of statistics to force a deduction about aesthetic similarities from the one hundred films women have produced at different times, in different cultures and countries, about the most varied topics and most diverse genres. Such an effort might be worthwhile if there were anything approaching equal participation of the sexes in the arts, but I doubt then if this would still interest us.

In addition, we should consider that until very recently, femininity was always defined by others, and that only now have women begun to comprehend themselves as social subjects and to throw off alien interpretations of their nature and being. The organized expression of these efforts is the women's movement, which from all sides and with dissimilar results and battles is feeling out the question of what women want, more than the question of what women are.

Women have just begun to *dare* to see themselves and others, society, with their own eyes; to compare alien opinions and theories to their own experiences; to formulate first concepts with the help of which we can begin to comprehend the nature of past feminine oppression, today's social contradictions, and our expectations for a different human future.

And in every woman's behavior toward herself and in others' toward women—in laws, traditions, and work regulations—nowadays we always find both images: woman as object and as subject; therefore both—the traditional and conditioned, and the politically new—will be present in work by women, including that of contemporary women filmmakers. It is yet to be seen whether women, when first given a chance to do whatever they want, will explode in never-before-seen forms, contents, and techniques—and it will then result from entirely different social conditions.

The visual arts at least tend to answer this question about feminine imagery with "yes." Women's preferences for certain genres, materials, and forms also seem to express particularly feminine aesthetic concepts; something like this also floats around in the women's movement, though it has been adequately recognized in the meantime that women have usually painted still lifes and portraits because they were *forbidden* to make studies of nudes, to say nothing of the barriers to sculpture.

This approach in film aesthetics is by its very nature senseless because we are dealing with standardized materials and equipment. But that does not prevent similar theses from being proposed in the area of film, claiming that women prefer, out of feminist conviction, video, documentary film, and semiprofessional work in groups with other women. Every such argument has economic causes but this is totally ignored. If one wants to work with film, video becomes a cheaper compromise, documentary films are usually cheaper than features; and the fact that some women filmmakers call on their women friends to help on sound, directing, and in other capacities stems from pure need.

So if for all the above-mentioned reasons we cannot speak of feminine imagery, and the women who film or paint, etc., interest themselves less in the question of whether their products are feminine, but rather in whether their products are authentic, then the penetration of the women's movement into the arts has made it possible for the first time, systematically, to recognize patriarchal ideologies in art works, that is to say, mostly male art works. The *absence* of certain sexist stereotypes which we could find throughout film history in films by women does not yet constitute a feminine imagery, but rather at the very most leads to attention to sensitivity for image-predominant ideologies.

Until now, with a few exceptions during the silent film era, film has been purely a male domain; and as such a widely distributed and immediate means of communication, it has also shaped women's images of themselves, their roles, their ideals, and standards of beauty. Women in film were for a long time the artistic creations of those who made the images.

We can perhaps measure the meaning of this indoctrination through false images if we consider that only about two percent of the population reads literature, and literary production has always been less standardized than film production; but nearly everyone shares in film culture through movies and today through television. Although the participation of women working in these media has grown in recent years, women still make up just a fraction of the whole and are almost never involved in decision making.

The women's movement in the arts now reveals the masculinity mania in art and is freeing the image of women from a "natural feminine state" and from an assumed "natural" relation to men visually as well. A very simple example of this is that in film even more than in reality women are expected to be shorter than men; for example, no serious romances could ever occur between partners of the same height, much less between tall women and short men. If this happens, it is always only comical and means that the *man* in such a relationship is not to be taken seriously. It is new that such a relationship today can be treated with irony, as in that TV news report showing a visit to Mao by Kissinger with his wife Nancy—a head taller than Henry; Mao, giggling, pointed repeatedly at Mrs. Kissinger while looking at Kissinger, as if Mao were bringing a good joke into politics. The newscaster announced this item with a slight smile.

In recent years, many Hollywood actresses have complained that scripts are no longer being written in which women appear. We at *Frauen und Film* have suggested that this could be perhaps unconsciously a correct and honest reaction to the women's movement. If one has nothing to say, one should remain silent; it is only in keeping with principles that women's roles get eliminated altogether.

I hope I have made clear thus far that the denial of female imagery does not mean that art does not vary according to sex, any less than it varies according to class, as socialist theory has analyzed. I do not mean by this that these aspects and others—national characteristics, for example—add up to determine a work of art, but rather that they enter into the formal experience that only an artwork makes accessible.

But just as a progressive social theory has led to a dogmatic aesthetics, that is, the equation of "social realism" with a thesis about knowledge (about how we experience the forms of knowledge), feminism has also had the tendency to make certain aesthetic categories a measure of the aesthetic experience. Thus spontaneity, in women not so much oppressed but rather socially patronized, has been sharply ideologized, and the form into which this spontaneity flows has been summarily declared to be art. This phenomenon is like the fact that science's being antipathetic to women has led to women's groups showing an antipathy to theory.

In a turnabout, social deficits are simply idealized and declared artistic victories. From such tendencies within the women's movement itself, then, definitions can be arrived at which always see women and their works only partially and not in terms of our whole living condition.

But underlying those sometimes so emphatically expressed women's demands for collectivity and spontaneity is also the wish to abolish the dichotomy which makes some responsible for the production of goods and the others for the arts. At the base lies the wish that it be the fundamental right of every person to work out experiences in every direction. In the realization of this demand, with all the catastrophes and horrors it brings, lies a piece of utopia; there is only rarely, very rarely, a lucky case when the joint work of nonprofessionals results in outstanding productions.

I have already implied that women today find themselves in a situation perhaps best compared to that of Kaspar Hauser or the Wild Child. We must first learn to see with our own eyes and not through the mediation of others. And when we have just first begun to talk, we still stutter and write no poetry. This leads feminist artists to conflicts for which there are no solutions and which affect them qualitatively totally differently than male artists.

The women's movement is striving to examine our fragmented history from the point of view of women's interests. So far there has been virtually no division of labor at this, only gargantuan efforts to gather individual insights piece by piece. The questions touch everyone existentially. The forms of confronting issues require again and again that we abandon our own line of work and choose between things of immediate importance to the movement and the requirements of our own work, which is in many ways, however, also based on the entire movement's insights. We are not only building a house, but simultaneously gathering and assembling the materials for it ourselves.

Women artists have worked not only on art but on the movement's pressing problems, always in the hope of soon making their presence there rather superfluous in order to be able to concentrate again fully on developing their own talents. Almost all the women's movements' projects with which we have meanwhile become acquainted are unpaid and have arisen from this inner contradiction, such as the first women's film festival organized by women filmmakers to familiarize themselves with otherwise inaccessible knowledge; the art exhibitions; the journal *Frauen und Film*, for work on which even today no one makes a penny.

Many film projects have also arisen in order to contribute to social campaigns, for example around Paragraph 218, contraceptives, etc., all born of the desire to support the women's movement in such a way as to have an immediate effect. But this often distracts from women artists' own projects, which are more complicated and stand in a much less direct relation to the movements. The pressure of making many such works without financial support, and often with untrained people, quickly leads to unbearable conflicts with the women filmmakers' own standards of excellence; and such films are frequently used in an official context against the filmmakers when they are applying for money.

Furthermore, the art and film market will scarcely allow even a temporary absence. Artists must rigorously pursue their own interests or else be lost. It means being torn back and forth between the women's movement and its demands and its advances on the one hand, and the conditions of artistic work on the other. This contradiction leads to nearly insoluble internal and external problems, which necessarily become apparent in our work. Besides, the competition in the free-lance world is murderous. This system again turns women filmmakers themselves into competitors, because in comparison to their male colleagues they receive fewer commissions to begin with and do not yet have a lobby of any sort.

Beyond this, many of the qualities which are encouraged in and through the women's movement, such as eliminating hierarchical behavior and irrational authority, and recognizing and paying attention to underrated abilities, are in actual work situations likely to result in catastrophe. Filmmaking conditions are so intertwined with the laws of the market that humane behavior at work is often interpreted as feminine weakness. Consider too that normal professional work teams derive from labor traditions which fully accept capitalist values.

In short, wherever women land, within a very short time there is nothing but confusion, shock, excitement.

If we also consider that many women, in keeping with their principles, propose to make films on subjects which have arisen from a movement which the ruling powers ignore or fight, then we can get a pretty good idea of what happens before productions, that is, where decisions about financial means are made. Examples of this are almost all of the works which came out of the campaigns against Paragraph 218. Because the political demands of the women's movement could not, in fact, really be theoretically grounded with the public media, this resulted in the semiprofessional works which I have already mentioned, often formally quite lacking. These works born of necessity have led, as I said, in definitions about feminist film to the sort of conclusion that feminist film is presumably "primarily interested in the documentary and mistrusts the power of fantasy."

Still other aesthetic points of friction have arisen in these confrontations. Quite materialistically and simply, the women's movement has begun with itself, with the female body, thereby exposing injustices and alien definitions. Now in many of these films, nude bodies and sexual organs play a role, these being filmed not to awaken erotic feelings in men nor to be sexually neutral or medically functional, but rather to picture the female body so as to lead women into the blank regions of unexplored subjectivity.

Because a female sex organ is immediately associated with pornography and thus banned from all public media, we can imagine the collisions between themes of this kind with public broadcasting stations, for the stations follow general guidelines which clearly forbid showing anything which violates customary moral feeling or which in principle challenges marriage and family. This challenge, however, forms a basis of the entire women's movement. On the international scale, this chapter of women seeing their bodies with their own eyes is far from having been written to the end; and it will become explosive anew when contributed to by our Arab sisters, who must struggle to win not only the filmic right to their own bellies but also even the right to their own unveiled faces. Not long ago a newspaper article mentioned that the Turkish censor had forbidden showing love scenes or women in bathing suits in films.

When we perceive our own interests, we do not express that only in tearing down ruling ideologies, but really concretely in confrontations at the work place, now among women filmmakers in the arts industry. To put it in other terms: women's most authentic act today—in all areas including the arts—consists not in standardizing and harmonizing the means, but rather in destroying them. Where women are true, they break things.

With visual material, this "breakage" has been the most progressive in analyses and the most diffuse in practice. It often makes productions disjointed and inconsistent, especially with women artists who have just begun to work, those not trained in and then building on an art tradition before joining the women's movement and then consciously distancing themselves formally from this tradition.

Of course, we also should not forget that there are women filmmakers and artists who because of personal distance from the women's movement remain altogether untouched by these problems and can for this reason often work much more effectively; unburdened by politics, they can get commissions and sit on certainty instead of on chaos. In contrast, feminist artists say with Bob Dylan: i accept chaos. i am not sure whether it accepts me.

Translated by Ramona Curry

Konrad Wolf

The autobiographical film I was 19 *(Ich war 19, 1967) chronicles the experiences of Konrad Wolf (1925–82) as a soldier in the Red Army that conquered Nazi Germany, the son of a leftist German Jewish family that had gone into exile in Moscow in 1933. After the war, he returned to Germany and took part in founding DEFA (Deutsche Film Aktiengesellschaft), the East German state film company. After completing his education in film direction in Moscow, Wolf went on to become one of the most important filmmakers of the German Democratic Republic, directing such films as* Stars *(1957),* Divided Heaven *(1964),* Mama, I'm Alive *(Mama ich lebe, 1976), and* Solo Sunny *(1979).*

On the Possibilities of Socialist Film Art: Reactions to *Mama, I'm Alive* (1977)

First, a short reply about passions. Passion has something to do with suffering: suffering for and with people, from time to time also suffering for and with the things we do.

Concerning the review's call for more passion in the feature film: I do not think that more passion can be achieved by people who work on feature films making their way back to the classrooms of their documentary film colleagues, despite the fact that various classroom desks have recently been offered to those of us in feature film. No passion can be achieved by having the amazed public watch tough guys sobbing on the movie screen or TV screen, for the most that one achieves by this is not the ardently desired "deep movie screen," but rather a "dripping movie screen."

Open laughing or crying in a film scene has rarely produced an adequate effect in the viewer. Usually, he is embarrassingly irritated. Has anyone seen Chaplin laughing? The hero Shukshin in *Kalina Krasnaya* and Paula in *Legend* made millions of people laugh and cry and led them to passionate pro and contra. Why? Because something extraordinary happened in normal, understandable life circumstances, because it has to do with being a person and becoming a person, where the most comical things crash up against the most tragic; because, under the conditions of our socialist reality, it has to do with nothing more and nothing less than life and death in both films. This is the greatest passion having an effect on the audience, and it remains so.

Now to a different topic. Matters of the day as seen in the example of our viewers' contentious opinions: an attempt to create a montage from letters, from the opinions of those for whom we make films and who, while not present here in the conference hall— are yet constantly in this hall.

The first letter from Neubrandenburg: "I was a Soviet prisoner of war for two and a half years and had an anti-fascist education, albeit a modest one. So I can tell what was dealt with honestly in your film. This honesty moved me most deeply. The film gets under your skin, that's simple and clear and right. I sat still during the showing and said to myself, 'That someone comes and can show how your heart felt back then, how cheerfulness and sadness, pain and joy, mental breakdown and understanding, life and death can lie so closely together, that is beautiful, that is moving.' The film is simple and great at the same time. . . ."

The second letter from Berlin: "About myself: I've been a member of the KPD [German Communist Party] and the SED [Socialist Unity Party] since 1931. In the Nazi period, I was in prison for nine years, in the concentration camp at Auschwitz, and I was liberated by the Red Army on April 22, 1945.

"I emphasize that I'm commenting about the film today only in a purely personal way. Your name was so far a guarantee of quality for me, and your films excited me. But I don't understand your new film *Mama, I'm Alive*. What do you want? What do we as a party and state want to proclaim and achieve? Do you want to show the complexity in the development of the young German soldiers in Soviet POW camps, how they became politically conscious people? Do you want to show that there were also weaknesses among members of the Soviet army? But what's the point of the film? Is it supposed to rescue the honor of the soldiers of the fascist army (*Wehrmacht*) who ended up in Soviet captivity?

"I do not understand this and unfortunately, unfortunately the opinion of many comrades was the same. Almost all of them were outraged about this, your new film. Unfortunately, I'll probably be the only one who writes to you so candidly, although I did not hear one positive opinion from the 200 comrades and FDJ [Free German Youth] functionaries who saw the film. The young functionaries were much harder still in their opinions.

"Well, good. Your film *Mama, I'm Alive*, will be officially premiered on February 24, there will be excellent reports about it, everything's great, then the film, after certainly not going over well with the public for very long, will gradually disappear or will be shown to special collectives at closed screenings. Is this what we wanted to achieve, is it all worth the effort? Surely, you're shaking your head as you read these lines and are saying, 'Oh, well, what does this comrade understand about our profession, he's just an old sectarian.'

"In the hope of soon seeing better works from you that are more useful for our cause, and wishing you success in this, I leave you with a socialist greeting. . . ."

Third letter from a student from Leipzig: "I'd like to share with you an experience that I recently had in Leipzig. Place: 'Friendship Film Theater.' Your film *Mama, I'm Alive* was presented. The movie theater holds about four hundred people. Number of people actually present: twenty-seven. This was the count on Sunday, March 6, the third day of the film's run, eight o'clock in the evening, i.e., at a time when the movie theater is almost sold out for mediocre films.

"I want to say what I think about this. There have been films about war for thirty years and longer. Our people are sick of them, they don't want them anymore, they're all the same, there's no difference between them and people are in fact deadened to such messages today.

"We've dealt wrongly with this important subject and, over the course of decades, have incapacitated the majority of people through collective voluntarism (the screenings are full of school classes and such on workdays) and television programs. Hardly anybody turns to this complex of problems of his own volition.

"A film, at the height of our time and under the conditions of our qualitatively higher level of society, must, if it is not to cause more harm than good, show the human in a higher quality as an active human acting with conscience, self-consciousness, individuality and love of mankind; it must finally credibly represent and reconstruct our condition with artistic mastery.

"I would like to thank you and your co-workers for your having done just this. With satisfaction, I did without the typically wooden and peppy DEFA dialogue and was delighted with the real, flesh-and-blood, believable characters. It now finally seems that things are on the upswing with GDR filmmaking. . . .

"I have understood your film as an important step on this path."

Fourth letter from Stollberg: "We, the majority of our colleagues from the EOS [Extended Upper School], thank you most of all for the many new questions and for the very sensitive and humane manner in which you treat problems that should move us all more than is generally the case.

"Unfortunately, a film such as this one (and this is also true for *Nackter Mann auf dem Spielplatz* [*Naked Man on the Playing Field*]) does not have it easy in view of the widespread leveling of many people's habits of reception as a result of the mass acceptance of ready-made films.

"Of course, there are some questions, here and there a contradiction, among the teachers of our school as well. But that is altogether desirable.

"What repeatedly moves me personally is the following problem: What do we have to do so that the senses of our young people become more awake, more sensitive?

"What do we have to do so that they will be less lethargic of mind and in their feelings, so that they become more active?

"Finally, how can we better develop an active relationship with art? The further, systematic development of their capacity for aesthetic sensitivity seems to me to be of crucial importance for real, genuine advances in this area. In any event, we somehow are running the danger, I believe, of a certain divide becoming not less, but greater, as is already appearing now between accustomed habits of reception oriented toward superficial, one-dimensional artistic progress. For us German teachers, but also for our colleagues the music and art teachers, it will depend, in my opinion, on our better attempting to allow people to experience art on the basis of the works currently in the curriculum.

"In so doing, we must still do much in order to sharpen our eye for artistic creation, first among ourselves and then among our pupils. We are often afraid of dwelling on a detail and of showing in what way something significant or even something entirely commonplace or entirely human is shaped. Somehow, we were and still are too much focused on the one-dimensionally ideological and still do not grant hushed tones enough room. Dieter Wolf *(Sunday* 15/ 77) ultimately states a bitter truth with his harsh judgment that stories are told so that they do not become lost . . . and the school system has hardly internalized aesthetic needs in this regard."

Those were four letters.

In the same school in Stollberg, tenth and eleventh grade pupils were confronted with two questions.

I would like to quote as briefly as possible one, at most two sentences from each.

Concerning the film: You have to think too much about questions that remain open, but you have your head full with the next essay examination topic. / You experience the events of war from a totally different perspective. / When the film was suddenly over, we were totally shocked. / It has to do with humanity despite the war. A film about the war but not a war film. / I can't say that I enjoyed the film, but it was remarkable. It didn't provide a happy ending, it shows how it really was in war. It causes you to reflect. / I was already prepared for the worst and then, when I left the movie theater, was relieved. It wasn't so pre-planned. / I rooted for the Red Army's struggle for liberation and detested the cruelties of the fascists, although they weren't shown directly. / The transformation of half of Germany was embodied in the transformation of the four soldiers.

Concerning what is desired in a film: Show problems of today's everyday life, especially critical problems, like what is really going on in workplaces, and do not gloss over anything.

Make a film about today, just as true to reality and as honest as *Mama, I'm Alive.* / Make films about contemporary times /. . . .

I would advise Konrad Wolf to make films about the present this realistically.

Films that clearly characterize and do not gloss over the conditions in our state. /

About contradictions of socialists organization, for example, black market trade, bribery money and disharmony in planning. /

About problems of the working class, but how they really are. Is that possible? /

About young people, especially their problems and happiness. /

About our class that has a test coming up soon and has to rack its brain over your film. What each person does individually with his free time and how people as a whole think about love. /

A film about people's life and thought in the GDR and the Soviet Union now, not in the war. /

A film about love that lasted through the war and yet is shattered. /

About socialist personalities and imperialistic ideology. /

About contemporary life, about our problems, but real ones! A film where nature and man are in harmony. / Exciting to the last minute and without humor getting short shrift. / The obstacles that our parents had to deal with in order to create our homeland for us. /

In films, problems should be treated that are of general relevance in our society; most of all, they should correspond to reality. /

Next proposal, a complete aesthetic program: exciting, gripping, dramatic, adventurous, realistic (if possible), show contradictions clearly. / A hero must endure many problems and heavy demands should be made of him. The just person should prevail in a film. / I like a film in which the main heroes overpower the negative characters in an unusual way. / I'd like to see a film where real problems of young people my age are portrayed without adornment. These problems shouldn't be treated so seriously, nor only comically, though. A film should cause me to reflect; that's why no pat solution should be shown and all conflicts shouldn't be resolved. /

A real love film by Konrad Wolf, since he understands people so well. /

There would actually be nothing to add to that.

Perhaps only the following: who is the viewer, our contemporary? Certainly not a ghost holding a club behind his back. Our contemporary, our viewer is our ally.

The viewers' opinions briefly quoted here are also a slice of reality, a slice of the aesthetics of today. In their contradictoriness and indispensable desire to behave contentiously, they express one of the most excellent characteristics and possibilities of our socialist film art in a society struggling for socialism. The wide-scale effect of film art surely has to do with its contentiousness and with new, even uncomfortable views of things past and present.

A further experience: Never before have I at the same time sensed unity, reciprocity, and dialectical contradiction between the shaping of the past and the present so happily and painfully as in these weeks when *Mama, I'm Alive*, has come to the screen. Many viewers were really favorably impressed despite some prejudices, reservations and skepticism. Many also made no secret of their disinterest and their rejection. One demand, though, stated adamantly and often aggressively especially by young people, really jumped at me: we reject even an ever so convincing, i.e., truthful film about the past if the present is not just as obliged to the truth and is not masterfully depicted with a love for humanity. Or words addressed directly to me: "You are unbelievable to me, even though you tell the truth about the war, if you do not portray our problems, our worries and our conflicts just as convincingly. Are you not able to do it or are you not allowed to do it?"

And finally: The mental potential of the viewers, their growing socio-political maturity, and their alert mind are for me no longer a question. They want to be challenged. We should be challenged (and subsidized less). Challenged to place ourselves before the dialectic of the present unreservedly and without half-hearted, debasing anxieties. The viewers are considerably farther along in their expectations, indeed in their demands than we are with our films about the present.

And if there is a censor—and he does exist—then it is these people, this class of workers fighting for its ideals. And perhaps there is yet another censor, as Eisenstein once put it, namely, the party document that is not registered with local authorities and to which political independents also feel duty-bound: the party document that lies hidden in the deepest pocket near one's heart: you must look straight into its eyes and you cannot faint-heartedly shirk your responsibility to it, that is, to your conscience and knowledge and to your political and moral responsibility.

I feel obliged to these two types of "censor." Without them, I will be able neither to live nor to work, since I know no alternative existence without the struggle of the class which I have to thank for my life in the narrowest and widest sense, and without the struggle of the class of workers who are producing new material and never-before existing intellectual and humanistic values.

And the most important thing: Let us finally stop endlessly talking only about films that do not yet exist. Let us make these films!

Translated by Lance W. Garmer

Rainer Werner Fassbinder

Of the most famous film directors of the New German Cinema—Alexander Kluge, Volker Schlöndorff, Werner Herzog, Wim Wenders, Margarethe von Trotta, Helke Sander, Ulrike Ottinger, among others—Rainer Werner Fassbinder (1945–82) was easily the most prolific, making over forty feature films between 1969 and his untimely death at age thirty-seven in 1982. He began his career in the experimental theater, and his early films owe a lot to the influence of Jean-Luc Godard and the American film noir. In the early 1970s, he became familiar with the American films of German émigré director Douglas Sirk (Detlef Sierck); Fassbinder then began to combine the "subversive" use of melodrama he found in Sirk with a Brechtian aesthetic of defamiliarization. In the late 1970s, he began his trilogy of films on the history of the Federal Republic of Germany (West Germany), beginning with The Marriage of Maria Braun *(1979), probably his biggest commercial success, followed by* Lola *and* Veronika Voss *in 1981. In 1980, he completed his fifteen-hour-long television adaptation of Alfred Döblin's* Berlin Alexanderplatz.

From The Third Generation (1978)

1. The German Feature Film and Reality

In contrast to Italy, where people like Francesco Rosi, Damiano Damiani, and others are so close to the reality of their country that their films actually intervene in this reality, so to speak, even, and indeed precisely, under the unambiguously commercial demands of a film industry; in contrast to America, where again and again films are made that force their way into the chronicle of current events with critical commentary, and here too without sacrificing the commercial aspects of an industry that in fact is commercial—how should it be otherwise; in contrast to France, Spain, even Switzerland, where Jonas will be twenty-five in the year 2000; in contrast to almost all the Western democracies, there seems to be a mysterious common interest on the part of various groups in the Federal Republic of Germany in making sure that this kind of film does not even get made in the first place.

For years this interest in preventing any German films from being made that might deal with German reality was guarded by nothing more than the assertion that German audiences were not interested in "that sort of film," an assertion that was simply believed and accepted by German producers, who in any case were confused and timid. Reality, everyone seemed to agree, was the province of television, which in turn is fortunately a public institution and as such committed to a balanced approach to reality—or is it a balancing act, an undiscriminatingly pluralistic approach, in which anything and everything has legal rights, especially the legal system?

Lest I be misunderstood, I should add that I do know of course that critical films in the Federal Republic—with whatever limitations; that varies from network to network—were possible only on television, or at least in collaboration with television. But I also know the context in which this criticism reaches the viewer and that it—the criticism—because of the specific composition of television's evening programming (how sad it should make us) almost at the moment it is formulated by Peter Alexander or Anneliese Rothenberger—I know, it can't get much worse, but isn't that nevertheless the way it is on the whole—is eliminated on the one hand (this sentence is all right, believe me, grammatically, I mean, right?) and that on the other hand more directors are in danger of succumbing to an aesthetic specific to television, which really exists, or, to put it differently, people who want to make movies for the cinema usually don't take the genre of television, which provides their bread and butter, quite seriously. Thus many, many people develop sloppy thinking habits, and this sloppiness surely has an effect on feature films these same directors may make later on, something that the audience at least senses, and that in the end can only prove harmful to the cinema.

Certainly this issue is far more complex in its entirety than what I have sketched here, you know what I mean? But until the very recent past it seemed fairly clear that German reality could put in an appearance in German films at most in more or less successful translations into the nineteenth century or the twenties, if at all. The most friendly reception was reserved for the kind of film that very skillfully avoided the risk that the viewer might be reminded of his own reality. (This sentence contains more truth than you would at first suspect. Read it again, preferably out loud, before the thought that I am being unfair has a chance to take root in your mind.)

At this point I could easily make the transition to a concrete discussion of the theme of my film *The Third Generation*, since the refusal by the media as well, and perhaps precisely by them, to deal with reality is to my mind one of the reasons why this very reality, this specifically West German reality, has not succeeded in conveying to the individual citizen what I consider the basis of democratic ideas in such a way that a real democracy could have established itself, one that was not merely democratic in name and in which the phenomenon of now almost incomprehensible violence in response to violence and still more violence could not have sprung up. But I won't get to this with my characteristic simplicity until somewhat later.

First I would like to formulate my hope, as well as I can, that these missed opportunities or omissions or desired and rewarded manifestations of cowardice will soon be more and more a thing of the past, that a situation may come about for the German film that will be more liberated, gratifying, and fruitful than one could imagine. I think, and please forgive me if I am wrong, that that last sentence slipped a tiny bit into cynicism, but just a tiny, tiny bit, right? Or is it possible that from the succès d'estime (and from the commercial point of view the bottom line was very satisfactory, unless the rumors are even less accurate this time than usual) of the films *The Second Awakening of Christa Klages* by my colleague von Trotta and *Germany in Autumn*, a film, by the way, which for minutes at a time strikes me as more terrible than terrible, something I expressed loud and clear from the beginning, which is documented, but still a film about which I decided, with a great Parsifalesque naïveté all my own, that is wasn't the obscene moments that made this film into a film that was interesting and important to many people (and for those who may not know it, I don't find it obscene that I play with my dick in front of the camera, but rather I find it obscene when people masturbate who would like to keep the existence of their dick a secret from themselves, but also don't have enough of a grip on their brain so that they could grab it and at least jerk off with it. It's surprising, and what an accomplishment, to see how much people have masturbated with their mouths, which, just between us sisters of the revolution, actually doesn't work, with the mouth, isn't that so, with the mouth. . . ?) I should have drawn a false conclusion? (This sentence is right, too, in some way, at least grammatically!) A conclusion, furthermore, which is also supported by the great commercial success of the picture *The Lost Honor of Katharina Blum*—yes, yes, self-liberation is also allowed to demand sacrifices, even intellectual ones, "God grant" that this may not be one of the unforgivable ones, one of those that are punished with black-and-blue marks on the soul.

So a commercial success for three films that confront the reality of the Federal Republic of Germany in three entirely different ways, here and now, a success, finally, that allows me to draw the conclusion that it seems to have become possible even here to pose concrete political questions using the medium of film, even and precisely cinematic film, and that the potential of the audience interested in film is large enough so that these three films may well be followed by other films, and that, in contrast to earlier, these films have a chance to reach the public. Just one thing seems very important to me, that one keep one's eye on the ball, so to speak, so that such films continue to be made on a broad basis and those who oppose making the cinema a center of communication not be allowed to use the simple absence of such films as a pretext for turning the tables and arguing that this absence automatically proves that the viewers are not interested.

This is one of the reasons for my determination to keep on making a film from time to time that is directly concerned with current political problems. I believe one can make such films more and more attractive, by means of casting and technique, and I believe that there are plenty of unambiguous moral justifications for this "speculation." If one thinks of the Italian cinema, for instance, time and again they use much-loved stars, like Franco Nero in Belocchio's films, Gian-Maria Volonté in Damiano Damiani's, or Rod Steiger in Francesco Rosi's, or, or, or . . . ; this list could be prolonged indefinitely, and in *All the President's Men* it was Robert Redford and Dustin Hoffman who gave the screen treatment of the

Watergate case not only their acting ability but also their glamour. I think I needn't say more on the potential question of why I want to make *The Third Generation*, a film concerned with a problem, that of terrorism and terrorists today, more or less current at the time the film is being made, a problem with which the inhabitants of this country and those who represent this state have not yet come to terms in any way, either practically or even just intellectually = ideologically.

2. A Film—a Title

The Third Generation could mean: (1) The German bourgeoisie from 1848 to 1933; (2) Our grandfathers, and how they experienced the Third Reich and how they remember it; (3) Our fathers, who had an opportunity after the war to set up a state that could have been more humane and free than any had ever been before, and what became of that opportunity in the end.

But *The Third Generation* could also mean the present generation of terrorists, if you accept the idea that there was a first and a second generation before them. The first generation was made up of those who were motivated by idealism, which combined with excessive sensitivity and almost pathological despair at their own helplessness vis-à-vis the system and its representatives to drive them almost "insane."

The second generation was made up of those who, understanding the motives of the first, generally defended its representatives, often as "genuine" proponents of justice; but this defense was slandered for so long and so intensely as fundamentally criminal that this generation's move into actual criminality and thereby into the underground occurred more ex post facto than in fact.

Whereas each individual citizen is somehow capable of mustering something like understanding for the actions and motives of the first and second generation of terrorists—or not, as the case may be—it is more than difficult to understand the motives of the third generation, indeed, perhaps it is impossible from the point of view of the two preceding generations; for the third generation of terrorists has, it seems to me, less in common with its predecessors than with this society and the violence it perpetrates, to whoever's benefit.

I am convinced they don't know what they are doing, and what they are doing derives its meaning from nothing more than the activity itself, from the apparently exciting danger, from petty adventures within this system, which admittedly is administered ever more perfectly and therefore alarmingly. Action undertaken in danger, but without any sense of perspective, adventures experienced in a sort of intoxication for their own sake—these are the things that motivate the "third generation." Nonetheless, the fact that this phenomenon exists exclusively in this country does of course have to do with this country, in fact has an alarming amount to do with this country, with its mistakes, its omissions, with the democracy it received as a gift, which one should not look in the mouth, the same as a gift horse, a democracy whose basic values are being allowed to degenerate more and more into taboos, a democracy that the state blindly defends against its citizens, and which besides—this is obvious—is in turn in blind agreement with this same citizen, who is so unenlightened (looking over the various curricula of all the various schools can really teach one what fear is all about) that he is incapable of noticing that this construct around him, this state, is becoming a tiny bit more totalitarian from day to day. And next time, friends, it won't last just a childish thousand years; the next time has already begun, secretly, softly and quietly, and the next time will be really long.

And, to come back to this, what a gift of God must this state see in a kind of terrorism that springs up without motivation and poses so little risk, even in the negative sense of being comprehensible. And in fact, if these terrorists didn't exist, the state at its present stage of development would have to invent them. And maybe it even did? Why not? What, for instance, was that business with the Gleiwitz transmitter, and how did the first Molotov cocktail get into the KI,[1] and the Reichstag, which burned down so photogenically—that's a story, too, and somebody in Prague indubitably requested help from Moscow, fortunately, but why? And what luck that even without having been summoned the Russians already had their troops well on their way to Czechoslovakia.

By the bye, so people can more readily form a picture of what it is like, *The Third Generation* is not a so-called political film; to me, every film is ultimately political. But I wanted to mention some examples of the films I feel indebted to for *The Third Generation*, and they would be *A Touch of Evil* by Orson Welles, *Flamingo Road* by Michael Curtiz, or *Conversation Piece* by Luchino Visconti.

---

[1] KI is short for Kommune I, the first radical commune in West Berlin in the 1960s. (Editor's note)

In this sense I also looked for actors who hadn't been overexposed by television but nevertheless had something like glamour. As far as the title goes, I'm open to persuasion, though *The Third Generation* seems attractive to me. It's accurate, besides, but be my guest; the film industry has its own laws, of course. Other suggestions for a title might be: "Grandchildren of Evil," Hangmen of Hope," "Slaves of Order and Tranquility," as well as "The Spreading Cancer—That's the Whole Thing." But there'll be time to chat about all this, though not to excess, face to face.

Translated by Krishna Winston

The Manifesto of Women
Film Workers (1979)

Not one woman had signed the Oberhausen Manifesto in 1962, and well into the 1970s the "New German Cinema" was almost entirely dominated by men. By the late 1970s, however, a number of women filmmakers—Helke Sander, Margarethe von Trotta, Ulrike Ottinger, Jutta Brückner, and Helma Sanders-Brahms, for example—had made films that had won critical acclaim. There was a new emphasis on gender in these films, and there were many connections between the filmmakers and the West German women's movement. In 1979, women film artists came together to call attention to sexism in the "oppositional" New German Cinema and to make demands on the West German film-subsidy system that provided the economic basis of that cinema.

Press Release:

In recent weeks the "Association of Women Film Workers" was established in Berlin.

On the occasion of the "Film Festival of the Filmmakers" in Hamburg, many women once again realized that alone in the name of women they cannot make any demands. For that reason an initial spontaneous reaction of the women film workers was the

MANIFESTO OF THE WOMEN FILM WORKERS

The Association of Women Film Workers takes the liberty of expanding the "Hamburg Declaration of German Filmmakers" to include the demands of women filmmakers. We demand: (1) 50 percent of all film funding, production sites, and documentation projects; (2) 50 percent of jobs and training positions; (3) 50 percent of all committee seats; (4) support for the distribution, rental, and exhibition of films by women.

Over eighty women film workers from the Federal Republic and West Berlin signed the manifesto.

From the charter of the Association:

1.1 Women film workers are all women who are active or are becoming active in the film branch or the audiovisual media;

2.2 Goal of the organization is to support, encourage, and publicize all films made by women which are indebted to feminist, emancipatory, and nonsexist content and intent;

—to list, catalogue, and collect old and new films made by women;

—to collaborate with and to support persons publishing information on women film workers and women in film;

—to support with advice and the ongoing exchange of information women's film projects and applications for subsidies;

—to cooperate with domestic and foreign institutions and groups pursuing related goals.

These goals will be concretely implemented through organization and realization as well as participation in education and training, likewise in every possible support of all activities connected with film production and exhibition. The Association will be selflessly active in the advising, support, and representation of its members, helping them to carry through the preparation and realization of their productions in the realm of film and the audiovisual media.

The Association actively pursues sexual parity in all sectors of film and the audiovisual media. It sees the demands of the women film workers of 3 October 1979 appended to the "Hamburg Declaration of German Filmmakers" as its central goal and works for their immediate realization. To the declaration of the women film workers of 3 October 1979 the charter has been appended and constitutes its essential component.

The women film workers meet once a month in Berlin, and beyond that, are starting to form project groups. A nationwide meeting of women film workers is being planned for the Berlin Film Festival.

December 1979, the Association of Women Film Workers.

Cynthia Beatt, Heide Breitel, Jutta Brückner, Beate Büker, Clara Burckner, Christa Donner, Sabine Eckhard, Margit Eschenbach, Ingrid Fischer, Monika Funke, Marianne Gassner, Katharina Geinitz, Erika Gregor, Renée Gundelach, Petra Haffter, Eva Hammel, Ulrike Herdin, Claudia Holldack, Ebba Jahn, Riki Kalbe, Christiane Kaltenbach, Barbara Kasper, Angelika Kettelhack, Brigitta Lange, Birgit Lelek, Henriette Loch, Christine Löbbert, Ursula Ludwig, Jeanine Meerapfel, Elfi Mikesch, Renate Merck, Karin Mumm, Anke Oehme, Ingrid Oppermann, Ulrike Ottinger, Reinhild Paul, Cristina Perincioli, Ulrike Pohl, Margret Raspé, Sigrid Reichert-Purrath, Gudrun Ruzickova, Hille Sagel, Helke Sander, Helma Sanders, Claudia Schillinski, Monika Schmid, Valeska Schöttle, Claudia Schröder, Barbara Stanek, Chris Sternickel, Ula Stöckl, Anneli Wagner, Hildegard Westbeld, Krista Zeissig.

Translated by Eric Rentschler

Jutta Brückner

After earning her Ph.D. in 1973, Jutta Brückner (born Jutta Haefs) (1941–) made her first film Do Right and Fear Nobody *(Tue recht und scheue niemand, 1975) that, like many of her films, is partly autobiographical and explores the relationship between gender, history, and the self. In her prize-winning* Hunger Years *(Hungerjahre, 1979), she continues with her examination of autobiography and depicts the experiences of a teenage girl growing up in 1950s West Germany. Brückner, also a widely published film scholar, is a professor of film and video at Berlin's University of the Arts* (Universität der Künste).

Women's Films Are Searches for Traces (1981)

Women are waking up as filmmakers and becoming aware of how society creates and regulates our sense of the media. In this media world, women, who have always been instrumentalized, even in most sociological investigations, because their forms of existence only assume a negative significance, are supposed to, suddenly and overnight, become active subjects. Behind the camera, pressed into modes of production bound in male modes of thinking and sensing which take apart and reassemble, they are now supposed to function as creators, to express something society has not allowed to exist ("feminist aesthetics"), neither in the historical public sphere nor in the intimacy of the private one. The transition from beloved and other-directed object to autonomous, self-directed subject occurs a little too suddenly so that it is not free of losses stemming from the frictions between employer and employee, crew and director, and films and audience. But, above all, women rub themselves raw. And the temptation is great to become daddy's sulky little girl, whose caprices are confused with autonomy, a role that we, after all, know well from our childhood reading.

I want to talk about the women who resist this temptation, however, and only these women. Even if one assumes that the time for women has come, because, among other things, the wretched lot of women still has more strength than the healthy state of men, one must say in the same breath that this society is still well enough organized and has the strength to do us in. And the instinct that defends itself against feminist radicalism remains firmly entrenched. For feminist films are not something that women could or would want to make only for themselves, they are not films for limited audiences or minorities, contrary to what one hears even well-meaning souls occasionally claim these days. Like every movement with an avant-garde impetus, women filmmakers seek to redefine history, including art history, going back all the way to the Western reflexive premise of *cogito ergo sum*. The aims of women filmmakers are expansive. This makes things difficult, but also more vital, because women, precisely due to their "lack," have not yet forgotten that there exists life which is more than the sum of functions, roles, and emotions. Capitalism as the mortal enemy of art as well as woman (Ernst Bloch) senses, with good reason, the all-out attack. The fact that women were permitted for centuries to partake of the fine arts as a recreational activity while their husbands pursued the more serious task of creating a society that denied this art any epistemological value and conceded it only an ornamental one, stems not solely from patriarchal arbitrariness but also contains an inherent logic that might now be turned against patriarchy. Namely, women may now assume an active role at the moment where an art form becomes accessible which virtually redeems their most crucial loss: prelinguistic sensory reality, the sensuality not only of the eye. Exposed to our collective conformity at the price of collective repression, we find in the cinema a space to wish for our own images, our own experience of lost speech and lacking images, because increasingly we were made into images instead of having ones of our own. We do not have this space, but we would like to have it.

This negative inventory hardly smacks of the carefree hours one supposedly now and again whiles away at the cinema if it is to survive as culture. Rather it is somewhat frightening. But the recognition of lacks is today the necessary basis for realism, and this does not exclude fantasy production. What does not exist in society should not appear in art as something real. Up to now women have refused to continue the sorry German legacy of making art into a substitute for meaningful social activity.

Women's films are searches for traces, affirmation of identity as film's theme and process, hopeful stories looking forward to a self-confident life, in which one can feel and think at the same time. Feminist aesthetics expresses how hard it is to see emotionally in an age where the eye has become the most abstract of all the sense organs and now carries objectification to hyperbolic extremes. It also expresses a process whose goal is in fact what fuels this process: feminist aesthetics. This much-discussed phenomenon is not simply there because women now have the opportunity to stand behind cameras. Damaged sensuality also reacts to a damaging reality in a damaged way. The films bear witness to things that one lives with at the price of sickness and dissatisfaction, not as the representation of feminist insights, no matter how important they might be as the replication of a certain syntax, but rather the integration of self-consciousness, a sort of seeing with one's head and stomach and knee. Perhaps there exist moments in this process where one gets a glimmer of what might be possible, if only.

When women's films here succeed in being radical, many people feel frustrated. Even the many yearning, intellectual men who love the cinema are scared away, because women insist on their desire to show things that all those people sitting in the dark of the movie theater who do not want to reconcile themselves to the reality of the functional, can only vaguely sense as a desire. Feminist films do not lend themselves to cult worship and cineastes, they are signposts on the road to a gradual liberation of individual and collective creativity and not the stimulus for cineastic celebration.

The difficulties, however, do not diminish even as we seem to become more familiar with the means and techniques of production. This is because women, whose self-confidence is only fragmentary in terms of what is acceptable in modern society, first of all have to organize themselves before they organize anything else, not their lives, but themselves: the connection of their stomach ulcer to the head busy adding up figures; the relation of the "neurotic" need to sleep to the demands of an overly organized shooting schedule; the bearing of the intimate desire to try and recover obscured notions of creativity on the exigencies of getting the product of these labors onto the market immediately, to make a profit or at least to break even. We are developing social resilience at the price of never really developing for ourselves the body of experience we are trying to document.

The path leads at once inward and outward, the gaze forward and backward, the search for traces into the past and into the future, the present as a moment of passage to that which is not yet, not real anymore. Gabi Teichert digs about in German history, we are digging about in ourselves as well and finding German history, also and even in the way we are digging.

The result is often the deadly silence that exists in the heart of a real hurricane, which does not only take place in the cinema, a very slow anger, but also an anger that painstakingly makes use of existing aesthetic forms, the anger that functions for us as an important gauge indicating that the principle of capitalistic rationalization, something we are at least in part subjected to in the filmmaking process, has not yet taken control over us from the inside. The leap from deficit to self-confident creativity has something suicidal about it. Women can tell you what kind of strength it takes to see through the schizophrenic strategy society demands of female artists. Persevering between pragmatism and utopia. The story of Münchhausen, who pulls himself out of the swamp by his own hair, is for women a political parable in which outside is inside, and inside is outside.

Women's cinema lives in and through contradiction, existing as a utopia in the never-ending process of coming nearer, constantly threatened by the social mechanisms that would like to extinguish its life, not only through active enmity, but also by passive nonacceptance. What is still at issue today is not so much the plain truth, but rather the lesser untruth. The undeveloped, whose forms we do not yet know and can only sense, is still not yet an alternative to what we know, but nonetheless not a deficit in the real, but rather in the possible.

Every step toward overcoming this situation becomes part of self-perpetuating strategies as long as they lead up the rungs of the ladder. And therefore even behind the important demand of 50 percent of all subsidy funding made by the Association of Women Film Workers lurks the danger that all these small steps up the ladder will end suddenly in a bottomless pit, that of the status quo.

It makes sense that women, who have been "behind" and "below" for so long, now also want to be "ahead" and "above." One must possess considerable autonomy to turn down an offered plate of sweets, knowing well it can only make one sick, instead insisting to one's benefactors that one has the right to eat a balanced meal as well. What strength it takes to express the truth unabashedly in the face of state television arrangements, the moral sensibilities of CSU-TV and listener organizations, also in the face of the conventions of established art, whose crisis is obvious, and—for usually this is most difficult—unabashedly to oneself as well.

Even with a new theoretical consciousness and a few lawsuits which have rattled social bastions, things have not gotten easier. The courage demanded here makes a mark on autonomous female individuals at the same time that it frees them: they are no longer lovable. The dialectic of the process—creation through destruction—does not only apply to a culture in which women will not, should not, cannot make themselves comfortable, but also to women themselves. No one is sure what the synthesis will look like.

One of its possible aspects might be allowing ourselves to get rid of our warranted inhibition about using such words as happiness and beauty—our inhibition about the words themselves and also what they signify.

Translated by Antje Masten

Wolfgang Kohlhaase

As a screenwriter, Wolfgang Kohlhaase (1931–) has been associated with some of the best-known films of the GDR. His writing career began early, when, as a student, he published in the youth periodicals, including Junge Welt (Young World), *the newspaper of the* Freie Deutsche Jugend (FDJ), *the official socialist youth organization of the GDR. From 1950–52 he worked for DEFA (Deutsche Film Aktiengesellschaft), the East German state-owned film company, and later became a freelance screenwriter and author. His first films, belonging to the genre of so-called Berlin films, were made in collaboration with Gerhard Klein and were neorealist accounts of youth in a divided Berlin (for example,* A Berlin Romance [Eine Berliner Romanze, *1955/56*], Berlin, Schönhauser Corner [Berlin—Ecke Schönhauser, *1957*], Berlin, around the Corner [Berlin um die Ecke, *1965]*). In his subsequent films, such as* The Affair Gleiwitz (Der Fall Gleiwitz, *Klein, 1960/61*), I Was 19 (Ich war 19, *Wolf, 1967), and* Mama, I am Alive (Mama, ich lebe, *Wolf, 1976), he continued exploring the effects of World War II and National Socialism. With* Solo Sunny *(Wolf and Kohlhaase, 1978/79), Kohlhaase co-directed his only film, which tells the story of a young singer in search of her own style.*

DEFA: A Personal View (1996)

The following is an edited transcript of an address originally made in German at the conference on East German Cinema held in March 1996 at the Centre for East German Studies, The University of Reading.

DEFA made about six hundred films during the forty years of its existence. Which ones will survive? The better ones, of course. One day these films will also be used as a source of information to help people understand what the GDR was: whether it was an epoch, a footnote in history or just a misunderstanding. In this conference we have been talking mainly about the political or philosophical context in which these films were made. But these films also show us other things: hair-styles, skirt-lengths, the girls people thought were beautiful in any given year. Everyday life is preserved in films and this is what gives the medium a different kind of significance.

DEFA films were made by three, perhaps four generations of directors. Here I can only speak for myself, or for the people I worked with, that is, from the perspective of my generation. How people reacted to the GDR, how they responded to its achievements and its failures varied enormously depending on how old they were when they began to confront the political world. So let me start by saying a few words about myself, without telling you my whole life-story.

I was fourteen years old when the Russians came. I can remember the day when they reached the Berlin suburb where I lived, it was April 24. It was quiet, you could hear the sound of gun-fire far off, and the twittering of the birds. At the end of the street you could see columns of Russian soldiers moving into the city; you didn't know whether or not to go and have a closer look. It suddenly dawned on me—at any rate that's how it seemed to me later—that I was one day older than the Thousand-Year Reich, I had survived it. And although we had no idea of what was going to happen, by the third day we had grasped one thing at least: this wasn't an end, it was a beginning. This was an amazing discovery, for the Nazis had declared that our demise would mean the end of the world. After us there would be nothing, only oblivion.

I had never believed this, perhaps for purely biological reasons; I was just fourteen and couldn't accept that everything would stop here. But of course I couldn't produce any intellectual arguments to refute this claim, and so it was a liberation in the truest sense of the word to discover that the Nazis had been lying. Here something was beginning. The sense of life that is born in such moments lasts a long time. It is a matter of luck, of course, when puberty and world history happen to coincide, as they did here. This feeling endured and became a part of my hopes—and the disappointments—that were to come; my reactions to everything were different from what they would have been if I had been ten years younger or ten years older.

How did I come to be a writer? I was soon back at school again; my main recollections are of black-marketeering during break, of noise and confusion, classes with eighty pupils, constantly changing teachers, in short, a place of enjoyment. We didn't learn much, but then we didn't intend to. One day it happened. A boy who sat behind me in class had written a thriller. I was astonished to realize that it was possible not only to read thrillers but also to write them. That same afternoon I sat down and began writing a thriller of my own.

It was set in London, in the fog. By the time I had reached page forty there were two houses that had burned down, eight dead bodies and no plot. I hadn't thought about what was going to happen, I had simply sat down and begun to write. So I abandoned that project and turned my attention to something that seemed to me more worthwhile. I wrote about my experiences of the end of the war. Again when I had reached page forty—obviously a highly significant number for me—I found that I had got to the end of my experiences and was confronted by the question: can one write about something that one hasn't actually experienced at first hand, or is that lying? I had been writing in the first person, after all. Finally I came to the conclusion that it probably was lying, not because I was such a high-minded fellow, but because I thought someone might read it and then point out that it wasn't true, that I had made the whole thing up. I felt so ashamed at the very idea that I stopped at page forty. There was no one I could turn to for advice. And so it came about that at a very early stage in my life I was faced with the problem of reality and truth.

Now that my interest in writing had been aroused I turned to the newspapers. With no previous training I wrote various articles, including film reviews. I went to see lots of films. Above all I wanted to write, and I thought that perhaps I could be a film writer. For me the real inspiration was neorealism which produced stories about the real world, the world I knew. Up until then I had seen the cinema as something exotic, about other people, not my world, in costume, as it were. I had enjoyed watching films but had never thought that I could have something to do with making them.

Then there was another factor: those first years after the war were bright years for me, for they were accompanied by a vast expansion of our awareness. The war, which until then had been something dark and incomprehensible that had led to catastrophe, became something we could grasp. Suddenly it was possible to discuss it, there were angles from which we could approach it, there were explanations. We were no longer blind. People began to write literature. The German émigrés returned. I had the immodest feeling that everything was happening on my account, all I had to do was take what was offered.

It was a time when doors opened. A whole generation was missing, the generation of the soldiers. The soldiers were either dead or prisoners, or they were brain dead. Whole areas opened up to us. If you tell that to people who are even only five years younger, they can hardly believe it. All you had to do was knock and ask whether there was anything to do. There was always something that needed doing. So at the age of sixteen I became a journalist and at twenty-three I made my first film.

It was wonderful. This state of affairs induced in us a feeling of responsibility for the future. We believed that all sorts of things had to be changed, why not the world? All that was needed was the will to do it. Later, as our horizons broadened and we started to look at things from a Marxist standpoint, we began to notice that a certain narrowing of vision was taking place. Marxism was often being interpreted in a rigid and dogmatic way. It was supposed to explain everything, but it could not. However, this realisation only came later, not right at the beginning.

By then we had made our first films and had acquired a certain degree of self-confidence. We didn't feel we had to accept every criticism, particularly when a film was going down well with the public. And we had allies—some of whom were politicians. It would be a distortion of the truth to suggest that it was always the politicians who were responsible for over-simplifying things and that it was the artists who had the monopoly when it came to sensitivity and seeing the world in a multitude of different ways. There were some of each in both camps. There were politicians who loved art and who had no wish to subject it to crude demands. And amongst my fellow film-makers there were those who were quite happy to resort to clichés.

However, the cultural policy of the GDR was governed by a rather limited, narrow understanding of the nature of art. Many of those in political office had spent more time in prison than in libraries. Their concept of literature was often purely didactic and, in Germany, there had been a long tradition of this. In the 1930s, Upton Sinclair was a much-read author in the German workers' movement. Gorky's most popular work was *The Mother*, a work that took you straight into politics. This attitude is understandable but it leads to a narrow view of literature and of art in general. For example, in 1938, when Hitler's shadow had long since fallen across Europe, a bitter argument broke out amongst German émigrés concerning Expressionism. The debate started in the periodical *Das Wort* which was published in Moscow and you can follow the argument there. Lukács was involved as were Bertolt Brecht, Anna

Seghers and many others. Expressionism was to be rejected because it represented an artistic position that was alien to real life and that was of no direct use in the political struggle. Brecht, who was not an Expressionist, was not alone when he put forward the view that it was more important to be united in the struggle against Hitler. One can understand people arguing about Expressionism, but it must be obvious to anyone that 1938 was not the ideal time in which to debate the matter through an exchange of letters in a periodical.

I mention this example just to show that certain misunderstandings, which had a long history behind them, were carried further in the GDR. However, Brecht, Seghers, Arnold Zweig, Heartfield, Eisler, Dessau, to mention but a few, also lived there. Because of these writers, who believed in socialism, we were not forced to adopt uncritically a theory which called itself "socialist realism." Many books have been written about this magic formula, but I have only really encountered people who have tried to explain what it does not mean. They wanted to rescue a concept that had been conceived in Moscow in 1934 and which had immediately been taken over by the wrong people. For them it meant basically a kind of idyllic naturalism: true to life but more beautiful. Once the manager of a GDR enterprise was asked how he would like art to be, and he answered, quite correctly, full of conflicts, but enjoyable.

Views of this kind were not enough when, as a government, you are in charge of running the arts. Soon artistic debates were taking place, but they all had a hidden political agenda. In the 1950s it was the so-called formalism debate, the offspring of a similar debate in Moscow. This affected not only people of my age, but also artists who had returned from exile abroad. They had to go through it all over again. Brecht's didactic plays, written in the 1930s, were now regarded as modernist. Now only the classics were accepted as suitable models. Nevertheless, despite all these arguments, we never lost sight of the belief that art, in all its multitude of different forms, should help us to understand the world. Nobody thought that after the end of the Nazi era there was nothing new to be learned.

Despite huge differences of opinions, there was, for many years, a kind of solidarity between art and politics. This applied to the film industry as well. So the damage that was done in the middle of the 1960s was all the greater when a rigid division of labor was introduced: there were those who made films, and there were those who banned them. Many things were destroyed at that time, including a common belief in the social relevance of our work. Film-making became a more solitary occupation. The history of the cinema shows us how productive it usually was when similarly motivated people were making films at the same time and reacting to each other's work. It was good for the cinema, the *Zeitgeist* was being explored. Filmmaking is a sociable affair, and the cinema is a place for communication, not for meditation.

DEFA was run on a budget. Every year it was allocated a certain sum, perhaps fifty million marks, and was expected in return to produce between fifteen and twenty films. The money would come the following year, even if the films had not proved to be successful in economic terms, that is, if they had not recouped the money spent on them. It was like the way an opera house is financed. So the film-makers had a degree of security. If a director was not successful, there was nothing to stop him carrying on making films, unless he had proved to be a complete dilettante.

You enjoyed a certain degree of security when you had a contract. Provided you didn't steal the silver, once you were employed, you were always given another chance. This caused some injustice. As hardly anyone was ever sacked, there was little room for new and young people. There were about thirty full-time directors and a production of about twenty films a year. They all got their money, though sometimes they weren't too happy about it. They wanted to work, not to be bribed. In the case of some of them we were glad when they just took the money, and didn't make a film. Looked at in hindsight this does seem rather strange.

The studio had a thematic agenda, with particular aims and projects for which certain writers and directors were needed. For instance it was decided that a film should be made about developments in agriculture or about the growing self-confidence of women at work. Material was collected, and *Dramaturgen* ("script editors") travelled around making reconnaissance trips. But in the end they usually made the film that the film people wanted, using the angle that fitted in with the studio's plan. So a film like *Alarm im Zirkus* (*Circus Alarm*, 1953) was supposed to be a film about how our young people's political ideas were shaped in the divided city of Berlin. And somehow that's how it turned out.

The importance given to work on the screenplay encouraged a certain division of labour in the artistic work. The type of film-maker which is so fashionable today, who does everything himself, was a rarity in those days. I'm still in favour of a certain division of labour, even today. There are only a few people who can do one thing well and even fewer who can do two. To write a book, to direct a film, perhaps even to drum up the finances for it, that is a lot to expect of one person. It takes time, it puts a massive pressure on him to succeed. If things go wrong, the greater the catastrophe is for him. When success, and failure, too, is shared, it creates a better atmosphere in both work and life. I was lucky with my partners: five films with Gerhard Klein, four with Konrad Wolf and things worked well with the others too. Billy Wilder once said that the problem between authors and directors was not that the directors couldn't write, but that they couldn't read. Mine could. In the long run you can only work successfully with people when everybody feels happy, not only yourself.

We had a saying: when there is a shortage of potatoes, there are sure to be some major discussions about art. The banning of ten films in 1965 was intended to impose some discipline on society when the country was going through a difficult time, politically and economically. The politicians used art as a medium for expressing concerns they did not dare to tackle directly. This had the effect of bestowing a greater importance on art. The lack of public discussion which increased over the years led the public to seek questions and answers in films and books or in the theatre. How otherwise are we to explain why the film *Solo Sunny* was a topic of conversation for many months? For the film wasn't just about how to survive as a singer when your singing isn't much good, it was about the individual and society, about the importance of having a dream, and it was about what Wolf called the creeping brutality of life. Without taking ourselves too seriously we did nevertheless have the feeling of having done something useful, as well as achieving success at the box office. We had ambitions for society, romantic ones perhaps. Volker Braun came up with the phrase "Haftung durch Reibung"—a phrase that means something like "people who rub each other up the wrong way stick together all the more." Well, we rubbed quite a few people up the wrong way. It was not comfortable but it seemed to make sense. Those in power expected a lot of art, but they feared it even more. In both respects they got it wrong. Our society was based on the principle of enlightenment; the search for knowledge was not forbidden and an understanding of history was encouraged. At the same time constraints were put on our thinking. In some areas people were supposed to think, in others they were expected merely to believe. This is enough to make people ill, it's enough to make an entire country ill. Thought is like light, it shines in every direction.

The politicians increasingly lost their sense of reality. By the time of the Eleventh Plenum, at which they banned, amongst other things, virtually an entire year's film production, they had cancelled reality. Political life suffered the worst damage. It was not possible to destroy the cinema totally. Not because film people are indestructible but because films arise out of actual physical contact with real life. And real life cannot be adjusted to be in tune with the demands of ideology. People experience reality at first hand. In addition, there was a new generation of people who experienced the country in a different way from us. This also tells us something about the demise of the GDR. It did not satisfy their needs in the way it had satisfied ours. These young people had grown up in a state which already existed, whereas we had the feeling that we had invented it and were making something of it. With hindsight everything looks inevitable. At the beginning it looked like, and was, a great adventure.

So far the discussions at this conference have concentrated on films in the context of contemporary history and cultural policy. That is important, of course, but I would like to add a few words about the moral and aesthetic intentions that motivated many of our films. It moves me when I look back at our attempts to portray the reality of people's everyday lives. We wanted to explore in film what occupied people for eight hours a day and took up most of their lives: the world of work. Often this was not what the public wanted to see. My father would come home from the factory and say: "When I put the television on, what do I see? Another helmet. And I've just taken mine off." And from his perspective he was right. No one goes to the cinema just to see themselves. The girl next door and the queen are both legitimate characters in films, representing the world we are closest to and that which is furthest from us, familiarity and distance, the attainable and the dream. I would never advocate leaving out the dream.

At home we had a photo of my grandmother in which she looked just as she had always looked. We all loved this picture. She had had eleven children, her health was not good, you could see this in the photo, and you could see the destruction life had wrought. We thought it beautiful. The one person who did not like it was my grandmother. It showed her as she didn't want to be. She had created a different picture of herself, a more flattering one. She had

had a hard life and she hadn't had that many opportunities, apart from that of having a better image of herself. What I am trying to say is that things are not simple for the so-called ordinary people when they see films about themselves. Sometimes films showing poor pregnant girls without husbands are praised by the intellectuals: at last, they exclaim, a film showing the truth about poor pregnant unmarried girls. But the poor pregnant unmarried girls don't go to see these films, they don't need to buy a ticket to see this reality. They go to see quite different films. We should not try to compare different kinds of film-making, and their different possibilities. When we began to make these films, inspired by neorealism, we were convinced that this was the only way in which to portray the truth. Filming in the streets, close-ups, raw material, professional actors working together with amateurs. A little older and wiser, having worked longer in the profession, we now know that you can tell lies with a camera in the street and that, conversely, you can tell the truth filming in a studio.

We were interested in such things. And we weren't constantly at war with the authorities. There were times when we had a good laugh. Now, at a time when people tend to see things in black and white, I would like to emphasise that even with a wall around your country you could still think for yourself. Of course today you sometimes find there are other walls than the one you had experienced before. You can also have walls around your head.

Making a film is a collective affair, and you need other people's money for it. Whether it be state money, as it was then, or a mixture of private or public funding, as is now the case, you find yourself having the same discussions, only the substance of the discussion is different. You're trying to persuade someone that you want to make a beautiful film. You cite your earlier films—a real problem for someone just starting out—banking on the persuasive powers of your rhetoric. It is easier and more legitimate for money or politics to have their say in the making of a film than when it is just a work of art produced by an individual. Friends who paint pictures have all, at some time or other, settled for a frugal life and painted what they wanted, the Berliners, the people of Leipzig, the Dresden school, the German tradition.

When we talk about censorship—and a lot has been said on this subject already—I would like to add that there was also a subtle form of censorship which affected films in particular. I am referring to lack of courage. The initial idea is often pretty imprecise. You try to explain it to someone, they look at you for a long time, understanding nothing, and you go home again. How do you manage to get a project started in the case of a film which no one wants? Where there is censorship I think it is exacerbated by the process of self-censorship. When works are banned it is done in order to teach people lessons. The banning of films in 1965 did not just affect the people who made them. Everyone was affected. But people can lack courage today as well. We are not, after all, living in a totally different world. If we think about conformity I dare say we can all come up with a few examples. It wasn't just an East European invention, it is the way of the world, the pressure to conform. I have not yet found that wonderful country where, if you want to make a film, someone says: here's the money—don't tell me what you are going to do with it. If I could find it I'd go there.

Translated by Margaret Vallance

CRITICS, SCHOLARS, AND THEORISTS

Enno Patalas

Enno Patalas (1929–) is one of the most important film conservationists and film historians in Germany today. His early achievements included founding the highly influential film journal Filmkritik *in 1957, which was intended to establish a leftist film journal influenced by Kracauer's sociological approach and was later concerned with aesthetics. In 1962, he and fellow film scholar Ulrich Gregor published* The History of Film (Geschichte des Films), *which has been revised several times and is considered one of the standard works. In 1973, Patalas became the director of the Munich Film Museum where, under his leadership, he was able to restore scores of important films of the early German cinema.*

On German Postwar Film (1952)

German Film Production since 1945

The first German film begun and completed after 1945 was premiered on October 15, 1946. Three films followed in the same year.

By the end of 1947, the total number increased to fourteen. Around this time, the first more detailed and comprehensive critical examinations of the phenomenon of "German postwar film" appeared in the German press. They are in part favorable or neutral, yet in part they also express displeasure and concern already and hint at the objections that were later to be raised by nearly all critics. Friedrich Luft begins an article by saying, "One cannot score a success with the small and random dozen German films such as those that have appeared in the different zones since the end of the war," and states in conclusion, "The beginning is crazy [. . .]. For two years of effort to achieve a new optical expression [. . .] a genuinely depressing result."

This negative attitude was increasingly prevalent in the following years. Especially after the currency reform, when the public also no longer accepted every new film without criticism, recognition grew that the German cinema had missed a rare opportunity for a new artistic beginning. This idea became the basis and quiet assumption in all discussions about the "German film crisis," such as those held on the occasion of "German Film Week" (September 29–October 5, 1950). Not only the critics, but also many people involved in film production expressed themselves negatively in interviews and responses to questions from the press. In the *Neue Zeitung* (*New Times*), Helmut Käutner commented unfavorably on the new German film activity and concluded, "Indeed, we have so much of which we may be proud. We're missing only one small thing: good German films."

Only individual representatives of production deny or play down the general mediocrity. Walter Koppel stated, "Everywhere in the world—it used to be like this in Germany, too—only a more or less minimal percentage of all films produced meet real cultural expectations. No one will be able to change anything about this in the future, either."

What objections are raised in particular? They proceed primarily in two directions: against the group of contemporary social problem films, which took their plot from the present or set their plot in it, and against "old style" entertainment films.

In his polemic "Salvation of German Film," the most comprehensive and most detailed examination of German post-war film so far, Wolfdietrich Schnurre, the film critic for the *Deutsche Rundschau* (*German Panaroma*), writes, "Spectacular and monumental films, crowd scenes, magnificent buildings, heaps of costumes—all this should be out of the question today." Gunter Groll, critic for the *Süddeutsche Zeitung* (*South German Times*), writes of these films that they "[. . .] float away from the present into a dreamland beyond all newspapers and are, as a result of desertion from reality, usually much sadder than they seem."

And after a side-glance at the contemporary social problem film, Groll notes, "From now on, nothing should any longer be shabby and miserable, but everything should be fine and jolly. The era of Marrakech and Gabriela dawned. Together with the many small innocuous films that everyone knows and the images of which resemble one another. From the Wailing Wall to prankish decorations, from ersatz coffee to breakfast champagne. [. . .] To many people, there gradually seems to be too much marra-kitsch and cheerful innocuousness." The list of critics who lash out at the flight into illusion could be continued indefinitely.

Contemporary Social Problem Film—Rubble Film

Next to these films that have no relation to the present whatsoever, there are those that—at least thematically—concern themselves with our times. Friedrich Luft's second charge is directed against them: "[. . .] [T]hey go at the present with artistically inadequate means, do not capture it, sentimentalize or contaminate it. Or they take refuge in worthless, frolicking frivolity and film melodies, now when they are least palatable."

Falsification of reality, artificial sentimentality, mendacious optimism, false reconstruction of pathos, and misuse of the present as a backdrop for old-style stereotypes are the charges that are then made again and again.

"Reality," writes Theo Fürstenau, "became sentimentally encrusted, and all élan died in the monotony of a studio workshop that was modeled after old cliché." Kurt W. Marek believes that the rubble films "most seriously discredit the contemporary social problem film that is so essential to us. They wanted to be realistic, but they recognized reality only as a prop, the ruins were nothing but a backdrop; bias and overdone pedagogy damaged the standing of the one, mendacity and the trade in sentimentalities discredited the others."

The Destruction of Language and Symbol

On various occasions, *dialogue* is cited as an example of the warping of reality and at the same time as a symbol of artistic weakness.

"What should be the easiest thing is the most difficult thing," writes Schnurre, "namely, to let people talk as they talk in reality. Everyone believes he has mastered this; and yet, it always turns into paper."

Kurt Lothar Tank devotes an entire article to language and film and writes there, "German film is lacking in language, real, natural language. [. . .] The exalted literary dialogue stands in contrast to the realism of the image."

As far as the artistic value of German postwar films is concerned, nearly all critics agree that—compared with the achievements of other countries today and with earlier German achievements—it leaves very much to be desired. After sketching the expectations that one needed to have of German postwar film, Schnurre poses the question, "And the people in German film, what are they doing?" He answers, "They are producing the most primitive mediocrity. They violate the most banal cinematic principles. They ignore dramatic consistencies."

Specifically, he mentions—starting with the view that "film language" is "symbolic language"—the "timidity of German film people about symbol and allusion" and their "predilection for directness": "People have [. . .] not yet realized that a skillfully photographed pitcher with moldy milk in it or the scruffy fire wall of a row house is able to express something more indicative than, for example, a massive offering of marauding film extras."

Next to the inability to "make things talk" and to allow real details to play a role as a vehicle for symbolism, the unimaginativeness in the choice of point of view and editing and the "flight into the wide-angle shot" are variously cited as proofs of artistic helplessness. The tendency toward excessive clarity and exaggeration are cited as being related to the "predilection for directness." Gunter Groll writes, "They exert themselves with German thoroughness. They hang the leaden weights of problems on everything. If they are playful, they are playful in such a thorough manner, sweating at it, so to speak, that it is no longer a real pleasure. If they are cheerful, then it becomes slapstick, and they push the slapstick to the limit. [. . .] Whatever they do, they exaggerate."

The Reasons for Mediocrity

Observers are less united in their view of the reasons for the predominant mediocrity than in their negative assessment of German postwar film. Two groups can be distinguished: the one seeks the primary reason in economic difficulties; the other considers intellectual deficiencies to be decisive. Between the extremes that want to admit only the one or the other cause, there are nuances of all sorts; some observers see both areas as being equally important.

Primarily those who are themselves involved in film production are of the view first cited (i.e., that economic difficulties are decisive). A distributor writes, "Have the production companies, the screenplay writers, the directors, and the cameramen who previously made films recognized as good suddenly become incompetents in taking up their work? This cannot be assumed. Thus, the only conclusion that remains is that external influences are affecting the quality of German film." One producer and director answers the question about the reason for the failure of German films: "Because we stumble from one crisis to another. First, it was the shortage of raw film material. [. . .] Now, it is the shortage of the German mark."

These arguments are continually countered with firmness: "To excuse oneself with 'technical difficulties' no longer works. Technical difficulties have nothing to do with trivialities and inferiority, even in the case of film production." "The lack of money alone is no reason to make bad films, since even bad films cost money, too."—"A shortage of material and money could be considered responsible for the fact that no films are made, but not for the fact that those that nevertheless are made are not good."

In another, indirect sense, material and money do seem to most observers to be important for the artistic success of film production as well: "The German producer is poor. He has no money to be able to plan ahead for the long term and thus to make good films." Films must be made "that, while not being able (or wanting) to make a claim to artistic quality, would fill the cash registers and thereby provide the prerequisites for a relatively secure basis of production, at least initially." The *Züricher Tat* (*Zurich Action*), on the other hand, treats these views with irony: "We have to make at least two guaranteed hit films with well-known actors in order to be able to afford an artistically valuable third one. Hardly any of these 'third' films was made—for most companies had already gone bankrupt with their two 'guaranteed hits.'"

The Fragmentation of the Film Economy

This brings up two additional sets of topics that take up much space in the discussion: public taste and the fragmentation of the film economy into small, enervated production groups. The fragmentation of the German film economy is two-fold: a horizontal one in the sharp separation of production, distribution and movie theaters and a vertical one in the large number of production companies and distributors. "People in German film circles have long realized that the fragmentation [. . .] has been pushed too far. This fragmentation will be increased even more by Lex Ufi,[1] which wants to sell the assets of the former UFA piecemeal. It turns out that the many tiny companies—the Western allies have already issued a total of more than 150 production licenses—are not strong enough to withstand crisis."

In the majority of other articles about German film, the fragmentation of the film economy is also cited, if not as a primary reason for, then as playing a role in the low quality of German film. The squeezing of German film by foreign competition is frequently named as an additional external reason. Rolf Meyer's commentary on the introduction by SPIO[2] of a quota of 1:2 for German to foreign films is cited as an example: "I see in this development the opportunity for German production again to work to a greater degree toward artistic quality. The continuing limited opportunity for German films to bring in money has led financers and distributors to gauge films exclusively according to their economic chances and to forget that the golden mean of the highest artistic intensity and of the greatest business success must be achieved in film." Various critics, though, do not permit any sort of external reasons as an excuse: "The senselessness of the discussion that is being held on the topic 'The Crisis of German Film' is quickly being exposed. For they start out almost exclusively with external factors. People speak in a discordant note of deepest embitterment of competition from abroad, bemoan the inadequacy of the material resources. [. . .] But no one stands up and admits that existing resources were squandered in a criminal manner."

Who Is Responsible for the Film Crisis?

Most critics mention the German film economy's economic difficulties cited as factors playing a role in the question of quality with-

---

[1] The "Law of UFA," that is, the law regulating the postwar break-up of the old Ufa film company in West Germany, which was a remnant of what was once Germany's largest film studio and production company. (Editor's note)

[2] "Spitzenorganisation der Filmwirtschaft," the Central (or High) Organization of the Film Industry, trade group that had existed since the Weimar Republic. (Editor's note)

out granting them crucial importance, however. If one wishes to bring together the various views on this topic on a middle course in order to come to a judgment that is as objective as possible, then one can say that the material obstacles, which doubtlessly were considerable, were apt to have a hampering effect on the joy of artistic creation and experimentation and to make the realization of cinematic artworks difficult, but that they alone do not explain the mediocrity of German post-war film. The essential reasons and deeper causes must lie in another area.

The majority of critics sees them in the realm of ideas or that of the personnel and in the inadequacy—professional, artistic or even character-related—of the people involved. The views diverge on which group of people involved bears the primary responsibility. Essentially, three groups can be distinguished: those who are involved for the most part economically (producer, financer, distributor, movie theater owner); those who are involved artistically or technically (author, director, actor, cameraman, editor); and—the public. The attacks of the critics are directed at all three categories; each group is accused of being responsible—at least co-responsible, but often solely responsible—for the artistic failure of German films.

As far as those involved economically is concerned, they are repeatedly accused of addiction to profit and the absence of a consciousness of artistic responsibility. Interferences—themselves impermissible—in the artistic production of films result from the attitude of producers and distributors who consider only profit. It is pointed out "[. . .] how little good it does German film that, lacking credit, it is financed by distribution: the distributor wants a hit film at any price and dictates his wishes pertaining even to the roles filled by the extras, to say nothing of the screenplay."—"If a producer were to engage in an attempt to take an artistic risk, be it with respect to the book or the roles filled, he would hardly find a distributor or other financiers who would be ready to take this risk."—"Good: if these producers functioned solely as financiers, there would be hardly anything to hold against them. But they do not think of contenting themselves in this manner. Not only do they put a bushel under the behind of the golden goose 'film,' but they also force it to swallow their prescriptions." People who make films also complain that they are abused by the distributor. The director Erich Engels states: "Most of the production companies are dependent, as far as the financing is concerned, on banking institutions for distribution. Distributors usually ask very rigorously what kind of film material is to be made and how, and totally refuse the loan if they believe that it cannot expect completely certain audience success from it. [. . .] What alternative does the director have in such a predicament but to choose the middle path between his artistic desire and the necessities to which he is subject?"

The producers and distributors defend themselves against these charges by pointing to the public "which wants it this way" and claiming that, in their view, artistic interests must therefore take a step back for the time being.

Yet, financiers are charged not only with lusting after profit and the infringements that result from it, but also with a "lack of financial sense" and a "lack of commercial instinct." In the critics' view, these manifest themselves primarily in inadequate research of public taste: "It is entirely incomprehensible that an industry that sets so much money into motion conducts no market research. So it can come about that a stockjobber, relying on his 'nose' and supported at best by a couple of suggestions by a distributor, becomes an art critic and finally even a book author and director." So much for those involved economically.

The Call for Screenwriters

One segment of critics sees the primary cause of the dreadful state of German film in a failure of the artists, authors, directors, and above all, the actors involved. The lack of authors who can write suitable screenplays is lamented most: "If only he (the director) had capable authors by his side! Authors who would write him interesting screenplays, gripping fateful images with a vision, penetrating the surface, of the man of our time. But the film director today must usually write his screenplays himself. This is a fact, difficult to change: The publishing houses and the stages are also not finding these authors." Several critics believe that suitable authors exist and that it only depends on interesting them in film: "It requires the combined effort of all persons involved, primarily, however, of scriptwriters, of authors who unfortunately are so often alienated from film today."

Named as reasons for authors' aversion to film are: too little compensation for screenplays; too great a risk for the author; and the continuing infringements by distributor, production and other parties during the writing of the screenplay. An author writes that script editors wish complete screenplays—instead of short exposés: "[. . .] but the risk for the author in this method is too great: If the screenplay is not accepted, then he has worked for months for nothing." In Hollywood, seven percent of the total sum is set aside for the preparation of the screenplay and 5% for the screenplay itself, i.e., a total of twelve percent. In West Germany "[. . .], on the other hand, [. . .] five-to-six percent is set aside for the screenplay, the rights and the film score composer. With such an apportionment of pay, the conspicuous lack of new artistic substance is no wonder."

Old Hands under Indictment

On the other hand, though, there is also frequent warning about the overestimation of the screenplay and it is pointed out that the form, which is determined primarily by the director, not the author, is crucial for the artistic value of film. How is it with German directors, though? "In whom, except Engels, Staudte, Fredersdorf, Baky, Käuntner and perhaps also York, does one notice that he has at all seriously racked his brain over an aesthetics of film? [. . .] Which of them is master of even the most important of all cinematic tricks: the art of allusion, of excluding and condensing, and of making the inanimate world come to life?"—"There are enough directors and camera people, understood in the sense of skilled craft. But artistic capability does not predominate here, but rather [. . .] an expertly grounded cadre of dilettantes, so to speak [. . .] They can direct, they can photograph, for sure; they can do it just like anyone else could do it who took the appropriate courses as long as they had."

Another area that is quite frequently treated critically in the press is acting. The charges here are usually directed less against the actors themselves, who are said to be only "wax in the hands of the director," than against bad casting and coaching. Particularly noted are the advanced ages of the stars of times past who, without regard to this fact, are repeatedly cast in the same roles and the absence of "new faces."—"The gaps that were produced by the departure of Paul Wegener, Emil Jannings, Heinrich George or the absence of Werner Krauss, Rudolf Forster and others have so far not been filled. Without any doubt, one can note the advanced ages in the ranks of our 'leading' actors and an absence of a stratum of actors who could step into the gaps. At fault here are less the actors [. . .] than the producers stuck in their prejudices about public taste

[. . .] who persistently fill their roles according to the same view-points as if time were standing still for actors." A career such as that of Aldo Fabrizi, who made a transition from the comic to character roles, "has no corresponding counterpart in Germany."

The Question of the New Generation in Film

Opinions about the new generation are divided. There are no enthusiastic voices, but some observers judge benevolently and wish for additional support: "They (Cornell Borchers, Jeanette Schulze, and others) are guarantors, certainly not of the future—but of the [. . .] expectation that German film will not remain a cinema without youth."

On the other hand, other critics are not reserved in their negative assessment of the achievements shown: "The young generation rare and weak. A new cliché—soon one cared no longer to see it."—"The lack of acting sense that is foisted upon a viewer here can hardly be outdone."

The fault for these serious shortcomings is sought among production companies, acting agencies, and directors: "Never [. . .] has [. . .] there been such a hopeless vacuum of a qualified young generation as now. What is the reason for this? The unscrupulousness with which films are hastily made in Germany today [. . .]; our producers' lack of artistic instinct and our producers' inability to discover real talents and natural abilities." The directors, on the other hand, attribute the blame to the financers who, appealing to public taste, always want only time-tested stars and box office magnets.

Is the Public to Blame?

With this, the discussion comes again—as it already repeatedly has—to public taste. Producers and distributors point to it in the face of nearly every complaint about artistic shortcomings of their films—insofar as they admit those shortcomings at all. In the press, nearly every conceivable answer was given to the question about the public's actual wishes. One extreme states that the public wants only good films; the other view says that there is no causal connection between public taste and artistic quality; finally, it is maintained that public success and artistic value exclude one another. In most cases, only biases are expressed and supporting evidence is absent; in other cases, the "proofs" are selected one-sidedly (repeatedly: either *Gabriela* or *The Third Man*). Only very few get beyond saying "the public is not as bad as people believe" or "the public is even worse." Since the extreme views are obviously refuted by the facts (nevertheless, they are constantly repeated), only moderate views are cited here.

They are represented most clearly by Gregor von Rezzori: "With all the nice intentions of 'educating' the public, it is only fair that the taste of the public is being taken into account. This public taste, though, does not wish, as it assumed, a particularly low artistic level (this ought to have been confirmed by the reaction to most German films). It's just that it extends over a specific, by no means small, and variable group of topics. Within the bounds of that which interests the public, the quality can be as high as possible."

Standing unspoken behind this view is also the one that films with contemporary topics that reflect the present do not appeal to public taste in any case. Yet there are the most varying opinions about this as well.

Thus, whereas some critics do not permit reference to the public as an excuse, other critics declare the "consumers" solely at fault: "The wealthy class consists of the nouveau riche. [. . .] The role that the public of the 1920s so masterfully played is now left to this class: to demand artistic films and, by means of knowledgeable criticism, to prompt new experiments. The uncontested artistic predominance of German film was the success that resulted from the public of that time. The man who today represents the dominant class also wants [. . .] to enjoy art, but his narrow-gauged concept of art ends with Marika Rökk, Leander, Moser and Lingen. [. . .] Thus, the German post-war film is bad because no German public is there to make it worthwhile. [. . .] It is not the film industry, but rather we who should change [. . .]."

With that, the most frequently articulated views on the topic of "personal blame" are recounted. Individual voices also direct themselves against other parties involved, such as against criticism in the press or church film agencies. Generally, however, even among those involved who come into question, the view prevails that their influence is too minimal to lower the quality.

The Creative Personality—Rare Commodity Even in Film

As far as the question of primary blame in the realm of personnel is concerned, a clear decision cannot be made after considering all of the arguments. It can hardly be denied, though, that those involved artistically, especially the directors and authors, could have achieved far better results with less mere routine and more "art." (Even the best will cannot produce the precondition for this—the most important one: talent.) On the other hand, it can be noted that the economically responsible parties, the producers and the distributors, by having placed financial considerations all too one-sidedly into the foreground, have done little to create for artists the basic working conditions for truly artistic activity. One must grant them, though, that the general economic and financial situations as well as the organization of the film economy are not suited to promoting consciousness of artistic responsibility and financial generosity.

Finally, there is a "vicious cycle" in which all involved—financers, artists and public—run around behind one another and where everyone is concerned with fulfilling the wishes of the man in front and with letting himself be led by the nose. They have been pressed into this cycle largely by their own doing, but also in part by a general development that is primarily determined economically and politically.

The dilemma of German postwar film ultimately consists in the fact that none of those involved musters up the courage to break out of the cycle. This means that the artistic "crisis of German film" is primarily a "crisis of personality" that is not restricted to filmmakers and the film public.

As a consequence of this, all suggestions to eliminate the general mediocrity through external measures influencing the film business have a weakness, namely insofar as the crucial move must be made by the persons involved. An attempt can, however, be made to create the preconditions that will allow talented cinematic artists to do fruitful work through a series of individual actions or else through more fundamental measures.

Ways out of the Film Crisis

The suggestions made for raising the level of film can be divided into two categories: The first comprises those whose representatives defend the basis of existing forms of production and believe it possible to lead film out of the crisis through individual measures of all sorts. The second type of suggestions want to build up a separate art film production independently of the existing industry (with its primarily economic orientation).

The idea of an economic reorganization of the German film industry stands in the foreground of many of the first group's suggestions; the economic reorganization is intended to result in an increase in quality, since the representatives of this view trace the crisis in quality back to a lack of money. The most frequently discussed suggestion of this sort was that of an indemnity bond in the amount of twenty million German marks that the federal government has assumed. In addition, there is a call for a change in Lex Ufi by means of which the assets of the West German rump of UFA—approximately thirty percent of former total assets—now in the hand of the federal government would be made usable for the German film economy. The value is estimated at fifty million in real estate, to which are added the box office receipts from UFA reissues—minus UFA's remaining financial liabilities, which would first have to be determined by a meeting of creditors.

Even if no critic rejects financial assistance measures for production on principle, various serious misgivings are nevertheless expressed. Theo Fürstenau writes: "[. . .] this is happening against a backdrop that does not appear very encouraging. This backdrop is the large number of productions that have developed in the confusion of the postwar years. Is it really responsible to spend even another penny for their existence? If millions from the federal government are now supposed to be misused to secure peace-time budgets for inferior films, then one must protest against it with all vigor. There is little to speak for the fact that the majority of film producers pursued other goals. [. . .] This has resulted in a difficult dilemma. For, on the other hand, one must help German film and may not allow it to go to ruin in its terrible state. On the other hand, though, it is difficult to stand up for German production as a whole." There are similar voices in great number.

Production on a New Basis

The suggestions that strive for a change or circumvention of the current production basis and call for *production on a new basis* are more comprehensive. They start with the consideration that financial motives always have priority over artistic ones in the existing order and thus hinder artistic film as a rule. "As long as private profit is decisive, costs will be in an inverse proportion to the artistic result. [. . .] Different foundations for work should be devised for film. There are only two ways to remove all kitsch from film:

patrons who support the good for the sake of the good or non-profit organizations not upset even by a failure."

This idea is repeatedly found in the press discussion. Against the first "way to remove kitsch," though, the objection is raised that hardly anyone in Germany would be in the position to play the role of the magnanimous patron if—as in the case of film—it is a question of sums in the millions. On the other hand, the second idea meets with more response. In this case, critics repeatedly point to the experiment that the French director Maurice Cloche successfully carried out, and they call for its imitation. After no producer wanted to finance his film about the life of the holy *Monsieur Vincent*, Cloche turned to the public and within a short time received 17 million francs in large contributions of one-thousand francs each. It was possible to find a distributor only through state intervention, since people were convinced that the film would be a financial failure. When success had refuted the doubts, Cloche wanted to make a second film; producers again refused financing, since they considered *Monsieur Vincent* to be an exception. The public also financed *Docteur Laennec* and helped it to become a success. With a third film, *La cage aux filles*, Cloche seized upon another form of contribution that was limited to shares of 250,000 francs each.

A Suggestion for the Promotion of Good Film

In a memorandum of the "International Promotion of Film Art" that they prepared under the auspices of UNESCO, Helmut Käutner and Herbert Seggelke develop substantially farther-reaching suggestions whose effects would not remain limited to Germany. They also think that the current film industry is only a hindrance to film art "because it fears every new path as an experiment." "Every artwork, though," they continue, "is also profoundly an experiment. [. . .] This is true especially in the advent of a new type of art that cannot yet function by relying much on experience and developed tradition." The authors assume that there is an audience in all countries that wishes artistically valuable films, but that this audience is not large enough to guarantee amortization in a national context. In order to bring everyone interested in film art together, there should be a separation of entertainment movie theaters and art movie theaters. In order to muster together the necessary number of moviegoers, the art movie theater should be made into an international institution. "The movie theater in the film production directed by UNESCO should offer a valuable repertoire of reissues, good documentary films and otherwise interesting films as a discriminating program."—In particular, the plan envisions for the "UNESCO Organization for the Promotion of Film Art" an executive committee, a committee of twelve internationally acknowledged artists, a dramaturgical office, international nonprofit production company, an art film distributor of the same type, and the contractual acquisition or establishment of art movie theaters in all UNESCO countries. Käutner's and Seggelke's plan is the only one that contains concrete suggestions.

Film and Reality

The way people think is reflected in everything that they create for entertainment and edification, which thus belongs to the wide area of "culture."

Among artistic forms of expression, film assumes a special position insofar as it is only in the rarest cases the reflection of the way of thinking of an individual or of a small number of people. A poem, a painting or a piano concerto are created by individuals who—insofar as they deserve the title "artist"—do not try particularly hard to satisfy the taste of the broad masses.

It is different in the case of film, which, already at its source, requires "teams" in nearly all cases as well as a large number of "consumers" who accept it. It must appeal to the taste and manner of perception of the "consumers," i.e., it must reflect their spirit. Applied to peoples, this means that "films reflect the mentality of a nation much more immediately than other artistic media," as Siegfried Kracauer expresses it in his investigation of German films *From Caligari to Hitler.* "Popular films," writes Kracauer, "or, to be more precise, popular screen motifs can therefore be suposed to satisfy existing mass desires." And further: "What films reflect are not so much explicit credos as psychological dispositions—those deep layers of collective mentality that extend more or less below the dimension of consciousness."

The history of motifs of German film *From Hitler to Dr. Holl* is not yet written; nor is it yet due as long as film, so far constantly cramped by reeducation regulations or lack of money, is in a position to reflect a way of thinking in only a limited sense. Nevertheless, initial signs are becoming apparent; one observer points to the "flight from the close-up to the wide-angle shot" and sees in it an expression of the flight of the individual into the masses. Here belongs the skewed relationship to reality that characterizes German cinema, the penchant for self-pitying black-on-black painting of some rubble films and for whining sentimentality, and finally the threadbare illusionism of "Everything will be better tomorrow" and "The sun shines after the rain." There are parallels in a hundred manifestations of daily life, from the soccer pools to the flood of magazines. They are indications that a large number of people have lost the correct relationship to reality.

Taste also demonstrates a regrettable flight from reality in its turning back to an outdated taste believed to be dead. The curliqued frill patterns of coffee cup sets, the furniture in the style of the founding years of the German Empire (*Gründerjahre*), the antiquated architecture, and the popularity that they enjoy bespeak of a startling absence of taste that would truly be in keeping with the times.

In art, the hoped-for engagement with our time has also remained absent. The oft-cited desk drawers of the "inner emigration"[3] were empty; German publishers published Hemingway and Graham Greene, the theaters performed Thornton Wilder and Arthur Miller.

Will German film be able to get past all this? Will it be able to raise the level of taste—even with better material conditions? Will it finally attain a genuine relationship to reality?

Translated by Lance W. Garmer

---

[3] "Inner emigration" refers to the assertion of many German writers and artists that they resisted the Nazis not by public resistance or by going into exile but rather by withdrawing into an "internal exile," writing only for themselves, only privately, in keeping with this idea of a private, as opposed to a public resistance. (Editor's note)

Theodor W. Adorno

Transparencies on Film

Children when teasing each other in their squabbles, follow the rule: no fair copycat. Their wisdom seems to be lost on the all too thoroughly grown-up adults. The Oberhauseners attacked the nearly sixty-year old trash production of the film industry with the epithet: "Daddy's Cinema." Representatives of the latter in turn could come up with no better retort than "Kiddy's Cinema." This cat, as once again the saying goes among children, does not copy. How pathetic to pit experience against immaturity when the issue is the very immaturity of that experience acquired during the adolescence of the medium. What is repulsive about Daddy's Cinema is its infantile character, regression manufactured on an industrial scale. The sophistry of the defenders insists on the very type of achievement the concept of which is challenged by the opposition. However, even if there were something to that reproach—if films that did not play along with business really were in some ways clumsier than the latter's smoothly polished wares—then the triumph would be pitiful. It would only demonstrate that those supported by the power of capital, technological routine and highly trained specialists could do better in some respects than those who rebel against the colossus and thus must necessarily forego the advantages of its accumulated potential. In this comparatively awkward and unprofessional cinema, uncertain of its effects, is inscribed the hope that the so-called mass media might eventually become something qualitatively different. While in autonomous art anything lagging behind the already established technical standard does not rate, vis-à-vis the culture industry—whose standard excludes everything but the predigested and the already integrated, just as the cosmetic trade eliminates facial wrinkles—works which have not completely mastered their technique, conveying as a result something consolingly uncontrolled and accidental, have a liberating quality. In them the flaws of a pretty girl's complexion become the corrective to the immaculate face of the professional star.

It is known that in the Törless film[1] large segments of Musil's early novel were incorporated into the dialogue almost unchanged.

---

[1] *Der junge Törless* (1965/66), a film by Volker Schlöndorff, based on Robert Musil, *Die Verwirrungen des Zöglings Törless* (translator's footnote).

They are considered superior to the lines by the scriptwriters, which no living person would ever utter, and which in the meantime have been ridiculed by American critics. In their own way, however, Musil's sentences also tend to sound artificial as soon as they are heard, not read. This may be to some extent the fault of the novel which incorporates a type of rationalistic casuistry into the internal movement of its text under the guise of a psychology that the more progressive Freudian psychology of the period exposed as a rationalization. Nevertheless, this is hardly the whole point. The artistic difference between the media is obviously still greater than expected by those who feel able to avoid bad prose by adapting good prose. Even when dialogue is used in a novel, the spoken word is not directly spoken but is rather distanced by the act of narration—perhaps even by the typography—and thereby abstracted from the physical presence of living persons. Thus, fictional characters never resemble their empirical counterparts no matter how minutely they are described. In fact, it may be due to the very precision of their presentation that they are removed even further from empirical reality; they become aesthetically autonomous. Such distance is abolished in film: to the extent that a film is realistic, the semblance of immediacy cannot be avoided. As a result, phrases justified by the diction of narrative which distinguishes them from the false everydayness of mere reportage, sound pompous and inauthentic in film. Film, therefore, must search for other means of conveying immediacy: improvisation which systematically surrenders itself to unguided chance should rank high among possible alternatives.

The late emergence of film makes it difficult to distinguish between technique and technology as clearly as is possible in music. In music up to the electronic period, the intrinsic technique—the sound structure of the work—was distinct from its performance, the means of reproduction. Film suggests the equation of technique and technology since, as Benjamin observed, the cinema has no original which is then reproduced on a mass scale: the mass product is the thing itself. This equation, however, is problematic, in film as well as in music. Experts in cinematographic techniques refer to the fact that Chaplin was either unaware of or purposely ignored these techniques, being content with the photographic rendering of sketches, slapstick routines or other performances. This in no way lowers Chaplin's status and one can hardly doubt that he was "filmic." Nowhere but on the screen would this enigmatic figure—

reminiscent of old-fashioned photographs right from the start—
have developed its concept. As a consequence, it appears impossible
to derive norms of criticism from cinematographic technique as
such. The most plausible theory of film technique, that which focuses on the movement of objects,[2] is both provocatively denied
and yet preserved, in negative form, in the static character of films
like Antonioni's *La Notte.* Whatever is "uncinematic" in this film
gives it the power to express, as if with hollow eyes, the emptiness
of time. Irrespective of the technological origins of the cinema, the
aesthetics of film will do better to base itself on a subjective mode
of experience which film resembles and which constitutes its artistic
character. A person who, after a year in the city, spends a few weeks
in the mountains abstaining from all work, may unexpectedly experience colorful images of landscapes consolingly coming over him
or her in dreams or daydreams. These images do not merge into one
another in a continuous flow, but are rather set off against each
other in the course of their appearance, much like the magic lantern
slides of our childhood. It is in the discontinuity of their movement
that the images of the interior monologue resemble the phenomenon of writing: the latter similarly moving before our eyes while
fixed in its discrete signs. Such movement of interior images may be
to film what the visible world is to painting or the acoustic world
to music. As the objectifying recreation of this type of experience,
film may become art. The technological medium *par excellence* is
thus intimately related to the beauty of nature *(tief verwandt dem
Naturschönen).*

If one decides to take the self-censors more or less literally and
confront films with the context of their reception, one will have to
proceed more subtly than those traditional content analyses which,
by necessity, relied primarily on the intentions of a film and neglected the potential gap between such intentions and their actual
effect. This gap, however, is inherent in the medium. If according
to the analysis of "Television as Ideology"[3] film accommodates various layers of behavioral response patterns, this could imply that

[2] Cf. Siegfried Kracauer, *Theory of Film: The Redemption of Physical Reality* (New York: Oxford University Press, 1960), pp. 41 ff.

[3] T. W. Adorno, "Fernsehen als Ideologie," in *Eingriffe: Neun Kritische Modelle* (Frankfurt: Suhrkamp, 1936), pp. 81–98. Based on an English-language original: "How to Look at Television," *The Quarterly of Film, Radio and Television,* vol. VII (Spring 1954), pp. 213–235, reprinted as "Television and the Patterns of Mass Culture," in: B. Rosenberg and D. Manning White, eds. *Mass Culture: The Popular Arts in America* (New York: Free Press, 1957), pp. 474–488. (Translator's note)

the ideology provided by the industry, its officially intended models, may by no means automatically correspond to those that affect the spectators. If empirical communications research were finally to look for problems which could lead to some results, this one would merit priority. Overlapping the official models are a number of inofficial ones which supply the attraction yet are intended to be neutralized by the former. In order to capture the consumers and provide them with substitute satisfaction, the unofficial, if you will, heterodox ideology must be depicted in a much broader and juicier fashion than suits the moral of the story; the tabloid newspapers furnish weekly examples of such excess. One would expect the public's libido, repressed by a variety of taboos, to respond all the more promptly since these behavioral patterns, by the very fact that they are allowed to pass, reflect an element of collective approval. While intention is always directed against the playboy, the *dolce vita* and wild parties, the opportunity to behold them seems to be relished more than the hasty verdict. If today you can see in Germany, in Prague, even in conservative Switzerland and in Catholic Rome, everywhere, boys and girls crossing the streets locked in each others arms and kissing each other unembarrassed, then they have learned this, and probably more, from the films which peddle Parisian libertinage as folklore. In its attempts to manipulate the masses the ideology of the culture industry itself becomes as internally antagonistic as the very society which it aims to control. The ideology of the culture industry contains the antidote to its own lie. No other plea could be made for its defense.

The photographic process of film, primarily representational, places a higher intrinsic significance on the object, as foreign to subjectivity, than aesthetically autonomous techniques; this is the retarding aspect of film in the historical process of art. Even where film dissolves and modifies its objects as much as it can, the disintegration is never complete. Consequently, it does not permit absolute construction: its elements, however abstract, always retain something representational; they are never purely aesthetic values. Due to this difference, society projects into film quite differently— far more directly on account of the objects—than into advanced painting or literature. That which is irreducible about the objects in film is itself a mark of society, prior to the aesthetic realization of an intention. By virtue of this relationship to the object, the aesthetics of film is thus inherently concerned with society. There can be no aesthetics of the cinema, not even a purely technological one, which would not include the sociology of the cinema. Kracauer's theory of film which practices sociological abstention compels us to consider that which is left out in his book; otherwise antiformalism turns into formalism. Kracauer ironically plays with the resolve of his earliest youth to celebrate film as the discoverer of the beauties of daily life: such a program, however, was a program of *Jugendstil* just as all those films which attempt to let wandering clouds and murky ponds speak for themselves are relics of *Jugendstil*. By choosing objects presumably cleansed of subjective meaning, these films infuse the object with exactly that meaning which they are trying to resist.

Benjamin did not elaborate on how deeply some of the categories he postulated for film—exhibition, test—are imbricated with the commodity character which his theory opposes. The reactionary nature of any realist aesthetic today is inseparable from this commodity character. Tending to reinforce, affirmatively, the phenomenal surface of society, realism dismisses any attempt to penetrate that surface as a romantic endeavor. Every meaning—including critical meaning—which the camera eye imparts to the film would already invalidate the law of the camera and thus violate Benjamin's taboo, conceived as it was with the explicit purpose of outdoing the provocative Brecht and thereby—this may have been its secret purpose—gaining freedom from him. Film is faced with the dilemma of finding a procedure which neither lapses into arts-and-crafts nor slips into a mere documentary mode. The obvious answer today, as forty years ago, is that of montage which does not interfere with things but rather arranges them in a constellation akin to that of writing. The viability of a procedure based on the principle of shock, however, raises doubts. Pure montage, without the addition of intentionality in its elements, does not derive intention merely from the principle itself. It seems illusory to claim that through the renunciation of all meaning, especially the cinematically inherent renunciation of psychology, meaning will emerge from the reproduced material itself. It may be, however, that the entire issue is rendered obsolete by the insight that the refusal to interpret, to add subjective ingredients, is in itself a subjective act and as such *a priori* significant. The individual subject who remains silent speaks not less but more through silence than when speaking aloud. Those filmmakers ostracized for being too intellectual should, by way of revision, absorb this insight into their working methods. Nonetheless, the gap between the most progressive tendencies in the visual arts and those of film continues to exist, compromising the latter's most radical intentions. For the time being, evidently, film's most promising potential lies in its interaction with other media, themselves merging into film, such as certain kinds of music. One of the most powerful examples of such interaction is the television film *Antithèse*[4] by composer Mauricio Kagel.

That, among its functions, film provides models for collective behavior is not just an additional imposition of ideology. Such collectivity, rather, inheres in the innermost elements of film. The movements which the film presents are mimetic impulses which, prior to all content and meaning, incite the viewers and listeners to fall into step as if in a parade. In this respect, film resembles music just as, in the early days of radio, music resembled film strips. It would not be incorrect to describe the constitutive subject of film as a "we" in which the aesthetic and sociological aspects of the medium converge. *Anything Goes*[5] was the title of a film from the thirties with the popular English actress Gracie Fields; this "anything" captures the very substance of film's formal movement, prior to all content. As the eye is carried along, it joins the current of all those who are responding to the same appeal. The indeterminate nature of this collective "anything" *(Es),* however, which is linked to the formal character of film facilitates the ideological misuse of the medium: the pseudo-revolutionary blurring in which the phrase "things must change" is conveyed by the gesture of banging one's fist on the table. The liberated film would have to wrest its *a priori* collectivity from the mechanisms of unconscious and irrational influence and enlist this collectivity in the service of emancipatory intentions.

Film technology has developed a series of techniques which work against the realism inherent in the photographic process. Among these are soft-focus shots—a long outdated arty custom in photography—superimpositions, and also, frequently, flashbacks. It is about time to recognize the ludicrousness of such effects and get rid

---

[4] *Antithèse: Film for one performer with electronic and everyday sounds* (1965); first broadcast April 1, 1966 by NDR III, Hamburg. (Translator's note)

[5] *Anything Goes* (1936; Paramount), dir. Lewis Milestone, with Bing Crosby, Ethel Merman, Grace Bradley *(sic!)* and others; songs by Cole Porter. (Translator's note)

of them because these techniques are not grounded in the necessities of individual works but in mere convention; they inform the viewer as to what is being signified or what needs to be added in order to comprehend whatever escapes basic cinematic realism. Since these techniques almost always contain some expressive—even if commonplace—values of their own, a discrepancy arises between expression and conventional sign. This is what gives these inserts the appearance of *kitsch*. Whether it creates the same effect in the context of montage and extradiegetic associations has yet to be examined. In any case, such cinematographic divagations require particular tact on the part of the film-maker. The lesson to be learned from this phenomenon is dialectical: technology in isolation, which disregards the nature of film as language, may end up in contradiction to its own internal logic. Emancipated film production should no longer depend uncritically upon technology (i.e. the mere equipment of its profession) in the manner of a by no means still "new objectivity" *(einer keineswegs mehr neuen Sachlichkeit)*. In commercial film production, however, the aesthetic logic inherent in the material is caught in a stage of crisis even before it is given a chance to really unfold. The demand for a meaningful relationship between technique, material and content does not mix well with the fetishism of means.

It is undeniable that Daddy's Cinema indeed corresponds to what the consumers want, or, perhaps, rather that it provides them with an unconscious canon of what they do not want, that is, something different from what they are presently being fed. Otherwise, the culture industry could not have become a mass culture. The identity of these two phenomena, however, is not so beyond doubt as critical thought assumes as long as it focuses on the aspect of production and refrains from empirical analyses of reception. Nevertheless, the favorite argument of the whole- and half-hearted apologists, that culture industry is the art of the consumer, is untrue; it is the ideology of ideology. Even the reductive equation of the culture industry with the low art of all ages does not hold up. The culture industry contains an element of rationality—the calculated reproduction of the low—which, while certainly not missing in the low art of the past, was not its rationale. Moreover, the venerable roughness and idiocy of such hybrids of *circenses* and burlesque so popular during the late Roman empire do not justify the revival of such phenomena after they have become aesthetically and socially transparent. Even if considered apart from its historical perspective, the validity of the argument for consumer-oriented art can be attacked in the very present. Its proponents depict the relationship between art and its reception as static and harmonious, according to the principle of supply and demand, in itself a dubious model. Art unrelated to the objective spirit of its time is equally unimaginable as art without the moment which transcends it. The separation from empirical reality which pertains to the constitution of art from the outset requires precisely that moment. The conformity to the consumer, on the contrary, which likes to masquerade as humanitarianism, is nothing but the economic technique of consumer exploitation. Artistically, it means the renunciation of all interference with the syrupy substance of the current idiom and, as a result, with the reified consciousness of the audience. By reproducing the latter with hypocritical subservience, the culture industry changes this reified consciousness all the more, that is, for its own purposes: it actually prevents that consciousness from changing on its own, as it secretly and, deep down, unadmittedly desires. The consumers are made to remain what they are: consumers. That is why the culture industry is not the art of the consumer but rather the projection of the will of those in control onto their victims. The automatic self-reproduction of the status quo in its established forms is itself an expression of domination.

One will have observed that it is difficult, initially, to distinguish the preview of a "coming attraction" from the main film for which one is waiting. This may tell us something about the main attractions. Like the previews and like the pop hits, they are advertisements for themselves, bearing the commodity character like a mark of Cain on their foreheads. Every commercial film is actually only the preview of that which it promises and will never deliver.

How nice it would be if, under the present circumstances, one could claim that the less films appear to be works of art, the more they would be just that. One is especially drawn to this conclusion in reaction to those snobbish psychological class-A pictures which the culture industry forces itself to make for the sake of cultural legitimation. Even so, one must guard against taking such optimism too far: the standardized Westerns and thrillers—to say nothing of the products of German humor and the patriotic tear-jerkers *(Heimat-*

schnulze)—are even worse than the official hits. In integrated culture one cannot even depend on the dregs.

Translated by Thomas Y. Levin

Gertrud Koch

Gertrud Koch (1949–) received her doctorate from the Johann Wolfgang Goethe–University in Frankfurt am Main. As one of the most important film scholars in Germany today, Koch has published books and articles in journals on feminist film criticism, film aesthetics, and film theory. Since her tenure as professor of film studies at the Free University in Berlin, a position she filled after the death of her predecessor, Karsten Witte (whose work appears on pages 307–13), Koch has been able to establish film studies as a major field of study.

Ex-Changing the Gaze: Re-Visioning Feminist Film Theory (1985)

Social movements of the 20th century, from the Russian Revolution through the proletarian mass movements of the 1920s up to the student movement and new women's movement have declared a particular interest in the cinema, motivated by the appearance of film as a mass phenomenon. Carlo Mierendorff, a German expressionist writer who became a leading social democrat in cultural politics and the resistance against Hitler, gives the following description of the cinema's audience in a programmatic essay of 1920: "They are the class of those who live without books. Those with a vocabulary of sixty words. (. . .) Those never reached by a literary author, perhaps by a newspaper, perhaps by a flyer, perhaps by a five-minute speech during an electoral campaign—before they re-emerge into anonymity. They belong to the cinema: where they feel free to come and go, as a matter of course; where they do not have to mistrust but may experience enthusiasm, pain, pleasure, enrapture (absorption?). An audience of millions which comes and lives and goes, which has no name and yet exists, which moving as an enormous mass is the shaping force of everything and which therefore we must get hold of. There is no other means but the cinema. (. . .) Whoever has the cinema has a lever for subverting the world."[1]

The politically motivated interest in the cinema as mass phenomenon, however, is inseparable from insights into the *quality* of cinematic fascination, insights that go beyond the mere statistical juggling with capacity figures of movie theaters. For anyone seriously involved with cinematic fascination, an investigation into the aesthetics of cinema became inevitable. Thus Béla Balázs writes in 1924: "I feel like the serpent tempting the childlike innocents to eat from the sinful tree of knowledge. For the cinema, up to now, has been the happy paradise of the naives, where you did not have to be smart, educated and critical; a dark space with the intoxicating atmosphere of a den of vice, where even the most cultivated and serious spirits could shed their educational obligations and standards of taste without feeling shame, where they could abandon themselves to raw, primitive gazing in naked, primordial childhood. (. . .) No, it is certainly not my intention to spoil your pleasure. On the contrary, I will try to stimulate your senses and nerves to an even greater capacity to enjoy."[2] Walter Serner, a literary intellectual recently rediscovered, focused as early as 1913 on the phenomenon of "primitive gazing." "If you turn around and look at what makes the last penny fly toward the cinema, into those strangely flickering eyes that point far back into the history of humankind, then it will appear, all at once, in big letters: Scopophilia (Schaulust)."[3] While the gratification of the scopic drive was perceived as the truly sensational feature of cinema, the attraction of film, of what could be seen on the screen, was embodied in the gaze: "This is what Homer attributed to Zeus: his eyelids move and all of Olympus begins to quake. Thus modern man: a batting of eyelashes, a nod of the lids, and a whole world starts moving."[4] (Egon Friedell in a speech inaugurating a Berlin movie theater in 1912). Writing in the journal *Die Literarische Welt* (1925), actress Yvette Guilbert gives a highly graphic description of "The Face of the Cinematographic Actor":

[1] *Hätte ich das Kino! Die Schriftsteller und der Stummfilm,* An exhibition of the German Literature Archives in the Schiller-Nationalmuseum Marbach a.N. (Stuttgart, 1976), p. 404.

[2] Béla Balázs, *Der sichtbare Mensch* (Vienna, 1924), p. 17ff.

[3] "Kino und Schaulust." Reprinted in: *Kino-Debatte: Texte zum Verhältnis von Literatur und Film 1909–1929,* ed. Anton Kaes (Tübingen, 1978), p. 53.

[4] "Prolog vor dem Film," *Ibid.,* p. 45.

"In the realm of the face, the eye and the mouth have their own language, and often the silence of the eye grimly drowns out any eloquence. The eye can speak, laugh and cry. It beckons you and turns you away. It encourages you and robs you of any hope. Listens to you and responds. Accuses and defends. Caresses and kills. It brightens or darkens, sparkles or freezes, beaming with life or braking in the moment of death. It may be the eye of wisdom as well as the cunning eye of mockery."[5] It is interesting that the earliest attempts to theorize film and the cinema already focus on issues of the gaze and scopic pleasure as dimensions specific to the cinematic medium—issues that were resumed, or rather reconstructed in a psychoanalytic framework by feminist film theory in the wake of the new women's movement.

The first films that were made in the context of the women's movement adhered rather to the tradition of the *cinéma militant* in that they were intended to produce an activist oppositional public sphere, addressed to a particular oppressed group. The interest in the cinema was primarily an instrumental one rather than an aesthetic one. This political impulse, however, led to a theoretical perspective directed toward and against the dominant cinematic apparatus, i.e., the question as to what actually constitutes the fascination and power of this apparatus, how patriarchal culture is reproduced in and by the cinema. Feminist theory has necessarily focused on the issue of identification, investigating the strategies by which identification predicates both cinematic production and reception. In this debate, two major strands of argument have been invoked: film aesthetic ones and psychological ones. In both aspects they resume observations of the earliest film theorists—a historical dimension which, alas, is hardly ever acknowledged or utilized.

One of the basic assumptions of film theory is that of the cinematic orchestration of the gaze. The recording apparatus of film, the camera, is analyzed in figurative terms—the metaphor of the eye. The camera-"eye" sees more than the human eye; it registers what Benjamin has called the "optical unconscious." Directed by the human hand, however, the camera-"eye" cruises through the world, transects it with perspectives, selects, focuses its gaze on particular things whose image it reveals to the gaze of the spectator. This conceptualization of the camera as an instrument of the gaze implies the connotation of the spectator's look as completely con-

---

[5] *Hätte ich das Kino!*, p. 277.

trolled by its guide, incapable of perceiving anything that had not been previously digested by the camera. The spectator—according to this conception—has no other choice but to follow the mercilessly segmenting gaze of the close-up; we cannot escape the pan through a space unless we close our eyes. The camera thus prescribes the direction of the spectator's gaze, its movements and foci, as well as the meaning that is to be distilled from the "optical unconscious." If we follow this model, only long shot and extreme long shot would grant the spectators the freedom of letting their gaze roam independently—a potential inscription which moved a filmmaker like Tati to a quasi-democratic program of film aesthetics. But long shot and extreme long shot in their way also predetermine the perspective of the spectator: we can neither change our position as with a tableaux exhibited in a museum, nor can we consider a tour backstage such as it exists, in virtuality, behind a proscenium stage.

British and American feminist film theory has traced this determination of the look especially in classical narrative Hollywood films—and shown how the look is constituted as a primarily male and patriarchal one and how the system of looks deployed by the film constructs the look of the spectator as one that is predicated on a male radius of perception. Crucial to this analysis is the concept of "suture," a term borrowed from surgery, according to which the spectator's perception is welded together with the orchestration of looks as prescribed by the camera, making us see a film "with the eyes" of the camera, the eyes of a male director. The formal analysis of the "suture" which film theory appropriated from Lacanian theory, however, was itself welded with the Freudian model of scopophilia and concomitant assumptions about its place in socialization. Laura Mulvey, in her now classical essay on "Visual Pleasure and Narrative Cinema,"[6] was one of the first to link the analysis of the orchestration of the look in narrative cinema with psychoanalytically defined needs in the spectator, such as voyeurism and exhibitionism, thus fusing two types of theories that are both in their way concerned with the issue of cinematic identification.

Mulvey's analysis in particular hinges on the assumption that the look which cinema organizes in a social form originates—in Freudian terms—in the scopic drive, which in turn is inseparable from the

---

[6] *Screen*, 16:3 (Autumn 1975), 6–18.

discovery of sexual difference, i.e., the woman's lack of a penis, i.e., an enforcement as a castration anxiety, thus setting off the formation of fetishes designed to contain the image of penisless woman. In her critique of classical Hollywood film, Mulvey proceeds from the observation that the legendary female figures on the screen—the Vamps, the glamourous stars, the beauties idealized to the point of grandiosity—are nothing but substitutes for the lack, elevated fetish-bearers who succeed in satisfying the scopic needs of the male spectator in offering up to his view what does not exist: the phallus.

The historical differentiation of voyeurism and exhibitionism along the lines of gender roles, which makes the woman the object and the man the active bearer of the look, consequentially predicated the aesthetics of narrative cinema on the patriarchal orchestration of the look. The spectator's identification is thus channelled into the cinematic image along the track of the male look, which posits the place of the woman in front of and that of the man behind the camera. Occasionally, the camera itself assumes a frontal position analogous to that of the spectators in the theater; it pretends to articulate their point of view. This camera position serves to present performances of female stars, song and dance numbers addressed to both the spectator and the male protagonist of the narrative. Even as such performances momentarily acknowledge the scopic economy of the addressee, they nevertheless mediate the allegedly collective view of the camera with that of the male spectator in the film, thus suturing the spectator into the film from an inescapably masculine-voyeuristic position. Only in rare moments is the woman granted a comparably orchestrated look at the man as the object of desire, when a male star is presented to the spectator in a comparable constellation—a constellation which, however, only reverses and thus reproduces the subject/object dichotomy of the dominant discourse.

The formalist analysis of the process of "suture" fuses implicitly structuralist (given the differential-linguistic premises of Lacanian theory) and psychoanalytic elements of film theory. For feminist film theory, this fusion presents a paradox which Mulvey herself as well as other feminist critics have since tried to address: If, according to the principle of suture, the spectator's look is inscribed in the filmic image in such a way that it is totally controlled, then this would entail a masculinization of the spectator position *a priori,* independently of the empirical spectator's gender. The over-determination of the look in classical narrative cinema caused Mulvey, in her initial essay, to exclude the female spectator altogether and to propose strategies of a counter-cinema that would turn its back completely on the patriarchal structures of narrative cinema, radically rejecting them in favor of new forms that would no longer depend upon the traditional collusion of spectator look with actor and camera look in cinematic identification.

At this point, feminist theorists have suggested practical consequences. If we accept the model of an inherently determined, closed-circuit economy of filmic production and reception, then only a qualitatively new production and construction of images can offer women the possibility to counter the patriarchal system. This strategy has led, especially in Britain and this country, to an increased production of experimental films, films that attempt a radical break with the mechanisms of identification deployed by narrative cinema. This break with narrative, however, has not necessarily liberated women spectators from the paradoxical construction of the gaze. As the analyses of dominant narrative cinema convincingly demonstrate, its aesthetic structures have indeed crystallized around the instinctual axis of voyeurism and fetishism. Whether this process can simply be reversed, whether the deconstruction of narrative forms which would release the Benjaminian "optical unconscious" as a medium of cognition could also achieve the emancipation of visual pleasure as a primary drive from its patriarchal encrustations including voyeurism and fetishism, remains to be questioned. The utopian vision of an emancipated (as well as emancipatory) "camera-eye" which can no longer be enslaved by the dominant patriarchal gaze is implicit in Mulvey's final plea: "The first blow against the monolithic accumulation of traditional film conventions (already undertaken by radical filmmakers) is to free the look of the camera into its materiality in time and space and the look of the audience into dialectics, passionate detachment." If one follows Benjamin's utopia of the emancipated camera-"eye," however, its implications seem to run counter to the distancing effect desired by Mulvey: "Thus, for contemporary life, the filmic representation of reality is incomparably more significant (than that of the painter), since it offers, precisely because of the thoroughgoing permeation of reality with mechanical equipment, an aspect of reality which is free of all equipment."[7] If one takes the metaphor

---

[7] Walter Benjamin, "Art in the Age of Mechanical Reproduction," *Illuminations*, trans. Harry Zohn (New York, 1969), p. 234.

of the camera eye seriously, then, in the final consequence, it will always remain the invisible, on whose visual trajectory the spectator becomes an "invisible guest" (Mulvey).

For the time being, the issue remains whether films by women actually succeed in subverting this basic model of the camera's construction of the gaze; whether the female look through the camera at the world, at men, women and objects will be an essentially different one. Moreover, one might add the question whether directions in feminist film aesthetics that focus exclusively on the role of the look in identification might not give us too narrow a perspective on what is at stake. In the historical development of film theory, phenomenological approaches to cinematic perception have been superceded by semiological ones that in turn have adapted a type of psychoanalysis based on structuralist linguistics. Yet there are a number of reasons for assuming that the phenomenological approach may still contain some useful and plausible observations, especially with regard to the issue of identification. In the model that I outlined above, identification is structured along the axis of voyeurism/exhibitionism, i.e., following the direction of the voyeuristic look toward the object displayed or displaying it/herself. If one were to modify this hypothesis with phenomenological analyses of the process of looking, one might come up with an explanation as to why actual women spectators tended to perceive these films not with consistent displeasure, but rather were able to identify subjectively—circumventing the masculine orchestration of the look, with the object of the look. For such a mimetic concept of identification one might further consult the findings of Gestaltist psychology.

The phenomenological approach might also elucidate another aspect of cinematic perception. If the perception of the individual image is determined by its construction within the individual film as well as the institution of cinema, spectators may get riveted to any detail within the frame, they may identify—in a sort of mimetic process—with a landscape, with individual objects or clusters of objects. This type of identification does not simply turn things into objects of the look, but implies a more emotional, one could even say, animistic relationship to the object. This particular aspect of phenomenological film theory was influential in the theoretical speculations about film of the Frankfurt School: From Kracauer and Benjamin to Adorno's essay "Transparencies on Film" (1966) we can find an emphasis on the dimension of mimetic experience which is inherent in cinematic images. The significance of psychoanalysis for Critical Theory can be gathered from the debate conducted by Adorno, Horkheimer and Marcuse with Erich Fromm and other representatives of the "revisionist" school. The conception of "Freudo-Marxism" developed by the former was based on a combination of the naturalist materialism found in the early Marx's *Paris Manuscripts* with Freud's metapsychology and his biologist theory of the drives, while the revisionists around Fromm were diluting psychoanalysis with the more pragmatic, therapeutic approach of ego-psychology. The significance of psychoanalysis for Critical Theory was primarily that of a theory of socialization that had as its object the instinctual nature of human beings and its fate in the process of socialization. Psychoanalysis was consulted as crucial authority on the social process of exchange with nature that took place within the subject him/herself. I am emphasizing Critical Theory's stubborn insistence on Freud's biologism because the *Dialectic of Enlightenment* focuses on aspects of the historical apocalypse of the total domination of nature and human beings. Adorno and Horkheimer project the writing of total and totalitarian domination onto the screens of the Culture Industry, which they describe as the agency in charge of perfecting the total domination of inner nature in gigantic dimensions. "[T]he whole inner life as classified by the now somewhat devalued depth psychology, bears witness to man's attempt to make himself a proficient apparatus, similar (even in emotions) to the model served up by the Culture Industry. The most intimate reactions of human beings have been so thoroughly reified that the idea of anything specific to themselves now persists only as an utterly abstract notion: personality scarcely signifies anything more than shining white teeth and freedom from body odor and emotions. This finally is the triumph of advertising in the Culture Industry: the obsessively mimetic relationship between consumer and cultural commodities even as they see through them."[8]

The elimination of the difference between consumer and product, between appearance and reality, between individual subject and society, is accomplished by way of the "iron bath of fun" in which everything is "subsumed by identity" (Negative Dialectic). In the social process the impersonations of the Culture Industry are absorbed by the audience into their "flesh and blood," aesthetic sublimation of the denigrated drives is replaced by crude suppression, by the reduction to foreplay, by the perennial repetition of the

---

[8] (New York, 1972), p. 167.

threat of castration. Under total domination there is no more difference between nature and society, since the latter posits itself as nature. Human beings are reified as empty monads on which the
machinery of Culture Industry imprints its patterns.

Such formulations tend to make psychoanalytic thought look
like a behavioristic stimuli-response model: society reproduces itself
in its individuals through a frictionless input-output process: the
final victory of socialization over instinctual nature. The prevalence
of the behaviorist model—in the chapter on Culture Industry—over
that of psychoanalysis does not necessarily reflect a change in
Adorno and Horkheimer's attitude toward psychoanalysis, but
must be attributed to the negative philosophy of history of the *Dialectic of Enlightenment* as a whole, which betrays its reductionism
all too strongly in such aporias.

In 1963, Adorno responded to his critics in a lecture, "Culture
Industry Reconsidered." While he maintained his and Horkheimer's basic analysis of the commodity fetishism inherent in all products of the Culture Industry, he somewhat tempered the thesis of
the total identity between products and consumers: "Only their (the
human beings) deeply unconscious mistrust, the residual trace of
the difference between reality in their spirit, explains why they have
not yet completely surrendered to the visions of the world as dished
out by the Culture Industry."[9] This fissure in the monolithic worldview of *Dialectic of Enlightenment* is due to a renewed recourse to
the category of the "unconscious" which counters the manipulated
consciousness. In fact, it is one of the basic assumptions of Critical
Theory that instinctual nature provides a pre-social potential
against the totalitarian infringements of the social process. Adorno
himself never went as far as Marcuse, though, who attempted to
spell out a positive social model on the basis of instinctual nature.
For Adorno, art and aesthetic experience was the only medium of
expression through which oppressed nature could oppose social restrictions and conditionings. Art is the wound that breaks open in
the margins where nature and society collide. It is therefore not surprising that when Adorno approaches film from the perspective of
aesthetics rather than that of economy and commodity fetishism,
the emphasis is on the category of experience.

In "Transparencies on Film" (1966) Adorno speculates on the
aesthetic dimension proper to the cinematic medium: "(. . .) the aes-

---

[9] *New German Critique*, 6 (Fall, 1975), 18.

thetics of film will do better to base itself on the subjective mode of experience which film resembles and which constitutes its artistic character. A person who, after a year in the city, spends a few weeks in the mountains abstaining from all work, may unexpectedly experience colorful images of landscapes consolingly coming over him or her in dreams or daydreams. These images do not merge into one another in a continuous flow, but are rather set off against each other in the course of their appearance, much like the magic lantern slides of our childhood. It is in the discontinuity of their movement that the images of the interior monologue resemble the phenomenon of writing: the latter similarly moving before our eyes while fixed in its discrete signs. Such movement of interior images may be to film what the visible world is to painting or the acoustic world to music. As the objectifying recreation of this type of experience, film may become art. The technological medium par excellence is thus intimately related to the beauty of nature (tief verwandt dem Naturschönen)."[10]

As this passage illuminates, Adorno conceives of aesthetic experience as the point where internal and external nature intersect. An aesthetic of film has to locate itself at precisely this intersection. The analogy of film to writing is a phenomenological one, not a linguistic one: the comparison invoked refers to the graphic figuration of writing, by way of a mimetic relationship. This distinction is extremely important because it contains the assumption that the aesthetics of film is characterized by a pre-linguistic, pre-symbolic dimension.

Psychoanalytic film theory, including Lacanian and feminist positions, traditionally privilege the symbolic dimension. Manifest content of images as well as formal structures tend to get read as signs of a symbolic order implicit in the materiality of the images. This means that most of these approaches analyze cinematically mediated experience in terms of phylogenetic and ontogenetic stages that presuppose a symbolic, linguistic competence. In psychoanalytical theory, however, these stages are preceded by nonlinguistic phases of experience.

The question would be whether and, if so, how film—and an aesthetics of film—contains and mediates elements of such experience. And I think it is no coincidence that Critical Theory—in particular

---

[10] *New German Critique*, 24–25, Special Double Issue on New German Cinema (Fall/Winter), 201. (see p. 269 in this volume—Editor's note)

Adorno, Benjamin and also Kracauer—grounds its analyses of the materiality of the filmic image in a phenomenological, rather than a symbolic framework. The fact that the reception of psychoanalysis in Critical Theory focuses on the "naturalist" theory of the drives, illuminates its affinity with anthropology, especially with insights into pre-linguistic realms of human experience. The concept of "mimesis," so crucial to Adorno's philosophy, is certainly related to anthropological material.

Whereas gestures are defined by social codes and conventions, i.e., a quasi-linguistic model of communication, mimetic expression, according to Helmuth Plessner, "conveys a meaning in that it articulates an emotion (a state of interior upheaval). Mimetic expression presents psychic content and physical form as two inseparable poles, a unity which cannot be split into a relationship of signifier and signified, (of shell and core) without destroying its organic, immediate and spontaneous quality."[11] One of the well-known shortcomings observed in actors of the silent screen was their indulgence in gesticulation—that they acted in exaggerated and theatrical style—but lacked the capacity of true mimesis. Silent actors we still admire today, such as Asta Nielsen, excelled in precisely this mimic capacity, in which emotional and physical expression formed a unity. Adorno describes the infantile dimension of mimetic expression in terms of the transition from a quasi-natural to a linguistic stage. In his essay on Chaplin he remarks: "Psychoanalysis relates the figure of the clown to reactions familiar from the earliest period of childhood before the ego is crystallized into a definite shape. However that may be . . . we will certainly learn more about the figure of the clown from children who communicate as mysteriously with him as they do with animals than by searching for a meaning in his actions which are designed precisely to deny that meaning. Only by knowing (if we knew) this language that clown and children share, would we understand this figure in which nature rehearses its shocklike departure."[12]

This is not too far from what happens with comedians like Laurel and Hardy who, failing to recognize the feet protruding from underneath the bedspread, start chasing the alien parts—not unlike the dog that tries to bite its own tail. Film seems to be a medium

---

[11] Helmuth Plessner, *Philosophische Anthropologie* (Frankfurt am Main, 1970), p. 61, p. 63.

[12] Theodor W. Adorno, "Zweimal Chaplin," *Ohne Leitbild: Parva Aesthetica* (Frankfurt am Main, 1967), p. 90 ff.

particularly well suited for the presentation of such mimetic expressions of the body—unlike the theater that has to resort to the enlarging interpretative gesture, to conscious stylization. Therefore one might more generally consider film as a medium which offers the aesthetic possibility to objectify modes of experience pertaining to the time before the "ego is crystallized into a definite shape." The "movement of images before the inner eye" (Adorno), the "equipment-free aspect of reality" (Benjamin) impart to the film experience a symbiotic sense of fusion, an absorption into images and their movement. If film attaches itself to such early layers of experience, then the issue of identification with characters in fixed sexual roles has to be reconsidered. For the spectator's pleasure can no longer be exclusively defined as that of the voyeur—whose look after all is intentional and directed—but would be complemented by that of the infant before language, propped in the mother's arms, who lets the world pass by, a world of which he or she is a part anyway. We may in fact owe the invention of the camera not to the keyhole but to the baby carriage.

The raising of the look changes in the field of vision, the tactile feeling conveyed by a subjective shot. The palpable sensation of drops may actually be a rehearsal of crucial optical/motoric experiences related to those awkward efforts that every human being makes when learning to move from a crawling to an upright mobility. In this process, the gaze is directed toward objects which the hand tries to grasp but fails to reach. If it is correct that in a socialization differentiated along gender lines, male infants receive more support in their motor efforts than female infants, then one might also understand the tendency in many films made by women to rivet the desiring gaze onto objects that are both beyond physical grasp yet fixed within the scope of vision.

A feminist film theory which, in the tradition of Critical Theory is interested in the aesthetic materiality of the film experience and not exclusively in the social and symbolic content of the films, could probably borrow more profitably from Jean Paul Sartre's *Existential Psychoanalysis* than from Lacan's. Sartre is interested in a "psychoanalysis of objects," of the material qualities which make them bearers of certain symbolic meanings: "A psychoanalysis of things and their material has to investigate the manner in which every object becomes the objective symbol of being and of relationship between human reality and this being. We even consider that it might be necessary, in retrospect, to discover a sexual symbolism in nature, but this would involve a secondary and reducible layer which presupposes a psychoanalysis of the pre-sexual structures."[13] I will withhold judgment as to the validity of Sartre's critique of Freud. Sartre's concept seems interesting in that it proceeds from the material property of things, that these things do not arbitrarily signify as symbols but contain an expressive/emotive force of their own, if you will, an aesthetic of their own. Only on the basis of these qualities can they become bearers of sexual symbolism. Why is water in Tarkovski's film *Stalker* transparent and fluid—whereas in Jutta Brückner's *Hunger Years* it is oily and choppy? What sort of personal differences bring about a choice to ascribe to water such different qualities? Sartre, hardly coincidentally, bases his concept on the analysis of aesthetic works, for in them content plays the dominant role.

Such modifications of the concept of identification make it possible to conceive of something like a female appropriation of cinematic images which claims its own access to narrative Hollywood films, against the structures of patriarchal cinema and by no means totally pre-determined by the latter. The phenomenological dimension, occluded in current psychoanalytic models of cinematic perception, needs to be reinserted into our analysis of the medium, whether historical or theoretical, if feminist film practice is to benefit from theoretical models beyond an abstract opposition toward narrative forms. Moreover, another look at Freud's speculations on bisexuality might be useful in understanding the gratification experienced by women even in their identification with the male look at the woman as object.

The theoretical discussion has so far yielded differentiated analyses of the patriarchal cinema, its aesthetics and its male spectators. This feminist advance in criticism, however, still does not fully account for the rather virulent conflicts going on at another level— inevitable conflicts resulting from the pragmatic political orientation of the women's movement, on the one hand, and feminist filmmakers' claim to autonomy on the other. Feminist film aesthetics cannot be normative in the sense that it would set standards as to what is feminism in film and what is not. The contradictions and conflicts involved in the reception—including theory—of films made by women for and by their female audiences have a history of their own which can only be understood through an analysis of the material at work in both production and reception.

---

[13] Jean Paul Sartre, *Das Sein und das Nichts* (Frankfurt am Main, 1967), p. 755 ff.

One might speak of a somewhat stubborn dialectics with regard to the success which women filmmakers have achieved in recent years in the sense that it led to an extreme differentiation rather than any unification. The increasing professionalization seems to have subjected women competing in the cultural market-place to similar mechanisms as their male colleagues. I am referring to mechanisms such as specialization, dissociation from others, as well as the reenactment of the split between art and commercial cinema. We cannot deny that the same process which, in economic and socio-psychological terms, could be described as "integration into the system," becomes the condition for women to be able to articulate themselves at all, beyond the small camp of an alternative public sphere. The meaning of the classically bourgeois term of emancipation—a movement from the margins of society toward its center—tends to fulfill itself with a vengeance. The tightrope act of the women's movement and professional women engaged in this struggle consists of trying to prevent themselves from becoming like those whom they fight, not in the usurpation of patriarchal power and domination but in its demolition. This is why the new women's movement—in Germany at least—has always tried to maintain a notion of subjectivity, as a force of resistance against the codes of the system.

In closing, I would like to discuss some of the reasons why a large part of women filmmakers, precisely because they are committed to such a notion of subjectivity, seem to have alienated themselves more and more from the political women's movement and why it has become more difficult for a female audience to understand the films in question. During the first phase of women's cinema, a period of *cinéma militant,* films were produced in a direct political relationship with the women's movement and would have been inconceivable without it. Spectators and filmmakers came from similar backgrounds and had immediate, short-term goals in common. A number of these films were conceived for purposes of agitation, information, for meetings and rallies, in short, they were addressed to an incipient oppositional public sphere. The objective of these films was a collective one: they were designed to express the general interest of all women, to accelerate and enhance the struggle.

On the other hand, the pragmatic feminist interest in an instrumental (and instrumentalized) aesthetics is aimed at a large public basis. Films guided by this interest inevitably confront a dilemma:

if they aim at the widest possible public resonance they have to make certain compromises; if they refuse to adapt to such standards they won't be able to realize their interest because they won't even reach a public. This dilemma is a generally difficult one for the artist, but it is especially hard on the feminist who cannot reconcile the political interest for public exposure with the principle of individuation and specificity that inheres in any radical aesthetics. The more radically a woman working in aesthetic processes of production maintains the utopian claim to autonomy, self-realization and emancipation of the subject—not only of the social conditions—the more radical this contradiction. The aesthetically most advanced films resist any facile reading, not only because they operate with complex aesthetic codes but also because they anticipate an expanded and radicalized notion of subjectivity. What is achieved in a number of these films is a type of subjectivity that transcends any abstract subject-object dichotomy; what is at stake is no longer the redemption of woman as subject over against the male conception of woman as object. What is at stake is less—and at the same time more—than the most general sense of the concept of subject: in the sense that Marx could speak of the working class as the subject of the revolution, in the sense that the women's movement could be the subject of the transformation of sexual politics. The most advanced aesthetic products represent a utopian anticipation of a yet to be fulfilled program of emancipated subjectivity: neither of a class nor of a movement or a collective, but as individuals, as concrete subjects they attempt to insist on their authentic experience.

Elfi Mikesch's film *What Would We Do Without Death* (1980) is certainly a film like that—a film about old age, but the old age of *a few* older women, a film as much about a particular old people's home as about one particular woman, Elfi Mikesch herself. Her film is irritating not only because it subverts the traditional codes of documentary and transforms them in an experimental mode, but because there is something that emerges from this particular cinematic form that transcends any mere reflection of reality. Therefore it is futile to argue whether this film is a realistic portrayal of a nursing home or even if it characterizes the situation of old people in an average nursing home. For what distinguishes Elfi Mikesch's film from a socially critical TV documentary is precisely the subjectivity of its aesthetic form. The luminous blue glass in the cupboard, the harsh silhouette of a chair on the balcony are sensuous impressions that transcend the mere reproduction of objects. What these images convey is a sense of fragility, a sense of lost time, of mourning and a holding-tight on life and the living. Elfi Mikesch's film is an emotive working-through of the experience of the imminence of death and the will to live, of the precarious existence of memories and their luminosity, whose continuity is disrupted by the course of time. On the level of aesthetic experience, Elfi Mikesch's film is a film against death. When she arranges certain images in tableaux, when she illuminates trivial trinkets as if they were precious vessels of memory against death, then it becomes clear that she expresses her own relationship to death and perhaps also that of a few old women.

The precondition for the understanding of radically subjectivized films is first of all a willingness to move beyond the construction of a collective ego to recognize the difference of the other, a subjectivity which lurks under the surface in a world of foreign images. The love relationship to a work of art is in this sense not much different from one between people: tension comes as a result of difference and the way in which I seek to mirror myself in the other, an other which looks back at me in all its strangeness.

Feminist aesthetics, I maintain, dare not fall behind the avant-garde, either in political instrumentalism or in an archaic primitivism, which would like to insinuate its way back into the Golden Age of the matriarchies of love. The socio- and art-historical genesis of so called feminine characteristics and idiosyncrasies cannot be captured in terms of the intuition of the "belly"—this holds for film as well as other areas. In film one must perforce control an eminent technical apparatus; one must, so to speak, break into the cave and conquer the industrial park of the patriarchal lion. Film is *the* art of the twentieth century par excellence. It exemplifies certain tensions in a particularly dramatic fashion: that between autonomous claims and market demands, between radical self-actualization and a technical apparatus, between isolated artists and an organized mass audience. Film is for this reason surely the most embattled sector—both ideologically and economically—of female art production right now. It stands as a symbol for hope: that women might exorcise the demons of the male technology while finding counter-images *(gegenbilder)* to those of the dominant male.

Heide Schlüpmann

Heide Schlüpmann (1943–   ) is one of the most important feminist film scholars in Germany today. In her early academic training, she studied philosophy with Theodor W. Adorno (whose work is included in this volume) and completed her dissertation on Friedrich Nietzsche in 1975. She has published in the areas of philosophy and film, feminist film theory, and the early German cinema in her book Unheimlichkeit des Blicks—das Drama des frühen deutschen Kinos *(The Uncanniness of the Gaze: The Drama of the Early German Cinema, 1990). She is presently an editor of the first feminist film journal in Europe,* Women and Film *(Frauen und Film),* where she began working in 1979. She has been teaching film studies at the Johann Wolfgang Goethe-University in Frankfurt am Main since 1991.*

Melodrama and Social Drama in the Early German Cinema (1990)

During the period from 1911 to 1912, film producers made a determined effort to adapt the cinema to the aesthetic cosmos of bourgeois culture. In so doing they were responding to massive attacks that had been launched against them by cinema reformers. They attempted to establish the "seriousness" of cinema partially through their choice of subject matter, drawn from the literary tradition. And yet the cinematographic appeal to classical literature did not immediately have the desired effect. A great many of the champions of culture saw the attempt to use literature as an affront to their cultural property.

German producers did not have any more luck in filming German history: *Theodor Körner* and *Der Film von der Königin Luisa (The Queen Louisa,* both 1912) met with little success among the guardians of German culture—the so-called *Bildungsbürgertum.* Film adaptations of historical events were criticized in drastic terms:

And now on to the German film dramas, the patriotic dramas that are supposed to take root in the German youth—it is a matter of educating the young people, the most important duty of the state. These films are *The Queen Louisa* and *Theodor Körner*.

Technically, they are below average. The images have neither depth nor breadth; one sees only fragmented details, never an overall impression as is offered to us in reality. Everything has an obtrusive effect. The content—what can one say about it? Certainly, no one would claim that Germany has no poets, no directors, no actors who could depict the great epochs of the wars of liberation and their decisive moments in a more worthy form. What we see here are tearjerkers à la *Gartenlaube*. We see the queen with her children four times. There is a scene with children in the *Iliad* as well, but the moment chosen for this is appropriate because Hector is being drawn into a fatal battle. Thus, without any such event, the scenes seem stale and inopportune; this could be any affectionate mother playing with her little ones.[1]

Certainly, the two films criticized here do seem wooden and stilted. And yet they also demonstrate the democratizing and demythologizing effects of the medium. Malwine Rennert, the critic cited above, finds fault with the technical limitations of the images, but more than anything else she misses "depth" for what seem primarily ideological reasons. The film makes the lives of the rulers appear "flat," commonplace, like those of "normal" people. In contrast to this, she extols contemporary French film production, the *film d'art*. This genre was making an impression at the time with its opulent sets and crowd scenes, and forcing the development of a German art film. Soon after this review, the first female critic of the German cinema transferred her primary interest to Italian monumental films. To the nationality-conscious, educated bourgeoisie (the aforementioned *Bildungsbürgertum)*, the suffusion of history with pathos in films like *Quo Vadis* (1912), *Cabiria* (1914), and *Caius Julius Caesar* (1915) seemed exemplary. History, they argued, should be presented as a sequence of great events, and not pulled down into the lowly regions of the mass-cultural everyday.

The historical film, as representative of a "lower" art, had a levelling effect on the subjects of high culture. In contrast, melodrama offered a genre which began to establish itself as one that lent the commonplace an "eventful" character. Melodrama represented the social problems of women in a stylized manner which lent them a

---

[1] Malwine Rennert, "Victor Hugo und der Kino: Französische und deutsche Filmkunst," *Bild und Film* II (1912–13): 129–31, 130f.

metaphysical dimension by focusing on the particular tragedy of a single and unique woman. The appropriation of the powers of the new medium, which were characterized as "monstrous" by the *Bildungsbürgertum* out of a combined reaction of recognition and anxiety, did not occur initially through the content *(Stoff)*, but through the style or "higher" form. Certainly, the development of a narrative cinema for a female public must have seemed suspect to the bourgeoisie: what would happen if large numbers of women saw their own reality mirrored in the movies? What if the repressive distribution of roles was not only discussed in bourgeois emancipatory movements, but also represented within a mass public sphere *(Öffentlichkeit)* by this soberingly "flat" medium?

In the course of the early 1910s, melodrama asserted itself against the documentary quality of the medium. A series of films were made in 1911 which constituted the beginnings of melodrama in German cinema. *Der Müller und sein Kind (The Miller and His Child), Im Glück vergessen (Forgotten in Happiness),* and *Tragödie eines Streiks (Tragedy of a Strike)* were all Messter productions starring Henny Porten and directed by Adolf Gärtner. In these films, the narrative cinema that was just establishing itself intersected with the inheritance of the so-called *Tonbilder* (sound images), which were first introduced in 1903. The Messter production firm was known for its *Tonbilder,* and Henny Porten made her first appearances in these one-reelers. The *Tonbild*—a combination of film and recorded sound—was a genre of the pre-narrative cinema for which Tom Gunning has coined the concept, "the cinema of attractions."[2] The cinema of attractions developed between 1895 and 1906 within the context of variety shows and yearly fairs. Its forms are those of exhibition, not those of voyeurism. It worked through visual effects in front of the camera, but also through effects created by the camera and through montage, and not least of all through the attraction of being able to exhibit reality. It did not yet subsume the new potential of the technical medium within the older interests of narrative. The attraction of Oskar Messter's *Tonbilder* lay above all in their connection of the image with sound. At the same time, however, these films banked on appealing to bourgeois taste through their choice of subject matter. From its prehistory in the cinema of attractions, the melodrama appropriated precisely this

---

[2] Tom Gunning, "The Cinema of Attractions: Early Film, Its Spectator and the Avant-garde," *Wide Angle* 8.3–4 (1986): 63–70.

moment that connected the "lower art" to the "higher" culture. Many *Tonbilder* draped the offerings of an "art of the body" *(Körperkunst)* in the forms of the classical opera and ballet, orienting themselves around images from bourgeois art history. For example, the attraction of *Meissner Porzellan (Meissner Porcelain,* 1906) lay in the movement of living bodies which appeared as the marionette-like dance steps of delicate rococo porcelain figures.

Like the representation of bodily movement in *Meissner Porzellan,* melodrama froze the movement of female (self-) representation at the beginning of narrative cinema. Just as in the *Tonbild,* the cinema of attraction had acquiesced to bourgeois culture through references to traditional art, in narrative cinema, melodrama acquiesced to patriarchal forms of culture. A hybrid form even before it insinuated itself into the cinema, melodrama abandoned the representation of woman's history in favor of the construction of a so-called "female perspective." In *Die grausame Ehe (The Cruel Marriage,* 1910), the story of a woman who killed her husband was presented in the form of a statement that she made before the court. The courtroom scene provided a dramatic framework for the story of the "cruel marriage." This framework represented the negotiations of men who judged the husband's treatment of the woman and made decisions as to her "fate." All that was left for her to do was to provide the "facts." This film demonstrates how, with the establishment of narrative cinema, there was a tendency to degrade women's history to the status of mere content for which male bourgeois culture provided the form of representation. To the extent that there remained, however, a tension between the represented story and the dramatic framework (as was the case in *Die grausame Ehe),* there was always a chance for the actress in the film to express an oppositional standpoint. This tension can be attributed to the collision between two media (literature and film) which also *implied* a collision between two cultures—classical bourgeois and modern mass culture. However, as opposed to the social drama which will be discussed presently, this tension was practically eradicated in melodrama, which only appeared to fulfill the cinema's promise to form a culture from below. Melodrama did not succeed in exposing the contradiction between a romantic concept of "popular art" and the modern art of mass culture. My thesis is that in the history of German cinema, the melodrama had from the very beginning a disciplinary function. It was not a genre that came from below, from the realm of the popular, but instead placed women's history in the service of nationalism and, later, National Socialism. The transition from Henny Porten to Paula Wessely was a seamless one.[3]

Melodramas have always had a second-hand effect. They did not build their tragedy out of life; rather, the tragic structure into which they compressed all reality ultimately consisted in nothing other than the collapse of a female narrative perspective within the restrictions of the dramatic form. The tragic element was an *a priori* attribute of the protagonist, before any particular content; it developed neither from the reality in which the film placed her nor from her story. Melodramatic heroines were static. They were not "narrators," but rather the representatives of an always already determined femininity. Even their aura of suffering did not refer to historical-social experience outside the cinema—precisely during this period, women were realizing that the feminine character was not a destiny—but this representation of suffering mystified the suppression of the female narrative perspective within the films.

The reactionary element in a melodrama like *Tragödie eines Streiks* (1911), a Messter production starring Henny Porten and directed by Adolf Gärtner, is obvious: the woman who, from the very beginning, has been in favor of order and against the uprising, is able in the end to convince even the male protagonist that social struggle will bring nothing but disaster. But she does so only at the cost of losing her child. Not only is the suffering of the woman in a male society transfigured by the melodrama, but the transfigured image of female sacrifice also serves to domesticate male oppositional perspectives. The actress, representative of femininity, i.e., of a male projection rather than an articulation of female experience, no longer represents her own narrative perspective, but enforces the dominant order. The "reason of the heart" (the title of a 1910 film) is thus transmuted from a historically specific voice into a projective defense, all in the name of a speechless female sensibility.

Henny Porten, the embodiment of this sensibility, already scores a victory in her initial appearance in *Tragödie eines Streiks* as the star who bows and smiles during the credits. The clumsy antics of the male protagonist are no match for her. He acts the communist official in a Russian peasant smock, proletarian cap, and wild moustache. Only at the outset are we treated to some snippets of "realism": the first shot, when life still seems to be in order, shows the everyday site of a proletarian one-room apartment which is at

---

[3] A popular actress in the Nazi cinema.

once living room, bedroom, and the woman's work space, as well as the nursery. The mother works at the sewing machine, her son playing at her feet. But when he falls ill, the film resorts to emotional, suggestive devices. It anticipates the dismal ending in that the camera devotes less attention to the details of the trip to the hospital than it does to the logo of a coffin manufacturer that has obviously been created in the studio.

The presentation of the strike must have seemed too "realistic" to the censors, since they excised the better part of it. Only one shot remains that shows the gesticulating labor force from above: a view from the position of dominance onto insurgent reality. The enticing image of woman in this film functions, analogously to the camera angle, to reinforce the idea of industrialization from above. One of the intertitles tells us that "light and power" are indispensable, thus putting in writing the admonition that was voiced by the female protagonist before the strike. The text has the effect of a caption that might come from the mouth of an allegorical statue representing "Electricity" that decorates the entrance of a power plant. The sequence in the hospital's operating room makes reference to the blessings of electricity; the operating table looks impressive in the bright light of the lamp. To the same extent that little of the text touting the indispensability of the new technology comes from the mouth of a real woman, so too the protagonist fails to communicate the view as the film proceeds that this technology could belong to women—or, for that matter, to the workers. The mother who fears for the life of her child sits waiting passively outside the operating room, a portrait of the madonna hanging above her head, and as the light goes out, the "god in white" appears in the doorway, ominously blood-spattered: the workers' strike is more than anything else a blasphemy against higher powers. It makes no difference if, in this context, the female spectator senses within herself a higher right *vis à vis* the "politicizing" man, seeing herself reconfirmed in her domestic concern for private well-being.

And yet, melodrama was not the only form in which cinema was oriented toward a female public. The social drama approached this public differently. Although the concept of the social drama stemmed from the Scandinavian cinema, Emilie Altenloh used it more generally in her 1913 sociological study of the cinema. For Altenloh, the term "social drama" referred to a form that related particularly to the life contexts of women.[4] In contrast to melo-

---

[4] Emilie Altenloh, *Zur Soziologie des Kino: Die Kino-Unternehmungen und die sozialen Schichten ihrer Besucher,* diss. Jena, 1914 (Hamburg; Medialaden, 1977) 58.

drama, social drama maintained a proximity to newsreels; its documentation of reality broke with conventional dramatic form. Altenloh described this similarity to the newsreel as follows:

> Viewed from one perspective, the interest in the cinematic image in German newspapers and newsreels is not so very different from the interest in German dramas. Certainly one important cause is the reference to the present. Film drama speaks to people in the context of their everyday lives.[5]

In contrast to melodrama, the social drama responded solely to an external censorship, one that restricted a genuine female narrative perspective, but yet did not force it to recede in favor of a stereotypical representation of femininity within a dramatized story. The social drama appealed to the curiosity of female spectators, and it gave the subjectivity of the actress a spatial framework.

The strength of the female narrative perspective in the social drama derived from its foundation in the forms of the cinema of attractions with which it entered into a pact against the bourgeois superimposition of the dramatic form. Although previously institutionalized, this form of the cinema no longer lent itself to the interests of a bourgeois cinema of entertainment *(Unterhaltungskino)*; from film to film—indeed, within one single film—the documentary qualities of the genre contributed to its theatrical effect. Social dramas did not transgress social gender roles, but they did illuminate them in a new way.

In keeping with the social division of gender roles, social dramas concern themselves with the theme of the mistress, on the one hand, and the married woman, on the other. But they also resist this division. *Heimgefunden: Von Stufe zu Stufe: Lebensberichte einer Probiermamsell (The Way Back Home: Step by Step: The True Confessions of a Model,* 1910) is one example of such resistance. Perhaps more than any other film, *Heimgefunden* shows how the independence of the story, in the face of attempts to dramatize it, is based on the continuation of elements of the cinema of attractions and goes hand in hand with the suspension of moral prejudices. The subtitle, *Lebensberichte einer Probiermamsell,* could have been taken from the enlightened women's literature of the period. The story of the film as well—a decent female employee allows herself to be seduced and becomes a mistress—corresponds to many cases

---

[5] Altenloh 57.

that were reported by the women's movement in their publications so as to set in motion emancipatory processes of reflection and self-reflection. The rehabilitation of "fallen" women, rather than their social condemnation, was the goal of radical sexual politics at the time. In 1914, for example, the journal *The New Generation (Die neue Generation)* published a series entitled *From the Life of a Prostitute, as Told by "Herself."*

The formulation "as told by herself" has the same effect as the subtitle *"True Confessions of a Model."* Filmed, on the one hand, with a documentary camera that utilizes the visual values of outdoor shots and directed, on the other, at sexual curiosity, the film maintains a complete distance from melodramatic elements. The female protagonist is seduced, but she is not presented as a victim who will meet a certain death; on the contrary, she will return to her family and marry her fiancé, as if nothing unusual had happened. Instead of representing patriarchal morality, her story conveys sexual and documentary attractions to a female public.

Heimgefunden tells the story of Elise, a girl from a simple home, who works in a dressmaker's studio. Her promotion to model *(Probiermamsell)* brings her into contact with upper-class customers. A count who comes into the shop with his matronly wife is less interested in the latest fashions than he is in the girl who models them. Elise agrees to a rendezvous, and soon thereafter becomes the count's mistress. He rents her an apartment of her own and provides her with clothes and jewelry. This helps her overcome her guilty conscience about having abandoned her parents and fiancé. While out for an evening of fun at Maxim's, she meets the engineer Natas, who makes advances toward her. The count surprises the couple when Natas is paying her a visit at home, and not only throws out his rival, but also decides to break with Elise. She switches over to the engineer, who turns out to be a less than serious candidate, eventually gambling away her jewelry. Thus disappointed, Elise longs for home. Her father shows her to the door, but her fiancé runs after her and prevents her, in her state of anguish, from throwing herself in front of a train. Eventually she and her father reconcile as well.

The narrative in *Heimgefunden* draws its strength from an undercurrent linking it to the cinema of attractions; in so doing, the film constructs the rudiments of formulating a first-person narration on the part of the female protagonist. Generally, the film is shot in tableau style, presenting its story in a simple sequence of scenes that are arranged and shot autonomously, emphasizing their visual values over their function within the film's narrative totality. "At home," as the intertitle comments, Elise is "her parents' sunshine," and also that of her fiancé. She is fascinating to the public as well. In the dressmaker's studio we are offered an insight into the working conditions and mode of production of a trade shop. Rows of sewing machines are set up, fabric and finished articles of clothing are strewn about, fashion drawings hang on the walls; we even catch a glimpse of a tailor's dummy wearing the design being produced at the moment. A number of women are busy working when a man, the boss, enters the room. A brief dramatic scene has been embedded within the presentation of the milieu, which is retroactively attributed to the supervisory male gaze. The boss scrutinizes his employees—he is looking for a new model, and suddenly chooses Elise.

The next scene provides another insight into the working world—it shows Elise in her capacity as a model. The gentleman (the count) who accompanies his wife spends more time looking at the young woman than at the dress she is presenting; he assumes the scrutinizing gaze of the boss. The count chooses Elise on the basis of her attractive appearance, obviously not in order to advance her socially, but to constitute her as an object of desire. A tantalizing detail: the count slips her a note requesting a rendezvous.

They meet in front of a cafe. The camera takes in the scene: gentlemen are waiting on the other side of the street looking steadily at the somewhat self-conscious, indecisive Elise as she stands in front of the cafe. The camera assumes the voyeuristically possessive male gaze, but, at the same time, pushes the woman into the open bustle of a big city—its interest in documenting the atmosphere outweighs the interest in formulating the male gaze. The count lights a cigar as soon as he enters camera range (his pleasure while waiting); he crosses the street, cigar in hand, while the camera remains fixed, recording the couple as they disappear into the cafe. Once inside, the man and woman sit at the window at equal distance from the camera, which reveals behind them the undulating traffic of the street and the flow of passers-by. The light from outside illuminates the faces of the lovers. A street scene follows as the two get into a cab, providing us with information on further developments in their relationship, but also allowing the camera to indulge in an elaboration of the street scene that had beckoned only indistinctly through the window.

Another scene that seems primarily to provide the viewer with narrative information is the following, in which Elise's parents and fiancé receive a letter from her, telling them about her new life. Even though Elise is not visually present, the scene centers around the written communication from her that the fiancé has received: "Forgive me, I have found my happiness; I won't be coming home anymore." The scene thus reinforces her fictional authorship.

The most elaborate scene in the entire film is devoted to the situation of the suffering mistress, a scene which characterizes the "milieu" just as it provides insight into the subjective perspective of such a woman—an attraction in its own right. Elise sits in her dressing gown in front of her dressing table mirror, which proudly reflects her new status. She takes up a small hand mirror. But instead of it affording a multiple view of her external features, she sees in it figures from her own inner life. Magically, there appear within the mirror's oval frame, in miniature and one after the other, her weeping mother who is wringing her hands, and then her angry father. The camera engages us through this minor bit of artistry; it shows us the conscience through a visual attraction rather than by means of the gesturally mimetic expression of an inner self. After this brief excursion into special effects, the film returns to her milieu. The door opens, and the count enters the room laden down with hat boxes and new clothes. The apparition has vanished, and Elise takes delight in unwrapping the packages.

This special effect is one example of how the film continues to develop its narrative on the basis of the principle of variety rather than subordinating it to the dramatic form. The conflict evoked by the old ties, despite the protagonist's clear decision to opt for a new life, is articulated by means of the montage of subjective images which preserves the unity of the woman's point of view. The autonomy of the scene supports that of the woman in the film; parallel editing would have withheld the realization of the reactions of the parents from the gaze of the heroine, and thus from her control. This would have also given an opportunity to the public to turn against the protagonist, to identify with the parents instead of with the gaze that their "lost daughter" directs upon them.

The film, far from reasserting the power of the moral superego over the narrator/heroine, goes on to show her and the audience the enticements of leisure. We are allowed a glimpse into Maxim's. There the women enjoy themselves at least as much as the men: they become exceptionally animated while drinking wine and champagne and dancing with one another. Elise too enjoys this unrestrained erotic atmosphere. Ultimately she is accompanied to the cab not only by her count, but by her new suitor as well. Apparently during the shooting of this scene, a crowd of curious onlookers was present—they stare curiously into the camera. As we know, early films were not self-conscious about the loss of illusion that might be generated by such narratively unmotivated attention. To the extent that the cinema drew its effectiveness from the element of attraction in the individual scene, the staring faces in the film merely reflected a fascination similar to that experienced by those sitting before the screen.

Although discovered in the act of being unfaithful, the woman is not represented as the helpless victim plagued by a guilty conscience. In view of all the indications that the enraged count will abandon her, she leaves the apartment. She seems helpless for the first time two scenes later, when the engineer imperiously demands her jewelry, her only joy, so as to meet his gambling debts. Intimidated, she brings him the jewelry box. Yet as soon as he is gone, she vents her indignation and decides that under such circumstances she no longer wants to continue leading the life of a mistress. The memory of her old way of life intensifies, and, as the intertitle reminds us, "Elise longs for home."

As if the two older lovers—both corpulent and sporting moustaches—were reverse mirror images of the father as moral authority, the film's ending enforces the father's disempowerment. "Get away, you miserable woman!" is his predictable response to his daughter's return home; the fiancé pleads in vain on her behalf. We see her leave the house through the front garden on an entirely ordinary late afternoon. In the next scene she is in an open field crisscrossed by railroad tracks. A train approaches in the distance, but even before the viewer has realized what the purpose of this walk through the field might be, we catch sight of the fiancé who runs behind her and takes her in his arms. The train passes by. This sequence in its entirety does not achieve its effect through drama, through the creation of emotional tension, but instead, once again, through the appeal of the outdoor shot of the railroad yard and the train roaring past. The dispassionate poetry of the camera's gaze, within which technology and nature appear momentarily reconciled, accompanies the heroine up to the very end. It could not be further removed from the suggestion of a higher power of fate that will ultimately catch up with the woman who has strayed from the proper path. At the end of this film, the desire of the men for the woman—now transferred from the lovers to the fiancé—is allied with the self-affirmation of her life against paternal authority. In the early narrative cinema that concentrates on social drama, the exhibition of the female body for voyeuristic male desire is not necessarily incompatible with the establishment of a female narrative perspective prompted by the appeal to a female public.

Marriage, which *Heimgefunden* no longer shows but instead allows us to imagine at the close of the film, would not reestablish the patriarchal order, but consummate physical love between social subjects. Other social dramas deal with ordinary married life in patriarchal society: narratives representing the lives of married women often display a similar blend of sobriety and fascination as do the stories of mistresses. *Perlen bedeuten Tränen (Pearls Mean Tears,* 1911) shows the development of the marriage of a lieutenant—from the delirium of the newlyweds, through the boredom of everyday married life, to the errant husband and the patiently faithful behavior of the wife, concluding with their reconciliation. *Um Haaresbreite (By a Hair's Breadth,* 1912) presents an upper middle-class marriage in which the husband's club is as important to him as his wife and his home, his child and domestic help. This creates problems. His male friendship is destroyed by the advances his friend makes toward his wife. The life of the family is repeatedly threatened by this male relationship which has turned into enmity. The security of the household rests solely on the self-assuredness of the wife.

Although both of the films discussed above are Messter productions with Henny Porten, the first directed by Adolf Gärtner and the second by Curt Starck, neither film represents the suffering of the married woman in a melodramatic way. Rather, the films narrate scenes from a marriage and offer descriptions of the milieu. The documentary camera counteracts a sentimentalizing perception of the staged drama of "real life." There is a wonderful street scene in *Perlen bedeuten Tränen* when the crisis in the marriage has reached its peak. The scene shows a jewelry store: the wares on display in the window can be gaped at in every detail. The heroine arrives and disappears into the store. The shot, which is photographically precise and poetic at once (an effect of chiaroscuro and multiple reflections of light), focuses the gaze on the woman's walk; it preempts the melodramatic sense of a "victim's gait" (she is selling her pearl necklace to pay her debt). *Um Haaresbreite* devotes considerable time to delineating the dramatic events between the rivals—the death of one man from the bullet of a poacher, the flight of the other who believes himself to be under suspicion of murder—tightening them dramatically. The film loses itself in the appeal of the landscape shots, the images of a seemingly endless flight and pursuit through the woods, fields, and river.

And yet, the form of these marriage films differs from the films about mistresses, and also from a film like *Die grausame Ehe*. In *Heimgefunden*, the dramatic form, as a framework for male judgement which restricts the female narrative perspective, becomes one element within the narration. *Perlen bedeuten Tränen* and *Um Haaresbreite* develop a new concept of drama out of an element of the story. Both films revolve around objects whose meaning transcends their narrative function and generates tension around the solution of their "mystery." The newly-wed young woman receives a pearl necklace as a gift from her mother-in-law along with a hand-delivered letter, telling her: "they always say that 'pearls mean tears,' but to me they have brought only happiness." From that point on, the female viewer will wait to see whether the superstition will be confirmed or whether the enlightened attitude of the mother-in-law will prove correct. In the end, the experience of the gift-giver rather than "popular wisdom" proves true, so that the significant object generates a dramatic tension in the minds of the audience which both responds to and criticizes a deep-seated belief in fate.

In *Um Haaresbreite*, the rival who is dying alone in the woods writes a letter that exonerates the husband. The wind blows the sheet of paper away. From then on the public wonders—will the letter be found, will it be able to fulfill its redemptive function? The couple's child, who is playing, picks it up and wraps it around a bouquet of flowers he has picked for his mother. In keeping with melodramatic convention, the pearls in the first film and the letter here generate the expectation that deflects the narrative from everyday life. Thus, the enjoyment of the individual scenes that have been meticulously observed and attractively staged and photographed is overlaid with an eagerness to find a solution to the "mystery." Inserted into a suspense-generating plot, the scenes finally take on tendentially a new quality that curtails the effect of the documentary camera.

This new quality lies in the stimulation of the voyeuristic libido without anything explicitly erotic being offered on the screen. The objects that are charged with meaning in the marriage stories tend to usurp the function of the suggestive scenes in the mistress films. Since bourgeois marriage is not an institution of sexual pleasure (on the contrary, it renders the married woman taboo as a public object of desire), the female protagonist cannot be staged openly as an attraction for the male gaze. The marriage films, therefore, relinquish a residual moment of the cinema of attractions, with which the female story had joined forces in opposition to the establishment of a bourgeois patriarchal cinema. The eagerness for the solution of the mystery revolving around the object thus replaces the erotic attraction that could be provoked by the heroine's negligée or by the hero's kiss upon her lips. But it is precisely this erotic stimulation that continues to have an effect, repressed and displaced within this eagerness.

It was more explosive for women than for men to be able to see the stories from everyday married life invested with this secret pleasure. Pleasure was defined as taboo for women within bourgeois marriage during the Wilhelminian period. The situation was presumably different for men, who had access to mistresses and prostitutes. For women, however, the repression of sexuality in marriage amounted to a repression of their sexuality altogether. How much more, therefore, it must have meant a rupture in their everyday lives to be able to observe in the cinema the complications of secret sexual expectation in married life.

This form of marriage drama transformed and contained the elements of the cinema of attractions that still survived in the early narrative cinema because it responded to the gaze of the female consumer. The cinema opened up the perspective of mistresses and prostitutes to women, who constituted a financially potent *(finanzträchtig)* public. At the same time, the cinema organized a perspective on marriage not only as an institution of reproduction, but also as the dramatic form of their sexual life. It thus re-channeled the sexual curiosity that was released for the sake of consumption.

Such attempts at rechanneling were not simply repressive, but also productive. The inclusion of erotic attractions in stories about women allowed the social problematic of the sexes to be rendered visible; by the same token, the dramatization of the female narrative by means of an objective correlative reflected the social relationship—the marriage—back onto repressed sexual relations. Fundamentally, *Perlen bedeuten Tränen* and *Um Haaresbreite* are about nothing other than the deteriorating sexual interest of the husband and his homoerotically-based leisure-time enjoyment. What the officer's casino is to one man, the club is to another; one relaxes with a ballerina, the other by going hunting.

The social marriage dramas mediated between a female narrative perspective and the cinema of attractions, and also between both of these and the dramatic form. In this mediation lay the real significance of the objects. On the one hand, they are everyday objects that play a role as props in the course of the narrative. On the other, they possess a fetish character insofar as they appear in place of the openly erotic attraction in the mistress films. They substitute for the sexual element repressed in the representation of the marriage: the happiness that the mother-in-law promises with the pearl necklace on the wedding day is a reference to what the bride anxiously anticipates before the wedding night. The rival's letter stands for the sexual desires that intrude into the marriage from outside, as well as for the mending of the damaged marriage bond. Thus the meaning-laden object occupies the sexual fantasy of the public. (A short pornographic film exists from the same period, showing scenes of a wedding night. The film is obviously a compilation of several scenes with different couples. The first scene, in which a newly wed couple enters the home and the bride receives a necklace, is taken from *Perlen bedeuten Tränen*. The original scene, which was very decent, now takes on a pornographic meaning through a montage sequence in which the man and woman first undress and then enjoy themselves in bed.)

This tension, this provocation of sexuality through a special staging of an object within the cinema of attractions, is not the only tension, however. It is not only their fetish character that lends the objects significance beyond their function in the plot. Their significance also originates in the fact that, in the privileged status of the object *vis à vis* the story, a moment returns that might be a refuge for the dramatic frame as the representative of patriarchal power. Displaced by the female narrative perspective on the level of dramatic form, it remains present in the film as an ominous substance: will the mother-in-law's experience be productive for the young woman, or will the pearls only confirm the repressive role of the mother in patriarchy, i.e., preventing her son from forming a happy relationship with the opposite sex? The meaning-laden object mediates between erotic attraction and prohibition, the id of the female viewer and her superego; it dramatizes the gaze that is cast upon the story.

Heimgefunden demonstrates how the narrative revocation of the authority of patriarchal censorship made possible a representation of marriage as a voluntary association for what Kant terms the "reciprocal use of the sexual organs." Thus the new medium of film was reacting to social changes that were pressing for a liberalization of rights within marriage, as was being demanded by progressive social movements at the time, especially the women's movement. Patriarchal violence is ascribed to the past; the films retain it as the pre-history of their story in the form of a pearl necklace or a letter. The patriarchal order appears not only as something that has been conquered, but is simultaneously present as something that has been internalized. However, while melodramas were, during the same period, already attempting to psychologize in a way that made external fate into an internal one, these social dramas of marriage attach the continuing presence of outdated powers onto what is objectively visible. In their foregrounding of such objects, these films place the hope for a release from the "return of the same" within the relationship between the sexes. The function of the significant objects oscillates between a release of the longing for earthly happiness and the blinding of sexual desire in the fetish object.

To the female public for whom the marriage dramas were chiefly produced, these objects ultimately stand for the male sex as patriarchal power and as sexual object. What seems to be at stake for the female spectator, who is uncertain about marriage and who seeks enlightenment or pleasure in the cinema, is that which the married woman is deprived of, that which seeks its satisfaction elsewhere, that which threatens and beckons outside marriage—that "beyond" which has been rendered socially taboo. The bourgeois appropriation of German cinema through the melodrama developed a repressive distraction in the sublimation of the female gaze and its erotic power. By contrast, the dramatization of the female gaze through the social drama tended toward a representation of male sexuality, of the man as sexual object. This tendency obviously collided with the influence of the guardians of bourgeois culture; social drama, unlike melodrama, disappeared from narrative cinema after World War I. Now the meaning-laden image world of film completely assumed the role of the taboo.

Translated by Jamie Owen Daniel

Karsten Witte

Karsten Witte (1944–95) received his doctorate from the Johann Wolfgang Goethe–University in Frankfurt am Main, where he studied literature. He moved to Berlin in 1979 and eventually became the first professor of film studies at the Free University in Berlin. He published articles and books on Nazi cinema, film theory, and Siegfried Kracauer; he was also involved in the gay-rights movement in West Germany. Witte taught at the Free University in Berlin until his untimely death in 1995.

The Indivisible Legacy of Nazi Cinema (1994)

Reflections on Methodology

Whereas scholars of Nazi cinema working in the 1970s focused primarily on the consonance between politics and aesthetics, more recent commentators have begun to consider the circumstances under which a seeming disparity between politics and aesthetics was both possible and productive. It is now no longer admissible to define a Nazi film's aesthetics solely by locating its systemic place. Instead of determining which features constitute a fascist film, we need to examine how films functioned under fascism, or rather, in the context of fascism. Can a common idiom be identified in the filmic language of the products of the Axis Powers, the German Reich, Italy and Japan? Did the general conditions of production under state control foster similarity or diversity? Did the national idiosyncrasies of stars and genres become unifying factors by way of co-productions or through the exchange of films between these nations? Did Ufa and Cinecittà have more in common with the Hollywood studio system than they might have wished to acknowledge?

Whether films of the Third Reich possessed a discernible common style has been an ongoing topic of debate. As long as the point of departure remained the system under which films were produced, the answer was clearly affirmative. However since the epochs that went before and followed Hitler have been factored into the equation, the answer is no longer so straightforward. Considerations of tradition and continuity have become pertinent concerns; the periods of transition have assumed a more decisive role in comprehending the parameters of 1933 and 1945, historical moments that previously could be so neatly demarcated. As the determining role of the Nazi system has been elaborated with more nuance and care, questions of form and aesthetics have likewise become more visible. A number of films from the Third Reich have now gained recognition as exceptions to what previously served as the rule. They have been located in the neglected output of certain directors and various genres. The popularity of these films has never been in question and it has remained constant. The fantasy productions of the Third Reich outlived the Nazi system as traces of a collective memory, leaving emotions with far-reaching and lasting repercussions in their wake. This accounts for the continuing commemoration of the era's stars, from the use of Zarah Leander's voice in Visconti's *La Caduta Degli Dei* [*The Damned*] to Fassbinder's portrait of artists as political tools in *Lili Marleen*.

Foreign Models, German Knockoffs

One of the Nazi regime's most glaring contradictions was the removal of modernity from public life and its simultaneous reintroduction by means of film and other mass media. Not only in the documentaries of the Bureau for the "Beauty of Work" can one detect a hunger for the functionalism of the ostracized Bauhaus. Conspicuous examples of classical modernist furniture and accessories from the 1920s can be located in the set design of many Nazi era films. Between 1933 and 1945, German culture and everyday reality were marked by what Hans Dieter Schäfer calls a "divided consciousness." The condemnation of American capitalism and the castigation of jazz as "nigger music" did not stifle the importation of Coca-Cola and Mickey Mouse, the circulation of swing records, or the screening of Hollywood films (which in fact did not really cease until 1941). The female players Marianne Hoppe, Brigitte Horney, and Paula Wessely became the ersatz versions of American stars. Hoppe was modeled after Katharine Hepburn and Horney yearned to be like Joan Crawford. Zarah Leander imitated Marlene Dietrich and Marika Rökk envied her tap-dancing idol, Ginger Rogers—to no avail, for these figures were at best imitations. Until Germany declared war on the United States, its audiences could compare the domestic output with the foreign competition. It was perhaps less important who was better. Rather, in a period of increasing political repression, the question on people's minds seemed to be: who offered greater freedom and autonomy?

Films promised women, who in the everyday reality of their life and work had lost a great deal, a much wider range of roles. This is particularly clear in the case of films modeled along the lines of Hollywood prototypes. Viktor Tourjansky often allowed Brigitte Horney to appear as a self-reliant (at times even rebellious) working woman, for instance in the disaster film of 1936, *Stadt Anatol,* which can be compared to W. S. Dyke's *San Francisco* of the same year. In the latter, the earthquake catalyzes a collective dream of reform; Clark Gable emerges as a savior from the rubble, as it were a father of Frisco's New Deal. In the German counterpart, the impetus for rebirth is likewise implicit in the catastrophe: Horney and Gustav Fröhlich go on to build a radical paradise.

Gustaf Gründgens made *Capriolen* (1937) in which Marianne Hoppe plays an American pilot. At one point she is interviewed by an American journalist (played by the director himself), allowing the influence of the Hollywood sophisticated comedy to resonate. The comedy of the image, which granted the performers room for improvisation, is transformed into verbal comedy. Jochen Huth and Willi Forst, the two great and neglected talents who wrote the screenplay, were also responsible for *Allotria* (1936). Here Renate Müller and Jenny Jugo demonstrated that women could be funny without losing their personal dignity or their social grace.

Hans H. Zerlett's musical, *Es leuchten die Sterne* [*The Stars Are Shining,* 1938], had the nerve to take on Hollywood choreographer Busby Berkeley and to copy his imposing mass ornaments. Zerlett had studied Warner Bros.' *Broadway Melodies.* In the film's center-piece, he attempts to transform an inanimate object into a set and the label of a bottle into a prop, to create a revolving stage out of the brim of a hat. The maneuvering of the dancers for a spot in the front row is also not missing in the convention-bound narrative which quickly enough disintegrates into a revue. The creation of a film in the studio guides the story, with all of the tried-and-true trademarks of the backstage drama. A star descends, a starlet is born. Prominent figures from the Tobis Studio appear throughout the film in cameo roles. Hans Söhnker, the notorious heart breaker, is among their number, but the starlet only has eyes for a member of the lighting crew. While *Nur nicht weich werden, Susanne!* [*Just Don't Lose Heart, Susanne!*], another meta-film made during the Third Reich, poses the ideological dilemma of what is the proper form of realism, *The Stars Are Shining* does away with that question altogether and unabashedly embraces illusion. Any interest in the real world disappears as the story celebrates the artificiality of the cinematic world with a variety of tricks. The woman is not married off to "nature"; rather, she remains in the happy family of the film world, wedded to "art" in a marriage of convenience.

Tyrants and Model Husbands

Heinz Rühmann is the star of *Der Mustergatte* [*The Model Husband,* 1937], a film directed by Wolfgang Liebeneiner. The latter, surely not without talent, made his mark initially as a specialist for comedies. Later he would gain political clout, creating epic tributes to great men (*Bismarck* [1940] and *Die Entlassung/The Dismissal* [1942]) and supporting state-administered murder (under the guise of "euthanasia") in the form of the film, *Ich klage an!* [*I Accuse!,* 1942].[1] *The Model Husband* was a huge public success, the function above all of its lead actor's performance. Millions wanted to be like Rühmann, to possess a self-deprecating wit that might allow people to slip by without being noticed. Helma Sanders-Brahms aptly described this figure as "a Mephisto through whom one might study the relationship of the artist to power, similar to the example of Höfgen-Gründgens in Klaus Mann's novel and István Szabó's film adaptation."[2]

As the model husband, Heinz Rühmann was finally able to remove the milquetoasty houseslippers which he had worn in the depression comedies of the pre-1933 era. The petty bourgeois beaten down by hard times metamorphosed into a perfect Englishman, at once a businessman, a sportsman, and a gentleman. He is the master of his own household and no longer subservient to the whims of foreign capital. While his bank works for him, he plays tennis. The self-confidence that the regime exuded during the Olympic Games seems to emanate from Rühmann as well.[3]

---

[1] After the war Liebeneiner would become a plier of hackish entertainment in West Germany, an exemplar of what Young German filmmakers would call "Opas Kino."

[2] Helma Sanders, "Ein kleiner Mann: Anmerkungen zu einem deutschen Publikumsliebling," in *Jahrbuch Film 82/83,* ed. Hans Günther Pflaum (Munich: Hanser, 1982) 52.

[3] At this point an Englishman still could be seen in a sympathetic light. Later, in 1939, as Great Britain stood at Poland's side, images of an amiable English diplomat in Helmut Käutner's comedy, *Kitty und die Weltkonferenz* [*Kitty and the International Conference*], would no longer find the approval of German censors.

Rühmann's establishment faces the threat of bankruptcy. Once the big businessman appears, however, dressed in a double-breasted power suit, all worries vanish. He saves the bank and strides through an effusive gathering of grateful employees. In Venice the model businessman will become the model husband—to the detriment of the woman, for he does everything possible to keep his wife at arm's length and to short-circuit her erotic energies. His jealousy becomes a test of love and the scene that the wife stages in this regard ends with her willing submission. It is not so much the transfer of economic strategies onto the private sphere that is comic here, but rather the rebellion of the wife against these strategies. A male outburst may be a pardonable mistake; a female revolt is a ridiculous failure.

In the screwball comedies of Gregory La Cava or Mitchell Leisen, a marital indiscretion served to call the institution of marriage into question. In *The Model Husband,* an indiscretion is simulated in order to support a somewhat shaky institution. Otherwise, this German comedy might become a melodrama. Rühmann must first ingest the courage for his indiscretion in the form of alcohol. He then feigns an act of adultery on a polar bear rug, playing a grotesque game of innocence in which this model husband regresses to a model child, albeit a child not altogether shorn of desire. If he must deny himself sexual release, he receives consolation in the form of voyeuristic pleasure. He rings for the maid, dragging her out of bed, relishing the sight of her sparely clad body while issuing the command, "About face!", and making sure that she is alone when she marches back to bed.

The conspicuous lack of social experience in German comedies seemed to ensure their public success. It certainly reduced the flexibility of the actors, who were obliged to limit themselves to the mechanical dictates of the confusion of identity, the exchange of social status, and the celebration of minor transgressions. In American comedies, the richness of social experience was the precondition for commercial success. This expanded actors' possibilities; they remained unfettered by dramas of confused identities and could admit a more dynamic range of responses into their repertoire of gestures. Within the realm of the aesthetic paradigm, the viewer (along with the actor) could gather new experience and find encouragement for self-improvement, something decidedly foreign to German films.

The Politics of Comedy

When the percentage of the total production represented by comedies drops and that of propaganda rises, do propaganda films take on the role of comedies? What was comic about the political and what was political about the comic films? If we pursue such possible connections, we need to discuss the structural relations between genres and their functional places.

The comedy, *Der Gasmann/The Gas Man* (Carl Froelich, 1941), is marked by a divided consciousness: on the one hand, it represents modernity; on the other, it uses anti-modernity as a comic effect. It presents the visual fact of "little people" living in developments designed by the architect, Bruno Taut, in Prenzlauer Berg, dwellings blessed with a benevolent light and a healthy use of space. The plot line, however, emphasizes that an atmosphere of suspicion and jealousy reigns in the buildings. A housewife with a refrigerator or even a new perm must fear the resentment of her neighbor. The camera invests more energy in capturing acts of domestic spying than in following the main storyline about accusations of espionage against the gas man (Heinz Rühmann) in this working class district of Berlin. The presentiment of state surveillance is ever present, appearing here in the express form of men in the notorious leather coats. A threat directed at the gas man by a tenant who cannot pay her bill ("A cousin of mine is a party member, you know!") is not effective, for the party member in question has already been established as a risible figure. What is effective is the onerous and paralyzing suspicion in the film which militates against any prospect of petty bourgeois happiness.

The *Revuefilm, Der weiße Traum* [*The White Dream*, 1943], directed by Géza von Cziffra for Wien-Film, was one of the era's largest box-office successes. Here the musical countries Spain and Hungary as well as the classical city of musicals, Manhattan, enter the picture. The film tells a familiar story about the rise of a great, true, and irrepressible talent who wins out over all challengers and challenges. The balletic camera movements suggest a desire for an existence not bound to the laws of gravity. This seems both removed from reality and nonetheless appropriately realistic. The entertainer in the stadium falls out of character for a moment and encourages the spectators to heat themselves with laughter instead of coal. At this moment the film industry's advice was very much in keeping with the realities of the winter of Stalingrad.

Exceptions and the Rule

While West German film of the Adenauer era maintained the illusions of the 1940s, East German film resurrected the realism of the 1930s which the Nazis had forsaken. In many cases the technicians from the old Ufa dream factory continued in the same jobs and the same capacities. They adapted themselves to the new environment and felt justified in their brazen postwar self-defense, transforming films made under the aegis of Goebbels into products of their artistic genius. The structure of the films, however, speaks a different language than their credits. Not all of the films produced in Nazi Germany were automatically Nazi films, but neither was every film banned in those days an instance of aesthetic resistance. The National Socialist system functionalized film as it did all the other media. It alone produced anti-Semitic hate films, the likes of which one will find no counterparts in Italy or Japan.

German cinema of the Third Reich had little to call its own. It was a borrower. It mobilized in order to immobilize. It employed a Manichean logic that reduced and simplified meaning. Appeals to the senses in the form of flags and masses went hand in hand with a profusion of dissolves. The visual symphony ended in a flood of images, a flood that involved an apotheosis, an ecstasy of annihilation. The attempt to fashion a sense for unequivocal images necessitated an assault on the senses, a barrage on the eyes and the ears. A media empire was an essential precondition for such an aesthetic campaign. The films made under National Socialism ultimately would play in about 27,000 theaters, whenever the German army had conquered new territory.

There were fascist films. And there were films made under various fascist regimes. One must always bear in mind the question of their form and function. Even if *Triumph des Willens* [*Triumph of the Will*] may not be shown in public, Riefenstahl's Olympia films are called documentaries and aired on the commercial station SAT 1 without a problem. They remain examples of a shocking and notorious power.

More recently critics have sought to discover exceptions to the Nazi rule within the cinema of the Third Reich, more often than not playing up the exception and downplaying the rule. No Wysbar, Sierck, Tourjansky, Hochbaum, Pewas, or Käutner will ever keep Steinhoff, Riefenstahl, Ucicky, Ritter, or Harlan in the shadows. This infamous legacy is not divisible. One either accepts it as a whole or one misunderstands it altogether.

Bibliography: Primary Sources

Adorno, Theodor W. "Transparencies on Film," 1966. Trans. Thomas Y. Levin, *New German Critique* 24–25 (1981–82), 199–205. Orig. "Filmtransparente" in Adorno, *Schriften 10* (Frankfurt am Main: Suhrkamp 1977): 353–61.

Adorno, Theodor W. and Max Horkheimer. "The Culture Industry: Enlightenment as Mass Deception," 1944. *Dialectic of Enlightenment*, trans. John Cumming (New York: Continuum, 1982), 120–31. Orig. *Dialektik der Aufklärung: philosophische Fragmente* (Frankfurt am Main: Suhrkamp, 1981).

Altenloh, Emilie. *On the Sociology of the Cinema: The Cinema Business and the Social Strata of Its Audience,* 1914. Trans. Lance W. Garmer. Orig. *Zur Soziologie des Kino. Die Kino-Unternehmung und die sozialen Schichten ihrer Besucher* (Jena: Diederichs, 1914), 23–43.

Arnheim, Rudolf. *Film.* Trans. L.M. Sieverking and F.D. Morrow (London: Faber & Faber, 1933), 5–14, 170–85. Orig. *Film als Kunst* (1932) (Munich: Hanser, 1974).

Balázs, Béla. "The Visible Human," 1924. Trans. Lance W. Garmer. Orig. "Der sichtbare Mensch" in Béla Balázs, *Schriften zum Film: Band I, Der sichtbare Mensch Kritiken und Aufsätze 1922–1926* (Budapest: Akadémiai Kiadó, 1982), 45–77.

Brecht, Bertolt. "The Three-Penny Trial: A Sociological Experiment," 1932. Trans. Lance W. Garmer. Orig. "Der Dreigroschenprozeß" in Brecht, *Schriften zur Literatur und Kunst I,* 1920–32 (Frankfurt am Main: Suhrkamp, 1967), 143–44, 164-98.

Brückner, Jutta. "Women's Films Are Searches for Traces," 1981. Trans. Antje Masten. Eric Rentschler, ed. *West German Filmmakers on Film: Visions and Voices* (NY: Holmes and Meier, 1988), 85–89. Orig. "Filme von Frauen sind Spurensuchen" in Hans Helmut Prinzler & Eric Rentschler, eds., *Augenzeugen: 100 Texte neuer deutscher Filmmacher* (Frankfurt am Main: Verlag der Autoren, 1988), 195–99.

Döblin, Alfred. "The Theater of the Little People," 1909. Trans. Lance W. Garmer. Orig. "Das Theater der kleinen Leute" in Anton Kaes, ed., *Kino-Debatte: Texte zum Verhältnis von Literatur und Film 1909–1929* (Tübingen: Niemeyer, 1978), 37–38.

Einstein, Carl. "The Bankruptcy of German Film," 1922. Trans. Lance W. Garmer. Orig. "Die Pleite des deutschen Films" in *Kino–Debatte,* 156–59.

Eisner, Lotte. "The Predisposition towards Expressionism," Introduction to *The Haunted Screen: Expressionism in the German Cinema and the Influence of Max Reinhardt* (1952), (Berkeley: University of California Press, 1973), 9–15. Trans. Roger Greaves. Orig. *L'Ecran démoniaque,* 1952.

Ewers, Hanns Heinz. "Film and I," 1913. Trans. Lance W. Garmer. Orig. "Der Film und ich" in *Kino–Debatte,* 103-4.

Fassbinder, Rainer Werner. "The Third Generation," 1978. Trans. in Michael Töteberg and Leo A. Lensing. eds., *The Anarchy of the Imagination: Interviews, Essays, Notes* (Baltimore: The Johns Hopkins University Press, 1992), 128–133. Orig. "Die dritte Generation" in *Filme befreien den Kopf: Essays und Arbeitsnotizen,* ed. Michael Töteberg (Frankfurt am Main: Fischer, 1984).

Goebbels, Joseph. "Dr. Goebbels' Speech At the Kaiserhof on March 28, 1933." Trans. Lance W. Garmer. Orig. "Rede im Kaiserhof, 28 März 1933." In Gerd Albrecht, ed., *Der Film im 3. Reich* (Karlsruhe: Doku-Verlag, 1979), 26–31.

Goll, Claire. "American Cinema," 1920. Trans. Lance W. Garmer. Orig. "Amerikanisches Kino" in *Kino–Debatte,* 146–48.

Groll, Gunter, Helmut Käutner and Walter Talmon-Gros. "Every Audience, As Everybody Knows, Has the Films It Deserves." Trans. Lance W. Garmer. Orig. "Jedes Publikum, bekanntlich, hat die Filme, die es verdient," *Film* (Dec. 1956): 6–7.

Harlan, Veit. "History and Film," 1942. Trans. Lance W. Garmer. Orig. "Geschichte und Film" in Siegfried Zielinski, *Veit Harlan* (Frankfurt am Main: Rita G. Fischer, 1981), 186–87.

Hippler, Fritz. "The Formative Power of Film," 1942. Trans. Lance W. Garmer. Orig. "Die formende Kraft des Films" in Albrecht, *Der Film im 3. Reich,* 144–48.

Hofmannsthal, Hugo von. "The Substitute for Dreams," 1921. Trans. Lance W. Garmer. Orig. "Der Ersatz für die Träume" in *Kino–Debatte,* 149–52.

Ihering (Jhering), Herbert. "An Expressionist Film," 1920. Trans. Lance W. Garmer. Orig. "Ein expressionistischer Film" in *Kino–Debatte,* 133–34.

Käutner, Helmut. "Gratitude Toward the Theater," 1945. Trans. Lance W. Garmer. Orig. "Dank an das Theater" in *Das Jahr 1945: Filme aus fünfzehn Ländern,* ed. Hans Helmut Prinzler (Berlin: Stiftung Deutsche Kinemathek, 1990), 76–77.

Kluge, Alexander. "What Do the 'Oberhauseners' Want?" 1962. Trans. in Rentschler, *West German Filmmakers on Film,* 10–13. Orig. "Was wollen die 'Oberhausener'?" in Prinzler/Rentschler, *Augenzeugen* 47–50.

Koch, Gertrud. "Ex-changing the Gaze: Re-Visioning Feminist Film Theory," *New German Critique*, 34 (1985): 139–53. (Orig. "Blickwechsel: Aspekte feministischer Kinotheorie," *Neue Rundschau*, Nov. 1983, 121–135).

Kohlhaase, Wolfgang. "DEFA: A Personal View," in Seán Allen and John Sandford, eds, *DEFA: East German Cinema, 1946–1995* (New York: Berghahn Books, 1999), 117–26.

Kracauer, Siegfried. "Die kleinen Ladenmädchen gehen ins Kino," 1927. Trans. and ed. Thomas Y. Levin in *The Ornament of the Masses* (Cambridge: Harvard UP, 1995). Orig. in Kracauer, *Ornament der Masse: Essays* (Frankfurt am Main: Suhrkamp, 1963), 279–94.

———. "Introduction," *From Caligari to Hitler: A Psychological History of German Film*, (New Jersey: Princeton University Press, 1947), 3–11.

Lang, Fritz. "The Artistic Composition of the Film Drama." Trans. Lance W. Garmer. Orig. "Der künstlerische Aufbau des Filmdramas" in *Filmbote* 20 (1924): 13–16.

Lukács. Georg. "Thoughts On an Aesthetics of Cinema," 1913. Trans. Lance W. Garmer. Orig. "Gedanken zu einer Ästhetik des Kinos" in *Kino–Debatte*, 112–18.

"The Manifesto of Women Film Workers," 1979. Trans. Eric Rentschler, *West German Filmmakers on Film*, 5–6. Orig. "Manifest der Filmarbeiterinnen" in Prinzler/Rentschler, *Augenzeugen*, 429–30.

Murnau, F. W. "The Ideal Picture Needs No Titles: By Its Very Nature the Art of the Screen Should Tell a Complete Story Pictorially," 1927. Trans. in *Theatre Magazine* (New York), vol. XLVII: 322 (January 1928): 41, 72. Orig. "Der ideale Film benötigt keine Untertitel" in Fred Gehler & Ullrich Kasten, *Friedrich Wilhelm Murnau* (E. Berlin: Henschel, 1990), 151–54.

"The Oberhausen Manifesto," 1962. Trans. Eric Rentschler, *West German Filmmakers on Film*, 2. Orig. "Oberhausener Manifest" in Prinzler/ Rentschler, *Augenzeugen*, 22.

Patalas, Enno. "On German Postwar Film," 1952. Trans. Lance W. Garmer. Orig. "Vom deutschen Nachkriegsfilm" in *Filmstudien: Beiträge des Filmseminars im Institut für Publizistik an der Universität Münster* (Emsdetten: Verlag Lechte, 1952), 13–28.

Rennert, Malwine. "An Abyss Not to Be Bridged." Trans. Lance W. Garmer. Orig. "Ein Abgrund, der nicht zu überbrücken ist" in *Bild und Film* II (1912/13): 18–19.

———. "War Films." Trans. Lance W. Garmer. Orig. "Kriegslichtspiele" in *Bild und Film* IV.7/8 (1914/15): 139–41.

Riefenstahl, Leni. "May the Strength and Beauty of Youth Have Found Cinematic Form." Trans. Lance W. Garmer. Orig. "Kraft und Schönheit mögen filmische Form gefunden haben." *Film-Kurier*, 31 Dec. 1937.

Sander, Helke. "Feminism and Film," 1977. Trans. Ramona Curry. Rentschler, *West German Filmmakers on Film,* 75–81. Orig. "Feminismus und Film" in Prinzler/Rentschler, *Augenzeugen,* 184–92.

Schlüpmann, Heide. "Melodrama and Social Drama in the Early German Cinema." *Camera Obscura* 22 (1990): 73–88. Trans. Jamie Owen Daniel.

Serner, Walter. "Cinema and the Desire to Watch," 1913. Trans. Lance W. Garmer. Orig. "Kino und Schaulust" in *Kino–Debatte,* 53–58.

Staudte, Wolfgang. "A Letter To The Central Military Commander of the Soviet Occupation Zone," 1945. Trans. Lance W. Garmer. Orig. "An die Zentral-Kommandatur der sowjetischen Besatzungszone" in *Das Jahr 1945,* 104–5; also in Eva Orbanz/Hans Helmut Prinzler, eds., *Staudte,* (Berlin: Volker Spiess, 1991), as "Ein Brief," 151–53.

———. "A Reflection: Befouling Our Own Nest?" 1964. Trans. Lance W. Garmer. Orig. "Eine Überlegung. Das eigene Nest beschmutzen?" in Orbanz/Prinzler, *Staudte,* 164–65.

Tannenbaum, Herbert. "Art at the Cinema," 1912. Trans. Lance W. Garmer. Orig. "Kunst im Kino" in *Kinematograph* Nr. 4 (1987: "Der Filmtheoreteiker Herbert Tannenbaum,") 47–48.

Wenders, Wim. "That's Entertainment, Hitler" 1977. Trans. in Eric Rentschler, *West German Filmmakers on Film,* 126–31. Orig. in Prinzler/Rentschler, *Augenzeugen* 279–86.

Witte, Karsten. "The Indivisible Legacy of Nazi Cinema," *New German Critique* 74 (1998): 23–30.

Wolf, Konrad. "On the Possibilities of Socialist Film Art: Reactions to 'Mama, I'm Alive.'" Trans. Lance W. Garmer. Orig. "Von den Möglichkeiten sozialistischer Filmkunst: Reaktionen auf 'Mama, ich lebe'" in *Film und Fernsehen* 10 (1982). (From the "Diskussionsbeitrag auf den III. Kongreß des Verbandes der Film- und Fersehschaffenden der DDR, May 1977.")

Acknowledgments

Every reasonable effort has been made to locate the owners of rights to previously published works and the translations printed here. We gratefully acknowledge permission to reprint the following material:

Alfred Döblin, "The Theatre of the Little People"; Georg Lukács, "Thoughts on an Aesthetics of Cinema"; Walter Serner, "Cinema and the Desire to Watch"; Hanns Heinz Ewers, "Film and I"; Herbert Ihering, "An Expressionist Film"; Claire Goll, "American Cinema"; Hugo von Hofmannsthal, "The Substitute for Dreams"; and Carl Einstein, "The Bankruptcy of German Film" originally published in A. Kaes (ed.), *Kino-Debatte. Texte zum Verhältnis von Literatur und Film 1909–1929*. Max Niemeyer Verlag, Tübingen (1978).

Emilie Altenloh, from *On the Sociology of the Cinema,* German original *Zur Soziologie des Kino*. Jena: Diederichs, 1914. Reprinted by permission of Heinrich Hugendubel Verlag GmbH, München.

F. W. Murnau, "The Ideal Picture Needs No Titles: By Its Very Nature the Art of the Screen Should Tell a Complete Story Pictorially" originally published in Gehler, *Friedrich Wilhelm Murnau,* Henschel Verlag, 1990. Reprinted by permission of the publishers.

Siegfried Kracauer, "The Little Shopgirls Go to the Movies." Reprinted by permission of the publisher from *The Ornament of the Masses* by Siegfried Kracauer, translated, edited and introduction by Thomas Y. Levin, Cambridge, Mass.: Harvard University Press, translation copyright © 1995 by the President and Fellows of Harvard College.

Bertolt Brecht, from *The Three Penny Trial,* originally published in *Schriften zur Literatur und Kunst I,* Suhrkamp, 1967. Reprinted by permission of Methuen Publishing Ltd.

Rudolf Arnheim, from *Film* © 1964 Carl Hanser Verlag München Wien reprinted by permission of the publishers. English translation by L. M. Sieverking and F. D. Morrow published by Faber & Faber, 1933. Reprinted by permission of the University of California Press.

Veit Harlan, "History and Film" originally published in Siegfried Zielinksi, *Veit Harlan.* Frankfurt am Main: Rita G. Fischer Verlag, 1981. Reprinted by permission of the publishers.

Max Horkheimer and Theodor W. Adorno, "The Culture Industry: Enlightenment as Mass Deception," in *Dialectic of Enlightenment,* courtesy of S. Fischer Verlag GmbH.

Siegfried Kracauer, *From Caligari to Hitler: A Psychological History of German Film* © 1975 by Princeton University Press. Reprinted by permission of the publishers.

Lotte H. Eisner, *The Haunted Screen: Expressionism in the German Cinema and the Influence of Max Reinhardt* © 1973 by the University of California Press. Reprinted by permission of the publishers.

"The Oberhausen Manifesto"; Alexander Kluge, "What Do the 'Oberhauseners' Want?"; Wim Wenders, "That's Entertainment: Hitler"; Helke Sander, "Feminism and Film"; "The Manifesto of the Women Film Workers"; and Jutta Brückner, "Women's Films Are Searches for Traces" from *West German Filmmakers on Film: Visions and Voices,* edited by Eric Rentschler. Copyright © 1988 by Holmes & Meier Publishers. Originally published in *Augenzeugen 100 Texte neuer deutscher Filmmacher* © Verlag der Autoren, D-Frankfurt am Main 1988. Reprinted by permission of the publishers.

Konrad Wolf, "On the Possibilities of Socialist Film Art: Reactions to *Mama, I'm Alive*" originally published in *Film und Fernsehen* 10, 1982. Reprinted by permission of Stiftung Archiv der Akademie der Künste.

Wolfgang Kolhaase, "DEFA: A Personal View" *originally published in DEFA: East German Cinema, 1946–1997* © Berghahn Books Ltd., Oxford. Reprinted by permission of the publishers.

Theodor W. Adorno, "Transparencies on Film" from *Schriften 10,* Frankfurt am Main: Suhrkamp, 1963. Reprinted by permission of the publishers.

Heide Schlüpmann, "Melodrama and Social Drama in the Early German Cinema," *Camera Obscura* 22 (1990). Copyright 1990, Camera Obscura. All rights reserved. Reprinted by permission of Duke University Press.